HOOKERS, ROUNDERS, AND DESK CLERKS

THE SOCIAL ORGANIZATION OF THE HOTEL COMMUNITY

Robert Prus
and
Styllianoss Irini

gage PUBLISHING LIMITED
TORONTO ONTARIO CANADA

Canadian Cataloguing in Publication Data

Prus, Robert C.
    Hookers, rounders, and desk clerks

Bibliography: p.

ISBN 0-7715-5743-4

1. Prostitution.   2. Prostitutes - Interviews.   3. Crime and
criminals.   4. Crime and criminals - Interviews.   I. Irini,
Styllianoss.   II. Title.

HQ117.P78   306.7'4   C80-094049-0

1 2 3 4 5   HR   84 83 82 81 80

Printed and bound in Canada

Contents

Acknowledgments

We first want to thank the hotel people—the staff and management, the hookers, dancers and other entertainers, as well as the rounders and the patrons—for all their assistance with this project. We not only appreciate the friendship they extended to us, but also the education they have given us. We ordered the material, situating it in a sociological cast, but they contributed the substance.

A number of people assisted us in various aspects of the projects, but we particularly want to thank Dianne McCulloch, Beverley Taylor, Alison Haworth and Barbara Prus for their contributions.

We are also grateful to the University of Waterloo and the Social Services and Humanities Research Council of Canada for the financial support they contributed to the project. While these grants were in aid of ongoing research, they greatly facilitated our ability to obtain depth in the project and to process the incoming material.

We would additionally like to acknowledge the assistance of the "Gage people" in seeing this project through to publication. The careful, thoughtful and pleasant assistance of editor Joan Kerr was especially appreciated.

Finally, we wish to thank the many friends, colleagues, and students who provided us with the day-to-day encouragement necessary to sustain a project of this nature.

ALL NAMES OF PEOPLE AND PLACES
HAVE BEEN CHANGED*

*Any resemblance to actual names of people or places is purely coincidental.

To those who constitute the Hotel Community.

Chapter 1

The Community

INTRODUCTION

This book examines the way of life of a group of people who together form what we call the "hotel community." It's a book about hookers and strippers, bartenders and cocktail waitresses, bouncers and desk clerks, bar patrons and rounders. However, in examining the ways in which these people work out their lives with one another, we gain some insight into the nature of group life more generally. Not only do we focus on the interpersonal relations of involved parties, but we also consider their careers and routines, and the subcultural elements serving to define the community as a distinctive way of life. In studying the interrelatedness of persons in this setting, it is hoped that we will acquire a better understanding of group life in both "deviant" and "straight" communities.

Being involved in a number of quasi-legal and illegal pursuits, the participants in the hotel community represent some of the rougher and better "action" people in society. Although many of the activities we will be considering have been discussed somewhat in other sources, we are particularly interested in indicating the ways in which persons who are involved in a variety of activities (deviant and otherwise) come together and jointly work out aspects of their lives. Providing an ethnographic account of the social organization of a hotel community, this research depicts the interrelatedness of involved persons and has particular significance for filling in missing materials on hustling and deviance more generally. For example, while some information is available on bars (Cavan, 1966; Roebuck and Sprey, 1967; Roebuck and Frese, 1976), hustling (Sutherland, 1939; Maurer, 1941, 1955; Polsky, 1967; English and Stephens, 1975; and Prus and Sharper, 1977) and prostitution (Bryan, 1965, 1966; Gray, 1973; and Velarde, 1975; Rasmussen and Kuhn, 1976), relatively little attention has been directed to the larger subcommunities in which these activities and the participants fit together.[1] Although the present material depicts only some aspects of the larger scene, it was approached in a manner somewhat akin to *Street Corner Society* (Whyte, 1943), *Elmtown's Youth* (Hollingshead, 1949), *Asylums* (Goffman, 1961), and *Tally's Corner* (Liebow, 1967), and is thus seen as contributing to the understanding of the underlife of the larger society.

In developing this monograph, we focussed on a number of basic themes in deviance emerging within the hotel community. On one level, material pertinent to the development and continuity of subcultures points out the significance of "interrelatedness" and the tendency of communities to "spill over" into one another. At another level, attention is focussed on the "career contingencies" of a

---

[1] Readers are referred to Orwell (1940), Hayner (1969), Stephens (1976), and Lilly and Ball (1978) for other statements on aspects of hotel life.

variety of "deviants" and the ways in which they manage their various involvements and hustles. Finally, in examining aspects of friendship and affection, loneliness and sexuality, violence and disruptions, some important themes in the social psychology of interpersonal relationships become explicit.

THE SETTING

Although we have collected some material through observation of a number of hotels and bars, many of which cater to strippers and/or hookers, a major source of our information comes from "Main" and "Central," two hotels in "Eastville." Both are located in a rough (quasi-slum) area of the city and both are well-known for catering to prostitutes and their clients, not only in Eastville, but among certain groups of entertainers and promoters throughout North America.

While Eastville seems fairly typical of mid-eastern cities, we have also attempted to gauge the representativeness of Main and Central by asking hookers, entertainers, and the like how these places compare with other places they have worked. Many of these people have worked in a variety of places across North America and their responses indicate that while one finds variations (for example, in hooking procedures and hooker-desk clerk relations in any large city), the situations at Main and Central are fairly typical; and that Main and Central are probably better than many other places for providing a cross-section of hustles and the actors involved. Although many of these people are highly mobile and make adjustments to any local/temporal conditions, they have a major advantage over most tourists. As "insiders" in the hotel community, not only are they more likely to be knowledgeable about ongoing hustles but they are apt to be more aware of the undersides of the hotels at which they work. Speaking very generally, there seems considerable agreement that the "normative frames" operative at Main and Central are reasonably compatible with those in effect at most "hooker bars" in North America.

Both Main and Central have cocktail lounges, rooms for rent, and feature exotic dancers — but draw a significant income from activities associated in one or other ways with prostitution. In both instances, the bar clientele is rather diverse; while one finds straight businessmen and blue collar workers in attendance and the occasional couple out for an evening, one also finds an assortment of "rounders" (streetwise individuals with other than legitimate means of support) present. One will also encounter the occasional "bum" who may have just cashed his welfare cheque, but these people are generally not tolerated in these hotels. University students sometimes visit these bars in small groups, but they do not constitute any significant element of the trade.

Fights are relatively frequent at both Main and Central and, over the years, a great many people have been injured as a consequence of these incidents. While many of these confrontations were between patrons, staff members have also been frequently involved either directly or in their attempts to "police" the area. For anyone regularly frequenting or working in these bars, violence, while not a way of life, is something they can expect to witness or experience with considerably more regularity than persons habituating many other bars.

Given the degree of sexuality and violence associated with these hotels, they are popular targets of the police. Although the police were successful in closing Main for a period of time, the general effect of police pressure on any such hotel is a temporary shifting of activities to other bars, followed by a return to "life as normal." While hotel staff will call the police in more extreme cases, they are in no way sympathetic towards them. Along with rounders and hookers, many of the staff have been arrested and some have been incarcerated; many are into drugs and gambling, and some deal with loansharks. Beyond this, many staff members are involved in a variety of quasi-legal and illegal hustles within the hotel setting. Finally, while negative attitudes towards the police are reinforced in this setting, many of the staff members' prior experiences involved unpleasant encounters with the law.

Recognizing the amount of "action" at hotels such as Main and Central, we do not intend to present them as "typical" bars. Thus, some of our efforts have been directed towards balancing out this aspect of the research by examining life in other bars. Nevertheless, many features are common to all bars in varying degrees, suggesting that research on "action bars" may be extremely useful in alerting us to some elements of group life that tend to escape our attention in more "sedate" settings.

APPROACH

The material on Main and Central and over fifty other bars and/or hotels was collected through observations and interviews. The community was initially accessed through the affiliational network established by one of the authors over five years of part-time and summer hotel work. Although he started as a barboy, he subsequently worked as a desk clerk, a waiter, a bartender, and a doorman at Main and worked for shorter periods of time in four other bars. Work observations were extensively supplemented by both interviews and material gathered by the authors as they spent time "socializing" with members of the hotel community at bars, in hotel rooms, in restaurants, at after-hours clubs, and at their homes. No attempt was made to conceal the authors' university identities and the relationships would be best described as informal, characterized by varying degrees of friendship.

As we became acquainted with more hotel people, we found our contacts expanding. Existing contacts introduced us to others and, with time, we found our overall project had expanded considerably more than we had earlier anticipated. As a result of these exposures to other bars and settings, we found that not only were we becoming more aware of the external activities of the persons at Main and Central, but that we were also obtaining a much more representative basis on which to discuss the hotel community.

By and large, the material has been organized around activities. By articulating the ways in which activities are handled we hope to indicate: how "social order" emerges in this seemingly disruptive environment; how persons become involved in the hotel community, and the conditions affecting their continuances and disentanglements; how services, legitimate and otherwise, are provided; how "suckers" are hustled, and the ways in which encounters with the police are handled; and how interpersonal relationships between the hustlers, the staff, and the patrons develop, and the implications of reputations and contacts for ongoing life.

In developing this material, an attempt was made to indicate the relatedness of persons coming together in an environment characterized by a number of deviant pursuits. This is, we think, an element of sociology which has been too frequently neglected. In attempting to account for particular forms of involvements, researchers seldom take the time to articulate the ways in which persons develop roles in conjunction with others. Although the progression is by no means automatic, as hookers, staff, and patrons spend longer periods of time in this setting, they tend to become increasingly caught up in the underlife of the hotel community: for all its roughness and lack of respectability, it becomes a regular workplace, and a home. While the hotel community does not necessarily exclude other activities or places, persons remaining in this setting over time are likely to find that it becomes an increasingly central element of their identities. Thus, if we wish to understand the career contingencies (Becker, 1963; Letkemann, 1973; Lesieur, 1977; Prus and Sharper, 1977) of deviants, it becomes critical that we take the time to examine the ongoing exchanges characterizing these subcommunities and the contingencies affecting persons' involvements therein.

AN OVERVIEW

To provide the reader with a sense of organization of the book, we would like to briefly highlight central aspects of each chapter. Following this introductory chapter, Chapter 2 focusses on prostitution. Representing a central activity in some bars and hotels, "hooking" is the pivot around which much of the social and economic life in those settings revolves. Hence, while prostitution is only one aspect of community life, it provides a useful starting point. This chapter involves a number of themes, reflecting the ways in which these women work out aspects of their lives both within and outside the hotel setting. In addition to indicating the significance of prostitution for the hotel community, attention is directed toward the hookers' procedures of locating and managing "dates"; the nature of hotel life they experience; their career contingencies (involvements, continuities and disinvolvements); and their entanglements in reference to pimps and "wives-in-law," boyfriends and husbands, families and children, and the hooker community. The briefer discussions of street hookers, massage parlor girls, and call girls serve to further contextualize bar hookers and thus promote a more general understanding of the "working girls."

In Chapter 3, "Working the Desk," we follow the hookers to the hotel rooms and thereby examine the role of the desk clerk. Using the preceding material as a backdrop, we see another side of the hotel community as concerns of "keeping order" and "protecting the girls" become prominent. In this context as well, we also begin to see some of the other hustles operative in hotel settings and some of the exchanges taking place between the hookers and the staff members.

Returning to the bar, Chapter 4 highlights stripping (or "exotic dancing"). In this chapter we not only depict some aspects of "putting on a show," and some of the problematics of mobility and respectability, but also discuss "hooking on the side," "career contingencies," and "love and sexuality," as these pertain to strippers. As stripping represents but one form of bar entertainment, some material on musicians is also presented, indicating more generally the contingencies affecting entertainers as they endeavor to fit into bar settings in reference to both on-stage and off-stage engagements.

Chapter 5, "Working the Bar," depicts some of the "behind the scenes" activities of bar staff. In addition to their responsibilities and services, a variety of hustles involving bartenders, waiters and barboys, waitresses and hat-check girls, dancers, and doormen, are examined. We also discuss the ways in which trouble is handled, and the career contingencies and social lives of persons legitimately working in "disreputable settings."

In Chapter 6, "Being Patrons," the emphasis is on the forms of bar patron involvement and the ways in which their lives and those of the hookers, the strippers and the staff become intertwined. Regardless of whether patrons are there as tourists, occasionals, or regulars, or are there for friendship, drinking, the floor shows, or to "get laid," they represent a most vital component of the hotel community.

"In Perspective," the last and the most theoretical chapter, articulates and synthesizes a number of themes emerging in the preceding chapters. Under the general rubric of "deviance as interaction," Chapter 7 considers deviance in respect to "normative frames," "interrelatedness," "careers," and "activity." This is followed by a discussion of the problematics of doing field research.

In gathering the data for this book and in presenting it, we have endeavored to "let the people speak for themselves,"[2] as we wanted very much to ground our analysis in the everyday experiences of the participants.

---

[2] While letting the respondents speak for themselves, we have done some editing of the extracts. All names and places have been altered, and in addition to deleting noncontextualizing repetitive or noninformative material (e.g. "uh," "er," "you know"), we were forced, given printing limitations, to omit a great deal more material than we desired.

Chapter 2

Hooking in the Lounge

A lot of guys ask me, "What's a nice girl like you doing in a job like this?" And they tell me that I look too innocent or that I shouldn't be doing this kind of thing. Usually I'll say, "What do you think I'm doing? I'm a hooker!" (hooker)

Focussing on the life-styles and operating procedures of the "working girls" in a bar setting, this chapter depicts one aspect of the hotel community as it is presently constituted. While relatively few places would be classified as "hooker bars" or "hooker hotels," we were able to access a number of these settings. Thus, although most of the material in this chapter comes from Main and Central wherein prostitution is a "featured activity" and one which affects the lives of most staff and patrons therein, we have been able to contextualize our material more generally. In addition to examining the hustles, career contingencies, and interactions of the "working girls," and the ways in which prostitution is assimilated in these two bars, we provide some indication of this activity in other bar settings. The chapter concludes with a discussion of hookers working on the streets, in massage parlors, and as "call girls," as we attempt to situate "bar hookers" in this broader context.

ATMOSPHERE AND ECONOMICS

A lot of hotels downtown, if you took the hookers out, they just wouldn't make any money, because hooking is so much a part of it. And it's good for the management because of the business, and it's good for the people working there because a lot of the guys will tip to impress the hookers. (hooker)

To a large extent, prostitution represents a central feature in the histories of both Main and Central. Although neither hotel appears to have opened with that as a goal, prostitution has become an institutionalized component of these hotels. While any number of hotels or bars may have been successful in disinvolving themselves from prostitution, the geographical location of these hotels, their reputations, and the interconnections of the people involved make this prospect unlikely for either Main or Central. Attempts have been made to eliminate prostitution from these hotels, but this element figures prominently in the general success of both Main and Central. The "working girls" not only promote a viable liquor trade, but also represent an important contributor to the financial well-being of nearly every employee from manager to maid:

If you took the hookers out, they'd have to change the whole hotel. It would have to be different. It just couldn't make it as a cocktail lounge. It would be impossible. He's tried it before, a couple of times, and he's brought high priced groups in. He thought, "We'll make this a really respectable place and get the girls out of here," but it just didn't work out. It just went downhill financially. . . . He's tried a lot of things, and none of them worked out and so he's gone back to the girls. (bartender)

A third bar, Hillcrest, with a similar reputation, has also found its economic life precariously dependent on the presence of hookers:

Look at this place. They told us, "Get the girls out or we'll close you down." We have only about half the regular clientele now. The money's just not there. . . . You still get guys coming in, looking for some action, but it's not like it was. I hope we can get back to normal pretty soon. (doorman)

The dependency is a mutual one, and the girls working these bars become sensitive to advantages outsiders may not readily appreciate:

I never worked in any other hotel. It wasn't necessary. A lot of people ask me, "Why do you work out of this crummy hotel?" But Central is so easy, you just sit there. Everyone who comes in, just about all the men who come in are tricks, and they all know that you're working there, and they sit down and you know why they're sitting down. If you're at another hotel they don't know for sure, so they try to feel you out and you're trying to feel them out, and they might think, "You don't look like a hooker!" Finally after talking to them for an hour, it might have been an interesting conversation, but then when they find out, they say, "Oh, well, you're really nice but I'm sorry, I don't pay for that sort of thing." So, at the Central it's so easy. You get lazy working out of hotels like Main and Central because it's so easy. . . . Girls that are barred and have to start bar hopping will tell you they'll do anything to get back in, because it's rough to have to go from bar to bar, and much more expensive. (hooker)

Whereas neither the hotel staff nor the management "sets up" customers with any regularity (most wish to avoid this function), and any client-hooker transactions are considered their own business, the girls are, nevertheless, apt to find themselves being screened to ascertain their acceptability. Desiring as much business as possible, the managers are also concerned that (1) the place not be too (obviously) cluttered with prostitutes and (2) the girls present themselves in an appropriate manner. These concerns seem largely motivated by the desire to maintain a satisfactory social atmosphere and to avoid trouble, especially legal entanglements. Hence, although procedures will vary somewhat over time and the girls may more or less freely move into these hotels, it is not uncommon to find them being qualified once it becomes apparent that they are there to work:

Maggie was discussing an interview that she had prior to starting at Main. She said that the interview ran about an hour and that the manager told her a set of rules that she was to follow. Such things as not being too obvious on the job and buying drinks, not beer, and also to take people upstairs rather than to a hotel on the outside. . . . Bea said that she didn't have an interview, but knew the manager at Main previously. When she was unhappy at Central, he said it would be okay for her to go to work there. (notes)

While the more overt presence of prostitutes promotes a definition of these hotels as "sleazy" by the respectables (some of whom "would not be caught dead in such a place"), the hookers' significance extends considerably beyond the social aura associated with these hotels. Not only do the establishments benefit directly from the business generated by the working girls themselves (representing a particularly loyal group of regulars) but they also derive business from their tricks, and the tourists, as well as from those regulars who like the atmosphere these places afford.

"WORKING GIRLS"

The (regular) hookers we are considering operate predominantly in cocktail lounges. Although most are involved in prostitution full-time (the major or exclusive source of income), not all work on a regular day in, day out basis. Excluding dancers and staff members who hook on the side, about 25-35 girls each work out of Main and Central in the average week, although they will not all be visible at any given time.[1] Generally speaking, the girls range in age from 18 to 40 and with the exception of a few "old timers" (55) at Central, the girls at the two hotels are more or less interchangeable. Typically, the girls will work out of one hotel for a period of time, sometimes for years. Not only does this enable them to develop a more stable clientele but, with time, they become meshed in the subculture of that hotel: it becomes a basis of friendship and assistance in a potentially hostile environment.

Most of the hookers are reasonably attractive by general North American standards. It would, however, be erroneous to assume that all or most of the girls have glamorous Hollywood faces or physiques. While many of their outfits do have an erotic flavor (party dresses or otherwise revealing outfits), much of their attire is relatively casual (office, shopping attire) varying in degrees of neatness and quality. Perhaps it would suffice to say that although a little more care may be devoted to promoting a "sexy" appearance than average, most of these girls would not stand out on a reasonably busy street:

> I was kind of surprised, myself, when I first started at Central, at how many girls were doing it. All kinds of girls, like some had some university, some really intelligent, nice quiet girls. (hooker)

> There are all kinds of girls, all shapes and sizes, and you look at some of them and you wonder, "How do they make money at that." You figure they must be in the wrong business. Somebody comes along and there they go. It's amazing. . . . I don't know what you consider ugly, but you see a lot of girls that look to me pretty ugly, sort of pushed-in faces or whatever, but they're making their money. You just wonder. And fat, some of them are really fat. . . . Like this one, gee, I wouldn't go and smell her, but she makes a lot of money. Even to look at her made me kind of sick, and this girl, she goes upstairs, back and forth, up and down, up and down, all night. I'm surprised she didn't lose more weight just walking up and down the stairs. (bartender)

---

[1] The number of hookers working at either Central or Main can vary considerably from week to week. We have seen weeks with as few as 10-15 girls working in the lounge or as many as 50-60. Even when the number of hookers working in a given bar is fairly consistent over a few months, some turnover is likely to occur on a week to week basis.

Although many of the girls at Main and Central (about 80 per cent at any given time) have "pimps," they solicit almost entirely on their own. These "kept men" offer virtually no assistance in any aspect of the hustle and are generally discouraged from frequenting these bars. While the hookers will refer "safe" customers to one another, they do not have anyone regularly setting them up. The staff may make occasional referrals but are generally reluctant to do so, since they feel that the risks are not worth the gains.

Being accessible, to a large extent, means being present. As persons more familiar with hotels can fairly readily identify hookers by observing their inter-actions with one another and with the staff over a period, and also by talking with regulars, a hooker's mere presence in a bar may be sufficient to attract prospective customers. And, unless the competition is stiff, the amount of time a girl spends in the bar is proportionately related to her success:

There are some very dedicated hookers. Like Mary there. She will be here from noon until closing time, day in, day out. If she's not in, she's out doing a trick and will be back shortly. She's always around. That's the kind of girl I'd like to have working for me. (doorman)

As simple as it seems, the first indicator of a successful career hooker is her continual presence in the hotel. Many long-term hookers do not, however, possess this dedication to their work. While some will work in a number of hotels in a day or week, and some will "do tricks" at home or through other arrangements, a number of hookers are available only on a haphazard basis:

Usually, I only work from 10 to 12 in the evening. If I can't make any money in an hour and a half or so, that's it. I forget about it. Unless I've got bills to pay. Then I'll be here more. (hooker)

I work when I need the money. My rent's due day after tomorrow so I figured I better hustle my ass down here. (hooker)

From the girls' point of view it's best to be in the bar when the prospects are maximized (highest trick to hooker ratio) but, lacking schedules, one finds a fair amount of guessing as the girls endeavor to find optimal times:

I thought it would be good tonight, but look at this place. Shit! It's just crawling with girls. I guess we all had the same idea. (hooker)

It should not be assumed, however, that quiet times in the bar are necessarily quiet times for the girls:

Carol said that Saturday is a very good day for regulars. She said that Saturday afternoons a lot of women go out shopping, leaving the husbands free and they come down in the afternoon. She says that on the average Saturday she can make about a hundred bucks just in the afternoon. There's always something in the afternoon, even though it's quiet businesswise in the bar. She says, "Later on it doesn't get any good until 10 p.m. In between that time it's not too good." There doesn't seem to be any connection between business at the bar and the money the girls are making as far as customers. Sometimes, when the place is packed, nobody's taking anybody out. Other times, there may be just a few people there, but they're taking the girls out. (notes)

SCREENING DATES

Unless they have specific reasons to believe otherwise, the girls view each patron as a prospective trick. Some prospects will be viewed as eager for action ("seekers") while others will be seen as needing a little encouragement. By and large, it is assumed that any man will "want to get laid" whenever he can and then it becomes a matter of coming to terms.

The girl will sometimes sit, on invitation, at a customer's table, but usually it is the customer who goes to her table. Typically, he buys her a drink and they may spend five to twenty minutes engaging in light conversation and mild flirting. During this time, both parties have an opportunity to assess one another.

For the dates these table conversations may not only represent a form of intimacy (for those so interested), but may also serve to qualify the girls. In discussing the music, her drink, the show, the club, and so on, the date will find out whether or not she is a "regular girl"; through selection, he may find a girl who best fits his notions.

If the girl is unsure about the man's identity, she may ask him if he is a police officer, request that he show some identification, or try to avoid him. However, if the girl decides the fellow is acceptable, she will try to get him to make her an offer (a strategy used to reduce the likelihood of being charged with soliciting). The transaction is further facilitated when one of the parties has chosen a table adjacent to the one the other party occupies. The man not only is less obvious in approaching the girl, but he or she can more casually involve the other in conversation.

Although seemingly a simple matter, and varying considerably from one girl to another, the screening of customers is an important element of the hustle. Not only are the girls wary about plainclothes policemen, but they are also concerned about the prospect's ability to pay for the session and that he be reasonably "safe" (non-violent). The following extracts indicate both the sorts of concerns the girls have and the sorts of approaches they encounter:

> You do get guys coming by who are just looking for a straight date. With them, you try to indicate that you're not here for fun, you're here to do business. You're here to work. You also get some who say, "Are you free?" and you say "No, I'm not free." Or they'll say, "Are you for sale?" and you say, "No, I'm for rent!" You also get people coming that you're not interested in. Then you say, "Well, look, I'm busy now" or "I'm leaving shortly!" or "I'm just not interested." Usually that seems to work. (hooker)

> Young guys especially are smart alecks, I can't stand smart alecks. People that are too aggressive or tough guys scare me. I don't want to go with them because they're usually the guys who were going to be lovers. They're going to show you how great a lover they can be. Forget it! I'm not interested in that. . . . A lot of guys, if I said, "I don't want to go out", or "I'm not interested", they'd say, "Well, why? I've got the money." I'd say, "Well, money's not the most important thing." I'd rather not have the money, there other things that are more important. They don't like that. Those kind of tricks don't understand. (hooker)

> I used to worry about them being cops, at first, when I first started and I didn't know who the cops were. But after a while you just know the face. It might've

been the partner, you know they change partners a lot, or maybe you've seen them at court or you've gone up to the police station and you just know the face. You can usually tell a cop. In most cases, you would just know, by the way he walks, and by the way he dresses and by the way he talks. When he sits down, you can usually tell. You do make mistakes, sure you do. I mean, a girl who's been there ten years makes a mistake. But basically, they're the same people. They have a few rookies come up every year, new faces, but that's one thing that I only worried about at the beginning. At the beginning, I talked to everybody. I've had five busts. I haven't had one in the last year. And most of the girls will tell you that. They don't get busted too often. So I never really worry. If somebody looks like a cop, and I'm not sure, I just don't talk to him. But there have been a few times when I was certain that guy was a cop, and turns out somebody else went out with him and he wasn't. So you say, "Oh shit!", but who cares. (hooker)

In spite of the value of screening dates, it should be noted that this is a stage easily omitted. When this is done, however, it not only jeopardizes the girl's operations, but also more blatantly defines the encounter as an economic exchange, stripping the relationship of any romantic overtones:

Some of these girls are so fast. Like I went over to this one table and I no sooner said, "May I join you?" and she says, "Do you want to take me out?" That's all she was interested in, just doing business. Just like that. (patron)

Should a hooker not be interested in a particular man, she may attempt to ignore him or refuse permission when he asks if he can join her at her table. This is usually sufficient and is frequently accompanied by the girls saying something like, "I'm busy right now", "Sorry, I'm leaving shortly". If the man is persistent the girl may become abusive towards him or call for assistance from the staff or regular patrons:

Maggie was having some trouble and called the bouncer over. Frank told the man to move, indicating that if he wouldn't, he would have to help him along. The patron appeared fairly drunk. He was tottering back and forth. (notes)

Usually, it depends on the guy. If he's decent, I'll be decent. Otherwise, I'll tell him to fuck off. Or if I'm in a bad mood, I am not going to put up with anything. (hooker)

Fees

Fees are usually arranged at the table, but seldom is money exchanged before the pair are in the room together. While the rates vary considerably, at the time of the research the girls generally settled for $30 to $60 for "a session." Sessions were vaguely defined in discussing prices with dates, but the girls generally meant one ejaculation on the part of the date or their typical 10-20 minutes with the date in the room, whichever comes first. The hookers will try to get as much as they can from a client for a short encounter and will generally charge considerably more for a longer date ($150-$200 for a two-hour session). As seen below, fees may vary with both the client and the girl involved:

I always had a straight fee, $40. . . . But if I wasn't sure, like if the guy was okay but there was something I didn't quite like, I made it higher. And then if he *went for it, well, I couldn't pass up $60, and then I'd go. But basically, when somebody sat down, it was $40. You have a lot of guys, especially regular tricks, who'll say, "Well, so and so went out with me for $35. Why don't you go for $35, or $30?" And you say, "Well that's so and so. Go out with her if you want it for $35." Then they say, "Well, what's so special about you?" "Nothing, but I've always got $40. Why should I make it $35 for you?"* (hooker)

I charge $80. I could get more tricks for $40, but this way I only have to do half the number of tricks to make my $80. (hooker)

While some of the clients may be open to more "extravagant" fees, others have very definite limits:

Forty dollars is the most I can spend. I only make about a thousand a month and I have a wife and three kids to support with that. That doesn't leave a hell of a lot does it? So forty, that's my limit. Like she has to live, but so do I, right? But, if some broad wants sixty, too bad, I can't afford that! For sixty dollars, I'll go in the can and whack off. I can't afford that. (patron)

Tom and Jerry earlier in the evening had been joking about the hookers, but later on, they tried to score at Main. Tom said that he knew one of the girls, Marlene, from before, and went to talk to her. He came back, saying, "She wanted $50, a flat 50! She wouldn't come down on that. That is too much." Then he and Jerry went off to the Central to see if they could pick up something a little more economical. (notes)

Although most anyone could arrange a "date" with one of the hookers, the girls are selective both individually and on a somewhat collective basis. Thus, depending on which girl one first approaches, the likelihood of being defined acceptable can vary considerably. However, once a patron has been turned down by one hooker, the chances of him being rejected by others increase:

I try to judge them by talking to them, to get some idea what sort of person they are, if they are acceptable. If I don't like the person, I ask them to leave. If another girl rejects the guy, I probably will refuse him as soon as he approaches me. The other girls will be looking at him the same ways, and if he doesn't meet their standards then he wouldn't meet my standards. (hooker)

Generally, through brief visits at one another's tables and/or the "powder room," the word that someone is significantly unacceptable will spread fairly quickly and most of the girls will try to avoid that person.

Although a number of bar patrons, particularly the regulars, are quite knowledgeable about prostitution in this setting, it should not be assumed that everyone with money "scores." Arranging a date with a hooker is not as easy as some might infer:

A man in his thirties, with whom I had earlier been speaking, went to talk to a couple of hookers. When he returned, he asked, "Hey, what do you have to do to get lucky around here?" "How do you mean?" He replied, "Well, I tried two girls already and struck out." "Oh yeah, what happened?" He explained, "The first one said she was just getting ready to leave, that she was busy." "Well, that happens, you know. What happened with the second one?" "She said, 'Thanks, but no thanks.' Like I know that I am not the most handsome guy in the world, but do these girls have to be so particular? Like, what the hell are you supposed to say to them?'' (notes)

GETTING A ROOM

The bar hookers generally arrange to meet their clients in hotel rooms. Although some will meet dates in their homes or "trick pads" (another apartment), it would be highly unusual for the girl to rent a room and proceed to take a client there. Typically, once an agreement has been made at the table, the girl will tell the man to rent a room in a particular hotel indicating that she will follow. This is an important point. The man will be on his own for a few minutes and if not sufficiently encouraged, may change his mind. It will also become evident to him that (unlike massage parlors) the girl's fee does not include accommodations.

The hooker's next sequence of activity depends, in part, on which hotel they have selected. In some cases, she will wait a few moments and then head to the hotel. After asking the desk clerk if Mr.---- (the agreed-upon name) has registered, she will proceed to his room. If he has failed to show, the girl has wasted her time, possibly a cab fare and will, upon returning to the bar, be forced to order another drink. Some of the girls do become visibly upset when this happens:

> We had just gotten into the lobby and were talking with a couple of dancers when Mary came up and asked if a particular name had registered. The clerk checked, "No, can't find anyone by that name here." "What?" Mary retorted, "Where did that motherfucking son of a bitch go? Look again. That son of a bitch! . . . Let me see those cards. . . . Here it is. Room 43. That's him, the son of a bitch. I'll take care of him." And off she stomped to the man's room. (notes)

A second routine involves the girl calling the hotel after she considers sufficient time for the man to be registered. If the man has checked in, she can proceed directly to the hotel. If not, she has only wasted the price of the telephone call and, if she has left some possession at her table while making the call, she can return to her table (tables vary in desirability, and the loss of a choice location could hurt one's business). In hotels using this system it is generally considered undesirable for the girls to go directly to the desk. All but the most careless or naive will first call the desk clerk for clearance:

> This one hooker was obviously pretty new at the game, because she went right up to the desk and asked what room a certain man had taken and when visiting hours were. She didn't go through the usual route and was very indiscreet about going upstairs. You don't go over and talk to the desk clerk and mention somebody's name out in the open, in the lobby, where the police could be sitting around or hiding. She seemed very new at this, asking about visiting hours and what not. That's not the way it is supposed to be done. (clerk)

Unless the desk clerk suspects the presence of police in the lobby, or the customer has left (or has registered under a different name), the call from the hooker presents no particular problems. When there is a discrepancy, the way in which the clerk responds to the call will generally clue the girl into the situation. If the coast is clear, the clerk will give the girl the room number and she can then proceed directly to the room.

IN THE ROOM

Not having collected any fees in the lounge, one of the girl's first tasks, particularly with a new customer, will be to obtain her money. If a specific price has not been arranged previously, that will have to be negotiated, as will any additional or unusual services.

When I first get in the room, that is when I collect, except for a few regular guys I know, they pay me after. (hooker)

Although the dates may have a variety of time anticipations regarding a "session," the girls generally operate within very tight time parameters:

They're very clean girls, but fast as they can do it. You could sit in the bar and time them, ten minutes. The girl would meet the guy, get her money, get all her clothes off, wash up, put her clothes on, all this in ten minutes! And you figure, in there somewhere, right, this guy just blew his load, in ten seconds, a minute. A lot of people pay big bucks to stay like half an hour. (bartender)

Usually they take about fifteen minutes in the room, and if they take longer, well it's more money. Sometimes you have problems with the guys not wanting you to leave, but when their time is up, you just tell them, "Well, I've got other customers waiting for me. I have to go do my work, I'm a business girl." (hooker)

Time is seen as money and, generally speaking, the girls endeavor to spend no more time than necessary with a date. Although longer dates may generate more take-home pay, they are usually not desired. Not only are longer dates likely to intensify problems associated with disentanglement but, being accustomed to quick turnovers, the thought of spending two hours or an evening with a stranger causes some of the girls to experience some anxiety:

Another type of date you try to avoid is the all-nighter. If you're with somebody, two hours even, you start to think, "Well, what do I do? What am I going to do with this person?" You're with a stranger and after half an hour or so, your superficial relationship runs out and you don't want him to get to know the real you. You want to avoid that, so it might be okay going out to dinner with the guy because you can talk about the meal and the place but when you're alone in the room, the problem's what do you do? Sure, it's physically easier, but mentally it's hard. You just try to avoid those prolonged sessions. But you pretty well have to make that same decision every night because somebody is going to come and they're going to want this longer type of arrangement. You have to just tell yourself "It's too difficult, it's not worth it." (hooker)

The hookers typically spend between 10-20 minutes in the room with a date. In general, those taking less time tend to be the more successful overall. They are also likely to be the more experienced girls and are less apt to have difficulties with their clients. While these limited involvements may be somewhat disappointing to some of the clients (certainly not all), they enable the girl to more readily "disentangle" herself from her clients. Thus, although she has made an agreement to perform in certain respects, she can in other ways invoke personal distance between herself and a client she finds in any way offensive. What may be seen as "cold" behavior, from some clients' perspectives, need in no way signify a "cold hearted" woman. For the girl, it may be a way of achieving acceptable distancing under otherwise intimate conditions. Any girl unable to situationally disinvolve herself from her dates is unlikely to be a successful hooker, and seems more likely to find herself in more than usual difficulties with the clients. Thus, not only is some prestige associated with the ability to efficiently dispose of customers, but longer sessions tend to generate concern:

> *Carol came to the desk. She was kind of worried and asked me if I had seen Maureen, a black hooker. I said I didn't know where she was. She asked me what room she was in, but I had just come on and didn't know. Another hooker, Rita, came by and I asked her if she had seen Maureen. By the time Maureen came down, about a half an hour later, Carol was really upset, "What took you so long? What were you doing?" Maureen replied, "Just taking care of business."* (notes)

Anticipating subsequent encounters with other clients, and feeling little obligation to any of the tricks, the hookers generally try to put stringent limitations on the extensiveness of any foreplay and actual intercourse:

> *The girl has to take the initiative and be somewhat assertive and telling the guy what to do. Otherwise, she'll have considerable difficulty just managing him, and then later leaving the room.* (hooker)

> *Kissing, well, that's one thing you are just never suppose to do, and almost every guy wants to do it. And you're just supposed to say, "Never mind, I don't kiss," right. And he says, "Well, why not?" Well, with most girls, you think well here's this complete stranger in front of you and you go down on him and you give him a blow job, and what's more personal than that? But it becomes regular, that it's not personal anymore, so what's left that is? Kissing. So then they treat kissing as something they really care about. It's the only thing left, right? . . . Well, I never felt that way. If I just couldn't stand him, like if they were ugly, or if they had icky teeth or bad breath, then I would just say, "Well, look, forget it, I don't kiss." But if he was a nice guy and I was being nice to him in every other way, if he wanted to kiss, okay. Sometimes the guy will sit down at your table and ask you, "Do you kiss?" If they've had experience with hookers and they know they don't, they'll ask you. So I say, "Yeah", and I did. It just didn't bother me, because . . . well, it's the same way with sex, I just blanked it out of my mind, like I'd be thinking about, "Like tomorrow I'm going shopping for groceries. What do I need?" or whatever. It was something, completely like standing away from myself for that time. I just wasn't there. I could do the same with tricking. I could kiss somebody and not put anything into it and just know it didn't mean anything. But most of the girls, almost all of them do not kiss. . . . It's the same thing with not letting anyone touch you, or caress your body, they just didn't want that. But I knew if you're going to kiss a guy, you're going to let him touch you. If that's what turns him on, of course he's going to get off faster. And if he thinks that you're enjoying it, of course he's going to get off faster. I mean, you fooled him. I mean, how does the guy know*

anyway, if you say the right things, and you make the right sounds, he'll think that you're really enjoying it. You can believe that he's going to come back and see you because he finally found a hooker that enjoys it. I mean, I've had a lot of guys convinced that I really enjoyed it. So, of course, they came back once a week, I had a lot of regulars. (hooker)

Affection is a very difficult thing for me with the dates. I try to avoid it as much as possible. It's too involving. It's too difficult to handle. It's too personal. (hooker)

While the preceding material provides a sense of detachment of hookers from their dates, the extract following denotes in sequence the ways in which depersonalization is managed:

I usually get the room number over the phone, and I usually talk to the guy. I'll say, "I'm on the way up, what room are you in?" He tells me. Then you go up, knock at the door. He opens the door or says, "Come in" and you walk in. You make small talk, well I do to start. By the way, I'm very shy, well, I was very shy. That's one thing this business has helped me in, I got over a lot of my shyness. As soon as I walk in the room I say, like "Hi, how are you?" You know, just small talk. And, usually if the guy knows anything about it, he'll have the money out. He'll be giving it to you or have it on the table. If I don't see it, or if he doesn't have it ready, I'll just say, "Can I have my money now please." He says, "Oh sure." and he gets it and gives it to you, you put it away. You start to get undressed, so he starts to get undressed or maybe he's already undressed waiting. Then you go and get a towel and you wash him off, and you wash yourself off. . . . So you've got the guy and you've just finished washing him off and yourself, along with a little small talk. Then you see, it depends, each individual case is different. It varies, but basically I ask the guy if he likes to be Frenched. You'd be surprised, there are some guys who don't like getting Frenched. They are terrified of the idea, "No, no, no!" So you ask him and he'll usually say, "Sure" or something, so you French him for about five minutes or whatever. Sometimes he's already got a hard on, sometimes he doesn't, it depends. And I usually liked the guy to get on top because it's easier for me, so I just say, "Would you like to get on top?" Usually, he'll say, "Oh, sure." Sometimes they won't, sometimes they say, "No, I'd rather you did." Then I'd say, "Okay, well, I'll start it off, you finish it." But I try to get him to get on top. A lot of the girls, however, liked to get on top because that way they have control. But not me, I liked him on top, because when he's on top he can control the way he wants to move. He knows what's going to make him come, you don't know. That way he's got control, you just go along with it, you're just there. So I like it better. But a lot of the girls like to be on top because they feel if the guy's going to do anything, they feel that they have more control. But I never worried about that much, you're usually lying near a phone and your hands are free. I'll make sure that my hands are free. I mean he can't do anything to me really. It's about ten minutes, that's basically all it takes, for a typical trick. Then what I usually do is I get up and I get washed and I come back and wash him, and light a cigarette. Then I'll sit on the bed and talk for another five or ten minutes, make him feel like he's getting his money's worth, especially if he comes faster. Like if you're there five minutes and he comes and apologizes for it. You say, "Oh, that's okay." Now, most girls will jump off, get washed, get their clothes and leave. I never did that. I always stayed and talked, because, well because I don't want to make him feel like he's a machine. A lot of guys, I don't know why they keep coming, but they will have gone out with hookers, different ones all the time and when they find that the last five or six have all treated them like that, they get mad and they might take it out on you. I've never had bad trouble. I've had a few guys who didn't like me, but with most of them, I found that extra five minutes, talking to him like he's a person, really helped. Most of them came back. (hooker)

When finished, it is conventional for the girl to call the desk for clearance. Then, she usually leaves first, the client following a little later. From the girls' perspective, it is largely sex without affection, a business transaction:

You think of it as work. They're strangers and you're providing a service. You want to do it in the most efficient way you can. Sometimes you're flattered when these people come to you, I suppose more initially. Later, you just don't think in those terms very much. You think in terms of the $40 or whatever it is that that trick might be giving you. (hooker)

A lot of people think that if you're in the business for sex, then that's where you get your sexual satisfaction. That's what they believe. Maybe a few do, but very, very rarely. For most of them, it's just a job and they don't feel anything. (hooker)

There is no emotional involvement with the tricks at all, not at all. And, on the girl's part, it is actually a lot better if they can stay apart from the dates, because if she gets involved with one person, then it is harder for her to work, because she has that person on her mind and she really can't concentrate so much on what she's doing. So it's better for her not to have any feelings for the tricks, and sometimes, it's kind of hard, because you find that the person is a very nice person, and the kind of person you figure you wouldn't mind being involved with, but you have to keep it on a neutral basis. (hooker)

DEVELOPING A STABLE CLIENTELE

Once a hooker ascertains that a date is ''safe'', she may endeavor to turn him into a ''regular.'' By dealing with regulars, the girls introduce elements of continuity and predictability into their lives in terms of both income and safety. Thus, even if business is slow or the competition keen a girl may, through developing regulars, establish a buffer against these elements:

The business was very slow Friday until about 10 o'clock and then things started picking up, but Sue Ann and Mary were quite busy. Sue Ann said that she hardly had time to sit down because she had already done four or five tricks since she came in, so she didn't seem to be suffering from the overall lack of business. A fair amount of business that the girls may have at any time would involve regulars rather than new people, so that things could be slow (in the bar) and they could still be making out in terms of their own business. (notes)

The regulars will call me sometimes. If I like the person I will give them my number, where they can reach me. I will also call them. But I don't want to become a regular call girl, because I don't want to take the risk of taking dates to my apartment. That way you would be too easily traced. I will go to other places with regulars, but nothing like what I did when I first started. Then I would go anywhere with persons I didn't know. (hooker)

Given the desirability of having regulars on which to rely, one finds the girls making concessions to their dates in attempts to develop and maintain prospects as regulars:

If the guy looks like a nice guy, she might try to turn him into a regular. Like say an average working guy comes in and sits down, and he's nice to her. Well, she figures she might charge him $30, a little less than what she ordinarily might. If he's been around at all and she gives him a good deal and he goes upstairs and he has a reasonably good time and he comes back, he figures, "Well, I'll go to her again." If he walks over to another girl she's going to say $40 or $50, he's going to think that $30 was pretty good, "I'll stick with her." A lot of times the guys will tip the girls an extra 5 or 10 because, "You were so nice." It pays off for the girl. She's been nice giving the guy what he wants, and now he's giving her a little more back. She's giving the guy a break, but she figures he'll be coming back to her. (hooker)

Part of being a hooker and keeping regulars is pretending sexual satisfaction with the tricks. Not all the girls do this, but if you want to maintain regulars, you have to. It is important that they think that you are able to relate to them sexually. (hooker)

I spend as little time as possible with the dates, but I want regulars, so it's necessary to have some patience, to treat them like human beings. (hooker)

Although the regular clients become more familiar with the hooking procedures than the occasionals, they also become known to the girls and the staff more than they might anticipate.

Often you tell the other girls about the tricks that you had. Or, let's say it was a particular girl's trick, you might say, "Well, Luis came in and you weren't here. I took care of him." You do pretty well know who's with who and if there are any regulars, the girls keep track of them. (hooker)

This fellow, we used to always joke about him. Everybody knows him. He's always wanting to be tied up to the bed or whatnot. He's in The Flamingo a lot. (hooker)

In a manner not unlike a pastor's concern with another pastor "stealing his sheep," the girls tend to become possessive of their regulars:

The girls can get possessive, very possessive. If the business is there and the money's all over the place and the guy goes with someone else, you don't care too much. But if you're sitting there counting your money, and you don't have very much, and if a familiar face comes in, and he's a date of yours, like there are some guys who just tend to go out with the same girl. If you see him, you pretty well have that money counted in your head. Then, when he doesn't go out with you, it makes you mad! And sometimes, you don't get mad at him, you get *mad at the girl he went out with. Why did he go out with her? The girls will fight over dates. If they have a date and he's been a regular of hers for five years, maybe he got a better deal, like maybe somebody's cutting their rates. Say she's asking 35 and you've been charging him 40 all along. You know he's not going to go out with you again for 40 when he can get her for 35. A lot of girls will fight, especially over good money, like two hundred dollar dates, guys like that. If you lose somebody like that and you've been counting on him once a week, and then suddenly he doesn't go out with you anymore, you get mad at the other girl. There's a lot of that, an awful lot of that goes on. . . . Like you just really get disappointed because as soon as I saw the guy's face, you know that is your money, and if he doesn't go out with you, that would be $40 that just went down the drain. But you find, even tricks that go out with you for a year maybe, all of a sudden they get tired of you. They don't want to go out with you anymore. They want something different.* (hooker)

In spite of the apparent advantages of regulars and the sense of possessiveness accompanying them, it should not be assumed that one must have regulars to be successful, or that all girls desire regulars:

Not all of them are interested in having regulars. A disadvantage to having regulars is that they get too possessive. The guy wants to know too much about your personal life, especially if they come into your home or what they think is your home. Then they want to know too much about you, especially if they're spending good money. Like a sugar daddy, a guy who maybe furnishes the whole place, then of course he wants to be there and he wants to know what the girl is doing. . . . With the regulars, usually, there's only so much you can talk about and so much you want to reveal about yourself. And there's only so much you care to know about them. Some people are just boring, and after you've talked about what they do for a living and what their social life is like and where they were raised and how they grew up, I mean, how many times can you talk about it? And then you get into feelings. And usually, if a guy keeps seeing you week after week for a year or two, he cares about you. You get into love things. I would never tell anybody I love him. I'd say, "I like you a lot, you're a nice person." I did, I had some tricks that I thought were really nice, but I still let them know that I was in this for the money, I was going out with them for the money, not because I enjoyed being with him. I might enjoy being with them, but I was there for the money. That was why I was doing it. And I had a few tricks who just got too involved with me and usually they were good spenders, a hundred dollars, and they'd call and I'd say, "Sure, I'd love to see you." Then I had to psyche myself up. As soon as I hung up I'd say, "Oh, shit, now I have to see Kevin. He's such a pain in the ass.". . . . that's the reason why the girls would probably avoid regulars. They've probably had them before and have found that it's easier to go out with a stranger, somebody that you don't know anything about who's interested in getting his rocks off, and that's all he wants from you. Regulars can be very tiring mentally. That's why a lot of girls would rather go out for $35 and know they're only going to spend 15 minutes than go out with a $200 date, because a $200 date needs a lot of time and a lot of talking and it's very draining emotionally. No matter what people think, hookers do have feelings. It can get tough especially if they're telling you what their problems are and you're discussing it, trying to help them. I've had a few *people who had me almost in tears. I've had a few tricks who have been in tears. And what do you do?* (hooker)

TROUBLE IN THE ROOM

In contrast to the seemingly haphazard linkage of violent exchanges with prostitution, our observations suggest that instances of violence are much more predictable than one might assume. For, while the girls anticipate more trouble than they actually experience, much of their difficulties reflect their own operating styles. Although some of the customers tend to be rowdy or otherwise difficult to manage, many of the difficulties the girls experience (and some much more frequently than others) reflect the casual and sometimes aggressive manner in which they relate to their dates:

I won't go past my time limit, which is half an hour and so if a guy is slower in getting off, that is just too bad. You tell them, "Your time is up." If they want to go longer, "It will cost you another $40" or whatever the arrangement might have been. (hooker)

I usually spend between 15 minutes and half an hour with a trick. It doesn't matter if he comes while I am washing him, it just means that there is less I have to do with him. (hooker)

They don't want to be reminded that they're paying you, and a lot of these girls do remind them. And they remind them by saying, "Don't touch me," when the guy would go and touch them, their breast or something and they'd say, "Don't touch me! I don't want anyone to touch my breast. Hurry up. What's taking you so long? Your time is running out." They do that. They don't worry about it taking longer, they say, "Look I've been here a half hour, I'm sorry. I've done my best." They figure, "Well, I've been paid for a half hour," and they just get up and leave. A lot of men say, "Hey, wait a minute!" Like to a hooker $40 is not a lot of money, that's the lowest, except for the girls who go for less. But for a guy, $40, especially if he's only making $200 a week, and maybe he has to explain to his wife why he's $40 short, is a lot of money plus the hotel, plus he hasn't even gotten off. They're not going to just say, "Well, sure." (hooker)

Regardless of who seems most instrumental in initiating a confrontation, hookers who take the time to try to "cool out" their dates seem more able to avoid intensive conflicts:

I've never had a trick beat me up or hit me. I've had a few get rough, or say they're going to get rough if I didn't do what they wanted, in which case you do what they want you to do. But some girls don't. They fight back. If the guy says, "Give me my money back or I'll kill you," some of these idiots will say, "Fuck you!" Not me, I just say, "Fine," and give it back. I don't know what it is, they just feel that they've earned it, and there's no way anyone is getting it back. (hooker)

Other elements affecting violent exchanges between hookers and their clients are discussed in Chapter 3, but the preceding material should sensitize readers to the negotiable quality of "violent encounters."

THE TRICKS

Having just examined a number of aspects of the hooker-trick relationship, we would like to briefly comment on questions of the sort, "What kind of man goes to a hooker?" We generally say, "Just regular guys." Before examining some other aspects of the bar hookers' world, we would like to explain this answer somewhat.

The "tricks" we have encountered come from a wide variety of backgrounds, ranging from unemployed males cashing their welfare cheques to factory workers, students, prominent businessmen and politicians, and extremely well-known entertainers. Further, while one is apt to encounter reports of "odd ball" interests, most customers seem interested in conventional forms of heterosexual experience. Additionally, our material suggests that although many of the patrons are reluctant to discuss their activities with their home and work associates, they seem unlikely to be acknowledged as "other than regular guys" among those with whom they routinely associate.

While suggesting that hooker patrons are by and large relatively unexceptional individuals in reference to their own groupings, it should also be emphasized that they are not a homogeneous set of people. In this regard, it makes little sense to talk about the "typical trick" as an analytical type:

There are so many different men you meet, there's no such thing as a typical trick. Well, there is, there must be a typical trick. I know I've done it. I can't remember all of them, there must be thousands. I know I have done it. (hooker)

There are all different kinds of tricks. Just like there are different kinds of people, well, there are all different kinds of tricks. Some tricks, they just want to go to bed, but you get other people who want to spend a little more and they want to spend a little more time talking to you. But I don't think I have ever had a trick that I could say is ever the same as any other trick. And they want different things. Some want half-and-half and somebody wants straight sex. Their preferences are different and the people themselves are very different. One person might want you to be very submissive and somebody else may want you to be very overpowering. They are just not the same, they just couldn't be the same. . . . And if they were the same, I don't think a hooker could stay in business long, because you would just be bored out of your mind. It would be like going to work everyday and doing the exact same thing everyday. I mean, if you are working in an office sure you sit down at a typewriter and you may type every day, but you don't type the same thing everyday over and over again. It's something like that. (hooker)

In addition to the usual assortments of "unexceptional" dates, girls working for longer periods of time are apt to encounter a wide range of unusual requests:[2]

One night we were talking about some of the different experiences we had, like this guy who wanted to be tied to the bed posts. He wasn't violent or anything, but that was what he got off on. . . . A lot of the tricks are not really harmful people. They just have different ideas of what they like and they don't want the wife and kids to know about it. . . . Like this one guy, he wanted to go over to his

---

[2] Rather than view these interests as the result of "perversions" and the like, we suggest that these interests reflect associations and the human capacity for self-reflectivity and innovation.

place and the big thing was all these costumes that he wanted me to wear.... One of the strangest things was when this woman tried to pick me up and I didn't know how to handle this situation. (hooker)

Another problem with the tricks is that some of them think that all the girls are the same, that all the girls will do everything, and that they are all into Greek, or S & M. And it's just not the case, but they all have their own ideas, and so when they get a girl in the room, they figure that she should go along with whatever it is that they want. Now if they would explain things to you at the table, it would be different, because you could tell them who is into this or that, but they often don't do that. They just expect that when they get there, they will get what they want. (hooker)

Although readers will probably think of more exotic "quirks" when unusual habits of patrons are discussed, many of the peculiarities encountered are relatively mundane:

Some of them want someone to talk to, and they maybe couldn't talk with their wives, so they needed someone to talk to. Some of them really don't seem to know their wives anymore. They will have the kids, and live with them, but they have different interests, and they just get to where it's not the same person they married, and they just don't know one another anymore. (hooker)

A personal dislike of mine is for the girl to talk while we're having sex. It is very definitely a turn-off for me and I just tell them to be quiet. (patron)

Some of the dates, they get to be a problem because they get too possessive. They fall in love with you and they want to hang around or get you out of hooking. Some of the regulars are bad that way. (hooker)

While the great variety of people a hooker may encounter requires some versatility on her part, it should also be noted that the patrons also not only undergo a learning experience in reference to dealing with hookers generally, but may have to negotiate their interests in respect to the particular hookers they encounter:

The guys that are new to it are very naive about the whole thing. Some of them are scared, they don't know what to expect. They think the hooker is really tough, but others expect a lot more than what they deserve. They expect a full romance for $40. But some of them have been going to hookers for years and years. (hooker)

After a while, you don't think in terms of romance or kissing them. You still look for somebody who looks good to you, but you have to forget the other things. They're just not into that. (patron)

As the chapter this far suggests, hooker-client relationships are simultaneously transitory and intense, intimate and impersonal, physical and social. Given these ingredients, in conjunction with the variable backgrounds and particular interests of the involved parties, it is somewhat amazing that hooker-client encounters proceed as smoothly as they do. While the hookers, as the generally more experienced partners, tend to dominate the relationship each exchange seems contingent on one or both parties making a number of concessions to the other. Further, although some males become disenchanted with "hooker sex" and may terminate these involvements, others will continue. While patrons may initially be surprised at the lack of affection in their associations with hookers, with time they either accept this as usual or pay more for "personalized attention" (and/or patronize girls who violate hooker norms in this respect):

> *Lydia's well worth the price. For $100 she's fucking wild! Just look at the jugs on her. She is really worth the extra. She'll show you a real good time if you are willing to pay a little more.... Sometimes Lydia will kiss and sometimes she won't. It just depends in what kind of mood she's in.... But it's funny, because you'll get a girl and she'll be sucking on your dick, and you figure she'll kiss, but they see it differently. Like you say, "How about a little kiss?" And she'll say, "Oh, maybe another time" or "I'm not in the mood for that today."* (patron)

Clients who wish longer dates, dinner dates, and the like, are likely to encounter similar problems. Thus, regular hooker patrons are generally persons who have come to terms with impersonal sex. While this may deter some males from initial and/or subsequent contacts, for others this may be a desired condition:

> *Before, I used to come down just now and then, but now, I'm making better money and I can treat myself more often. I haven't found a (straight) girl that I really love, and this way, I get to try out a lot of different girls. If she treats me well, I might go back to her, if she doesn't, then I'll try somebody else.... I tried two black girls. I wanted to see what they were like. They weren't bad, they weren't good.... Carol over there, I've tried her three times. The first time, she was just super. I could not believe how good she was! The second time and the third time she didn't seem as satisfying to me, so after the third date, I let her go.* (patron)

In discussing men who have exchanges with hookers we should also recognize that there are some interested males who simply do not know where to find hookers (in spite of rumors to the contrary). Others, it seems, are reluctant to visit bars known to cater to prostitution. Still others, on visiting such places, may be reluctant to approach the girls and/or follow through with a transaction.

Thus, in addition to "interest," it is also necessary for would-be patrons to know where to find hookers, to feel able to approach them, and to overcome the "disrespectability" (and dishealth) conventionally associated with intimate contact with prostitutes. Conditions of greater "drift" (Matza, 1964: Prus, 1978), wherein persons experience lower levels of "moral accountability" (as suggested by drinking activities, stag parties, solitary travel, and other conditions providing autonomy and freedom from responsibility), are conducive to initial involvements with hookers. Subsequent involvements may arise under similar conditions, but concerns associated with overcoming the "hooker mystique" are likely to be less prominent.

In discussing hooker patrons, it also seems useful to consider prostitution as a "form of entertainment." The concept of entertainment is developed further in Chapter 6. Just as some people develop interests in music, drinking, partying, and "amateur night" shows, for instance (and may anticipate some realization of these interests in bar life), we would suggest that some people develop interests in sexuality, companionship, and romance, and may envision some prospects for realizing these interests in their relationships with "working girls." Few patrons seem likely to cite hooker encounters as those they would most prefer but, just as persons might prefer "live bands" to "canned music" in actualizing their musical interests, so might persons prefer sex with a hooker to another form of sexual activity in realizing their sexual interests. Further, although some men may seek out hookers in the same way people might seek out other forms of entertainment (ballet, jazz, football games, and so on), a customer may stop at a bar to meet a friend, to unwind, to have a drink, or to watch the dancers, and find a particular hooker unusually attractive, or find that as the evening progresses his interests become aroused. In this respect, hooker patrons seem not unlike diners in a restaurant who, on getting cues from, or curiosities aroused by the sights of other diners, may decide to sample an unanticipated or previously undesired dessert; one's decisions to become involved with a hooker may be more situational and negotiable than commonly supposed. Additionally, while some hooker customers will have been bar regulars prior to involvements with hookers, others tend to become more involved in the hotel community as a consequence of their hooker involvements. Working girls can serve as a "drawing card" and, although some hooker-interested patrons may later become involved in the other entertainment offered in the bar (drinking, music, dancers), the hookers' entertainment functions should not be overlooked:

> *Bars are lonely places. A lot of people seem to be joking on the surface, but you find that a lot of them are troubled by a lot of things. A bar is a place where people can live out some of their fantasies and be more of the kinds of people that they'd like to be, than they can at work, or with their families. . . . At Main, you find quite a cross-section of people and these people might all disagree on just about everything. The one thing that draws them all to Main is their desire for pussy.* (musician)

CAREER CONTINGENCIES

The term "career contingencies" (Becker, 1963; Prus and Sharper, 1977) is used herein to refer to the situational elements affecting entrance, continuity, and disinvolvement from a particular activity. Although our dominant focus is on the interrelationships of persons in the hotel community, we also have gathered some data in respect to the, "What's a nice girl like you. . . ." question of seeming interest to so many people. We have no simple answers, but would like to indicate some of the contingencies affecting women's involvements in prostitution. In doing so, it is important to emphasize the extent to which initial involvements can be understood only in the context of the larger subcultural setting in which the prospective novice finds herself. Certainly, one may speak of women who are in one or other ways more vulnerable to hooking involvements, but any attempt to explain their involvements only by reference to their "backgrounds" or their "personal qualities," neglects the role of other persons and subcultures predating the individuals' involvements.

People often think of prostitution as a "sexual phenomenon," but we would suggest that only in defining it as a "social phenomenon" can one begin to understand the career contingencies of hookers. Thus, while the situations and the form of prostitution (bar hooking, street hooking, massage parlors, call girl operations), will vary somewhat over time, it is important to recognize that career prostitution is not the simple act of exchanging sexuality for money. It is a way of life. Consequently, anyone becoming involved is forced to come to terms with the other people associated with prostitution. In this section, the focus is on such things as "fitting in," "interpersonal entanglements," and the "hooker community." These elements may affect not only one's "initial involvements" but also one's continuity as a hooker.

GETTING INVOLVED

Not unlike Bryan (1965) who studied call girls and Gray (1973) who studied teen-age street hookers, we found that, prior to their own involvements, the bar hookers had generally established contact with someone who was already involved in prostitution. Some girls were introduced to the life by pimps attempting to "turn them out," while others were introduced to prostitution through hooker friends they had met in other settings. Still others became involved in the hotel community as strippers, waitresses, or bar regulars, and then "drifted" into hooking. It should be emphasized that not all girls who have the opportunity to become involved in prostitution do so. For example, and contrary to what one might think, the pimps are apt to have "low batting averages" in this respect. While by no means comprehensive, the following extracts provide a sense of the involvement patterns:

> Ruth said that a friend, a younger girl around 15, had gotten caught up with these people and was instrumental in turning her out as well. Through this other girl, she became acquainted with people in the life. She said that the first time that she had engaged in sex for money she was very upset with herself afterwards. She felt quite shaken by the whole thing for the next couple of days. Afterwards, however, she didn't feel that sense of shock. She said also that she is with another guy right now. She said that he is taking money from other girls, but with her it's a better type of relationship. According to her, he never asks her for anything and if they're together they do what they want to do, without him making any demands on her. It seemed to me that this was the same sort of routine that she had just gotten out of, but she did not define it as such. (notes)

> Vicki has been hooking for about four years. She said that she had gotten involved through a group of friends. She had seen the sort of money they were making and she felt, with their encouragement, that she could do just as well. She indicated that at the time she was rather naive about sex, but was impressed with the money. She said that for her first trick, she went along with another girl. (notes)

> Most of them meet a guy and go into it in order to be with him, "If you want to be with me, you've got to make money, just hand it over." (hooker)

LEARNING THE ROPES

As the following suggests, many girls may be at a loss over how to go about "turning their first trick." Procedures vary considerably by setting and by practitioners, but unless a prospective hooker has someone to show her a way of handling dates, her involvements may cease at that point:

This other hooker took me to do a trick with her. He was a Japanese, which might have been a break for me. I didn't realize it at the time, though. She just called him from the lobby of the Cabana Hotel and said "I've got a friend with me." It worked out that he'd give us $40 each. But she talked him into it. He didn't realize he would have two girls at the time he first talked to her, like then she was to go for $50. On the way up I said, "I don't know what to do. Like I've never done this before." She said, "Don't worry, just do what I do." Now, this is a very shy girl. It took me three years to take my clothes off with the lights on with my boyfriend. So we went in his room and she's talking to him, and she starts to take her clothes off and he starts to take his clothes off and I took my clothes off. And you know how doubles work, one girl's working on him, Frenching him, and the other girl's kissing him, and then we changed places. And I got through it, I did all the things I was supposed to do, it was just very mechanical. I think I was in shock. I just did it without thinking. I just did it, did what I had to do, and we got dressed and said, "Thank you very much" and left. And that was it. It was late at night so we didn't really go out anymore after that. Then I was on my own. That was the last time she took me with her. From then on I got my own tricks. She took me to a bar where she worked in San Francisco, and I just took it from there. I really just kind of played it by ear. (hooker)

Not unlike card and dice hustlers (Prus and Sharper, 1977), hookers are apt to find that "learning the ropes" is an ongoing experience. Not only will they find themselves innovating as they endeavor to expedite their hustle, but they are also likely to find that they learn from others both by occasional tutelage and through listening to others discuss job problems and remedies. Their learning is not, however, confined to the handling of tricks, but also involves coming to terms with the work setting, the pimps, and their "colleagues."

"FITTING IN"

In addition to overcoming concerns about hooking for a living and learning how to hustle, the girls are also faced with the problematics of fitting into the hotel situation. Although it is easier for an experienced hooker to adjust to the bar setting, any newcomer is apt to be defined as an "outsider." Unless she has people to "qualify" her for the "locals," a prospective hooker has to come to terms with the animosity commonly directed towards "the competition" before she can effectively work as a hooker:

With a new girl, the girls would notice her right off, she might get away with one or two tricks, but afterwards they want to know, "Who is she?" and they'll complain. If she goes to the washroom, they may follow her and tell her to leave. Unless she has a wife-in-law it may be difficult for her to get in. (hooker)

She took me in and told me, "Okay you sit on this side of the table, facing out." You never walked across the stage, that was the rules, you always walked around. You always tipped the waiter. . . . And I didn't know anybody. The girls look at you funny when you're a new girl. They're wondering, "Here she is with Sherry. She must be her wife-in-law." I didn't know that then, but they all assumed that I was with Hogey. At first, nobody talked to me, they left me kind of on my own then too. And after a few days one of the girls got friendly with me. (hooker)

One cannot keep track of the subsequent activities of all the girls who do not "fit in" particular bars, but it is apparent that a number of girls do not last. Some will go on to try other bars, the streets, call girl set-ups and the like, but we suspect that after an unsuccessful encounter or two of this nature, many careers in hooking are aborted:

Lately, I've run across a lot of girls getting out of the massage parlors. . . . They come into the hotel and sit down. When they first come in, they usually sit at the bar. It's sort of, "Oh, hi, how are you? What are you doing?" this and that, you just sort of talk to them about things. They you get a little bit out of them. "Where'd you work before?" "I was in Paradise Place." God knows how many there are on the drive. So they say, "I was just in there a couple of months. Wanted a change, you know." You figure she hasn't been there that long just from the way she talks. She doesn't really know what's going on. They never last, these girls never last. . . . There are little rules that the hookers have themselves, not really that they enforce them, but there are just little things that they never do, like take another girl's trick, or something like that. When these new chicks walk in and do this, they're going to get a talking to. They'll say, "You want to stay here, fine. You stay over there. Don't come near us, and don't take any of our tricks. Regulars or nothing." (bartender)

A lot of the new girls coming in just can't take the police action. They're just fine until they run into that and then boom, they don't know what to do. The regular girls don't like the new girls at all. Some of these girls have been here for like ten years and all of a sudden this new little broad comes in and here she is cutting in on their action. Like the regulars might figure the guy is coming towards them and then all of a sudden, this little girl makes a play for the guy. Well, that's going to get them a little bit upset. They'll get her in the washroom and either punch her out or tell her that either she gets out or she gets punched out. (hooker)

In addition to reconciling oneself with the other hookers, "fitting in" also involves coming to terms with the bar staff and management. We will be discussing this in Chapter 5, but clearly this is another important aspect of "fitting in" the hotel community.

ENTANGLEMENTS

If one wants to understand the girls' involvements and continuities in hooking, an examination of the affiliational networks in which they find themselves seems essential. In this regard, we consider the relationships hookers have with pimps, boyfriends and husbands, families and children, and the hooker community more generally.

PIMPS AND HOOKERS

In spite of the seeming lack of assistance the hooker receives from the pimp, the pimp-hooker relationship is one of the most powerful in the hooker's world. He is her major financial beneficiary and, regardless of whether or not he introduced her to hooking, he is likely to want her to continue this pursuit as intensively as possible. Thus, he becomes a central figure promoting continuity in the girl's career as a hooker. It should be noted that, although not all girls will be working for pimps at all times, almost all career hookers will have worked for a pimp at some point in time. In spite of their significance for prostitution more generally, we found that black pimps (or "players") spend very little time in bars such as Central and Main. Not only are the pimps more obvious in predominately white bars, and more able to avoid legal hassles by avoiding hooker's bars, but the management in such places tend to discourage their presence:

> At different times, some of the pimps will call me, wanting to get their girls in. Sometimes they get a little nasty if they are turned down, sometimes they get a little threatening as well, but I don't take them too seriously. . . . I don't want the pimps in the bar where the girls are working. It makes it too difficult for the girls to work when the pimps are there. So I tell them, "It is either one or the other, if she is here, you can't be here; and if you're here, then she has to go." (manager)

> We also get a few black pimps, not too many in this bar, but you see them around because the girls are with them. They're dressed like they're on t.v., with the gold watches and the big floppy hats. Dressed real well. At different times I thought I might go and talk to them, but they would say, "Well, who are you?" If you say, "I know your old lady," they figure you're a cop or something. Pimping, that gets them five years right off the bat, so they want to be careful about who they talk to about what they're doing. (bartender)

As a result, the players generally represent "behind the scenes" actors. They do not arrange for dates, or handle troublesome dates:

> The pimp doesn't really do anything for them. He doesn't set the girls up or protect them or anything. It's, "How much did you make?" And if there's a bust, "Well, don't call me." They don't want to get busted themselves, so they stay away from it. They'll see the girl once a week, or whatever, to collect, but they don't want to be bothered with the details. (hooker)

White Pimps

As the bulk of the discussion focusses on black pimps, it may be useful to briefly discuss white pimps. Less obvious than the black pimps, the white men can more readily fit into ongoing bar life. As a result, they can be fairly instrumental in defining the social life in some hooker bars. The white pimps with whom we are familiar might best be characterized as "rounders," street-wise people involved in a variety of hustles. Typically, they initially drifted into a pimping relationship with an established hooker through tolerant affiliation in the hotel setting. Given a hustling orientation, they subsequently tend to seek this type of relationship with other women:

> Sam, Lucky, Felix, there are a number of them, people in the hotel who have girls working for them. They got involved with some hooker and then she started giving them her money. A good deal. After, you start looking for it, trying to get a girl to go to work for you. (rounder)

Lance is a half-assed hustler from away back. He was always into something, gambling, dope, pool, whatever, so if he can get a girl working for him, so much the better. He'll take it whenever he can find it. (rounder)

We will be discussing other aspects of "rounder" involvements in Chapter 6, but it may be sufficient to note that white pimps are a minority and for the most part they avoid "black" hangouts. As Milner and Milner (1972) note, one does find the occasional white pimp who hangs around and otherwise emulates black pimps, but they tend to be rare.

"PIMPS AND HOS"

Of all the relationships in the hotel community, the one we have had the most difficulty coming to terms with is the (black) pimp-hooker relationship. Not only does one face the problem of dealing with all the sensationalism associated with these relationships, and the difficulties piercing extensive "facades," but there are a number of other themes such as the "black culture" and the "drug culture" that make these heterosexual involvements particularly complex. An illustrated commentary (Hall and Adelman, 1972), and an anthropological account (Milner and Milner, 1972) of pimping are by and large consistent with the sort of information we have encountered, but do not reflect the sort of issues we wanted to examine. Consequently, we would like to discuss some dimensions of the pimp-hooker relationship that seem critical to understanding these associations.

First, although drugs and/or force may be used in turning some girls into hookers, and while some pimps may sell girls to one another, the relationship generally reflects a voluntary, albeit sometimes naive involvement on the part of the female:

The pimps don't want their women on drugs, because that makes it more difficult for them to control the women, and it's also going to take money out of his pocket, so a little grass, a little coke, but nothing really heavy, because then the woman is more likely to turn on him if she needs a fix. (pimp)

Sam (a white pimp) estimated that perhaps ninety per cent of the girls in the Central or Main had black pimps. He said that predominantly, these girls were impressed with the fellows, that they drove big cars, had plenty of money, and wore flashy clothes, sort of the man-about-town, going to the races, and whatnot. Initially the girls, the ones that went into this, tended to be impressed, falling in love with the guy. Then he would farm them out, over a period to time. Depending on how much money these girls brought in, the pimp would spend more or less time with them. He might also establish some sort of competition so that the girl that brought in the most money was the favorite lady or bottom lady for that period of time. He said that the pimps did not try to set the women up, but rather would drop by once a week to collect. In the meantime, they would be running around with other girls trying to set some more up. He also said that it wasn't unusual, if there was a breakup between a pimp and one of the women he had with him, for him to take back furs or whatever he had given her and then turn around and give them to another girl, saying that this was especially for her. He also mentioned that among the black pimps there was a lot of switching around. The women might be with one guy for a while and then become involved with another one. He also said that you wouldn't see them hanging around the hotels where the girls work. They would just visit the girls at their places to pick up the money and spend the night. Sam also mentioned that one of the black pimps had called him earlier in the day, asking him if there was room for another girl at the Central. (notes)

They have different styles. Some of them make you think, "Oh, I don't really want you for your money, baby, I want you for you. 'Cause you're so nice, and we can do so much together, and I'm getting money from these other three, so why would I need yours?" They make you believe that, until a certain point, when all of a sudden, he wants money from you. (hooker)

Secondly, while pimps commonly attempt to recruit girls into working for them by impressing them with their money, charm, and thoughtfulness, and will often involve others (for instance, other hookers) in introducing new girls to their world and neutralizing it for them, the girls typically become involved in hooking out of a desire to help him. Although the "lines" employed by pimps will vary considerably among the practitioners, and may be adjusted from one female to the next, many of the ploys utilized by the players have been worked out and tested by others. Knowing his objective in establishing a relationship, and equipped with a spiel and an ideology challenging and reinterpreting conventional morality, players are advantaged vis-à-vis their targets. While a confidence-game model (Prus and Sharper, 1977:2) is exceedingly relevant, it is also apparent that involvement in prostitution provides a sense of identity (Klapp, 1969). As the woman helps her man out, she tends to become further obligated to him. As they "plan things together," she develops a sense of purpose, such that while she is helping him, she is also working "for them"; her working (as a hooker) makes it possible for them to exist as a couple:

What a woman does with her body, that's kind of her business, and the way that she uses it, that's her business. So it really doesn't matter if a woman is out whoring for her old man or whether she's out working her ass off running around as a waitress or working her fingers off as a typist, it's the same kind of thing. If she's giving him her money, then she's supporting him, and it doesn't make any difference how she's doing it. (pimp)

As the girl becomes more involved with a pimp, she is more apt to be exposed to other persons whose perspectives envision her relationship with her pimp as normal and desirable:

There's sort of a black culture, like heading down to the Ebony or the Jungle Drum; I was into it. I was with a black guy for nine years and had a lot of black friends, so I was kind of into black culture, black music, and black actors. You just knew more about them. You were just more up on the latest facts, or whatever, just from being around black people. (hooker)

At the Jungle Drum, all the hookers are well dressed and everybody sees what you're wearing, the way you're looking, and how well you're doing. The girls always try to outdo each other in diamonds and clothes, to show that you're a better hooker. And the same with the guys. . . . A lot of the girls want to go out with black guys. Now if they've been through all those ones in town and there's nothing there that they want, so when some out-of-towner comes in and sits down and they see him, well, "So and so's here from L.A., there's this really cute guy, from L.A., is he ever sharp!" And they all want to run down and see him and see which one he's going to pick to go to bed with that night, or the next night, how much it's going to cost you. Some guys will use that too, you can't go to bed with them unless you give them a thousand dollars first, or whatever. So they are into blacks. (hooker)

Thus, although the prevailing image of a pimp-hooker relationship is that of the player solitarily involving the girl, our data suggests that other people are exceedingly relevant in promoting and sustaining hooking careers.

Making it Together

Not unlike other couples, a pimp and his "ho" can make plans together and make the scene together, with the girl taking some pride in what she has done to make the union a viable one. The relationship is more than this, however, and concerns with companionship, affection and money are relevant:

I think that's part of what they're looking for in the pimps, a companion, a sexual companion. Somebody to comfort you, to come home to and to cook for, and most of them, believe it or not, really deep down, would like to find somebody that loves them and would marry them and look after them. When they heard that we were going to get married, they really didn't believe it. Some of them said, "I hope she knows what she's doing." Then we got married and they were all so happy for me and they said, "You lucky bitch, I wish I could find somebody." (hooker)

They're there for that every third night, somebody to sleep with and somebody to be there in the morning, and somebody to call every night when you come home, because most of these girls live alone. And maybe fun to plan for every third Sunday, you know. But, a lot of these guys are rough. Pimps aren't like the image people have of them, beating girls up usually, or even saying "You'd better have $200 or else!" There are some like that. They're a little harder to work for, because that's what they really are like. But most of the guys aren't. You may have the occasional fight, but you don't really get beaten up or that often. But that's life in general. (hooker)

You make your own money. You give him money, but if it's your bill week, and the rent is due and your phone bill and whatever, okay, this week is your money for your bills. You make it for yourself. The rest of the time, it's not like he sees you every night, anyway. He may have 3 or 4 other girls, maybe you see him every third night. . . . You still talk to him every night and tell him how much you made. And when he comes to see you on Friday you have that much money to give him. . . . And you still have to ask him (it's not like you can go out and spend what you want) "Is it okay if I go and buy a new dress today?" (hooker)

I didn't mind giving him the money, I sort of figured that we were building something together, and he had all these plans. Then after, I figured, "Well, I'm not getting anything out of this." No love, no affection, not even a shoulder to cry on. I remember one night, I had got beat up and I needed some help, I needed him to come and pick me up, and he says he couldn't. Then, when I got home, he was angry at me, "Where were you?" And it turned out that he was just watching t.v. all during this time. (hooker)

The Wife-In-Law Enterprise

If the player is to be successful by the standards of the pimp community, it is necessary for him to have more than one girl working for him. That is, if he is to have the big car, clothes, diamonds, drugs, and such things associated with a successful "man on the street."

The situation is especially difficult for the novice player. It takes money to impress the girls, but it takes girls to make the money. Some men never overcome this dilemma. Further, as losing a girl can jeopardize one's position, particularly when one only has one or two hookers, one starts to see the sense of urgency characterizing pimps whose "old lady" appears likely to terminate the relationship. Even in larger "stables," where a pimp's resources are more extensive, the loss of one girl may threaten his financial position. The recruitment (finding and keeping) of one's ladies is, thus, an ongoing enterprise.[3]

It should not, however, be assumed that only the pimp is interested in recruiting additional workers:

When I first started, there was no way there was going to be any other girl, but towards the end I was trying, "Please can't you find somebody else, just to relieve some of the financial burden." But it takes money to make money. In order to get girls, you have to go out every night and spend money in those clubs, you have to dress well and look like you've got money, then you can get girls. Because the way they get girls is say, "Okay, baby, you don't have a color t.v. with so and so? Well, I'll make sure you have a color t.v., I'll make sure you have a diamond ring." A pimp has to make them believe that's what he's going to do for them before he can get them to take their money and give it to him. And he just wasn't in the financial situation where he could go out and fake it. Towards the end, I was even naming girls. "Well, he said, "You know the girls there. You know the girls who are on their own at the moment, maybe you can do something." I never came right out and said, "Well Pete's a really nice guy, why don't you be with him." But I'd sit there and talk about his good qualities and how he was the kind of guy that a lot of them were looking for, somebody who you could really believe cares about you. (hooker)

The pimp's main lady, she'll keep an eye on the new girl, and if she turns three tricks, they'll expect her to have the right money, the minimum of what the other girls in the place are charging. And if she comes back with less, they'll think she's holding out on them. That's a way of him keeping track of the girls, without him actually being there himself. (hooker)

Any woman succeeding in luring another girl into the "family" will likely be well received by her "old man". Terms such as "bottom lady" or "main lady" are used in reference to the girl who is seen as his major partner in the enterprise.

Given our emphasis on monogamy, one can see where the "wife-in-law" phenomenon can be simultaneously both a lever working in favor of the player and

---

[3] The parallel concerns of pimps and clergymen are striking vis-à-vis the continual pursuits of finding and maintaining a dedicated following. See Prus (1976) for a fuller discussion of religious recruitment.

a source of animosity. Sometimes a pimp will be successful in giving the impression that he has a relationship only with a particular girl. But such information may be difficult to conceal, particularly among the more experienced girls and those who "make the scene" at certain discos and after-hour bars. Players may elect to make their prowess known to their girls, but in any event once it becomes evident that two or more girls are wives-in-law, the elements of competition surface:

> There's a kind of competition between wife-in-laws, or girls who try to be wife-in-laws. They already know the girl and they know the guy she's with and they try to outdo each other. It gets to a point where, if they work in the same place, which is a very bad situation to be in, they could tell on each other, "She spent an hour with this guy." or try to make more money. If she makes $800 a week, and I make a thousand a week, I'm a better ho. . . . They call each other "hos." There's a girl in Central who says, "I know I'm the best ho in Eastville." And she does make damn good money because she just turned anything and everything and would work till five in the morning, just to make more money than her wife-in-law did. I guess she felt he would appreciate her more because she was better. And they do that, the guy can say, "Well, shit, you only made $200, and she makes $300 a night!" He can exaggerate it too, to make that other girl feel bad so she'll make more money, or just feel bad, one or the other. (hooker)

Choosing

As "hos" become more familiar with the game many realize that they have a considerable amount of bargaining power and may elect to "choose" their pimps. A girl may have left a pimp or may decide that this new man is more to her liking than the present one:

> When the girl choose a guy, they give him so much money, $200 or a thousand, whatever his quota is or whatever they settle on. Also they have to pay off the guy to leave. Most of the pimps will try to outdo each other as well, just as the hookers do. Like Ron, for instance, if you're going to choose him, you talk to him. He'll say, "Okay, in order to choose me, you've got to give me a thousand dollars. Show me how much money you can make." So she'll work her ass off for a week, or however long it takes her to make her thousand. Then she goes up to him one night and says, "Here's my thousand!" He says, "Okay, now you're with me. . . ." Now if you're a good money maker, well, he doesn't want to lose you. So if you tell him, "Okay, I'm leaving you," some of them are civil about it, "That's fine. You owe me this much. You've been with me this much time. . . . I've done this much for you, I've bought you a living room set, or whatever. You owe me this much money." Then if it's okay with the second guy she's going to, okay. Sometimes it isn't, and they will have fights about it, "She's with me now. She doesn't owe you nothing." The second guy wants that money too, the thousand or whatever the price is. But they don't all charge you for leaving. In some cases it doesn't matter. It also depends on how long you've been with him, and some of them do care about the girls. (hooker)

> It's a bit of prestige if they can take some guy away from another girl. He may have two old ladies working for him, but if she can horn in on the action and get his attention, or whatever, where he's neglecting them, I guess that's sort of,

"Hey, I'm better than you, baby!" .... *And the first girl knows that he's going to be inclined to spend more time with the bigger money maker or be nicer to her, plus keep reminding the first girl that she makes less money, etc.* (hooker)

Thus, an unsatisfying relationship with one pimp is unlikely to be sufficient to disinvolve a "ho" from hooking. Although the girls have much more power in determining relationships than might be commonly assumed, a player learning of a girl's free status may attempt to charm her into selecting him:

Ruth said this other pimp was trying to talk her into going with him, that he had big plans for her, and she said she didn't want to go. She's pretty street-wise, so she would know what was going down. Some of those guys think that they're sweet talkers and they can talk you into anything and you're going to believe it. But once you've been around just a little while, you know pretty much what's happening. But it's still kind of amazing that the girls will sort of leave one guy and they get involved with another guy that seems to be the same, like, "I've got plans, baby." (hooker)

The other pimps, they really won't go on somebody else's territory. Like they might talk to you and say, "Well, my old lady's doing better than you," where they may try and raz you, but they don't really make a big play for you when you're with somebody else. (hooker)

Further, while it is considered poor form for one player to poach on another's property by approaching a girl directly, one of his "hos" may attempt to steer a disenchanted hooker in his direction.

Terminating Relationships

Insofar as a pimp finds his relationship with a hooker profitable, he is apt to want it continued. The subculture in which the relationship occurs also supports the idea of a plurality of hookers for one pimp, thus making it easier for him to tolerate a particular girl with whom he might not be so enamored in other ways. The female, however, is likely to find it difficult to have a simultaneous relationship with two or more pimps. Further, as her affectionate relationship is expected to be confined more exclusively to this one person, she is likely to want to terminate the relationship more quickly than does he. Recognizing her particular financial contributions and the prestige accruing from a "larger stable," a player may use force and intimidation when his charm seems ineffective (the two should not be seen as exclusive):

Some of them can be pretty rough, and they'll threaten the girls and all, and some of them just do not want to let the girls go. They'll do whatever it takes to keep her, and if she leaves, she may not leave in such good shape. So some girls, they may want to leave their old man, but they might be really terrified of what he might do. (hooker)

As "disenfranchised" pimps lose both money and "face" (a poor manager) they will likely experience some moral indignation when facing a threatened or actual loss. When a termination occurs, the "release price" is helpful, not only in "cooling a player out," but also in reaffirming his value in the community. As with other relationships, the "pimp-ho" relationship is subject to considerable vacillation vis-a-vis termination as players and hookers attempt to come to terms with their lives and the relative payoffs they associate with one another:

> Bea told Kate that Polly had taken up her old man again. It appears that Polly had gotten back with a black pimp that she had had before. This pimp also has Karen and a couple of other girls working for him. Both Bea and Kate said that it was dumb to get connected with a pimp and Kate said, "I just don't understand, it is just crazy to give your money to some guy...." What was interesting about this was that both Bea and Kate have been involved with pimps at different times in their careers. When they get intimately involved with a pimp, it makes sense; but when another girl becomes involved with a pimp while they themselves are not thusly involved, they tend to become very suspicious of the arrangement. (notes)

> The pimp I just left is a real motherfucker! There are good pimps and bad pimps and he is a real motherfucker! Denise and I were both with this pimp and we had a few fights over him. Well, eventually Denise left this pimp and so did I. Now, he has no one, which is what he deserves! The pimps generally show the girls a really good time when they're getting to know them. At first, they're really good, they're really nice to you. They take you to all the best places and what not. . . . After we just broke up, he came back to me saying that he realized that he was wrong. He said that he was sort of crawling on his hands and knees and that he just didn't have any pride where I was concerned, that he just needs me. He also told me that he has big plans to take me to Vegas, which I don't believe. He also calls my home and bothers my parents, trying to get a hold of me. I guess he is just not ready to let me go. (hooker)

> The pimps, they find little ways of holding on to these girls. Like, they're nice to them right, they buy them stuff, they give them a line and sometimes kick the shit out of them, whatever. It does happen that way. They buy them all kinds of nice stuff. The girls actually pay for it themselves, but they're too stupid to realize it, "Look what my old man gave me, a big diamond ring!" It took her like two years to get it together to pay for it. They do get punched out a lot, but they always go back to them, all the time. All of them go back, it don't matter, "Oh, I'm never going back." Give her two or three weeks, "Oh, well, it didn't work out alone, I'm back home now." (bartender)

Not only are the players concerned about their girls leaving them for other pimps, but they also tend to be concerned about the girls becoming "independents" or leaving them for others. The latter occurrences are insulting not only for the immediately affected players, but to the community of pimps more generally:

> Nancy discussed some trouble she had been having with a black pimp. She said that part of the reason she thought that he might be upset with her was that she had been trying to take away one of the girls that he had. Nancy indicated that she is bisexual and was having a bit of a fling with this other girl inferring that he was worried about her taking this girl from him. . . . She added, "It is really dumb for a girl to go and work for a pimp. At different times I've tried to help girls get out of that situation, but they wouldn't leave because they said they were in love. The pimps are really good confidence men. They give a girl a big rush for a week and then try to turn her into working for them." (notes)

When they started hearing about me and Dave, that was the greatest insult to Benny and all those other guys. Not only was I leaving him, that's a "no, no," but I was leaving him for a white man! It was like, "Kill the motherfucker, because he's white! That was a terrible degradation. How could I, I mean imagine. . . . But that's how they felt about it and probably a lot of the girls felt I was very strange too. Why? What could I possibly see better in a white man? They all liked Dave, but they didn't know him. What could I see in him? But I used to tell them, you just keep going around and around, you can go through all the black guys in the city. You're just looking for something, and whatever it is you're looking for, you're not going to find it there. Most of them are looking for security and love, and you're not going to find security and love in the black guys, the black pimps. It's just the culture that's there. It's just not going to change. It was the same ten years ago and it's going to be the same ten years from now. (hooker)

BOYFRIENDS AND HUSBANDS

While hookers may occasionally meet men outside of the hotel community and develop something of a double-life in this respect, many of their relationships with "straight guys" seem doomed to failure. Not only are they likely to have difficulty explaining their work to many "straights," but as they become more immersed in the hotel community and the black culture, they are less likely to find more conventional males attractive:

If a hooker finds a guy, then he has to understand that she is a working girl and they can't be hung up on that. (hooker)

Some of them will have boyfriends on the side, as well as the pimps. They wouldn't go to the places where the pimps would go, but they'd go to clubs, and maybe run into a guy, usually a black guy too, and maybe he's a pimp too, but he's just in town for a visit, or whatever. Just a good looking guy and he has money. And of course, as long as nobody can go back and squeal on them, and he's good looking, he can take her home for the night, why not? A free fuck, it didn't cost her anything. . . . But if he's a pimp here in town, and if they can get a guy for free, they don't respect him as much. That lowers him in class. If they can get him for free and actually come home and screw him, then they don't have as much respect for him as they would if he would say to them, "Oh, I'm sorry, but you have to pay me for this." They call them chippie scores. But why not, they get horny too, just like normal people. Most people think that hookers get their sex through tricks, but it's very different. (hooker)

Hookers really don't care for straight guys. They're in a different world. They're in the action, in the life. They're into dope, theft, all the things straight people put them down for. (hooker)

As the girls become more involved in "the life," they tend to have less opportunity to become involved with straight males. They become more dependent upon the hooker community and the culture to which the pimp exposes them. Given their working and leisure hours, they're usually with him, the other girls, or other people in the hotel community.

For straight males, one of the problems of dating a hooker is that of overcoming the concern that the girl is having sexual relations with a large number of men. Even those who go to hookers on a somewhat regular basis may feel that it's all right for the girl to be involved in prostitution, provided they're not personally involved with that girl. But as they become more involved, they may want the girls to be much more selective in their clientele. Not only would this represent a basis for any number of arguments, but precludes prospects for a relaxed, intimate relationship.

A more convenient type of relationship for the hookers is that of becoming involved with hotel people, particularly staff people and rounders. These men do not only know of hooker activities, but are generally more accepting of these activities than most outsiders, as their hustles are more apt to parallel those of the working girls:

One of the hookers from Central said that she usually takes her tricks to The Flamingo. She met her boyfriend, who is now a waiter, here, when he was working at The Flamingo. (notes)

I used to go out with a lot of the hookers. . . . It was just a fling, that's all. I'd go out with them for maybe a month, and bang, they'd be somewhere else doing something else. . . . A lot of them do get mixed up with people who work here. They often try to keep their little thing to themselves, but it usually gets out and people find out about it, but who really cares? I don't care if this hooker screws this waiter. It doesn't matter to me. The only person who's probably going to get her head kicked in is her, if her old man finds out about it. Like while they're going out with this guy, a lot of them still have their old man. They've got to go back to their old man. If she doesn't, he'll look for her or have somebody looking for her. . . .

The staff don't really get jealous of the girls when they're dating them. It's none of their business. All they really want is to get screwed off the broad, that's all. The odd time, they'll get jealous. Jack is one who gets emotionally involved. He's a fuck up. He just can't fuck a broad. He thinks he can just screw the broad and it's over. But, a lot of times, he's running after the broad, but he tries to make it look as if she's running after him. I've seen him get so fucked up over a hooker he'd be crying. He just couldn't handle it. He wanted the girl, but she just wanted to screw him, that's all. She just wanted to get laid too, but meanwhile she's laying everybody else. She's a hooker, she's got an old man, she's got shit like that. He got messed up like that a few times. You'd say to him, "She's just a whore." He'd yell, "Don't call her a whore!" If you did say anything, he'd punch you out. (bartender)

Jack, a regular day desk clerk, has gone out with a number of the hookers, Glenda, Freida, before Roxanne, and I guess some other ones too. One of Jack's former romances involved the woman who is now with the old manager. She was Jack's old lady. There does seem to be some moving around of persons to one another within this same environment. Keith, the new manager, his girl was a hooker before. I don't know what she is doing now. When the place closes, they go down and drink. She was with one of the waiters who left some time ago to run a craft shop. (notes)

While some playful flirting may take place between any hooker and staff member who find one another congenial, one also finds that some of these relationships eventuate in serious romance (and the occasional marriage). Particularly interesting in this respect are the ways in which "sexual propriety" is defined. Thus, while hooking (as work) generally remains an acceptable activity for the female, other non-shared sexual activities are disapproved in ways not dissimilar to those typifying more "conventional" members of society:

> I was at the desk talking with three girls. One of them a stripper, Bubbles, was sitting on the desk talking to me when Maggie came down from a trick. When she saw the three girls there, she said to Bubbles "You better not be messing with him!" She was quite upset. Bubbles looked uncomfortable and kind of moved off the desk. Maggie hung around until the other girls had all left, then she said, "What the hell is going on around here?" I said that nothing was going on and that she just had to trust me. . . . Another time, I was talking with Myrna, another stripper, and Maggie had just come down from a trick. She was angry again, saying, "That one is mine, you better leave him alone." (desk clerk)

FAMILIES AND CHILDREN

Few hookers openly disclose their activities to their parents. Other relatives (sisters, cousins, for example) are more likely to learn of these involvements, but generally conceal their knowledge from the parents. While some girls find safety in moving to other cities, their links to other people in the hotel community (especially their pimps) may make this option untenable:

> Most of the girls' families, say the ones that live in the area, they don't know what their daughter's doing. Most of them will have their suspicions, but then they think, "My little girl couldn't be doing that," and so they seldom really confront the girl with that. Sometimes though, you will have friends or neighbors dropping by, and that creates a bit of a panic for the girl, and then she'll say "Oh, uh . . . I'm just visiting" or "I was just waiting for somebody here." But, it is a problem, she doesn't really know how to handle it. So sometimes, neighbors or maybe other members of the family may know what's going on, but may not actually tell the parents. (hooker)

Children represent special difficulties for the hookers. While some will leave children with relatives or full-time baby sitters, others keep their children with them. In varying degrees, these women lead double lives, as they try to keep the children from learning more fully of their hooking activities. It should not be assumed, however, that all hookers are careful in the ways in which situations are handled, particularly on those occasions where the children are seen to interfere with the woman's social or work life:

> Most of the girls have children and some, most of them, will have babysitters for the week and perhaps see the children on Sundays, or maybe for the weekend. . . . There is one who takes her son to the restaurant. He's about ten years old, and she just takes him to the restaurant near Central and she'll be there talking with the other girls, talking about business and different tricks and whatnot. She just feels that he accepts it. Other girls have told her that she shouldn't be bringing him here, but she says that that's the way she wants to

bring him up. . . . A lot of them will tell their children that they're working as waitresses or something in the evenings. But with the baby it's kind of awkward because you never really know who's child it is. (hooker)

THE HOOKER COMMUNITY

On examining affiliational networks among the hookers, one finds them, for the most part, not unlike those characterizing secretaries in an insurance building or workers in a factory. While they share a number of common concerns, such as being pressured into buying more drinks than they want or being afraid of certain customers, they also have "best friends" and preferred others with whom they clique.

Friendship networks at work are somewhat in evidence as the girls visit one another's tables, as a means of relieving the monotony, but the networks are often much more extensive than this. Not only do girls refer desirable dates (wanting variety) back and forth amongst themselves, but the girls will eat together during and after work hours, go shopping, and meet outside the work setting to celebrate events such as birthdays and Christmas. In casual settings some of the time is spent discussing tricks, the management, staff people, and other work-related themes, but much of the conversation is oriented towards families and children, night clubs, music, astrology, movies, and other "mundane" topics.

From outside appearances it would seem that the girls do spend a fair bit of time "gossiping." Nevertheless, these exchanges are functional not only in relieving boredom but also in keeping the girls informed of changes taking place within a potentially hostile setting. While the girls vary considerably, in the extent to which they are close to one another, closeness also has a situational quality to it. Thus, one finds that those occasions generating fear, distrust, and animosities of hookers towards their patrons (all common concerns) are highly conducive to promoting a sense of closeness:

Vicki said that following Joan's death, the girls were all scared and suspicious and that they would only go out with trusted regulars. She also said that the girls were really close at that time, and often checked with one another regarding dates, and would walk one another to the hotels, frequently waiting while the other girl did the trick. (notes)

We were talking with a couple of hookers at a restaurant when Bea rushed in saying that she had just about gotten killed. She was all flustered and claimed that some guy had been strangling her. She was saying that she had gotten roughed up pretty badly and that she didn't know what all was going to happen to her, she thought that she was done for. This other hooker, Kate, exclaimed, "What the hell did you do to get him upset with you like that?" Bea said that she didn't think that she did anything and Kate said, "You must have done something!" She was getting angry at Bea, saying that Bea should have had enough sense to try and cool the man out, to try to talk to him. She was saying that it was Bea's own fault. Bea then said it was another girl's regular and that he had been drinking and had gotten violent with her. Kate said, "I still think it is your fault. If you handled the situation the right way, you wouldn't have had this problem." Bea was still moaning and groaning, how it hurt when she bent over, and this and that. Shortly after, Maggie came in, aware that Bea had had some trouble. Maggie was quite annoyed with Bea, because she had earlier advised Bea not to get involved with that particular trick. Bea was moaning and groaning, but she was not getting much sympathy. Maggie felt that she was stupid to try to do the trick and Kate felt that she was stupid because she hadn't tried to cool the guy out. Bea also received some advice on what to do at this point. Maggie said for her to go home and forget about it. Kate said to go right back to work before she started thinking about it too much. Otherwise, she said, Bea would be too anxious to go back to hooking. Kate then related a similar experience, saying that that was what she had to do, before she lost her nerve. Bea said that she would go back to the bar but would not look for any tricks. (notes)

The knowledge that persons are engaging in illegitimate activities also promotes a sense of closeness:

Freida called me over and asked me to tell Sue Anne that the guy she was with was a cop. I went over and whispered this in her ear. She shook her head. When I returned to Freida, she said, "Well, I told her, and if she doesn't want to listen, well I guess that's her business. . . . I really don't care for Sue Anne that much anyways, but she is another working girl." (notes)

The following extracts indicate a number of norms operative among the bar hookers. Particularly noteworthy in this sense is the shared definition of "sex as work." While unsuccessful hookers tend to be dismissed as incompetents, any girl thought to violate the "business ethics" of the hooker community tends to be shunned:

The standard minimum fees at Central are $40. You try to get as much as you can. You don't go for less than that. Any girl who does will get into trouble with the other girls if she undercuts their fees. (hooker)

A girl will not be well thought of if she goes accepting too little money for a date, where they break that rule that they accepted too little money. Then the girls will get upset with them. If they're having sex in cars, that's bad! That'll get them a bad reputation. Or if they're going to the guy's house, that's bad, because all these things, they put pressure on the other girls to do that. So that if a date says, "Well, I can get so and so for less money," you have to pretty well say, "Well, there you go," or if he says, "Last time we went to my place," with another girl, then you have to explain to them that's not what you do. You see, it makes it more difficult for the other girls, so they don't like it. Also a girl can get looked down upon if she kisses her dates or if she spends a lot of time with them because the other girls don't want to do that. Some of the girls are also looked down on because they're unsuccessful. They'll hold that against you. Or if the girls are poor dressers, and maybe they don't look very good, the girls will talk about that. Different times they will find things to criticize about each other, it doesn't matter who they are. (hooker)

Some things that affect the girl's reputation are her relations with pimps. Like, some of them have been through them all. Like Bea, she's been through all of them. Sometimes the girls will wonder, "Is she a threat?" because she's after this one and that one, she never seems satisfied. . . . Another thing is how hard working the girl is. Does she turn a lot of tricks? Does she make a lot of money? That's an important thing, how much money you can make . . . the pimp, if she's working with a pimp, it really doesn't matter how she makes the money, but did she make it or didn't she? (hooker)

Like other collectivities, this grouping also has an ongoing and sporadic set of internal conflicts. They are, however, not only as vocal as most other groups but, given the settings in which they find themselves, are also somewhat more inclined to engage in physical violence than are members of some other groups:

We've had girls fighting in here with each other. The girls just walk in, "Boom, boom, boom, that'll teach you." They also have these little rules among themselves, like you don't rap off about another broad you don't figure you can handle. Things you really shouldn't do, "no no's" you call them. Like talking about somebody else's old man. A lot of girls get their heads kicked in for that, or grab at somebody else's trick. Like this girl makes a date with so and so and this guy goes up and all of a sudden another girl grabs him. A lot of broads get their heads beaten in for that. You don't do that. (waiter)

Thus, while a girl may be ranked on looks, social skills (at hooking), loyalty, and monetary success, she will also be accorded prestige for being able to handle trouble.

LEGAL ENTANGLEMENTS

Although hookers tend to despise and fear the police, ~~their job requires~~ that they ~~work in spite of the possible hazards~~ arrest may entail. They may derive some comfort from the presence of other working girls but, to a large extent, concerns with the police occupy a prominent position in their mind only when something happens that makes the prospects of arrest more obvious:

The worst part about prostitution is the bust, where you have to go to court, that whole thing. . . . It is really embarrassing in court, it really is, because you are there in front of the people and they have all of these lies and the judge is saying, "Is this right?", and so you are supposed to agree with everything to make it better. So you agree, "They found me naked." "I asked the guy to go upstairs." But it isn't true. The judge says, "Is that true?", and you think, "He is a lying son-of-a-bitch," and then you say, "Yes." But you can't do much else. I got busted one time I was coming out of the room, and I had already gotten my clothes on. I had my money and everything else before he stopped me. We can get dressed much more quickly than the guys do, because they are just putting their shorts on or whatever. I was just coming out of the room and I saw the cops. They say, "Hold it." Where do you think you are going? You are being arrested!" I said "What do you mean? I am not even in the room." He said, "That doesn't matter!" In the court, in front of everybody, he says that they caught me naked. What can you do? They show the money to everybody, the money I had received. (hooker)

Something else is that if you hear something illegal going on in the city, and you report it to them, you can get your case off. Anything, guns, drugs, if you do it, you are going to get off. I have been told, "You help us find anything and you are off the hook." (hooker)

The busts do get to you after a while, because they keep track of them. . . . Anytime you get arrested, it's a big hassle, but after a few convictions, they can get a little heavy with you. That's why I'm trying to get out of it. The judge gave me a break last time, but next time, I might be in real trouble. (hooker)

Although "getting arrested" has the effects of deterring some girls from continued participation in hooking, for those who survive this ordeal, it establishes them as more of a "pro." They become more firmly embedded in the hooker community. "Getting busted" seems an inevitable aspect of career hooking and although it is not a sign of prestige, it tends to make persons more "police wise" (aware of their "actual" modus operandi) and negative in their attitudes towards the police. Persons returning after a "bust" are thus seen as having survived another induction into the career and tend to be seen as a little more "solid" than the uninitiated:

I've been busted about 7 or 8 times. Five the first year, and the second year about twice, about 7 or 8 altogether. My lawyer said, "You just never plead guilty. If you're going to be found guilty, fine. But let them find you guilty, don't ever plead guilty." I have two convictions and the only reason for those are because I owed my lawyer more money at the time. I had three cases that were all put together on one day, and my lawyer wasn't there. I didn't call him to come and defend me because I owed him money. So I just had three charges and what you do is make a deal with the prosecuting attorney or whatever. If you plead guilty to two, they'll drop one. If I would've said, "No, I'll plead guilty to one and drop two," they probably would've done that too. I just wanted to get out of it. . . . I had a good judge too that day, I knew he was an easy judge. You know the judges. You know which ones are on the hookers' side and which ones aren't. He gave me two $50 fines, a $100 in all. . . . The first time I was ever busted, they took me out in the car where they write up your ticket, and they said, "I guess we'll have to take you to the station." "Oh, I don't care." I sat very calm on the surface, but inside my heart was pounding away. They took me over to the police station and told me they were going to keep me all night and all that, but they didn't. All they did was sign you out on your own recognizance, that's all. (hooker)

As with most other aspects of the hustle, girls getting busted are apt to find that they cannot depend on their "old man." Any help they do receive is much more likely to come from a hooker friend (sometimes a wife-in-law), than from the pimp:

The pimps are of no help in making bail, they are not seen. They don't want anyone to know. The cops, that's the thing that they love. They don't really want the girl, they'll even make deals if the girl's in a heavier charge, a coke bust or something. They would let her go if she'll tell them who her pimp is, who's the coke dealer in that town, who's got the guns and all that. They'll tell her, "You can get off." Of course she doesn't know everything and she has to be careful. . . . That's why a lot of girls don't get too friendly. You have to be careful who you say what to, your name might come up! But forget about him bailing you out! If you go to jail, don't call him from jail. You've got to worry about the phones being tapped, he's not going to help you there. . . . The only thing he helps with is your rent or your bills, or if you're starving because you don't have any food in the house, maybe he'll come over and bring you some. That's about it. (hooker)

In addition to formal sanctions, it should also be noted that the "long arm of the law" is capable of exerting informal pressure on careers of "troublesome" working girls. Thus, while some girls have been prevented from working certain bars because of violations of bar rules, the police may also inform bar managers that the presence of specific girls in their bars would be detrimental to their interests:

> *Most of the girls who've been barred at Central have been barred because the cops have something against her. Like maybe they told her to plead guilty in a case that came up with them and she didn't. Maybe they're really harassing her and they'll go to the manager and just say, "I want that girl barred for two weeks." The manager doesn't want any trouble, so out she goes. She'll just go to another bar.* (bartender)

MEDICAL COMPLICATIONS

In spite of the seemingly common expectation that concerns with venereal disease would be somewhat commonplace in hooker bars, we have found that, in a manner much like concerns with the police, concerns with venereal disease tend to be sporadic and situational. Overall, the general attitude of the hookers, staff, and patrons is a very casual one, with the general affirmation that the girls hooking from the bars are "clean":

> *These girls are very clean. They're a lot safer than most of the girls that you would be able to pick up at some bar for free. It's standard procedure for the girls to wash both the date's genitals and their own before sex. Afterwards the girls always wash themselves as well. They don't worry too much about the guy then. They let him wash himself once the act is over. . . . The girls also get frequent check-ups.* (patron)

> *I asked Mike about VD concerns on the part of staff having sex with known hookers. He said that some of the girls were thought to be poor risks by the type of clientele they had, indicating that the more selective girls were, the more likely staff members would think they were safe in having sex with them. He also mentioned that he thought they got checked out now and then. Mike said that he only thought of using a safe in terms of preventing pregnancy, that he really wasn't concerned about getting VD, that one just went and got a needle. He said he never gave it that much thought and that he just doesn't worry about it.* (notes)

Just how regular these check-ups are remains questionable. Some girls do go for weekly checkups, but we very much doubt this of others for whom the keeping of any appointment seems unlikely. Nevertheless, as a general rule, the girls do wash their own genitals and wash and inspect those of their dates before engaging in sexual relations. It should be noted, that although these visual inspections can be misleading, some of the girls place considerable faith in them. Many of the girls also require that their dates wear safes, but clearly this is not always the case. The following extracts will provide the reader with a sense of the dynamics involved in the situation:

I've never had anything, any kind of venereal disease. I've been lucky, because most hookers have had it, a number of times, at some time or another, and crabs and everything else. I never had, I don't know why, because I don't use rubbers very often. . . . Using rubbers is another one of the things a lot of the girls do. I think it's a very good thing to do. But I had so much trouble getting them to use rubbers, especially with people that I'd been out with a few times before, I just didn't have that big a turnover, or new faces. . . . At first I didn't use rubbers. Then I decided one day that I should, (although) I've never had a dose. I tried a few times and some guys just flatly refused, no way! Some guys, who you don't know, when they sit down and are talking to you, will ask, "Do I have to use safes?" Then there are some guys who would only go with safes. And they'd ask you, "Is it okay to use a safe?" or "Do you have any on you?" Fine. It's much cleaner, it's much safer anyway. It didn't make much difference to me. Some guys would go along with it and, "Well, if I have to" and I'd make up a story that I was off the pill and didn't want to get pregnant. But they just didn't enjoy it and then it took them longer. And that's something I didn't want, because you had to be there a little longer. So I have used them, but not most of the time. A lot of the working girls do. A lot of them won't go out with any guys otherwise and they'll tell them at the table. . . . But, that's another thing that guys get mad at. There are girls who will agree to anything at the table, "Yes, I kiss", and "No, I don't use rubbers", until they get to the room. And then they tell the guy, "Okay, you can't touch me, I don't kiss, you're going to have to use a rubber, and you've got 15 minutes." Of course, the guy is going to get mad. If you tell him at the table, that's different. When I was using rubbers, I said, "Look, I'm telling you right now, you have to use a rubber. If you don't want to, then just don't go out with me." "Okay, that's fair," he agrees to it at the table. But if you're going to wait to tell him until you get him in the room, then you might have the guy say "Okay, forget it. Give my money back," or you might have a guy get upset and get a little rough with you. A lot of the girls cause their own trouble. (hooker)

You just hope that you don't get it. Knock wood! We have this one doctor we go to, and every Saturday morning, I will be there. But some of the girls only go now and then, or only once. He would teach us how to look for VD and crabs and such. What you sort of look for is a sore, if his testicles are inflamed or red. You sort of give your customer a hand job, and if he has VD, well then you might get some signs. Usually by the time you have finished that he has a hard on, he is pretty well ready to go and that is one reason you are there for only five minutes or so. So it works out good that way too, but you have to be careful of the guy who says, "Uh, don't touch me, I am sore." Them, I have to check even more. . . . Also you leave the minute that guy comes. So you not only check him for VD, but what you are up there for is to get him to come. And if he comes while you're checking him out, great, you can leave! Sometimes they really get mad in that situation, but that was the deal, until they came. That is something you learn over time, and you find the less you get the guy inside of you, the less likely you are to have any problems or get sore, or whatever. So you try to do as much as you can by hand. Then if he has a hard on and gets on top of you, he comes very shortly, to where he is not doing very much to you. And that is good too. (hooker)

DISINVOLVEMENT

Although we are focussing on disinvolvement more specifically in this section, we wish to call attention to the inseparability of "involvement" and "disinvolvement." Thus, a review of the preceding material will suggest a number of points at which persons might become disinvolved from hooking and a number of contingencies promoting disinvolvement throughout one's career. Consequently, in this section, we would like to emphasize some other themes not so obvious in the preceding material.

DISENCHANTMENT

Although the life of the hooker seems an exciting one to many people, it can also "wear away" on persons. In addition to the problematics of respectability, and the legal and medical complications entailed in their work, the girls may also find themselves disenchanted with the "material" with which their job requires them to work:

> One of the hookers, after coming out of the room, started talking to me. She said that she had just been insulted by one of the customers. I asked her what he said. She said that the guy told her that she was an asshole to be hooking, that she was young and pretty and should be a secretary or something like that. (notes)

> Your attitudes towards men are often negative. Sometimes they try to be too accepting, they'll say, "Well, if I were a woman I'd be doing this." But it's not that easy, and you don't want them to be too accepting of you because they don't really understand all the things that have happened to you. So sometimes, it bothers you if they're too accepting of what you're doing, and yet at the same time you don't want them to be intolerant or looking down on you.... There was a while when I found myself really hating men, and I guess part of it is all the types you see. For a while I was wondering if I was gay or not. I didn't become involved with any of the girls, but it's something that you wonder when you find yourself hating men like that. It's not a lasting thing, but at times you wonder. (hooker)

> For the longest time, I took a very negative attitude towards sex. Because when you're working, you're typically very neutral towards the person. Like if a guy wants to take you out and have dinner and all, that's fine, but you really don't want to have sex with him. It's kind of interesting, because you can go to work and get paid for it, but in other situations, it's different. I just took a very negative attitude towards sex. Sex just wasn't appealing to my senses anymore. Like I would get invited out for dinner and so forth, but I just didn't get involved in sex with them. (hooker)

LEAVING THE CAREER

While it is not uncommon for many girls to leave work for short periods of time, disinvolvement is by no means as simple as outsiders (and the girls themselves) generally anticipate:

Most of the girls I know are 26 or 28 and have been in the business for 10 years, and they don't see an end to it. They say they'd all like to get out, that they're going to leave, but if they've been doing that since they were 16, what else are they going to do? Like, I've worked in an office and I know I couldn't go back to that. I could if I had to, but I wouldn't want to. And most of them haven't even had that experience. So what are they going to do, go out with no experience? So they just stick with it. It's the only way they know how to make money. They know what they're doing and their friends are there. (hooker)

There are so many times you'll be talking to the girls and they'll say, "Well, I'll just be working here a couple more months until things work out." There are so many times you hear this and then you see them there for years and years. Usually, they have plans of getting out in the near future but these don't work out. (manager)

There was one girl that I got to straighten up, to square up. She had two kids and she was with this guy and was very unhappy. I'd talk to her and she'd say, "I'm thirty years old and what kind of life am I giving myself? What kind of future do I have?" She finally talked her way right out. She left the business. I don't know what she's doing now. After she left, she moved in with a trick, and he looked after her, kind of a sugar daddy type, he paid her rent and looked after her kids. There was no love there or anything, just some kind of security for her. Then she got mad because he was still going to Central and going out with one of the girls. That broke up and she kept in touch with this other girl that I know. She left him. Then one day, about a year after she left, she came back to Central. She figured she'd come back and make some money. Things change so much around there. Things don't stay the same. Basically, the girls are there and the tricks are there, but so many things happen, like staff changes and rules, and new girls. She came back and sat down. She's a very pretty girl, always made a lot of money, but business was slow. So she sat there for three hours and not one guy talked to her. She was very upset and she just couldn't understand why anybody wouldn't talk to her. Finally, she got a date and sent him to the Lion's Castle. When she got there, he wasn't in his room. She just came back and said, "Well, that's it," and she never came back. (hooker)

Even when more extensive disinvolvement from prostitution occurs, "career girls" often do not leave the hotel community. Rather, many of their alternatives tend to arise from within other sectors of the hotel community. In this sense disinvolvement is often less dramatic than might be supposed:

Maggie is quite an accomplished booster and although she has been hooking for quite a few years, she is presently more or less disinvolved from hooking. (notes)

A number of the strippers have been hookers before getting into stripping. Some of them are still into hooking quite extensively, but others do so only rarely or occasionally. (notes)

This one girl, Sheila, left the business. She just fell for a trick. The guy was giving her the old charm routine and it worked. I got to know him quite well because he'd come in the bar a lot and he'd say, "Gee, I'd really like to get hooked up with this one. I'd really like to take her out," and whatnot. The fact of going out with a hooker and having to pay for it kind of hit him too, but he did the odd time. He took her out a few times and it was always just because he was really hung up on her. This went on a few times, and then one day she came in and she said that she was living with him. She said, "Hey, you know Leon. Well, I'm living with him now." She stayed on for about 3 or 4 months afterwards as a hooker. I guess they wanted to get a little ahead financially and then she was going to stop and get a regular job. He was the manager at The Flamingo and she moved in on that too, sort of helping him out there. She's not hooking right now. She's working as a desk clerk now, but you couldn't really say that she's out of it, because she's still in that environment. (bartender)

Even those who quit tend to miss aspects of "the life." One's former life is not totally left behind:

I know that I would never go back to Central and sit there again and become one of the girls. But I enjoy seeing everybody and they all can be so friendly, saying "Hi," and telling what's going on. If I had to, I could turn a trick, it wouldn't bother me, I could do it. But I would never put myself in that situation again. (hooker)

There were times, I'd think back and I'd wonder, well, "Is Susan still with so and so and is Janet still doing this or that?" You do get to know the people, and you do miss them. You wonder what are they doing, and how are things working for them. (hooker)

I saw a man I knew was good for $70, that I could've got $70, and I know it's only 15 minutes. But I didn't want to go through what I had to go through for the 15 minutes. (hooker)

Finally, just as becoming involved in prostitution seems largely dependent on having friends "in the life," disinvolvement seems contingent on having supportive others on the outside. While extensive disenchantment with the life or troubles therein is conducive to thoughts of disinvolvement, successful disinvolvement attempts vis-à-vis a straight life seem contingent on the hooker's establishing (or re-establishing) a trust relationship with an outsider. These others may be family or friends, but an understanding acceptance in conjunction with timing (disenchantment) seems most effective:

The only one in my family I could turn to is April. She knows what I've been through because she's been a working girl herself. She was heavily into heroin, but she got herself dried out and together again. Then she got a straight job and about a year later, she got married. . . . I didn't know anything about this until after I got back home, and I think she saw a part of herself in me. I remember how she was when she came back, sort of withdrawn, not wanting to talk to anybody, and not being able to comprehend what they were saying, because she was a completely different person. I thought about this when I came home, and I thought, "I will just lay it on the line, but she beat me to it, "Well, what were you up to?" I said, "Uh, how do I tell you this?" And she said, "Look, if you were going to say you were a hooker, just come out and say it, because I was too." And I was the one who said, "Oh, no, don't tell me." But it was a lot easier, and I knew that I could turn to her for help. (hooker)

So when I was having this trouble, I came home and I just had to tell my parents. My mom, she didn't help at all. She got upset and was crying, but she didn't help. My dad was great. He said that I would always have a home with them, that we all get ourselves into difficulties now and then, and that we should try to sort out our lives for the future. He loves me, and he cares. I have thought of going back different times, but one of the things stopping me is that I don't want to let him down. (hooker)

Scott knows what I was doing. He had been in the hotel scene too. So it was good that way, he understands things. . . . It was after I got involved with him that I got out of it. . . . It's good, because I don't have to worry about keeping things secret from him. It's a problem with the family or the friends sometimes, but not with him. I don't think I could have made it, say with somebody who was uptight about the whole thing. (hooker)

The working girls may establish intimate relationships with unknowing straights. While these relationships may also be instrumental in effectively disengaging a girl from prostitution, they may be subject to considerable anxiety:

He figured that Tamara had been working as a receptionist for a business firm, and she can't let him know otherwise. He is very straight, and she worries about that, because he would dump her like that (snap!). So even with me, he can't find out what I am doing either, like not her long time friend, because he would get too suspicious. (hooker)

I don't know if I should tell him or not, but I think that if I do tell him, I'll lose him. And I think that he's the biggest thing keeping me from going back to hooking right now. Also, I don't want it to be something that he can throw back at me if we're having an argument. My mother does that to me now. Also, if I told him, and his parents found out, that would end any liking they have for me. (hooker)

At home, I try to avoid all conversations about hookers and things like that, because I'm sure that I'll get myself in a corner. Like they will be saying things, and I know that it just isn't that way, or the way they made it seem in some movie we watched. But if you say anything, if you seem to know more than you're supposed to know about things, then people are going to start to wonder about you or how you know these things. (hooker)

HOOKING IN OTHER BARS

As a means of situating the preceding material within the broader context of hooking in bars, it seems advisable to distinguish between "hooker bars," "bars popular among hookers," and "non-hooker bars." Most bars seem best described as non-hooker bars. One may find women working out of these bars on occasion, but their presence tends to be infrequent and erratic:

We get the odd girl in here, but none of them stay very long. This crowd just isn't into it, and the guys here, well, there's so much free stuff available, they're just not used to paying for it. (manager)

You don't find hookers in bars like this. There's not enough action. It's not like Central or Hillcrest. It might be kind of interesting if we had them here, but we don't. Maybe some guy will pump a chick full of booze, and take care of her that way, where he's buying her drinks all night, but not a regular hooker. (bartender)

Although hooker bars, such as Main and Central, are popular among the working girls, they are less common than "straight bars popular among hookers." Whereas a number of hookers are more or less continuously available at hooker bars throughout business hours, the popular straight bars tend to be considerably less obvious, and may be popular in spite of attempts on the part of management and staff to prohibit prostitution in those bars. Thus, a few girls may routinely work these bars, but the girls working these bars are more likely to develop a circuit-like bar routine.

In contrast to "hooker bars," most other (straight) bars preferred by hookers have high traveller ratings (**** ratings), are within walking distance of one another, and cater more to travelling businessmen and conventioners. While a bar's reputation and the relative prominence of prostitution therein is much more instrumental in denoting a "hooker bar" than is decor, size of the hotel, or traveller ratings, in general the management (and staff) at the larger, more prestigious hotels tend to discourage obvious patronage by the working girls. These hotels are generally more discriminating in their bar clientele, but this reflects the proportionately greater revenues typically derived from other services, such as room rentals and restaurant businesses. In spite of the problems of entry, however, the trade potential the travellers represent defines these hotels as worthwhile spots in which to work:[4]

The Supreme always has good money in it, if you can get into it. But you've got to be good looking and very well dressed, where you really have it together, to work at the Supreme. Because if you don't, they will put you out on your ear, just like that. . . . The Tri-Star is another place, and the Lexington. The people there are very nice, and we usually have a lot of fun there, drinking and carrying on, but a lot of the girls don't go there because it is too far from downtown. A lot of the girls don't like getting out of their territory, so they will stick right downtown at the Crystal, the Fairly, La Paloma, the ones that are more or less within walking distance, because a lot of them don't want to put the money out for a cab, and a lot of them don't have money for a cab because their pimp wouldn't give it to them, so if they don't get a trick, then they just don't have the money to go anyplace. . . . At the Supreme, if you leave with a date, well you don't come back the same night and it is even better if you stay away a couple of nights before you come back. And at the Fairly, the same kind of thing. If you take them up to the rooms, don't come back afterwards. And the management really doesn't tell you this or the staff, but you hear this from the other girls, so you sort of learn what the rules are that way. . . . Also you can't have tough looking girls. They would rather they charged that extra and have them look good than have some rougher girls coming in and charge less. But some of the girls look so obvious. . . . The Supreme is a difficult place to work in because the security is very tight, but any time I decide to go to there to work, I make damn good and sure I'm dressed in my best clothes. It's a place you just

---

[4] While some of the women working from these bars feel more comfortable in these "classier" and more "respectable" settings, many of these hookers also lack the contacts enabling them to more fully access "hooker bars."

can't go walking into work in a pair of dress pants and shirt. They just won't let you in. At the Crystal, you could go in with a nice pair of dress pants and a nice shirt, but at the Supreme you have to dress to their standards. You have to dress high class. And you have to be very meticulous and not sort of flashy where you are too obvious. And you can go in there and make a killing that way. . . . Downtown you could dress that way and do quite okay, but in some of the hotels, you just would be asked to leave, "Sorry, you don't meet our dress codes." (hooker)

"Bar hopping" may seem a more interesting way of working as a hooker, but it has definite drawbacks:

It is hard to go bar hopping. It's costly, and you waste your time, and you are buying drinks and cab fares, and you really don't know where you stand a lot of times. So it is nice to stay in one bar and work there for a while. Because some nights you will be putting out $20-25 just on cabs. (hooker)

At the Copycat, it's really hard to get in, and then if you have any trouble, that makes it more difficult too, because then you don't have people that you can turn to for help. So if you are working in a bar, it's nice to know that you've got friends and that they won't turn on you or call the police, things like that. . . . If you know the people in the hotel, or if you know there is somebody around in the hotel who can give you help if you need it, then you are more likely to go to that hotel. And if you go to another hotel, then you are completely on your own. (hooker)

In addition to coming to terms with the staff and patrons of a new hotel, a girl working a bar circuit also faces the task of dealing with other hookers she may encounter. They may resent her presence and make it more difficult for her to work "in their territory":

If you want to know the rules about a particular place, you have to get in with the girls. Some of the girls will have a very difficult time getting to talk to the other girls because some of them don't want anything to do with an outsider. They figure this is their territory and they just don't want to do anything that might make it easier for other people to work there. But myself, I'm usually able to go and talk to people and people seem to accept me pretty well. . . . Sometimes you can tell just by looking at them; but if you see her and she goes and comes back, then you might go over and sit down and say, "Hi, how are you?" and maybe make some comments about her clothes or something, but along the way letting her know that you're a hooker as well. If you can do that, make some compliment to them, then they may open up to you a little bit. And so you get to talking and maybe you don't talk that much about the place itself, but just some little things to where they're feeling a little more relaxed and talking with you. Then if you both order drinks and the waiter comes over and she goes to get her money, well you pull yours out and you say, "That's okay, I'll get it." It always helps if you want to find out what is going on and that sort of becomes a cue where you just don't have to come out and ask them what's happening, but they know that you kind of like to know what the score is. And they prefer to have it done that way than rather you lay money on the table, like you're trying to buy information, because where you're putting money on the table it is not very personal and it is not very discreet. The other way, you can build up your relationship with that person. . . . . And you have to make it very clear that you're not a cop and that you are not there to try and find out other information because you are a police officer. That is hard to do with some of the girls because some of them have been busted so many times that they really don't want to talk with anybody for fear they're a cop. (hooker)

While the work habits of the migratory bar hookers tend to be less settled than those routinely working from particular hooker bars, with time the "bar hoppers" tend to find themselves more intensively involved in the hooker community. Eventually they are apt to define one or two bars (wherein they find one or two sympathetic and helpful staff people) as home bases. In general, however, the extensive interrelatedness of hookers to staff that one finds in hooker bars does not exist in these other settings.

In an attempt to further gauge the representations of Main and Central as hooker bars, we not only asked the more travelled of our respondents how these places compared with other "hooker bars," but also sought out contacts in other bars so labelled. In general, we found the operations at Main and Central fairly typical of other hooker bars. The bars vary somewhat in respect to decor and rules, the cost of drinks, the "going" prices for the girls, and "appropriate attire." However, those bars in which prostitution represents a prominent element tend to operate in ways similar to Main and Central.

Bar hookers are hustlers. They may come from a variety of backgrounds, but regardless of their means of introduction to the hotel community, career hookers are first and foremost "hustlers." As hustlers, they vary with respect to dedication, awareness, contacts, and sophistication, but their overall exposure to people "in the life" results in a set of orientations and practices which while promoting shared sentiments in the hotel community, tends to distinguish them from "straight people." Further, while one can relate aspects of their lives to those of people in other work/love/sex contexts, these women find themselves immersed in a setting in which a number of everyday contradictions are strikingly apparent. As a result, they are faced with the problematics of dealing with seeming dramatic incompatibilities such as "good times and disliked work," "love and impersonality," "being somebody and being outcast." Consequently, regardless of the bars in which the girls work, they find themselves forced to deal with somewhat similar aspects of their lives.

WORKING THE STREETS

To more broadly contextualize the preceding discussion of prostitution, we sought out information on working girls in a variety of settings. Thus, we endeavored to make contacts with hookers on the streets, in massage parlors, and those operating as call girls. Although discussing prostitution in some of these other settings may seem to remove us somewhat from the hotel community, our research suggests, to the contrary, that bar hookers (and the hotel community more generally) are best understood within this more general context.

Generally speaking, outsiders seem to regard "street hookers" as the least respectable category of prostitutes and this view tends to be perpetuated by academics writing on the subject. In part, this reflects the "youth" and "tough-ness" of street hookers in contrast to popular images of "call girls." In part, it reflects the "disrespectable" settings in which people working the streets find themselves. This view also reflects the notions that these girls are indiscriminate in their acceptance of tricks and that they are willing to indulge in a variety of sexual practices at very "cheap" prices. While there is some validity to these images, we would like to present some material which indicates the ways in which street hooking is related to prostitution in other settings.

One finds women of a wide age range hustling on the streets but overall these hookers tend to be younger than those working in bars. While some street hookers have worked in bars, parlors, and escort services, or may be doing so concurrently, "underage" girls may find themselves excluded from these other settings. Con-sequently, they are more likely to concentrate their efforts on dates they can arrange on the streets or in area restaurants. In general, street hookers are a little rougher than the girls working the bars but, lacking the protection the bar provides, have to be more self-reliant in dealing with troublesome situations.

Using data derived largely from an institutionalized juvenile population, and focussing largely on involvements in street prostitution, Gray (1973) notes that while the girls she studied had become disenchanted with their relationships with their families, all knew, on an intimate level, persons involved in prostitution. She also found that prior to these involvements the young hookers were not as singularly opposed to prostitution as may be commonly supposed. While these girls seemed aware of many negative aspects of prostitution (such as arrest, venereal disease), these concerns were balanced out, not only by the prospects of making good money, but also by attraction to "the fast life," "liking her pimp," and "seeing prostitution as a way to be somebody important."

Our material is consistent with Gray's findings. The hookers tend to learn about hooking from their friends and although their interests are very much contingent on their contacts, tend to be attracted by the life. Most of the people with whom we have had contact further indicated that at the time of their involvements, they were disenchanted with their former situations and/or felt little accountability to other people. While hookers may work both bar and street settings more or less concurrently, the girls working the streets more exclusively, not unlike those working bars more exclusively, tend to be introduced to prostitution by friends (girl friends or boyfriend pimps):[5]

> I got it into through a friend. She got me started. She took me on my first dates. I did it together with her. We worked people on the streets and in cars. (hooker)

> The girl that got me into it was a girl I met in training school. . . . We got along pretty well. Here's a poem (love poem) she wrote to me. (hooker)

> That same night, after I lost my job, I thought about the advantages and the disadvantages of it and to me it seemed very rational in my mind. . . . Like most

---

[5] Only a minority of hooking careers seem traceable to reform schools. However, of the girls having been to reform school, a seemingly large proportion may be involved in prostitution before or after their school experiences (Davis, 1971; Gray, 1973). Training school subculture also seems conducive to lesbian involvements, and would seem to account for some of the overlap between these two sets of activities (see Giallombardo, 1966; Carter, 1973).

of the books I have read, the hooker is a sweet innocent little girl at first and she knows nothing about nothing and she gets talked into or tricked into it by the pimp, that is sort of the common stereotype. You know, the girl comes to the big city and she doesn't know what all is happening. Whereas with me, I sort of looked at it and said, "Well, I am not sweet and innocent. I know about the whole thing. I knew there was good money in it and I knew it was easy work, so to me it made sense at that time. One of the things that sort of kept me from being more positive towards it was that the rest of the society doesn't really accept that. The hookers in their own group they are very accepting of it, but the rest of the society really doesn't go for it and that was something I thought about too. But I did know a couple of working girls who would help me out, and I knew more or less what was going on there. (hooker)

BEING ACCEPTED

Any girl could attempt to work as a street hooker, but those intending to work the streets, not unlike those working bars, are apt to find initial acceptance problematic:

The girls don't like new girls. It's different if you have been working and you leave, and then you come back, but if you just start out new, they really don't want to accept you. They don't want anybody that might cause trouble with them or them with the cops or maybe they think you are going to cause problems, or with your old man or whatever. They sort of worry about a girl being like a candy ass if she meets the cops, where she folds and tells them everything. And the girls they really don't want trouble and they really can't afford it, so they don't like new girls because of that. And the competition, a lot of the girls don't like the competition. Some of them, they don't care about it because they figure that they can be successful regardless of what the competition is like, but some of the other ones resent any competition. And the girls more or less pick their own little areas and if anybody comes into their territory, then they really get hot about that. You see after the girls has been there for awhile, well it's okay, but at first, there's that real strong sense of resentment. (hooker)

One of the biggest problems a new girl would have would be dealing with the people on the street, because if she didn't have an old man, she might have to deal with a lot of heavies. Also dealing with the other people on the street, the dates or whatever, you don't have five minutes to talk on the street, so you have to be able to deal with people very quickly and get everything settled, very quickly. . . . In the bar, you do have more time to talk with people, but on the street it is very fast and if somebody comes up and talks to you, you have to know what you are doing. Also you have to watch that you are not too obvious, because you are going to get busted. . . . In talking to people, you have got to be able to say, "Yes, I am a hooker, and this is my price for such and such a period of time," and that is it. Very much a yes and no kind of thing, because you don't have that time to talk. Also you have to settle on what hotel you are going to, or are they wanting to go to their room or whatever. You have to be able to quickly get the information. A new girl won't know the hotels and she won't know where to take the dates. . . . Or they may not know how to handle tricks that are into S & M or other kinky things. You do get different kinds of people and some of the girls are into things like that, but you could see where a new girl wouldn't know how to get out of situations, that she wouldn't be able to handle or she wouldn't like. . . . If a girl is just starting out it might be useful to work for a man so that she has time to get adjusted to the situation and learn what is happening there. I found it was useful to be with Errol for a period of time. After I knew what was happening, I didn't need him, but initially it was a big help, people knowing I had an old man. Otherwise they will come on to you. It is not just something you say, "Well, I am going to do it," because you have to have some contacts and some idea of what you are getting into. (hooker)

I think if I had gone down and started by myself, I would have really been scared to start off, and I'd really been worried, and uncomfortable and I would have kept a lot more to myself. But with Shelley there, I had more courage or more nerve than I would myself, so I would do things that I wouldn't have done if I had been by myself. And Shelley told me, "Don't take any shit off those girls downtown, you know, you don't have to do that. You just stand up for yourself." And she said, "You have to let them know that you're not there to play games and that you're not there to be walked over by them." And the word also gets around there that if you're not a pushover and you stand up to somebody, the other people will know about that and they will kind of respect you for it too. . . . Being with Shelley was good for me, because they accepted her and they figured that she wouldn't bring someone in who wasn't okay. . . . Being in the area for a year or so, and being busted at least once, is almost necessary to being accepted for a new girl. The thing about being busted is that the way they figure that you don't go running to the cops about things, that you don't like the cops. . . . If a girl has been busted too many times, though, that can be a problem because then if the cops see you with them, then they are more likely to run you in as well. And you can't afford to get busted in the first place. But if you can stay around two or three years, even if you've not been busted, they are likely to trust you. But if you have been around two or three years and not been busted, that really is miraculous! It would be really difficult for a new girl to say, "Well, I am going to be a hooker," and just go down town and work because there would be so many things you wouldn't know about. Like Shelley said, if I wanted to come out, she would help put me out, that is the term they use. So I had a big advantage over a lot of the girls who had just come down and they really didn't know what they were getting into. . . . She helped me in the bar scenes, and on the street, and even working on the phone. (hooker)

CRUISING

Although street hookers tend to develop characteristic styles of hustling tricks, one finds considerable diversity within their overall procedures. For instance, some will stroll up and down particular streets individually or in groups of two or three; others will situate themselves in particular enclaves or store entrances; still others will spend a fair amount of time being accessible in area restaurants and bars. To some extent, however, working the streets is contingent on "being visible," a quality that can work for and against the working girl:

One of the ways you could check the girls out was by the shoes they were wearing and lot of them would be wearing heels even when it didn't seem appropriate. It just seemed so obvious that you figure, well the girl is almost telling you, "I am a hooker." A lot of the girls want it to be obvious. But if you wear spikes on Delta, then you know pretty well that you are a hooker. It can be hard to tell sometimes, some of the girls working in the office, whatever, they might be dressed much the same way. . . . The other thing is that if you aren't dressed like a hooker, then you might have a problem making money. This one night I had on what I call my "little girl peasant outfit". It is kind of cute, white, and gingham, but nobody even approached me. I never made a nickel that night, so you think more in terms of something that would be somewhat appealing to people. (hooker)

While customers will often approach the girls, if competition is keener, or business is too slow, or the situation is considered more tolerant, the girls will approach prospects:

You have to be accessible, you have to be where the guys are. If they are in the hotels or the streets, well that is where you have to be. Also to be successful, you can't hang around with your pimp or a group of girls, you pretty well have to be by yourself or maybe with another girl, just the two of you where the guys might be willing to approach you. (hooker)

A lot of the girls in the winter hang out around the sports arena, because a lot of the men coming to the games wouldn't bring their wives with them, and if they're there for the night, like out of town, they might like a girl. Also the bars in the area and the Tri-Star, they will be there after the game. The big problem is getting into some of these bars because a lot of them, they don't want hookers around, so the problem is being accepted. . . . On the street, the business is a lot better in the summer time. In the winter, not as many people are out on the street, so business is slower, but a lot of the girls can't get into the bars, they are too rough-looking, and they just wouldn't fit in a lot of the bars. So the arena was good in this way, because a lot of men are real sports buffs, and they will travel to other cities with the teams, so in the winter, the arena's a good place to be. (hooker)

If a car stops, I just ask them what they would like. Or sometimes, I'll say, "Do you want to go out?" And they will say, "Like, how much?", "What will you do for thirty?" And what I try to do is to get the price up to $30 or $40, although sometimes I'll go for as low as $25 or even $20. Sometimes, they want to go for the whole night, and then it's like $100 or more. (hooker)

In the winter, you get yourself a warm coat, really warm, and you just do not sit down. You walk around and try to keep warm that way. You just don't sit down, or you might freeze your ass off if you do. You just keep walking around until you find someone. You will also stop at a restaurant and have a hot chocolate or a coffee to get you warm. (hooker)

As with the bar hookers, once a prospect seems interested, the street girls attempt to settle on a price and then direct the date to a hotel room:

The Denver House is a dump. It is clean, but not what you call your classier hotel. And a lot of the guys downtown, well, if they are going to pay $50 for a *girl they don't want to pay another $30 or so for a room and they go there because it's cheap. . . . A lot of the girls, they will have their preferred hotel where they take their tricks because then you get to know the rooms and the situation and they get to know you. . . . Usually it is the guy who goes and gets the room. What I do is call ahead and get the room number. Then you don't even have to stop at the desk. You just go shooting up to the room. It is good to have it set up that way because you never know who is going to be around the lobby or whatever. . . . The desk clerk can be important because you never know exactly what the person will be like when you run into them, like they might be the perfect gentleman helping you with your coat and helping you into the car and everything, but when you get into the room you just never know what they will be like, so it is good to have that desk clerk there and know that you can rely on him to help you out. . . . As you're wandering out you leave the guy a couple dollars, "Catch a cab," or "Have a drink on me," or something. You want to do that, because if there is any trouble in the room, then you know he is going to come and help you.* (hooker)

Some of them don't want to go to hotels, they're too cheap! They just want to have sex in their cars. So you might do it in the car, but it's risky, so you don't like to do that very much. (hooker)

Once in the room with the date, the street hooker's procedure is similar to that of the girls working from bars. Their first concern is that of collecting their fees, and then they try to leave as quickly as possible, with a minimum of personal (and physical) contact with their customers:

Always you wait until you are in the room before you exchange any money because if you exchange money, let's say before you go to the room, the chances you get busted are a lot greater. . . . Usually I spend about 15 to 20 minutes in the room. You have to watch you aren't too quick, because it really annoys some people, it really does! But some of the girls don't care if they have regulars or not. They are in the room and out of the room and back downstairs as fast as they can. (hooker)

Kissing the dates is one of the things you try to avoid. A lot of them have bad breath, beer or cigarettes or whatever. And I smoke myself, but if the guy has been drinking and smoking, it is just yuk to kiss them. It kind of tastes like shit. And some of them, when they breathe on you, you just almost pass out. . . . Some of them, before you go up, they ask you if you neck or kiss and I just tell them, I prefer not to. The way I look at it, is, if you are on the pill and if you have a safe, then you have very little to worry about in terms of getting pregnant or VD or whatever, but if you are into kissing a person, then you might spread VD that way. And, like, with oral sex I always use the safe with them. . . . I would rather give oral sex than kiss the person because it can be very impersonal and to kiss, well, that is practically all that you have got left. (hooker)

The hookers don't want to be friends with their tricks. They just get used to the idea going and having sex with them and then leaving them. It's just like so much money that is waiting for you to get it. (hooker)

Given the similar procedures and concerns of street and bar girls, it should not be surprising to find that the sorts of problems they encounter are also similar:

Another problem is getting them to use a safe because there are some really obstinate people. They say, "I never use them," or "I don't like them," or whatever and I tell them that I'm not only concerned about my own welfare but also with theirs. (hooker)

Some of the problems that you have come because they want their money back, and you figure that you deserve the money, especially if you've had a bad night, well you just don't want to give anything away. I can't say that I was ever beaten up badly, but there were times that I could have gotten out of it, but I just wasn't going to part with the money. (hooker)

If they came once, well that was pretty well it, especially for some of the older guys who wouldn't be able to get it up for the whole evening, so there is no point in trying with them. But with the younger guys, they figure that hookers were all night sex machines and if you were up there for half an hour well, they pretty well got their half hour's worth. . . . It also depended upon whether they were a meek person or whatever, because those people, well, I say, "That is it," and away I would go. But if somebody seemed more aggressive, then I might stay longer because some of them, you are afraid of what they might do to you if you got them fairly angry. (hooker)

Our research also suggests that street hookers, and girls working out of a number of bars, are more likely to steal from their dates than are hookers extensively working out of particular bars. However, in all these settings, some men (for example out-of-towners, highly intoxicated) are defined as safe "marks" by all hookers:

If a guy had a lot of money and you knew he was from out of town, where you probably wouldn't see him again, well, you pick up whatever you can and take his wallet, whatever you can. And some of them flash their wallets in front of you, that's something you should never do, open up your wallet to a hooker. And the hookers, they might not be too smart in terms of all the things that are happening outside their world, but what's happening inside their world, they know those things pretty well. And with the tricks, I have stolen wallets myself, and you'll be talking to them, just small talk, "How long are you staying?" and things like that and he is saying, "Well, I am only going to be here for the night and I am leaving in the morning." Well then you know that it's a probably good bet for you to try and take whatever you can. And like if a guy's got a lot of money, well take his wallet, to hell with him. He probably won't even realize until the next day when he goes to pay for breakfast or something, and a lot of the guys never report it. So it's not that risky to do. So I have never had any trouble from anything like that. Some of the hotels are good that way, because I'm not there all that often. (hooker)

Like the bar hookers, the street girls also acquire regulars. However, this is dependent, to a very large extent, on the girl establishing a relatively stable work routine in respect to location and/or times:

Regulars, if they like you the first time, they will probably ask you out again. Like they will know where to find you, and you may give them a number where they can call you, and sometimes you'll get their numbers. (hooker)

As with the bar girls, the street workers also exercise some selectivity in their dates:

Different times, like at the Oasis, you will see a guy, and one girl will turn him down, and that is pretty well the end for him, because the other girls figure their standards are as good as the one who refused him. Like if the other girl has turned him down, then you think that he's a little strange, or isn't up to par, or he's a cop, something like that. (hooker)

Liz, a black hooker, was talking to a prospect, asking him, "Do you want a special?" The man indicated some interest, but said that he wanted her for the night, offering her $60. "Sixty dollars," Liz yelled, "You want a fucking free broad!" Then she turned towards us, "He wants a fucking free broad! Sixty dollars for the night, what does he think I am!" The man sort of cringed and quietly left. (notes)

Although most of the street hookers also have pimps, they lack many of the sources of protection to which girls working in bars typically have access. Thus, while some of the bar girls are "tough individuals," one finds more overt indications of toughness among the street hookers:

We were walking down Delta Drive when we heard some yelling and screaming up ahead. It was Heddy, she was angry at this one man on the street. Apparently, he indicated that he was going to make a citizen's arrest because she had solicited him. But she turned things around on him, "What are you, a motherfucking cop? Let's see your badge. Are you impersonating a motherfucking cop? I'm going to have you arrested for impersonating a cop." Heddy had a rolled up newspaper in her hand, and was using it to hit the man as she bawled him out. She attracted a lot of attention and another street hooker, Sadie, a much smaller girl, also joined in the offensive. Heddy was still screaming, "He's impersonating a motherfucking cop," and Sadie was swinging her shoulder bag at the man. At this point, the man seemed to be getting even more intimidated by these two girls and started slowly running down the street. Heddy spotted a police cruiser, "Hey, there's a cop, I am going to have you arrested," continuing to batter at the man with this rolled up newspaper. The man then ran across a lane of traffic to jump in a cab with the two girls in pursuit, banging purse and newspaper against the cab. The man seemed genuinely frightened by the two women. (notes)

HOOKER COMMUNITY

Not unlike the bar hookers, street hookers can be seen as constituting a community unto themselves. The community is characterized by certain cleavages (for instance girls working for pimps vs. independents) and cliques (for example small groups of girls who frequently work together), but certain sentiments such as not interfering with another girl's hustles, maintaining impersonality with one's dates, and not informing on other girls are generally acknowledged. Thus, although the hookers may not be intimately knowledgeable about girls outside of their particular cliques, they tend to know of another by reputation (the extent to which a particular girl is seen as realizing commonly acknowledged sentiments):

You know the girls you work with, in say the downtown area, but you really don't know a lot of things about their past, like their families, or children, or even their real names. They might mention little things, but you really don't know much about where they're from. And you just don't tell them that I lived here or there, or my dad works at this or that. (hooker)

The biggest thing giving a girl prestige is how much money she makes. Some of the girls resented me because of that, because they had been working for a long time and I hadn't been in it long and I was making better money than they were. . . . Money tops the list, then your outward appearance, and if you can get along with the people better, that is good for your reputation too. . . . Where you're not getting upset about things, and where you're cool, and where you have got guts to stand up to people, that gives you a lot of prestige, because a lot of girls don't have the guts to stand up to people. Also they figure that if you run into some trouble with the police or whatever, and they see you can stand up for yourself, they figure that you probably aren't going to snitch to the cops like some candy ass would. Or if you run into a trick and he gives you a rough time and you can stand up to him, then they respect you for that too. Because they figure you are being more of your own person and that is something they respect. . . . Another thing is helping out the other girls. That is something that you don't really expect them to do, but if somebody is helpful to the girls, well then they do look up to her because of that. Where you appreciate their feelings. . . . Also they appreciate if you don't walk on their territory, their ground. They don't want you stealing their tricks, like Leila who was always cutting in other people. She didn't have any friends around the area. The only person she really had to fall back on was her old man because she was always stealing tricks and if he wasn't around, then she was in a lot of trouble because the other girls would be willing to beat her up because they resented her. . . . Another important thing is who the girl has for her pimp. Some of the pimps are just pricks, and they just beat up on their women and the girl gets nothing for it. The girl may not have a place to stay and maybe she has to sleep in the subway or whatever. Where the pimps do not treat the girl well, those girls have very little respect. But where their pimps are better respected, then the girls are more respected. (hooker)

The existence of sentiments of this nature not only affects who is likely to be accepted in this setting, but also provides guidelines for working girls to strive towards in "being somebody" among their peers. It is also apparent that as girls become better acquainted with other street people, the street becomes a less hostile setting in which to work. Not only may girls find friendship and opportunities as a consequence of ongoing relations, but they are more likely to find that they have others to assist them in times of trouble. In part, however, a girl's opportunities to become involved in other affiliational networks and hustles will depend on her willingness to associate with street people other than her initial introductory contacts. Unless a girl is willing to become something of a "rounder," street hooking can be a rather precarious enterprise.

"PIMPS AND HOS"

The street hooker-pimp relationships were very similar to those we encountered in bars, and those described by Gray (1973) in her depiction of street hookers. Thus, although players and the street hookers are reported to have some violent exchanges, their relationships were generally defined, at least initially by the hooker, in romantic terms. The girls turn most of their money over to their "old man" who manages it and them. As with the bar girls, the street hookers saw their status as partially contingent on which pimp they were with, and how well they took care of their "old man." Also like the bar girls, at any given time, most of the street hookers were likely to be working for black men. A minority were working for white men, and another group of hookers worked independently. Overall, the (black) pimps were a little more in evidence on the streets or in restaurants than they were in hooker bars, but the street hookers were also almost entirely on their own in all stages of dealing with their tricks:

> The pimps just don't hang around that much downtown. I remember reading an article in the Eastville papers and they were talking about this billiards parlor with the pimps sitting with their women on their knee, setting them up. It just doesn't happen that way. You will see the pimps downtown sometimes, but they are not with their women and setting them up. And the girls don't sit on their knees and he doesn't meet her after every trick and get her money or whatever. He may meet her at such and such a time and pick up some money and if she is around he will get it. But it is not like they said in the paper. The pimps don't want to stick around. . . . The idea that the pimps help the girls, well that is the biggest bunch of bullshit I have ever heard in my life. It might happen once, now and then, but he really doesn't do a thing for the girl . . . but some of these writers have such vivid imaginations that you just wonder where they ever get them from. . . . You also get people who suggest that the hookers don't know what is going on, but I would tell you that the girls do know what is going on. Like, they have to know what is going on, to be doing that. Some of the girls might be very naive about certain things, and they might seem stupid because they don't have very much education, but they do know what they are doing and they do know what is going on that street, because when you put them on the street, they do very well. And a lot of other women, they just couldn't make it on the street. (hooker)

Some of the hookers become involved in hooking through earlier romantic encounters with players, but we also encountered hookers who became involved with pimps subsequent to their hooking involvements. In part, these reflect the recruitment practices of the players, but they also reflect the definitions "of the life" to which the hooker becomes exposed:

> He asked me if I wanted to go out for dinner and he showed me a real good time. He seemed like a real nice person and then after a while, I got to like him because he was really nice to me and then he was asking me, "Do you live with anybody?" I said, "No, I live by myself." He says, "Well I bet you're really getting some heavies." I said, "Yes I am," and then after that it sort of became common knowledge that he was like my old man. And that's one of the things that really flies around the streets. And a new girl, the minute she gets a man, well everybody just lays off. . . . It is kind of the same thing as with the girls and their territories where the guys don't move in on somebody else's territory either. (hooker)

> At first, he treated her really nice but then after, if she didn't bring home so much money, he got really rough about it. And some pimps are like that, but

pimps are all different types and there aren't that many who are handsome or the good looking hunks like you see on TV. Some of them are good looking, but some of them, it isn't the good looks, it's the things they can offer a girl. Like if he can offer a girl nice clothes or a nice car or a nice place to live or if he is a more considerate guy that will make up for a lot of things. But the TV image of the handsome pimp, that is just a lot of garbage. It just isn't like that most times. (hooker)

When I first went to Eastville, just the people I was with, I thought I had to have a man. That was sort of the ideal that I was given. I felt that was the right thing to do. I really didn't think that you could work without having a man. Then after, when I saw how things were, I sort of said, "What the hell do I need him for?" So when he hit me, that ended up just being my excuse for leaving him because I thought, "There is no point continuing this. He really doesn't love me," and so when he hit me, I said "Well, that is it!" But I was in love with him at first and it took me a while to realize what was going on because I was still quite naive in the situation. (hooker)

From the player's perspective, his task is not only to encourage his ''hos'' to bring home as much money as possible, but also to deter any disenchanted worker from departing:

Some of the girls are dedicated workers, but a lot of them are there working because their old man told them to be and they know that if they go home without any money, or not enough money, then there is going to be a little bit of shit going on. (hooker)

Fergie had a couple of girls working for him, now and then, but not as much as he would like. . . . He tried to get me to work for him and was promising me all these diamond rings, and a big car and all these pretty clothes and all that shit. A lot of the guys do that. But a lot of the girls are afraid to leave their old men, because some of the guys, they are not the kind to let the girl just get up and leave. They would make threats, and some of them would be like this one I was telling you about, they probably would carry them out. . . . Something else that you will get is where the girls will get together and beat up on another girl, doing the pimp's dirty work instead of the pimp himself going and beating up on the girl. Also like some of the girls themselves, they might be stronger than some of the pimps. So these girls they could, you know, do a good job on somebody. Like this one girl, she used to beat up Micki all the time for Hugo. (hooker)

One of the problems a girl has if she wants to leave a pimp, and she hasn't been able to stash any money away, she wouldn't be able to pay him the release price. And if she just takes off, she is going to get into a little bit of shit with him, and he's going to try and catch up with her and get back at her for taking off. (hooker)

CONTINUITY

Troublesome clients, legal hassles, and the problematics of acceptance by the hookers and other street people all serve to promote a relatively high turnover on the part of new girls. At the same time, however, if a newcomer becomes accepted by the hooker community, and gets "caught up in the life," disinvolvement can be difficult. "Getting connected" is an exceedingly important aspect of sustaining one's involvement in prostitution, but so are one's involvements in other aspects "of the life:"

Sometimes working as a hooker can be very trying, where you have all these people coming on to you and getting heavy at times, but other times you think, "Gee, this really is an easy job," because you're making good money, and you're really not working all that hard, and you're meeting a lot of different people, all kinds of different people. And I don't know of another job where you meet so many different kinds of people as working as a hooker. And then, from the other girls, you learn all kinds of ways of making the job better, like ways of meeting tricks, and getting out of trouble, and ways of making more money or collecting from the guys, or dealing with the police. You just sort of keep learning ways of making the job easier as you go along. And then, you use certain lines with the tricks, like that you've got a daughter to support, and that is usually good for more money, especially with the older guys. Like the younger guys don't give a shit, but the older guys, some of them are softies, and they'll tip you a little, "Well, it must be difficult to support a child on your own." . . . So you'll be listening to the other girls, and you'd be learning from them and they'll be learning from you, and that's interesting too, because the older girls will learn from the younger girls too, because they'll be running across situations that they didn't experience before. . . . And there were things that Shelley would say she never thought to mention to me until that problem occurred, and then she would explain how to deal with that situation. Also Shelley was good in another way too, because if something bad happened, she'd try to make me feel better about it by explaining things to me or joking about it, making it seem like it wasn't as bad as I thought it was before. Like this one night, when this big jock did a heavy on me, and left me in the hall with my clothes ripped off and no money, and no friends, because I was at the Copycat, where I didn't know anybody. And I was feeling really low after that, and Shelley came along and when I told her, she says, "Don't feel too bad, I'll bet every night when he gets home, his old lady really kicks the shit out of him." It just seemed so funny, the way she said, it, and you get laughing, and you sort of get over it that way. . . . Usually, what I would do if I had some bad trouble, was the next day, when I was back working, she'd wait for me when I went to turn a trick, so it wasn't too bad that way. But this one day, I had some trouble, and I was alone with another trick and I was shaking so badly that even the trick picked up on this and asked me about it. So I told him, and he seemed quite sorry for me and told me not to worry, because he was not at all like that, and even that reassurance helped. (hooker)

It is really very fast, because there is always something going on, somebody calling you and wanting to know if you want to go out or you want to go shopping, or some date is coming by, or you want to go to the disco, and so you don't have very much time to yourself, and you really don't have all that much time to think about anything else except hooking or something to do with the people you are working with. (hooker)

If you get really down, then you take some pills to perk you up. It may seem like a stereotype, but it's a very common thing when you're in that world. It's very *much a part of it, the pills, the acid and all. So when you're down, you're really not down for long because there is always something to perk you up, and you can always get pills. And if you're really nervous about something, you can get some downers, or if you're feeling low, you can get some speed. You never really have to worry about feeling down. Because you know that someone would suggest you take a couple of pills or something. It was all part of being a hooker I guess. It all went along with it because you're not supposed to really feel down. And a lot of the times when you're working you're too smashed to really care about things. . . . I never really thought of the effects of the drugs, I just never really thought about it. It was just something that was there. And there, drug use, it's very casual and it's part of being alive and if you're too hyper, you just take a couple of downers or valiums, and there is always something there for you. Or if you take too many downers, you take a couple of uppers to get up again. I really can't believe the money I spent on drugs, a lot more than I should have. But everybody was like that.* (hooker)*

Even when a girl becomes disgruntled with the life, her ability to leave the life reflects not only her ties to the hooker life-style, but also the receptiveness she encounters on seeking out other options. Having worked as a hooker, however, she knows that she can become re-involved:

It was dad who really helped me in terms of getting out of it because I knew I could depend on him and different times I wondered if it was just my mother, if I would be able to have gotten out of hooking because my one sister, I really couldn't tell her because she was just like my mother, and she would throw it back in my face. . . . That can make a big difference, if you have somebody that you think you can count on when you are leaving. But in our family I was the one who you would think would be the least likely one to do anything like that. (hooker)*

There have been times when I have seriously thought about going back, like last Saturday. Doug and I had a big argument and I just about went up and packed my bags and headed off. But that is an important relationship to me. So, you get to the point where you say, ''I've got to go back,'' but then I think about Doug and that sort of keeps me going even though I think about going back. (hooker)*

MASSAGE PARLORS AND ESCORT SERVICES

Although we had hoped to be able to provide more material on massage parlors, like many of those involved in commercial sexuality we felt the squeeze of two Eastville morals crusades. Thus, while we encountered some people who were reluctant to discuss their activities in the bar setting, we found this particularly problematic in the context of massage parlors wherein raids and arrests were much more commonplace. We had developed a number of seemingly promising contacts among parlor people, but saw these sources "dry up" before we had an adequate opportunity to pursue them.

The "massage parlor" phenomenon represented a significant form of prostitution in Eastville from 1972-1977. Although the parlors employed a variety of profiles over this time, and increased in number to over 100, their basic operational format was relatively constant. The parlors had a basic fee for "a massage" (for instance, ''$20 for a half hour or $30 for a full hour''), supplying a private room and masseuse. The customer selected from the girls available and the two proceeded to the room. Although some parlors paid the girls a percentage (anywhere from 20 to 50%) of the initial fee, in other cases the girls were totally dependent on the ''tips'' they made from ''extras.'' These extras, the parlors contended, were entirely between the girl and the patron, and they consequently should not be held accountable for anything occurring in private between consenting adults. Thus, any extras were to be arranged and negotiated once the parties were inside the rooms:

You made your money on the extras. They'll pay their admission fees and after they're in the room, whatever services you can give them, that's your money. I was just there for a couple of weeks, I didn't find the money very good, and the manager was wanting me to go to bed with him. That's why I like it better on the street. It's more straightforward. They know what you're doing and that the price is for everything. Sometimes the guys in the parlor get upset when you tell them that anything else is going to cost them extra. (hooker)

In general, the operations of the Eastville parlors appear consistent with those reported by Velarde and Warlick (1973), Velarde (1975), Bryant and Palmer (1975), and Rasmussen and Kuhn (1976). While Velarde provides more indication of specific parlor practices, we particularly recommend the Rasmussen and Kuhn article as a source depicting the negotiation tactics and problematics of parlor encounters. The negotiable ''extras'' are clearly the means to financial success, but they also tend to complicate parlor procedures and business in general as the workers find themselves suggesting complete satisfaction while trying to avoid charges of solicitation.

The available literature on masseuses (Velarde and Warlick, 1973; Velarde, 1975; Bryant and Palmer, 1975; and Rasmussen and Kuhn, 1976) suggests that the girls working in massage parlors initially tend to come from a wide variety of backgrounds, but are likely to have been previously involved in other forms of prostitution as massage parlors achieved greater notoriety. This pattern also appears to hold for Eastville girls, but our data on this is highly impressionistic. Many Eastville residents seemed uncertain of ''what massage parlors were all about'' as late as 1975. Newspaper advertisements for masseuses were the type that could attract relatively naive girls, as Velarde (1975) suggests. Subsequent media coverage of massage parlors, parlor signs and window-dressing personnel (such as girls standing or sitting in the doorways, wearing provocative attire) would make it difficult to assume that prospective employees were completely unknowledgeable about parlor work.

Further, while we were not doing research on massage parlors in the earlier years of their existence, the links between massage parlor workers and the hotel community appear considerably more extensive than that suggested by the earlier mentioned literature. Thus, in addition to outlining some aspects of parlor practice, the following extracts provide further indication of the interrelatedness of persons involved in a variety of forms of hustling:

June, a stripper at Main, said that while in high school she was quite heavily in the dope scene to the point where she lost interest in school and dropped out at grade 10. Her parents were becoming rather upset with her drug habits and ''hanging around with the wrong crowd,'' so June ended up leaving home at *this time. She then moved in with her boyfriend who was her "dope connection." They were not making out very well financially and June decided to try to obtain employment in the massage parlors. She saw the advertisement in the newspaper stating that no experience was necessary and that training would be given. Noting that she "was not a virgin anyway," she decided to try it. The first ten days in the massage parlor were spent in training which June described as rigorous and extensive. This training was given by owner/operator who gave the girls instructions on how to massage, and a list of rules which they were required to follow. These rules were generally aimed at preventing arrest from undercover policemen known to investigate the parlor from time to time. The rules outlined the order in which the girl would dispense her services (massage first, sex later), the amount of time she would spend massaging (no less than 30 minutes), and what she would say to the customer (no direct propositions, no mention of "extras" until the late stages of the massage) and standards of cleanliness . . . . June notes that it was not very difficult to convince the customers to ask for extras since after one half hour of rubbing by a nude attendant, the customer was usually sexually aroused. Near the end of the massage, while she was placing her hand near the man's genitals, she would ask the customer if he would like a "local" (a hand massage). When he agreed to this she would mention that certain gentlemen had given her tips of $20 or $30 for these extras. At this point the customer would usually proposition her, saying that he would give her money for a hand massage, thus legally clearing her and the parlor. June said that some of the other girls performed more extensive sexual services such as sexual intercourse and fellatio, but she herself preferred to stay with "hand jobs." The girls did not receive a salary, obtaining all their income through "tips." June said that she was happy with this arrangement, claiming to make about $400-$500 per week.*

After the body rub parlor closed, June found making a living rather difficult. She had not saved any money and ended up drifting around the city, occasionally turning a trick. She found hooking on her own rather difficult, noting that she missed the protection she had in the massage parlor (from the owner and the bouncer). Occasionally she encountered some of her old customers on the street, but she was not able to build a regular clientele. June became disenchanted with street hooking and when an old girlfriend from the massage parlor, who was now stripping, suggested that June try stripping, June agreed. She was introduced to an agent and June began stripping. She said that she was rather nervous about stripping, expressing concern about her competence in relation to the other dancers . . . . Her concern was justified, she was dismissed the next day. Apparently, the management thought she was too amateurish and didn't fit in with the overall show the other girls were presenting. (notes)

As we walked down the street, Nancy (a Hillcrest hooker) talked to a number of the hookers. She said that the main effect of closing the massage parlors on the strip was that of turning the girls on to the street. She added that a good number of girls working in massage parlors were regular hookers and that while they would run two separate shifts, a number of the girls would stay for both shifts, doing doubles . . . . Nancy was also saying that her "old man" managed a massage parlor, the Pleasure Principle, but that it had gotten closed down a month or so before. (notes)

Betty works at massage parlors every now and then. If there's nothing going on in the hotel, she gets into a massage parlor. I don't know how they work it out, once they're in there, but somebody had taken a photograph of a chick inside a massage parlor for the papers. It was Betty, sitting there with her legs crossed, skirt hiked up a little. (bartender)

Existing somewhat concurrently with, and as an alternative to, massage parlors are a number of "escort services." Some operate on a "dial-a-date" basis wherein the customer never actually visits the shop, but calls the agency which in turn contacts the girl and has her meet the man in his hotel room or other prearranged spot. It is then her task to collect the agency's fees and arrange any extras on the side. In other cases the agencies attract patrons off the street and offer them a photo album of ladies from which to choose. The agency collects a time-based fee and arranges for the chosen girl (or an available substitute) to meet the customer at the agency office. As with the massage parlor, the fees are for the introduction and the girls' time; anything else is "between the two people themselves." Unlike massage parlors, escort services typically do not provide any rooms for the patron's convenience:

Lorraine and I decided to visit the "Date's Delight" escort service merely to gain some surface impression of the place, but the manager assumed that we had gone there so that Lorraine might be signed up and began explaining the operation to us. He showed us an album with pictures of about 20 girls, and another ten or so names and descriptions listed without pictures. I recognized a few of the girls as street hookers. . . . The rates listed were $50 for two hours or $60 for three hours of the woman's company. There is no guarantee as to the sort of services that might be involved and the only thing the manager said he would do is to introduce these two people, wherein she agrees to spend that amount of time with him. The client waits until the girl comes to the office and then they leave the office, before discussing whatever arrangements they wanted to make, where they wanted to go, or whatever. He also said that the girl would be guaranteed the basic $25 just for coming down, and that they required the basic $50 deposit from the man, and so even if things didn't work out she would have that $25. Anything else would be worked out between the two people involved. . . . As we were talking, it also became apparent that once the girl walks in, she has very little choice. She doesn't see the person beforehand, and although he gets to pick her, the best she can do, upon arrival, is to refuse to go out with him, in which case she would not get her money. She is much more locked into sustaining the particular relationship than are girls on the streets, or in bars. . . . These girls also have no built-in protection because nobody but these two people may know where they are going. (notes)

CALL GIRLS

The term "call girl" has been generally used to refer to "high class" hookers. These girls are thought to be discriminating in their clientele, and more discreet in their contacts and procedures. They typically entertain customers in their own apartments and, as a result, are less visible and seem somewhat removed from the bar or street hookers. Additionally, the call girl is thought to cater to wealthier clients, and to arrange her appointments over the phone, rather than by meeting men on the streets or in bars. Our material suggests that there is some truth in these statements, but that a number of qualifications are in order lest we unduly glamorize the call girl role. Certainly, there are some women who closely approximate the call girl ideal. It seems, however, that most "call girls" are not as readily distinguishable from the other working girls as might be supposed. "Call girl" is a much more relative term than is commonly assumed and, although call girl operations suggest a particular style of prostitution, the "call girl-common prostitute" distinction is not as useful as some might infer:

> *A lot of the girls, they have their phone business. So if things are slow in the bar, they'll make more use of these, or maybe you'll have a couple of really good regulars that you see every Tuesday or so. But at this bar, it's so easy, you don't have to worry about the phone and all.* (hooker)

> *Most girls have some phone tricks. Like Petra has her phone as well, but not all that much. At work you have your own little group of friends, usually a small group. You get along with the other girls, but you really don't talk to them about their business. . . . Ronni and Mimi also do some work by phone, but they spend more time working on the streets. . . . Typically, what I do is sit around until 7 o'clock and if nothing is up through the phone, then I go to the bars on the Delta or get on the street.* (hooker)

> *With the phone, and working downtown, and going out to the airport, and so forth, we found that we made a lot of money. . . . Some of the girls really didn't have that choice because if their man is downtown, they sort of were obligated to work downtown because he wanted to know where they were. . . . They have to work just a certain place because that's where their old man told them to go.* (hooker)

Thus, while some girls will work more exclusively off the phone, most girls working in bars, body rubs, and on the streets will develop regulars and some may develop a significant phone clientele over time, on this basis:

> *Nellie works as a hostess in the day, and works as a hooker in the evening, from the phone. It's funny, because most of the girls figure that she has gone completely straight, but she kept her telephone regulars, and between what she makes working as a hostess at the club and hooking in the evenings, she is doing pretty well. . . . She had been getting a lot of heat from the cops on the street, so she figured that she would try to clean up her act a little.* (hooker)

> *Opal got her clients from the body rub she worked in. It was a good place to build a book, arranging to meet the better customers at her place.* (hooker)

Given the concern with developing and maintaining a steady clientele, "the book" becomes the single most important characteristic distinguishing "call girls" from other hookers. Any girl possessing a good book (one listing many viable clients) can operate as a call girl. Whether or not she can maintain her clientele or avoid legal entanglement are other issues. But a call girl without a book can be likened to a train without a track. Books may be purchased, stolen or developed, but they are essential if one is to operate as a call girl:

The book to a hooker, who keeps a book, it is her most prized, valuable possession. It doesn't matter if you have a ring on your finger that is worth $10,000, it is that book that is the most valuable, the most prized thing that you have. (hooker)

The book is something that's not talked about. It's kept pretty quiet, because you don't want too many people to know that you have a book. That can get you into trouble, so maybe just a small number of people know that you have a book. . . . You don't want it known that you have a book because you don't want anybody to go running to the police. The book has to be pretty well kept up to date and you don't want the police coming and busting you or going through your place with a search warrant, because that book can be very incriminating in itself. (hooker)

If a call girl has a good book and clients that have money, then she has a good set up. But if she has a little book, like thirty or forty names in it, then she is probably not going to make that much money. Some girls try to work off a book that is very small but it is just not possible. You have to have a big number of customers, you have to have that volume, just to keep you going. . . . Some girls don't keep that much information on their clients so that it isn't much help to them when they are working on the phone calling the clients. Even things like favorite drinks and what the guys like, it really helps. (hooker)

Apart from the direct purchase of a book, which usually involves a trust relationship being established on the part of the vendor, books are either developed by a girl working with an established call girl (Bryan, 1955) or by building a list of regulars by working in bars, on the streets, or parlors. Not all hookers working in these capacities desire to become call girls, but if a girl is able to work in a certain city for a period of time and takes enough interest in her dates to establish regulars, she will be on her way to effectively becoming a "call girl."

Insofar as one may meet wealthy tricks in bars, on the streets, or in parlors, a certain amount of "luck" is also reflected in finding exceptionally lucrative tricks, often termed "sugar daddies." Although not as important as a good book, one or two generous clients can move any hooker towards call girl status:

If you can get a sugar daddy, a special regular trick, well you are on your way to becoming a call girl. If you have a guy who will pay the rent and stuff like that, well that's a real advantage. Then if he gets you a few referrals that's really great, because usually they're good, but you can't depend on the referrals. But if he's doing all the other things for you, who really cares? (hooker)

One client like that can really make a big difference, because you knew he was good for $500 every week. And he only missed once in a year. It is so good because some girls might only make $500 in a week. You know you have that $500 coming in, like money in the bank, so it is just such a big help when you are working. (hooker)

Sugar daddies are really important. If you have a sugar daddy, you've got it made. He will take you out shopping, or give you extra money to buy new clothes, lots of things like that. Or they might take you out for the day, and leave you a little bundle for your week's expenses. So you might not have to work that day, and then in the evening, you see the other girls, and, "I did such and such today." (hooker)

Although the possession of a good book tends to ensure a hooker of success as a call girl, her continued success is contingent on being able to maintain that listing of clients. A girl relying more heavily on the generosity of a particular date is especially vulnerable, but the girls generally tend to be concerned about keeping their better regulars. As a result, they cater more extensively to these clients than they would were they to meet the same men in other settings:

A lot of girls don't take the time to get phone numbers or addresses or get in touch with people. Because you can sit at home at your phone, and if things are slow, you just get on the phone, calling them up. . . . We would also write down the days they are working, the days they are off and different places to get a hold of them and different things that they like or dislike. We would just sort of keep a page for every person. Also you write down what they looked like, because a lot of times, if you just had the phone number, you might forget who they were. . . . And you usually write in the times when their wives are in, and maybe fake names you use if you are calling them at business. Sometimes they will give you code names to use, or files if they're doctors or lawyers, just so that you would know what to say when you called them. (hooker)

If you want to keep regulars, then you pretty well have to show that you are experiencing sexual satisfaction with them. Otherwise, they may not feel that they mean as much to you as they would like to. So it is important in that situation to let them think that you are getting something out of the relationship too, beyond just the money. . . . Some of the girls don't want to have regulars because they figure he will get to know her too well, because over time you do get to know a person. But, with me, my regulars were pretty good because one guy was paying my rent and another guy was bringing my chesterfield and so forth, another guy brought me a big chair, and another one brought me a new carpet, and I never bought my bed or my lamps. So the regulars, they can really be an important thing to you. (hooker)

Whether a girl is attempting to further develop her book, or is simply faced with the prospects of replacing lost regulars, the acquisition of new regulars represents an integral component of a successful call girl routine. A few girls may obtain a significant number of referrals from existing customers, but most call girls are likely to spend some time in accessible locations in an attempt to ensure an adequate business:

You have to keep looking for new people, because they come and go, and if you lose one good one, you almost have to replace him with two. If he's a good paying customer, and trustworthy, he's not that easy to replace. . . . Referrals aren't all that common. Sometimes, you'll get a trick, who'll send some friends over, but a lot of guys have a wife and kids, and they really don't want to talk about it with other people, because the word is going to get around. Some people do that, but you couldn't rely on that alone to keep you going. Even if you have a good book, the referrals probably won't be enough to keep you going, let's say at the same levels. (hooker)

*If you want to be a call girl, you've got to get the clientele from somewheres.
Getting a book built up is not an easy thing. . . . And if you go to the bar or a
hotel, a lot of the tricks you will meet are travellers, people that weren't very
regular. You want people who are in the area, or are passing through quite
frequently. And they have to be people who have the money to be a regular. A
lot of people you meet are people you never see again, or maybe not for a long
time, not regulars. So it's not so easy to build up a good book. . . .* (hooker)

In contrast to other contexts, girls working more exclusively as call girls tend to
acquire certain skills in using the phone. Thus, although the call girl may receive
inquiries, she is also likely to promote business by calling dates when things are
slow:

*When I'm on the phone, I'm the sweetest thing, I don't talk like I am now, but
very soft and little girl like. The men like that. . . . There are little ways of
talking on the phone. You don't use certain words on the phone. When you
are on the phone, you want to make everything seem casual, so you might say,
"Do you want to go out?" But you try to avoid mentioning sex, or anything
very explicit.* (hooker)

Further, although girls using hotel rooms may also receive assistance from other
people in the event they encounter troublesome dates, girls working from their
own homes seem less likely to be involved in violent exchanges. This may reflect
greater screening of dates on the part of girls working out of their apartments, but it
may also reflect the more considerate treatment accorded dates in these settings, as
well as the date's perception that he is dealing with a ''high status call girl'' rather
than a ''cheap street hooker'':

*I think it is easier for a girl working off the phones to make more money than the
girls on the street. But if a street girl is more dedicated, or has more regulars,
she can make out pretty well too. But I haven't found that a lot of the girls really
are that dedicated. If a girl is working for a man, she is not going to have that
much money in the end, but she is probably going to be more dedicated, getting
on the street, on the phone, and going to work, so she'll probably make more
money.* (hooker)

While some call girls may be particularly anxious to distinguish themselves
from the ''ordinary street hooker'' or ''house girl,'' the differences may be less
significant than might first seem. Additionally, to the extent call girls are involved
with pimps and their culture (see Greenwald, 1958; Bryan, 1965), they are apt to
be seen as ''just another ho,'' and judged by their ability to produce. Overall, they
appear ''classier,'' and tend to be better educated than the bar or street girls, but
insofar as they share acquaintances in both the black and hustling cultures, the
differences diminish. The call girl routine may seem more attractive to the novice
and as a result it may seem to be an easier way for some girls to ''turn out.'' It
appears, however, that the style with which one operates depends to a large extent
on her contacts, and those of the persons with whom she becomes connected:

*I've seen a lot of people in books talk about a lot of different kinds of hookers,
but what I say is that you have a hooker and that is all you've got! They have got
different styles of working. Some work on the streets, and some work in the
bars, and some are on the phone, but most of them, they have some calls and a*

lot of them who are "call girls," they will be working in bars or on the streets. It really kills me to see people saying, "This hooker is a call girl," or "This one is a street girl," because it's just not true. Like I have worked the streets, I have worked the bars and I have worked off the phone. . . . I have worked off the phone more than anything else, but if I hadn't gotten a hold of my book, I would have been on the streets a lot more. There is just no way around it. Some weeks I only made it out to the street maybe one night and I worked at home the rest of the time. But some people, they want to put us like hookers into a bunch of little packages and it just doesn't work that way, because a girl if she is a hooker, she can work out of any number of places and she will be sure to be where the business is. (hooker)

I found that no matter how much you learned or thought you knew already, there was always more to learn. And you'd find that different girls from another city would come to work in Eastville, and they would explain what they were doing, their hustles and ways of making money. So they'd show you that and we'd tell them what we were doing, and no matter what city you work in as a hooker, you find that in some ways, the hookers do stick together. . . . It doesn't matter if you're talking about call girls, or street hookers, or girls from bars, because you can usually find them in an after-hours disco or somebody's house where they're getting together. And the girls from the rubs will be into it too, and I don't think I know a girl who has just worked from the phone and hasn't worked in one of these other places. And if they're at the same party or disco, and the girl's well dressed and all, she'll be accepted, it doesn't matter where she works. (hooker)

Given the significance of contacts for involving women in particular styles of prostitution, and the tendency for career hookers to have some experience with a number of settings, it seems analytically unsound to place heavy emphasis on typologies of working girls. The girls come from a variety of backgrounds, and the relationships they have with parents, friends, pimps, and so on, can vary considerably from one girl to another and for one girl over time. However, as they become more involved in prostitution "as a way of life," they achieve a considerable amount of "cultural consistency" in their orientations towards this activity. Some hookers may work from particular bars for months and years at a time, but there is sufficient mobility among the hookers (and pimps) to promote continuity within and across North American cities. The bars, for example, may vary in decor, clientele, entertainment, and staff management rules and practices; nevertheless, many of the fundamental aspects of hooker procedures and bar life remain. Likewise, the girls working on the streets, in massage parlors, and as "call girls" share more commonalities with bar hookers than might be expected. Not only might the same girls be working one or more settings, on a sequential or concurrent basis, but they tend to associate with one another in other settings such as after-hours places and discos.

In concluding this chapter, it should be emphasized that the hookers' "story" does not end here. While this chapter has focussed more extensively on the hookers and their activities, the working girls are embedded in ongoing sets of interpersonal relationships with other participants in the hotel community. In looking at the girls' lives, we obtain glimpses into the lives of those with whom they are involved; but as we examine the activities of these other people in more detail, we will learn more of the "working girls." The lives of the participants of the hotel community are much more interwoven than terms such as "hookers," "rounders," and "desk clerks" imply.

Chapter 3

Working the Desk

Working the desk at hotels catering to hookers and/or strippers involves more for the desk clerk than would normally be expected in many "straight" hotels. In addition to renting rooms, answering inquiries, and catering to the residents, these clerks also act as protectors to the strippers and hookers and as general enforcers of hotel rules. Further, while the ongoing hustles place the clerk in a position of having to manage impressions vis-à-vis the police, they also present him with opportunities to greatly augment his legitimate salary. And his social life may become more complicated, given opportunities to become personally involved with the strippers and hookers. While most of the material introduced reflects occurrences at Main, some material depicting hotel practices more generally is also presented.

KEEPING ORDER

Given the accessibility of hotels to the public, desk clerks are likely to encounter a wide variety of persons. Thus, in addition to dealing with the hookers and their tricks, the desk clerks at Main also face the prospects of coming to terms with an assortment of people off the street, as well as guests, strippers and their fans, other staff and management, and the police. In the process of dealing with this mixture of characters, the clerk is expected to maintain the social and legal reputation of the hotel, to protect hotel property, and to protect the residents.

TROUBLE OFF THE STREET

Located in a quasi-slum area of the city, some of the trouble desk clerks experience stems from people coming in off the streets. In this sense, clerks at Main are especially likely to encounter a variety of "loiterers," including "drunks," "bums," the curious, and males "looking for a little action." While the clerk has some latitude in the ways in which he responds to these situations, he is nevertheless expected to keep the lobby relatively "litter free," lest he unduly offend prospective or present patrons or inadvertently permit disguised police observation:

A man came up, drunk, but well-dressed. He had been beaten up pretty badly. He came up to the desk and he just stared at me. I asked him what he wanted, but he didn't say a word. He stared at me. I asked him if I could do anything for him. He just stared at me. Then he just went away without ever saying a word. (notes)

A middle-aged woman came in, around 6:30 in the morning. She said that she wanted a room. She also wanted a discount on the room, indicating that in return, she would do me some personal favors. She talked about how her husband wanted to kill her, adding that her boyfriend was waiting in the car. (notes)

A customer told me that a drunk was sleeping downstairs in the lower lobby. I went down and found a man, about 65, sleeping under the phones. The stench was horrible. I woke him up and told him to go outside. As he was getting up, he said, "I ain't a bum, I've got money," and he showed me twenty dollars. I said that was fine and led him out the door. Then he did something really strange, he kissed my hand! I found that extremely upsetting and went back upstairs in a daze. Later, when the day clerk came in, she said that there was a drunk in the lobby. It was the same man. I woke him up and led him out the door again. (notes)

While proportionally few of these encounters involve physical violence, violent confrontations are by no means rare and add an element of danger to an already unpredictable setting. It should be noted, however, that while the clerks are apt to feel especially apprehensive at times during which they are unable to expect assistance from others in the hotel, to a large extent any violence encountered reflects the ways in which the clerk responds to the situation:

This drunk came up to the desk asking for a girl. I told him I couldn't do anything for him. Then he started rambling on and on, and I was getting so upset with him that I started yelling at him, "Get the hell out of here or I'd beat the shit out of you!" He staggered away. (clerk)

This guy came up to the desk, a big guy about 6' 4", 300 lbs., a big gut hanging out and was throwing around orders, acting tough, trying to intimidate me. There was a patron, a very small man, there with a pizza. This big guy had asked if he could have a piece of the pizza saying that he would buy it from him. The small man said no, but left the pizza with me at the desk, saying he would be back in a minute. When he left, the big guy looked at me and said, "I'm taking a piece." I said, "No, you're not." He started acting tough and saying he would do what he wanted. The bartender Rocky, was there and he was looking at this man. He wanted to deck him. I didn't want that to happen so I told him, "It's okay, I'll take care of it." The guy eventually left without too much of a problem. . . . Rocky was telling me of some fights at the desk, saying that the night shift was the worst. He was saying there were attacks on people by total strangers. They would come up to the desk and start antagonizing you and start fighting with you. He also told me about this desk clerk who was stabbed there a while back. He was on a night shift, he was sitting talking to some guy who seemed very pleasant but when he turned his back for a minute, the guy stabbed him in the back. That desk clerk is now doing time in jail; he was convicted for pimping and living off the avails of prostitution and so forth. It shook me up a bit because it's not the safest job in the world I have up there. (notes)

TROUBLE WITH GUESTS

The location of Main and the relatively poor quality of the rooms influence the type of clientele (non-tricks) the hotel has. Generally speaking, these customers represent more of the "down and out" segment of straight society. When the guests (predominantly males) are intoxicated, their behavior is more unpredictable than usual:

> *This drunk came in, staggering all over the place. Before I got a chance to say anything, he showed me his key saying he had a room up here. He said he was staying for a few weeks. I offered him some help getting up to his room. Then he looked at me and said I should know better. . . . This same man was drunk again tonight. He came in about three in the morning with his face covered in blood. He was in a fight. I asked him, "What the hell happened?" He replied, "Why don't you get on the phone and get a jug for you and me?" I said, "I don't have those kind of connections." He accepted this and went up to his room.* (notes)

MANAGING HOOKERS AND STRIPPERS

Along with the task of keeping the guests "in line," the desk clerk is also required to see that: (1) there is no soliciting in the lobby, on the part of hookers or strippers; (2) no rooms are rented to hookers; and (3) no men gain entry to the strippers' rooms (lest it appear that they are hookers and the hotel a brothel). While these rules are less frequently violated than those discussed earlier, they do represent disrupting elements in the desk clerk's routines:

> *The stripper that was there last week, Patty. She was really bad for that, she was flashing around there with no clothes on making propositions out in the lobby, discussing prices. You have to keep an eye on them because if a cop comes in you can be in real trouble. Also sometimes a hooker will be just dragging in guys dead drunk, in order to do business. She'll drag him up there and try and convince him, because the guy may not be too sure if he wants to go through with it. I get really nervous when that happens. Sometimes, when she's yelling and fighting with a guy trying to get a room, I tell her to take the guy outside because she can't do that here. Then she'll get mad at me and start yelling at me because I've ruined her trick, but you have to do that because what she's doing is too dangerous.* (clerk)

> *Otis checked the fire escape doors to see if they were closed, because he thought that the strippers might have their boyfriends come in through the back.* (notes)

> *Cynthia, a newly arrived stripper, asked me if she could have her boyfriend over night. I told her she better not do that or she and I would both get in trouble if the management found out.* (notes)

Although the desk clerk is entrusted with enforcing hotel rules, the rules are not always enforced. The owners and managers, the rule creators, have the most licence in violating them (for example, going into the stripper's rooms). Other employees or friends of the management may also be allowed liberties on occasion, provided it can be kept discreet. Similarly, the desk clerk may allow an acquaintance (friend, rounder) to visit a stripper's room, or he may do so himself, if he believes it can be done without the management's awareness (this is more easily accomplished on Sundays and night shifts when management is absent):

Quite often the managers, owners and their friends will visit the stripper's room. For instance Vito the manager slept overnight in Liz's room, Jim the doorman visited one stripper's room for a few hours and later slept in another stripper's room for about an hour. They really don't seem to pay too much attention to their own rules. (notes)

PROTECTING THE GIRLS

While desk clerks working in quasi-slum area hotels can expect problems with "drunks," "bums," and the like, a good proportion of the trouble clerks at hooker hotels encounter is related to prostitution. Further, although he may not anticipate it, an important part of the clerk's job is that of acting as a guardian, ensuring the hookers' well-being during their visits to the rooms. Reflecting the hotel's financial dependency on this activity, the clerk's concerns for the girls assume both legal and physical dimensions, as both legal indiscretions (or patron complaints) and instances of extensive physical injury may draw unwanted police attention to the hotel itself.

Clearance

Given the illegality of the services the hotel provides in conjunction with prostitution, an important task of the desk clerk at Main is to minimize the hookers' exposure to the police. While hotels systems vary, the girls at Main will phone the desk clerk for clearance (indicating the absence of legal threats in the lobby) before they go to the date's room and before they leave the room after turning a trick. He may also help the girls to "cover up" other incriminating evidence, but it should be noted that in those matters he is also dependent on the girl's co-operation:

When the hookers are finished with their tricks in the room, they call me at the desk and ask if the coast is clear. Not all do that, but most do. (clerk)

Just before the police came up, one of the hookers had called me and I said it was all right for her to come up. I was afraid that they would see her coming up and that would cause some trouble, but she spotted them and didn't come up. After they left, she came up and she and I kind of joked about what happened. We decided to set up some kind of cue system to warn her in case this ever happened again, so that when she asks for the room number, I'll give her a cue so she would know not to come up. In the meanwhile, the police wouldn't know what was going on. (clerk)

Trouble in the Room

In addition to routine clearance concerns, the desk clerk is also expected to provide assistance to the hookers should they encounter difficulties with their clients. The hookers may solicit the desk clerk's help in several ways. For example, in addition to asking his opinion on the suitability of her date, a girl may also ask the clerk to "keep an eye out" for her if she suspects trouble with a particular client:

One of the hookers approached me after her date had got the room. She asked me if the guy seemed all right, or did he look like a cop? And I said, "No, he was okay," and she went into the room. (notes)

More of the usual things that happen. Like two hookers did a trick and asked me to watch out for them. I haven't been mentioning that lately because that happens very often. (notes)

If a problem in the room materializes that the hooker cannot resolve herself, she will often pick up the phone and ask the clerk to come up to the room. In extreme distress, the hooker may knock the phone off the hook. When the desk clerk answers and hears no reply, he assumes that the hooker is in trouble and hurries to the room. The desk clerk may also come to the hooker's assistance if she spends an unusually long time in the room or if her date leaves before she does (it is customary for the hooker to leave before her date):

When I first started today, the first minute or so, I heard buzzing for a telephone call on the switchboard from one of the rooms. I picked it up and said "Hello," and there was no answer. I said, "Hello," again and there was still no answer. I figured there was trouble and told the woman who I was taking over the desk from to get help. I took the passkey and went to the room. (notes)

This hooker's date left before she did and went downstairs to the bar. I waited for a few minutes after this, because about 99% of the time the hooker leaves before the date does. I called up to the room to check to see if she was all right. (notes)

When answering a distress call from the room, the clerk will usually attempt to handle the situation informally with the aim of neutralizing any potential violence. And he is usually successful, since the mere prospect of a third party becoming involved in the girl-client relationship often resolves the difficulty. In such circumstances, the date may not only be outnumbered but, finding himself in a discrediting situation — caught with his "pants down" so to speak — is often surprisingly docile. However, much like the police answering domestics (Parnas, 1967), clerks have little idea of what to expect when they respond to distress calls. Further, while they try to handle incidents informally (as do the police, Bittner, 1967; Black, 1970; Black and Reiss, 1970), they have much less authority than do the police:

I got a call from one of the hookers and was on my way up when I met her. She said that it was all right. Apparently, she had problems collecting, but as soon as she got on the phone, that cleared up the problem. I guess it comes as something of a surprise to some of these guys to see a third person involved. (notes)

Actually, very seldom do you have to get physical. . . . You put yourself in the position of the guy who's renting the room. He's often kind of drunk anyway, and the girl picks up the phone, the guy has underwear around his ankles, lying in bed and this stranger comes charging through the door. It kind of puts the man on the defensive right away. He is not likely to cause any problems. Any reasonable person under those conditions would be scared and wouldn't want to take it any further. He would probably give in. But, if the guy is willing to fight, you know you've got a crazy guy on your hands and then you should not hesitate to use anything to hit him. . . . If you're going into the room, and you can get a jump on the guy, then you have a very big advantage over him. But, when I go into the room, I try to minimize the involvement I have with the hooker. If the guy asks you, "What are you doing here?" You say "Well, you rented the room, but you can't take a woman up here and beat her. I've got nothing to do with her, but you can't beat up people in the room, it's one of our policies." (clerk)

The desk clerk will answer distress calls by himself when he is alone after the bar has been closed or when he feels he can handle particular clients by himself. However, when he anticipates more trouble than he could reasonably handle, he will request help from other staff people:

Two men registered, saying, "We're just a couple of farmers out looking for a good time." Then a couple of girls went up to their room. Later, one of the girls called on the phone, asking for help, saying that they were having trouble with these guys. So, the bouncer and I went up to the room and found two hookers and the two guys when we walked in. One of the hookers said, "He is the trouble," pointing to one of them. "Not him, that guy is all right, he is a nice guy," pointing to the other guy who was pretty drunk and was sitting down, with a big smile on his face. Then the bouncer said, "What's the trouble?" And the girl said, "He won't let us leave." The guy causing the trouble was sitting on the bed. He said, "Oh, we are just out for a good time." The bouncer took the man out in the hallway and asked him, "What's the problem?" The guy said, "Well, you know, the girls didn't want to do it for a long time. We were taking too long. That was the problem, the girls wanted to take off." The bouncer said, "Well, you had better let them go. If you want to give me trouble, go ahead." And the guy said, "Well no, we are just out for a good time, we don't want to cause anybody any hassle." That kind of ended the argument. The girls went downstairs, and as the guy returned the key he said, "Hey, no hard feelings, we are just a couple of farmers out for a good time, that's all." (notes)

When I opened the door one of the girls was trembling and covering up her front with a towel. She was wimpering and crying and seemed really terrified. The manager and the bouncer came running up and she said that this guy had tried to kill her. The manager told her to get her clothes on and get out of the room. She wasn't very coherent, but she went to the washroom and put on her clothes. Through all of this, the guy was lying in bed, covered up in blankets, with his hands behind his head and a big grin on his face. He was pretty happy about it. Anyway, we all left except for the bouncer. He stayed in the room and talked to the guy for a while. A few minutes later the guy left. The hooker said that this man had her pinned against the bed and was strangling her with one hand and masturbating with the other. The hooker was still pretty terrified so the woman that I relieved from the desk took her to the bar to have a drink and calm her down. (notes)

Violence in the room is far from randomly distributed and the operating styles of the hookers influence the extent to which the desk clerk will have to intervene. Those prostitutes who request assistance less often are usually in better favor with the desk clerk than those calling for help frequently:

There's certain hookers that you expect more trouble with their dates. Some are very smooth and you're unlikely to have any problems with their tricks. Bea and

Samantha often create problems. . . . Some, such as Sue Anne, handle people better and are more careful about who they take into the room. . . . Something else, though, a lot of times the same man will be a regular to one of the girls, or the hotel more generally, never no problems, and then with Bea or Samantha, someone like that, you start to have problems with him. (clerk)

In addition to trouble arising from hooker-patron relations, the desk clerk is also expected to ensure the well-being of any resident strippers. Dancers commonly have unwelcome fans following them to their rooms or men propositioning them in the lobby and the desk clerk is expected to steer these troublesome persons out of the area. As the dancers often carry money and other valuables with them, part of this concern reflects prospective theft:

Some of these dancers, they always have guys hanging around the lobby. You know, calling the girls on the house phone, or waiting for them. And it's not good, because you aren't supposed to have them there because you never know what they're up to. (clerk)

DEALING WITH THE POLICE

The desk clerk at Main is also required to deal with police inquiries. In such cases the desk clerk acts as spokesman for the hotel, and is expected to give the impression of legal propriety. Additionally, he will frequently warn others in the hotel so they can also foster this image. This is a very crucial aspect of the clerk's job and if neglected may lead to his arrest and the closure of the hotel. Typically the desk clerk divulges as little incriminating information as possible, while endeavoring to appear co-operative:[1]

When I was working at the desk, the police used to harass you a lot and they'd come up and sort of look around. Check this out, check out the rooms, and then they'd come back, look around the desk, pull the drawers open, "Let's see what's here," kind of thing. What could you really say to them? (clerk)

One of the cops came up, flashed his badge, and looked at the register. I asked him what he was looking for. He said he wanted to see if anybody was staying a couple of days or by the week. Actually, he was looking to see if I had rented rooms two or three times, which we usually do if it's busy. But then, the desk clerks start a new sheet, so they can't tell how many times you've rented that room. (clerk)

A well-dressed man came up to the lobby and asked me if there was a phone at the desk he could use, because it was too noisy at the bar. I told him there wasn't. He then asked me if I could get him a girl. I told him that I couldn't. He then left. Emile, who had been in the lobby while this was happening then told me that the man who had just left was a "narc" whom he had seen bust someone for smoking a joint on the street the other day. (notes)

Today, the police came up through the back entrance. If they had come up through the front entrance, I would have seen them, but they came up through

---

[1] Readers may refer to Goffman's (1959) discussion of the significance of teamwork for impression management.

the back, through the side doors. The upstairs maid saw the two policemen standing on the second floor of the main lobby (apparently waiting for one of the hookers to go up). She came downstairs, looking frightened and told me about the cops. I got on the phone and warned the management. Realizing that the maid had seen them, the police left by themselves. Following this, the manager came up and talked about checking the doors, to make sure that they were locked, to see that there is no way for them to come up through the back. The story got around about the police coming through the back and it became the topic of conversation for the rest of the evening among the hookers. One said that she was not doing anything wrong and wasn't doing anything against anybody's will. (I mention this because this is the very first time that I have heard any sort of justification like this, any sort of philosophical comment on what they are doing.) (notes)

Although their presence is generally resented by staff people, the police are of occasional assistance to the desk clerk:

Mitch said that if he finds a drunk sleeping in the lobby he will occasionally call the police to have him removed. He says that it depends on how hard a time he thinks he will have or how dirty the guy is, or how he feels at the time. (notes)

One time I almost got it really good. This was close. Some guys rented a room, and took a chick up. Apparently the chick screwed them around and left. There were these three very big guys, looked like football players. They came down and said that they wanted their money back. I say, "I can't give your money back. What do you mean give your money back? You rented the room. You used the room. That's it." One of the guys started coming around the side of the desk and the two in front and one was going to come over. They were going to kick the shit out of me and take every cent that I had. So I had a bottle in one hand. I was going to smash one of the guys and try and make a break for it, which I doubt I would've got anywhere anyhow. But just as these guys were going to come over the desk, two cops walked up the stairs. "Hey, Rocky. Everything all right?" Is everything all right? (laugh) "Everything's great!" I thought, "Am I glad to see you!" First time, right! "Good to see you. Come on up! Everything's cool." (clerk)

Where legal entanglements arise from patron complaints, rather than direct police observation, the (frequently) relatively disreputable status of the complainant is a point in favor of any accused or otherwise implicated persons:

A man who was very, very drunk came to the desk asking for a room. I gave him a room and he said that he was having a girl come up a little bit later. When she arrived, she asked if I would keep an eye out for the guy because she was kind of concerned about him being drunk. She didn't know what he might be doing. Sure enough I got a buzz on the phone and I rushed in to check it out. It was around closing time and Rocky was in the lobby, so we went in together. I knocked on the door and the guy opened it. He said that Connie, a black hooker, had stolen his wallet. I said that I didn't believe him, that I didn't think she would do that. While we were talking, she got dressed and left. Then I closed the door, leaving the guy in his room. I thought that cleared up the situation, but later on he came out of the room and he said that he wanted to call the cops. I tried to talk him out of it, saying that I was sure that she hadn't taken his wallet, that he must have misplaced it. But, he insisted on calling the cops, so I asked him to go back to his room and I said I would put the call through. As he was going back, Rocky was with me, and he said, "I think we can handle this ourselves." And when the man picked up the phone to make the call, instead of dialing the police station, I put Rocky on another line on the desk. Rocky answered it, saying, "29th Division, Sgt. Moon speaking. . . . What is this you're saying? You took a prostitute up to your room? Sir, did you know that you could be charged for that?" So Rocky was asking these questions and sort of messing up the guy's head. Then he said, "Well, I will send a cruiser as soon as I can," and hung up. Rocky and I had a good laugh about that. After a while, Rocky took off, but then, about an hour later, this drunk came out of the room and said he wanted to call the cops again. At this point, I was alone and was getting worried about messing around too much. So I told him to go back to the room, and this time I put the call through to the police. They came down and went to his room. Now, at this time, the manager had come up and when I told him what happened, he said, "Well, the guy was drunk, we will just say that you just came on the shift, after the trouble had taken place." The police were in the room for about ten minutes and when they came out, the manager asked them what the problem was. They told him that this fellow had accused this hooker of taking his wallet. The manager said, "Well, I have just come on and we don't know what's going on." The police didn't say much more, they just left. About five minutes later the man came out and left. (notes)

TIPS AND HUSTLES

Working in a "sleazy hotel" may seem a relatively risky and unprofitable enterprise but desk clerks, like other hotel staff, are apt to find that one's "take home pay" is not limited to one's salary.

While presented with many opportunities to engage in job-related hustles, one of the most reliable sources of "extra income" is tips from the hookers. It is customary at many of the hooker hotels for the hookers to tip the desk clerk for his services. Being aware of the money hookers make, desk clerks frequently feel entitled to a "piece of the action" for their services. Although not all clerks accept these tips (in part because it places one in danger of being arrested for "procuring," "aiding and abetting," "living off the avails of prostitution," and the like), it is very tempting to do so since the tips typically amount to a considerable sum by the end of an afternoon or evening shift. Also, anyone not accepting tips is likely to encounter pressure from other desk clerks since his refusal to accept tips makes it more difficult for other desk clerks to justify their "fees":

Harriet said that she really wanted everybody to have to pay the $2 tip, that all the hookers should have to pay the $2 for the services rendered by a desk clerk. She claimed that the main obstacle here was Don, because he didn't want to charge the girls. He said they were all his friends and he knows them all. But, she said, in any other hotel they would have to pay the $2 and they had better start paying at this one too. (notes)

A hooker came down and didn't tip the desk. Mitchell said, "Aren't you forgetting something?" She said, "Oh yeah, sorry Mitchell. I forgot." And then she tipped him. . . . Mitchell was saying that he might let a new girl or a girl who just comes here occasionally by without paying the tip. But, he added, if she's going to be doing any amount of business out of this hotel, then he makes sure she abides by the policy of tipping the clerk. If they don't tip, he lets them know that then they are on their own with their dates. (notes)

Beyond accepting "tips" from the hookers (and an occasional patron), the major job-related hustles of the desk clerk are those of "rehashing rooms" and stealing from the patrons. Although the rehashing of rooms may represent a significant expense to the hotel, as rooms are typically rerented over the afternoon and evening shifts, desk clerks have opportunities to pocket the money for one or more rentals over their shifts without drawing undue attention to their activities:

You'd get some money from the girls or you'd be rehashing the rooms, and you'd make a lot of money that way. You might give a guy a room on the first floor, where it's handy. When he comes out, you run in there and make up the bed. Then you rent it out to another guy. And everybody wanted to work doubles. "Oh, yeah, I'll work doubles," because you figure that's another $200 to $300 right there. So if somebody wanted a day off for any reason, you'd want to get it before anybody else because the money was just so good. . . . The manager downstairs knew what we were doing so we had to kick him a little money in terms of room rentals too, but I don't think he realized how strongly we were going on this. So he knew we were stealing and he wanted some of it, so fine, we'd give him a couple of rooms and $30 or whatever it was and would just take off more for ourselves. (clerk)

Although the failure to report room rentals represents another instance of "trust violation" it contrasts with Cressey's (1953) explanation of embezzlement for, while he argued that activities of this nature represent a solitary response to a non-shared problem, our data suggests that some forms of "embezzlement" may be learned from co-workers:[2]

There was some trouble with the room keys. I was ten dollars short on the night because a couple of people had done me out of the deposits for the keys. A couple of staff people told me that sometimes I should pocket some room money for myself. Say you know a person is going to be in there for a few minutes, like a trick, all you have to do is forget the card. You just get the guy in and out and make yourself a quick fifteen, just for pocket money. . . . Rocky mentioned that he had taught LeeAnne, another desk clerk, how to steal a room. He asked me if I knew how to do it. I told him that I did. (notes)

In hustling the patrons, desk clerks may variously shortchange customers, fail to return key deposits, roll drunks, or cover up in-room thefts by a hooker or rounder. Typically, hustles aimed at patrons require some impression management (Goffman, 1959) on the part of the desk clerk as he attempts to cool out distraught targets. For example, in dealing with patrons who have been short-changed or who have had their money stolen, the clerk may suggest that they may

---

[2] Our observations of employee theft both in reference to the desk and the bar suggest, as do Vaz (1955) and Horning (1971), that there is often group support for individual theft, and that in some cases this support may be quite extensive, provided that the theft does not jeopardize other employees.

have lost their money in the bar or at other hotels or go through the pretext of helping them search their rooms for the missing valuables. It should also be noted that to the extent targets are intoxicated, the (allegedly) sober desk clerk would have an advantage in establishing definitions of the situation, be it for the patron or any inquiring parties:

> Mitchell said that he systematically rips off patrons by telling them that the room is $2 more than it is. In that way he keeps the key deposit. He also explained how I could rip off the customers for the deposit. He told me that I should tell the customers the price of the room was the total of the price of the room plus the deposit. Thus, when they returned the key I could keep the deposit myself. (notes)

> Lance, a rounder, told me that he dropped some valiums in a guy's drink and was going to the room to roll him. He gave me $10 and told me to cool the man out if he asked me anything when he woke up. (clerk)

> Eric was telling me how he made a few extra bucks on the night shift. One of the things he did was to check out the rooms looking for keys that people may have left. He said that he might as well get the deposit money as the maids. . . . He also says that if he gets someone who is really drunk, he will, under the pretext of helping the man to the room, remove his wallet. He says that he's managed to score a few times that way. (notes)

Although these are the major job-related hustles in which desk clerks participate they are likely to find that their job generates a wide assortment of contacts and opportunities to get involved in a variety of other hustles.

RELATED THEMES

Although somewhat abbreviated, the following discussions of friendship, alcohol and drug use, and messes and maids, provide further insight into the life experiences of desk clerks and their supporting staff. While removed from much of the action in the bar, these positions, nevertheless, afford occupants opportunities for relaxation, entertainment, and "worldliness."

FRIENDS AND SUCH

As the desk clerk has verbal contact with most of the strippers and hookers at Main, he was a better opportunity than most employees to become acquainted with the girls. Not only are they in a position of mutual accessibility and tolerance, but the hookers' dependence on the desk clerk for assistance promotes familiarity, the girls finding it in their best interest to be on good terms with the desk clerk:

> The hookers have to pretty well be nice to you if they want any protection, because you kind of control what happens to them if there is trouble. It's really up to you whether you want to help them. You can also ruin their dates too, by not giving the guy a room, or not letting the girls go up if you get mad at them. I can really affect their business. That's why most of the girls there are on good terms with me. (clerk)

In general, the relationship of the desk clerks and the strippers and hookers at Main can best be described as casual, varying in degrees of friendliness. One finds a considerable amount of playful flirting and, on occasion, these relationships may become more involved:

> *Tim was telling me that he met Stella (a hooker) while he was working the desk. He took her up to his place a few times and later on it developed into a more serious relationship. Stella ended up being Tim's "old lady" for a period of time. . . . Most of the desk clerks have become romantically involved with hookers. Many of these relationships were very brief, but some were pretty serious. The romances involving hookers also seem to last longer than those with the strippers who typically only stay a week at a time.* (notes)

ALCOHOL AND DRUGS

Given the accessibility of both illegal drugs and alcohol and the clerk's relatively unsupervised position, it is not uncommon to find desk clerks working while in varying degrees of inebriation. This is in spite of discouragement on the part of management who, over the years, have dismissed several desk clerks because they were found to be intoxicated:

> *Often desk clerks will smoke pot, or take uppers, or drink on the job. And off hand, I don't know of anyone who doesn't and works here. There's nobody to watch you, and it gets kind of boring, so you can do it, especially on the night shift.* (clerk)

Generally speaking, the desk clerks perceive themselves to be competent while in these altered states of consciousness; alcohol, speed and marijuana being the principal drugs used while on duty. These drugs are used variously to promote alertness, to relieve boredom, for entertainment, and as a means of being sociable:

> *The use of drugs in here is something that is almost taken for granted. It's something that has been going on for a long time. Some of the older people talking on the subject say that they have been doing things like grass for a long time, long before it became popular in the 60's and 70's. I have trouble staying awake for the day following a night shift, and as "matter of fact" advice, several people here told me that I should get some "Bennies" to stay up. It's like a home remedy someone might give you for the hiccups; using drugs is a very-taken-for-granted thing.* (notes)

> *Later on that evening, I asked Vince if he wanted to smoke up a bit with me after he finished work, which was about 1:30. We did and he hung around the lobby pretty well all night. Then Tim came in and we smoked some more.* (clerk)

MESSES AND MAIDS

Few people seem able to work in this environment without experiencing some effects of prostitution or the hotel setting on their lives. Thus, although they play a less prominent role than the desk clerks, the maids at Main also become exposed to and sometimes involved in the ongoing activities:

This one young man had four hookers go to his room. He wanted to be tied and beaten. The hookers tied him up, took all his money and left. . . . Apparently he got off on that, and came back again. This time he paid these hookers $300 to beat him up again, and they left him tied up in the room. When the maid came in, she found him naked and tied to the four bed posts. She got quite a shock. (notes)

Toda, the new maid, is becoming pretty well-known by all the staff. She smokes grass a lot while she is working, and will often smoke up with the guys at the desk. She is fitting right in, in that sense. (notes)

This one maid, I don't know what she was like before, but she's quite a character now, and the strippers at different times will fool with her. Like this one time they were stripping her while she was going about her work in the hallways, sort of throwing her clothes around. She seems to take it all pretty good naturedly. (notes)

It is conventional for the desk clerk to tip the maids. Say five dollars after a shift. This is for cleaning up the rooms and for kind of helping out in various ways. Say, for example, that the maid cleaned the room, and it was re-rented, with the clerk pocketing the money. (notes)

DESK WORK IN OTHER HOTELS

In an attempt to gain a broader appreciation of desk work, we talked with some desk clerks, bellhops, and security officers in other hotels. Although prostitution is unlikely to become a prominent feature in major hotels (chain, prestigious hotels), many hotels have some contact, welcome or otherwise, with the working girls.

CLERKING

While clerks in smaller hotels serve in a number of capacities, desk-clerk work in larger hotels is much more delimited. As a result, desk clerks in these latter settings may engage in extra job-related activities, but their major activities centre around room-related bookkeeping, switchboard operations, and information services:

Here, the traffic is so heavy, you really don't have time to do much else. The accounting system is quite complicated and between that and the switchboard and the guests, you are pretty well tied to the desk. (clerk)

The phones and guests coming in can make it hectic sometimes. It's really hard to keep up on what else is happening in the lobby. . . . They really don't expect us to do much else. (clerk)

Handling Trouble

While clerks at larger hotels are less likely to be responsible for handling any trouble arising in the hotel, and are less likely to encounter trouble ''off the streets,'' they are not immune to troublesome events:

It's kind of funny because even though this is supposedly a high class hotel, you find that if people get kicked out or if something goes wrong, they can get violent. Like I had this one guy who was going to throw one of the stand-up ashtrays at me. He had this thing picked up and over his head and was ready to throw it, when the security officer stopped him. So you can never tell what's going to happen and, like I say, this is one of the best hotels. (clerk)

Sometimes, let's say before the security people arrive, we also have to watch people in the lobby because sometimes we get people who are not guests hanging around the lobby. Sometimes they'll just be sitting down but you also might have some drunks coming in and you're expected to take care of that as well since it affects the hotel's image. (clerk)

Patron complaints are generally dealt with more graciously at the "more respectable" hotels and, should the situation threaten to become more volatile, the clerks are more constrained in the ways they respond:

We have just a lot of little complaints from customers. . . . The big thing is just to stay cool under these circumstances and also to just try and show them that you are trying to do something about the problem, that is, that you're not ignoring their complaint completely. That usually cools them out. (clerk)

Bellhops

Entrusted to perform a variety of desk-related service jobs, the bellhop's role can best be thought of as supplementing that of the desk clerk. While primarily responsible for helping guests with luggage, the bellhop is also responsible for running messages back and forth to the rooms, informing desk staff and maids of vacant rooms and/or those in need of cleaning, informing guests of the location of facilities, and assisting security guards when the need arises:

We more or less do all the little things that have to be done. We give messages, clean up the lobby, pick up and deliver laundry, those kinds of things. The thing about this job is that there's variety in it and you are not always doing the same thing all the time. (bellhop)

They expect us to be really friendly with the people. If there is any way that we can help them, as long as it's within hotel policy, we are encouraged to do that. (bellhop)

Much like desk clerks at Main and Central, bellhops in large hotels are assumed to be informed about "action events" occurring in town and within the hotel itself. Thus, they may be approached about such things as "hookers," "action," and "swinging bars." Some bellhops do take advantage of such opportunities to "make a buck on the side," but they are generally discouraged from doing so by both management and fellow workers:

I pretty well try to avoid having anything to do with the girls because I found in the long run it just doesn't pay to get involved with the hookers. . . . Over the years, I've known quite a few guys who've gotten involved with the hookers that way and they would maybe make arrangements with the girls to meet tricks because often you'll be getting guys who'll be asking you if you know where they can find a girl. They're from out of town and they're looking for a girl and they figure maybe the bellman might know of a little action. That is something that you'll see at different hotels and here I'm talking about the classy hotels, like here, where I work. You'll find some of the bellmen having these arrangements with the girls, but different times when they're found out about, they get fired or say the hooker gets busted, then she may get the bellman into trouble saying that he set her up. You really can't trust these hookers. So some of them, they're figuring they're making good money on the side and it's fairly easy just doing that because you're not actually doing so much work, just making a telephone call, but it's not worth it in terms of all the risks that you have to take and maybe get caught or loose your job or something. And to loose a steady job in hopes of making ten bucks here or ten bucks there, I don't think it's really worth it. Then if you get fired, or if you get a reputation like this, then you're going to have problems getting jobs in the better hotels in the area. (bellman)

Although desk clerks and bellhops at the larger hotels are not apt to be as heavily "into the life" as are desk clerks at hooker hotels, their access to a number of the "behind the scenes" aspects of their guests' lives does promote a more general awareness of life:

You see a lot of things in this job, like how doctors, businessmen, and politicians live when they're off stage. You get to know what people are like. (clerk)

In this job you get to meet a lot of people and you get to meet and make a lot of contacts with different people doing different things. Like even on a day to day basis, you don't know who you're going to meet next, a bum or a millionaire, because you've all kinds of people coming through the hotel. (bellman)

SECURITY WORK

Insofar as the desk clerks at smaller hotels constitute a significant aspect of that hotel's "peace-keeping" and "security force," it seems instructive to briefly examine the role of the security staff at larger hotels vis-à-vis these functions. Although neither small hotel desk clerks nor larger hotel security officers have the authority of police officers, they are expected to protect hotel property and guests:

We're not police here, we're not out to arrest anyone or put them behind bars. Our job is to protect the guests and make sure nothing happens to them that the hotel could be held responsible for. (security)

The main duties of the security guard is to protect the hotel property and the guests. . . . We have over 30 floors and since it is that large, then it's everybody's obligation to do as much as they can to make the service personal. . . . We patrol the halls, occasionally checking the doors as we make our rounds, trying to determine if everything is all right, check for smoke, loud noises, things of that nature. (security)

Like the desk clerks in smaller hotels, security people in large hotels generally try to handle trouble informally, and are likely to refrain from calling the police unless the situation seems likely to "get out of control":

In terms of my staff, I want people who are able to deal with situations with tact and diplomacy. I need someone who's able to reason with them. Someone who's very good at the public relations end of the industry. I really don't need a big person, or a strong person, because a security person is not there for the purpose of throwing people out. . . . You try to avoid getting into conflicts with people. You don't want it to deteriorate to that point. (security)

Usually we don't like to call the police, especially if we think we can handle the situation ourselves. But if you do have more serious problems, then you call the police. Like, sometimes you'll get someone who refuses to leave when you ask them to and they'll say, "Oh, I've got these rights and these rights," and so forth, and so you want to be a little more careful. So you'll call the police, and when they come down you say, "I want this person out," and they will just escort them out and that's it, because you have to watch that you don't get involved with assault charges, things like that. (security)

Overall, the kinds of trouble security people in large hotels encounter is very similar to that experienced by desk clerks at smaller hotels. Both are expected to: prevent drunks and other "no accounts" from loitering on the premises; prevent and squelch disruptive activities involving outsiders and residents; and prevent theft involving guests' possessions. The role of security officer in larger hotels would also include bar-related security and employee theft. Desk clerks in smaller hotels may also help with trouble emerging in the bar, but would only be concerned with employee theft to the extent particular instances interfere directly with their jobs.

Not unlike smaller hotels, those larger establishments situated in downtown urban areas or rougher sections of the city are also subject to visits from "drunks," "panhandlers," and other "vagrants" on a daily basis. Regarded as a liability to hotel property and image, these persons are encouraged to vacate the premises as quickly as possible. While image concerns generally prevent guards from being as physically and verbally aggressive in removing such persons as are clerks at some of the rougher hotels, they are no less persistent:

You have to expect it in this area. Winos always congregate downtown. Basically we try to remove them with as little trouble as possible. We try not to get too physical with them. We try to talk them out because the other will look bad for a guest that's just checking in, seeing some security guard beating up on a bum. (security)

With drunks, you don't want them to get out of hand, but at the same time you try to treat them as pleasantly as you can because you're concerned about the hotel. So you try to avoid fights and treat everybody with respect as much as you can. What I try to do is put myself in that same situation and I'd rather have somebody there talking to me than someone who's throwing me around and pounding me out. (security)

Another set of potentially troublesome non-guests are the "working girls." While one finds some staff people at larger hotels who are interested in generating a little action with the hookers, most of the staff and security people at the more prestigious hotels try to discourage hookers from working on the premises:

Because this hotel is on Delta Drive, hookers are one of the problems we have. Our job is to try and keep it out of the hotel because the girls might like to work out of it or maybe get their tricks to use the hotel. . . . I'll just talk to her trying to give her the impression that I've recognized her. I'll ask how they like it at the hotel, if they're registered here, etc. . . . . The idea is to let them know that you are keeping an eye on them. You want to get to that stage where they're willing to leave voluntarily without creating any sort of scene or any hard feelings. (security)

Now if the girl is very discreet she might be able to work out at a bar for a while, but it certainly is not our policy to condone these activities. I know all the major hotels in Eastville and their policy is to discourage hookers. When you let the hookers in, you get all the other riff-raff, like dopers, thieves, and whatnot. (security)

It is noteworthy that most deviance (prostitution-related or other) involving residents and visitors is handled informally. The material also suggests that persons working in "sleazy hotels" are doubly disadvantaged vis-à-vis handling trouble. Not only are desk clerks likely to find that they have to handle trouble alone, but patrons and visitors may feel that they need be less responsible for their actions in rougher hotels.

Having had some opportunity to envision "desk clerking" in a larger context, the reader may find the following extract useful in summarizing and sharpening aspects of desk work likely to be encountered in hooker hotels:

I was talking to Fritz, a desk clerk at the Flamingo. Their operation is similar to what we have at Main. We also know a lot of the same girls, because they've worked a number of hotels in the area, or they'll direct their customers to certain hotels where they figure the protection is better. . . . He was telling me about an incident in which a girl was badly injured before he could get to the room. It created problems for him because the police wanted to investigate the whole thing. Mostly they seemed concerned about getting a conviction on the offender (a trick), but because of that incident, a lot of things they did came to the surface. . . . Like us, the girls direct their dates to that particular hotel and then call to see if he's arrived. They are also concerned about keeping things reasonably discreet. . . . From the way he described things, their procedure for answering distress calls is much like ours, where you get help whenever you can. He also noted that he expected to have more trouble with some girls than others, stemming from the ways the girls treated their dates. He said that you couldn't rely on that alone, but that some girls got into a lot of trouble a lot more often than other girls. . . . Fritz also said that after working there for a while, you got to know the girls and that the job gave you an opportunity to get to know some of the girls pretty well. . . . He was also saying that they made money with the $2 tip and would occasionally pocket some of the money made in recycling the rooms as well. . . . In discussing trouble, he also noted that the girls would try to help one another out, even if they don't like one another. That's something else I've found to be true. . . . Like us as well, the trouble with the hookers is just a part of all the trouble they are exposed to. They also have problems with drunks, and the police, and people hanging around the lobby. (notes)

Working as a desk clerk in a hooker hotel can be both a boring and a risky enterprise. At the same time, however, this position also represents a work place which is lucrative and which also provides extensive opportunities to become involved with the people and activities constituting "the life." Clearly, desk clerks at hotels catering to prostitution can become integral components of the hooking scene. Not only is it financially beneficial for the clerk to become involved in accepting tips, but he may also find it tempting to become personally involved with the girls. Additionally, the job demands that the clerk also regulate the girls' activities and provide protection for them in the event of trouble. The clerk may become involved in other hustles, and he may set up dates with hookers (although we have found the latter to be relatively infrequent), but the significance of the hooker-desk clerk relationship extends beyond that of simple exchange. As clerks spend more time in the hotel, they are likely to become more embedded in the staff, hooker, and rounder aspects of the hotel community. Through tips and other considerations, the hookers can make the desk clerk's role a more profitable and entertaining one than would otherwise be the case, and, thus, may be highly instrumental in sustaining his involvements in the hotel setting. Not unlike the fence who can seem to facilitate the career of the burglar (Shover, 1972), the desk clerk (by providing tolerance, friendship, and physical aid) contributes to the hookers' continuing their activities on both a day-to-day and long-term basis.

We will be considering other interconnections of persons in the hotel community in chapters 5 and 6 but, even at this point, the significance of examining deviance involvements in a group context should be apparent. Neither initial nor sustained involvements in deviance can be explained by exclusive reference to the properties of the individuals involved.

Chapter 4

Providing Entertainment

Moving back into the bar area, this chapter examines the ways in which the entertainers fit into the hotel community. Although the analysis of entertainers is not limited to "strippers" (or "exotic dancers,"), this chapter focusses most entensively on this particular group of entertainers. Not only do the exotic dancers represent a more significant element of entertainment at many bars but, compared to other performers, they offer more contrasts (in terms of respectability, intimacy, and distancing). We first look at what is involved in "putting on a show." Subsequent material examines "initial involvements," "stripping as a way of life," and "the stripper community." The focus then shifts to a consideration of "love and sexuality" as experienced by the dancers. The chapter concludes with a discussion of other entertainers in the bar.

STRIPPING: AN OVERVIEW

The term "stripper" is a very broad concept covering a number of types of entertainment in which performers (typically female) in some state of undress (supposedly erotic) are featured.[1] The amount of clothing removed can vary considerably, as can the amount of dancing and the nature of any activities and/or props involved in the performance. In addition to bars, night clubs, and hotels, one will also find strippers in burlesque theatres, carnivals, and stags. In general, the dancers tend to be rather mobile and, with the exception of "house girls," seldom remain in one spot for more than a week or two at a time. "House girls" (often mistaken for hookers) are regular features at bars. They will remain at one place indefinitely. Compared to the girls on the road, the house girls have more security in their work and can establish more regularized work and social routines. They are, however, typically paid a lower salary than the regular touring girls (say $150-$300 compared to $300-$600).

Working conditions (dressing rooms, number of girls working a bar), and the number of shows required can also vary quite extensively. Thus, while the girls typically develop acts of about 15-25 minutes, some adjustment to each new spot is necessary. Further, although dancers' and other entertainers' roles are somewhat akin to staff roles, mobile performers tend to view each place as "just another bar," a place to work for a period of time: although they may become quickly

---

[1] For other sociological statements on stripping, see: Boles and Garbin (1974a,b) for discussions of strippers in club settings; and McCaghy and Skipper (1969), Skipper and McCaghy (1970; 1971), and Salutin (1971) for portrayals of strippers in burlesque theatres. Also see Misty (1973) for an interesting and insightful biographical account of stripping.

assimilated in particular bars, their anticipated mobility promotes concerns different from those characterizing the regular staff or the bar hookers discussed earlier:

If things work out well, fine. If not, well you will be leaving in a week, anyways. It's not always that simple, but that's sort of how you look at it. You figure you can put up with a lot of things for a week. (dancer)

PUTTING ON A SHOW

As a means of introducing the strippers, we first provide readers with an indication of what is involved in "putting on a show." Considered herein are concerns with "getting bookings," "costuming and preparations," "intimacy and distancing," "troublesome audiences," and "legal entanglements." These elements do not totally define the role of the dancer, but represent fundamental themes affecting stage performances.

GETTING A BOOKING

While some agencies book other entertainers as well as strippers, many agents concentrate exclusively on this aspect of entertainment. And, if one has forty or more girls whom one can book into places on a regular basis, it can be a profitable full-time enterprise. For their services, the agents typically receive 10% of the strippers' salary from the club into which they are booked (if a girl gets $500/week, the agent would get $50). When two agents are involved, the commission is usually split on a 50-50 basis. Although most dancers work through agencies, girls newer to the business, or those feeling particularly confident about their talents and contacts, will book themselves into clubs. They may or may not negotiate for the additional (10%) agent fees:

I do my own booking. I used to work with Arnie, but I found that different places wanted me back, so I figured I might as well have the agent's fees. Now I do my own booking. I get around a lot, so that helps. I'm thinking of becoming an agent myself. (dancer)

The first year I worked, I was without an agent and, like I said, I wasn't making any money. It's much better if the girl has an agent because he can represent you wherever you go and demand your money. But I look at it this way, like he and his family are relying on me, they're living off me. I let him know that, because if you don't stand up to these people you'll just get sort of pushed aside. They treat dancers like puppets anyway, or mechanical devices. (dancer)

Although one obtains a sense of club-dancer relations from bar observations and in talking with the dancers, time spent with agents was also useful in illuminating some of the issues involved in "getting a booking":

If you're an agent, you have to know the girls and you have to know your hotels, what type of girls would fit into which kind of hotels. . . . A club also gets what they can afford too. So if somebody wants a girl for $275, well, you know that they are not going to get a top girl. You have to explain to them that if you are paying beer prices, then you really can't expect to get champagne. Sometimes *you tell them that if they pay more, they will get a better girl and it's better for business.* (agent)

It's much easier to place white girls than dark girls. Colored girls are not wanted by most places. Some will just tell you, "No colored girls!" The colored girls are kind of necessary to me, because if I took them away, there would be such a shortage of good reliable dancers that we wouldn't be able to operate. So I need them and you try and get the clubs to accept them. If the colored girl is young and pretty, well they'll get away with it, but as she gets older and a little sloppier, she's going to have problems before the white girl will. . . . The colored girls are on the whole better dancers, but I think that it's a vicious circle. I think that colored people have been pushed around and they carry this chip on their shoulder. They always act as if they are the star or, if anything happens, they can't control their temper. They bring a lot of this on themselves so when I go through that two or three times, then you think, "Well I don't want another colored working here." I have some very nice colored girls working and I'm not saying that the clubs don't take any at all, but a lot of clubs don't want any at all. A lot of clubs don't want a colored clientele and they feel that if they have colored girls there, then they will have a more colored clientele. And white people don't like going to a club where there are a lot of colored people. (agent)

Although club managers may independently like to hire girls they can assess for themselves, few are able to maintain a regular stream of performers. Further, while photos may be considered a second choice, these may not only be misleading, but are apt to be available for only the more established girls. This means that most of the bookings are made by the agent, with the girl and the club becoming acquainted only by reputation or at the time of her arrival:

You can't tell that much from the photos. They may have a deadpan face, no act, no talent, or no rapport with the audience. The days have passed when a girl's able to get by on her good looks alone. There might be a few people who would be turned on by that, but a lot of people want to see someone who can dance or relate to them or put on a show. It's really escalating right now, everybody wants more of a show. You've got to involve the audience. You've got to look at him and him and him, you've got to make everyone feel that you would like to be with him. And while you're doing a show, you're not doing a show for yourself. It's no good looking at the ceiling while you're doing a floor show. You have to look at the guys. You can be ugly, but that's what you have to do. (agent)

We don't use photos that much, but it's nice if you have them because you can give them to the clubs and they can look at the girls and make their choices that way or they can also put them up on their billboards just inside the clubs or on the outside and attract customers that way. For the higher priced acts, though, usually the places do want photos. (agent)

The girls can choose their spots somewhat, either in advance ("don't send me there") or occasionally following a booking, although the latter is more disquieting to the agent.

After a series of disappointing clubs a dancer may decide to change agents in hopes of bettering her work settings.

COSTUMING AND PREPARATIONS

The costumes the girls use can vary greatly, from the casual dress of the ''go go'' dancers to the elaborate costumes and props of the more established professionals. Most of the girls are handicapped by problems associated with travel since few have their own cars:

> *You need a gown or a jumpsuit or something, a bra, little panties, and a g-string. You can either make the things yourself or rearrange underwear that was already done, or go out and buy it ready made in a specialty store. And, you might use stockings, I haven't used stockings for a while. You can usually do it sitting on a chair, take your stockings off. People are kind of fascinated by that. There are other things like, girls do things like oil acts, lotion acts, I haven't really gotten into that. I feel a little dumb sitting up on a chair putting oil all over my legs. There are girls that can do an oil act real sexy. And the rug act, and negligees are a good standard. . . . I like using pasties. They look nice. When you take your top off that's all there is, but when you have all these sparkly things on, then you're not standing there with nothing.* (dancer)

> *Right now, I am carrying six costumes with me. That is more than I need for a place, but I don't always have a chance to go to my home base every week and you try to keep alternating back and forth. It depends on how many shows you do in a day. If you do more shows in a day, then you might be using all the costumes in a given day. Otherwise, you might have enough costumes for two days. Usually I don't spend that much on my costumes. The most might be $50.* (dancer)

> *If a girl is just starting out, then you don't expect her to have too much in the way of costumes but if she has been in the business for a year or so, well, then you do expect her to have more variety. . . . The price of the costumes, well, that will vary in part with the girl's imagination. And, some of them will sew a lot of their own costumes. . . . The girl's wardrobe is also a sign of whether she's wanting to go someplace, if she's serious or dedicated to her job as well.* (agent)

Although one cannot separate the performance from the audience, there are certain aspects of preparation and presentation worth accentuating. Of particular significance to exotic dancing is the music and the choreography. As with costumes, the degree of care exercised in the selection of the music and the extent to which acts are developed can vary considerably. Thus, while some shows are carefully planned, occasionally with the assistance of a professional choreographer, others are left to the moment:

> *I vary my songs within the set. When you're dancing there's an exciting part, a sensuous part, and you can't have that going for the whole set, like the whole twenty minutes, or whatever. So you put your act in order and you work out your music. Like I said, the costume is a big part of the show, it's what people first get an impression of. So at the beginning you might put a little peppy music on to sort of introduce your costume. Music to take it off to. The first couple of songs are kind of a little happier, livelier music. Like the first song will be the fastest probably, and the second one will be more like an intermediate and the third song will be the slower one and the fourth song will probably be the*

slowest and most sensuous overall. Sometimes I switch it around so that my third song is the slowest one while my last one would be more of an intermediate pace, but not that fast. A lot depends upon which theme I'm trying to portray in that particular set. (dancer)

I don't have a planned routine, I just kind of improvise, do whatever seems to be the best at the time. Whatever makes me feel good in terms of the music. . . . Getting the right music is no problem, I can dance to nearly anything. (dancer)

Other concerns with preparation are related to dressing rooms, lighting and other stage conditions, and the music; one's "accompaniment" can be highly instrumental in portraying desired images. However, the conditions under which the girls work are often far from ideal:

In The Tower, you have a very small dressing room. They have nails all along the wall and you have all the clothes all over the place, so when you walk in with your costumes, you are wondering where you are going to hang anything. And the door opens in, to make it even more difficult. You're always picking up something, while you're knocking something else over. (dancer)

The stage conditions can make a big difference to putting on a performance. If the stage lighting and conditions are good, almost anybody looks good strip-ping. At this one place they have a plywood stage and a white light, one bulb right above a very small platform. The owners are always complaining about the girls, that they can never get any girls that are worthwhile. The lighting works against the girls. None of the girls are perfect and where the dancer has this bright white light, no one is going to manage in that setting. (dancer)

The different places we work, we don't always have an M.C. to announce us. Sometimes they'll just have like a tape set that you can announce yourself on the tape. But you always know before what's going on, because your agent will explain to you what the setup is, if they have a jukebox or whatever. You have to have the right equipment, like if you're going down, and the people are using records and not just tapes. Myself, I don't at all like going up without an announcement. It seems too cheap to just run up there. (dancer)

HANDLING THE CUSTOMERS

When they are watching the show, it's like every man is a dreamer and he can hope that he gets something like this and wouldn't that be nice. It's sort of a fantasy that they can enjoy while watching the show. (dancer)

"Putting on a show" is by no means limited to the manipulation of stage conditions. The material following focusses on "intimacy and distancing," "troublesome audiences," and "incidents," all of which introduce problematic elements into dancing routines.

INTIMACY AND DISTANCING

A very important aspect of "handling customers" is what might be termed "the management of intimacy." Exotic dancers (like other performers) are likely to be better received when the audience experiences a sense of rapport with the performers, but, insofar as undressing in front of other persons is considered an "intimate self-revelation," with a variety of sexual connotations, they are faced with the task of keeping intimacy within personally acceptable limits. While their acts entail some "counterfeiting of intimacy" (Boles and Garbin, 1974), performers face the problems of dealing with those who have been stirred by the presentation. This concern is particularly relevant for exotic dancers working in clubs (rather than theatres, carnivals, and so on), wherein off-stage contact with patrons is not only more extensive but can dramatically influence their on-stage reception. At issue, here, is not only the performer's personal integrity but also the audience's satisfaction with the way in which they were treated in the process. Although distancing seems somewhat problematic for all dancers, it is important to recognize that concerns with distancing vary somewhat by both audiences encountered, and the desire of the dancer to orient her show to the audience.

Congenial audiences make stripping a more pleasant experience but few dancers can expect this reception at each place they work. Not only is there likely to be little transference of reputations from bar to bar (as the girls may work any variety of circuits, or some scrambling thereof), but the dancers preceding them establish a framework by which the current performers tend to be judged. While they may have a week or two to consolidate themselves in a bar, the problems associated with obscurity are likely to plague all but the best-known performers throughout their careers. Further, an act that was "a success" in one place may be unworkable (due to stage conditions) or a failure (different audiences) in another:

> *The audience can be very different. Some places, each time you take off a piece of clothing they clap, and they're really pleased with what you're doing, they're very appreciative. When you come out, they applaud like mad, and with each piece of clothing that comes off, they applaud. This kind of builds up over the act. Here, it's different. Here, you have to pretty well force the people and remind them to clap. Today I haven't been doing that very much, because it's the end of the week and I just don't care that much.* (dancer)

> *One of the customers was saying that he quite prefers the stripteasers to the type of show on tonight. He said, "There is no striptease here tonight. It's one song, no dress, two songs no pants, three songs, no girl. . . . I like the real striptease where they come in dressed and they leave a little bit to your imagination. Take off a glove, take off a top, a little tit here, a little flash there. It is much more exciting that way." However, in discussing the same performers a short time later, another patron indicated "I really like this group of strippers. No fooling around. They get up there, take their clothes off, and you see what you want to see."* (notes)

Audience responses can affect the dancers' performances, but it should also be noted that performers can influence the ways in which they are received. In general, the dancers appearing to be more attuned to their audiences tend to be better received:

> *Before I really got into doing shows, really got into playing up to the audience, I used to think about just about anything but what I was doing. I used to think of my grocery list, what I was going to do the next day, and how much money I was*

going to put in the bank the next afternoon, and how much money I had saved. And then I realized after a while you've got to have your mind on what you're doing, or else it's a waste of time. You shouldn't even be up there. And there are times when I slip, like this afternoon, I was not into it, I really had to work to make myself get in the mood. Now I think I can basically concentrate on whether the audience is enjoying the show or not. Sometimes though, I really get paranoid about it. I see people sitting there, looking kind of bored and I really worry whether they really enjoy the show or whether they're just sitting there, waiting to see if another girl comes on, or something like that. (dancer)

With a lot of the local girls, it is not that they are bad dancers or that they have bad bodies, it is just that their attitudes are so bad it makes them very difficult to work with. They feel like they are doing everybody a big favor because they are there. Stripping is no different from any other form of entertainment. You are there to entertain the audience, not the audience is there to entertain you. Whether you are having a bad day or a good day, it's your job to be able to smile and relate to the audience and a lot of the girls figure, "Well, you're just lucky I'm here." She doesn't smile and she's sort of arrogant and she looks down on them, like they're all jerks. Well, that's going to show. (agent)

While keeping oneself extensively removed from the audience is a reasonably effective way of neutralizing intimacy, few club dancers find this a satisfactory or desirable method by which to handle their relations with customers. It is, of course, impossible for the dancer to be fully receptive to all the whims of the patrons, but it is also very difficult for the performer to remain totally aloof from the audience. Not only may the physical structure of the clubs provide opportunities for patrons to approach the dancer as she goes to and from the stage, but the management may, in varying degrees, encourage the girls to mix with the customers. Additionally, if she desires some company or a drink, or has "nothing to do between shows," the dancer may return to the bar, again becoming accessible to interested persons:

Sociability is a problem, because if you are too distant from the people, they won't treat you very well when you are on the stage, and you can't afford that. One of the things you might do if they say, "Hey, come and join us," or whatever, you say, "Fine, I will be there, but I have to get changed." You just never make it back down. You only choose the people you want to sit down with and you have to judge by sort of looking at them and just seeing how they treated you at first, who is decent and who isn't. Like some of them, you can see from a mile away that they are noisy or rowdy, by the way they are treating other people, or they are yelling or whatever, and they are the sort of people I try to avoid. (dancer)

You try to make a good impression, being friendly with them, smiling at them, just kind of seeing what they're like. If you're in a rough place and you come out and realize that you can't really be too sexy, you kind of put a limit on yourself. There are certain things that I can do at Central and get away with that I could never do at Sarah's. At Central, I could do a stocking act, and no one would bother me, but if I ever tried it at Sarah's, I'd be afraid somebody would try and get up on the stage with me. You kind of gauge your audience, just how far you can push them. And you have got to stay right behind that line. (dancer)

Skepticism represents yet another form of distancing. While the dancers very much appreciate fanfare, most, through experience, learn not to "believe everything everyone tells them":

The lines people give you. I was working with a girl who must have been about 180 pounds, a filthy looking girl, terrible looking, bare feet, dirty bare feet at that. She was up dancing and this guy is saying how good I looked, but how she looked terrible. Going on and on, and I was believing him. I was eating it up, I thought, "Wow!" Then when I had to do my set, she came down and sat with him. I was up there doing my set and I heard, "She's terrible. She's a lousy dancer." I was kind of listening and thought "Aha!" That's when I realized you don't believe anything anybody tells you. If someone gives me a compliment, I just smile. (dancer)

Apart from the performers' interests in isolating or exposing themselves to off-stage bar life, it is important to recognize that one finds a body of regulars at most strip clubs:

The regulars, those are the ones you have to watch out for, because they pretty well live in the hotel with you, and they can give you a really hard time. (dancer)

Whether so desired by the stripper or not, these regulars provide evaluative continuity between shows and over her stay. While the positive or negative responses of the other patrons have a fleeting quality to them, the responses of the regulars can effectively determine whether or not she enjoys working that particular bar. These people are likely to be aware of her bar activities and will often try to involve her in their pursuits. Although the girls have very little basis on which to assess the desirability of these prospective companions, the extent to which, and the ways in which, they mix with the regulars (and the staff) can have important implications for their reputations in the bar. First, should a girl remain more aloof she is more likely to maintain an aura of mystique, but she is also more apt to be typecast as "snobbish," or a "cold bitch" and may find that her act is received accordingly. If she mixes more extensively with the regulars and/or the staff, she seems more commonplace, and her habits (drinking, swearing, hooking on the side) and companions (bikers, the bartender) become much more instrumental in defining her place in the bar. While some of these activities and involvements sometimes disappoint or disgust some patrons ("Ah, she's nothing but a fucking biker broad!"), any friendship ties a stripper establishes can provide a basis of support (ensuring her of some fanfare as well as being a buffer against negative responses). The girls remaining more distant are less likely to find themselves in a series of awkward situations. They are, however, also unlikely to have much support in the event some difficulty arises.

TROUBLESOME AUDIENCES

It is easy to live with compliments; but cold, demanding, and sometimes insulting audiences represent an important element in the life of a stripper. Not only does she sometimes find herself the only female in the bar but, while on stage, she is the obvious centre of attention and, as her act proceeds, has little to hide behind. While negative responses are likely to be particularly difficult for the novices to handle, the often unanticipated poor receptions tend to bother even the most seasoned performers. As the following materials suggest, there is no totally satisfactory way of handling these obstacles. While attempts to ignore the comments or to lose oneself in the music or the routine seem among the more workable, it is difficult to endeavor to entertain a group of people and remain insensitive to their responses:

> *If the audience is cold towards me, I really don't bother with them. I just concentrate on the music. Sometimes, they will say to me, "When you are dancing you really don't look at the people." And that is true, because when I am dancing, I concentrate on the music. If you pay attention to them, a lot of times they will take advantage of it, "Take it off!", "Show some beaver." So it is better in a way to just stay with your music. . . . Then it doesn't matter so much what they say or what they do. You can lose yourself in the music. And sometimes, when I am dancing I will feel like a princess in a white dress doing ballet. It is that kind of feeling.* (dancer)

> *The audience can make or destroy your show, and some people are out to destroy it. They don't like to see you having a good time. For example, I might say to somebody, "Would you like a milkshake," and they'll say, "No, I don't like chocolate." Which really burns me because I'm not black, yet some people think I am. Another time I threw my glove at a fellow and he picked it up with his tie, like I had bugs or something, like he might get warts by picking up my glove with his hand. So I just picked up my glove afterwards and said, "Come back when you grow up." When I do a show I try not to be raunchy. Like I'm not raunchy, am I? I know I'm not raunchy, maybe a little kinky, but it's all an act, anyways. It's not the real me. People, they sort of think that however you are on the stage, that's the way you are, that's what you're really like. They just don't know the other sides of you.* (dancer)

> *They're all different types of persons. Maybe someone is clapping. Well you just smile at them a lot because you want them to keep clapping. You kid around with them. Somebody is sitting there kind of unmoved, then you might imitate them or wink at them. They may just like that, everybody wants to be part of the show. If they are really glum, you might tease them a little and if they don't respond, then you know their mind is on something else. They're really not interested. So you just kind of swallow your pride and look the other way. But you have to keep smiling at everybody. . . . The people who are being sarcastic, these people you can either ignore or just smile at them. You don't want to respond to any of their comments. Like someone called me Skinny and said that my nose was bigger than other parts of my body, and I just smiled at him. You can't let them think that they're getting results.* (dancer)

A few dancers indicated problems with men in the audience masturbating during their performance, but this is less common at strip clubs (and even many theatres) than might be supposed. One will occasionally notice someone in a washroom cubicle seemingly relieving himself after a show, but overt activities tend to be infrequent:

> *No, I've never come across any guys jacking off. There are guys that do it, I'm sure, but I told my agent that I didn't want to work in any places like that, and if he put me in any places like that, well, I wouldn't be working with him any longer.* (dancer)

Nancy asked me if I realized what she was doing when she made a particular gesture to this older man at Sarah's. "He was really going to town underneath the hat on his lap." (notes)

At Dixi's, there was a guy in the first row masturbating while I was doing my show. In this place they have ropes that hang down and what I did was to kind of bend over in front of him, leaning over him, holding onto the rope, to give him a little extra thrill, but what happened, my hand slipped and I fell right into this guy's lap! (dancer)

Male patrons are not the only ones perceived as offensive or troublesome to the dancers. Although one finds relatively few female patrons at strip clubs, many of the dancers reported these as instances of troublesome audiences:

You also get some women, though, who are also problems because they come in and they make very lewd remarks during your show, and that's pretty hard to take, coming from a woman. Sometimes the guys will come on to you too strong and they'll be all trying to touch you and sort of groping at you. I don't like that either. I don't put up with that, I've hit guys because of that. But women coming in, that can be a big problem too. I think that they're just jealous or maybe they're gay or something." (dancer)

Women in the audience can be the worst and sometimes they will make comments, "Look at the small boobs on that one," small bum, or whatever. Sometimes I answer back, and sometimes I just try to ignore her. (dancer)

You get other problems too. Like this one older woman, she was about two hundred pounds, she was hassling me from the audience, saying, "I can do better. I've got bigger tits than you!" I turned around and said," You're tits are flab! They hang down to your waist. And, if you think you can do better, why don't you come up here and I'll give you the thirty-five dollars." After a bit she left and never came back. (dancer)

INCIDENTS

The distinction between a troublesome audience and an "incident" is not as obvious as it might first seem. Most dancers are apt to encounter some unusually dramatic incidents during their careers and, while some of these are entirely outside their control, other events can become more significant or more intense as a consequence of the ways in which the performers respond to the event:

I've also had people throw things at me. That is very insulting, that is the worst. That burns me up, but you can't let them see that. Something like that is dangerous, you could get hurt. Not only can they hit you with it but you could step on a coin and slide off the stage. At one place, it's a working man's bar, there were a bunch of motorcycle guys and they got very rowdy and started throwing things. First, someone threw a coin. I heard a coin hit the stage, but I kind of ignored it, kept on going, thinking it will stop. And then I heard some more, like pockets full, and then I saw a cigarette coming at me and I just put my robe on and walked out. (dancer)

I walked off when I was working at Spring Gardens. I had taken my gown off and laid it across the chair. But someone took the gown and started throwing it around. And they'd spilled beer all over it. I got it back finally, and I didn't have my robe with me, I'd left it upstairs, so I had to wrap this gown around me and tried to walk off the stage, through the crowd and get back upstairs. Then someone came up behind me and grabbed me so hard that he left bruises on my thigh, and I turned around and slapped him across the face. I think it shocked him. I think I was supposed to enjoy that! When I went back for my next show and was doing a floor act, somebody came up to the stage. I had just taken my bra off and he just came and grabbed me. I was so mad, I just couldn't believe it! I just totally lost my cool. I jumped up and I put my robe on and I got down off the stage. I was going to pick up a chair and hit him over the head. I was so furious! I was going to try and kill him. I was so mad and furious and insulted, and the fact that no one else did anything made it even worse. And then I stopped myself, and I was shaking. One of his friends was sitting there and they saw me reach for the chair and they grabbed my arm, ''Don't, don't. He's drunk. We'll just get him out of here.'' (dancer)

In some of the bars it gets a little rough, in terms of fights. It's still a scary thing. I'm still shocked when fights start. At Sarah's they had three fights one night while I was there. I was doing my floor act when one of them started. I just sat up there and watched and waited for it to go away. You can usually tell when it's going to break into a full-fledged bar-destroying fight. And it just seemed like one involving two guys, so I just sat there and waited. When they finished, I finished my show. If they were near the stage or something I would just get up and leave, I mean leave the bar. . . . There are times when I really wonder what I'm doing up on the stage. You think, ''I've got to be crazy to be up here!'' Sometimes you'll see somebody who is acting really belligerent and it gets a little bit scary, especially if it's a really big guy who is really drunk, and you don't see any allies in the crowd, like you can pretty much pick out the people who would help you if you had trouble. And the waiters are not always there, a lot of the waiters run the other way when there's trouble. It gets a little scary sometimes. . . . Every once in a while it does really scare me, because when people are drunk, you can't tell what's going to happen. (dancer)

LEGAL ENTANGLEMENTS

Exotic dancing flirts with the law as well as with the patrons. While the customers typically respond favorably to a more explicit show, a dancer attempting to please her audience in this way is more apt to run afoul of the law. Morality interpretations, however, very much represent the whims and interests of the local police and judicial systems, making it more difficult for a girl to know when she is likely to be "busted" for an "indecent performance." In general, the clubs like whatever shows "make the cash register ring," but until the performer is warned (much more common than arrest) by the local morality officers, she may not be able to accurately gauge "how strong" her show is in the local context:

There are three no-no's in stripping. Three things that generally are not allowed. One is audience participation, either having a guy on the stage or going into the audience and having them undo your bra or otherwise involve them in the act, that's not supposed to be done. Another is insertion, using a dildo, or otherwise simulating intercourse. The third thing is simulating oral sex. (agent)

So I got a call from the management. Big Betsy's been picked up, she's in jail. But not only did she let the guys rub their face up against her bosom and such things, but she smoked a cigarette in her pussy. What the club didn't tell me was that she had been doing that all week! The place was just packed, they were making money hand over fist. It's sort of funny how the management didn't know anything about it until it happened, and then they weren't there, they didn't see it. I bailed her out, but she blew it on me, she skipped bail. I lost four hundred dollars. . . . Another girl, the management called and they said, "You know, she's really fantastic. We'd like to hold her over, but do you think you could ask her to cool her show just a little bit." I said, "Well, what is she doing?" I said, "You know the rules. Tell her what she can do and what she can't do and work it out from there." If she's doing spreads or whatever, they can see exactly what she's doing, because they're there. Then I had her in another bar after that and she got busted on a Friday. What she was doing was inserting cherries and ice cubes into her pussy and then popping them out into the audience. She was laying on top of this grand piano, popping ice cubes into the audience. The morality did not appreciate it. . . . The other problem is that the criminal code is very vague in reference to obscenity, so by and large it is up to the local morality squad. It's their decision, what they think represents obscenity, what constitutes a gross or an obscene performance. You don't need to be nude to be gross. (agent)

So here I get busted for using a dildo, right. So, the next night I am at this stag, and who is there, but the police chief. So I ask him, "Is it okay to use this, because I don't want to get busted again." He says, "Yeah, its okay with me. The boys want a show." So there you have it. The same precinct, but different places. One place it's legal and the other you get busted. (dancer)

GETTING STARTED

Much like the hookers, the girls involved in exotic dancing are often asked, "What's a nice girl. . . ." Although there is some glamor associated with stripping, it is also considered a disrespectable occupation by most people in society. Thus, while providing some contrasts with hooking, involvement in stripping suggests some similarities as well.

Few girls, it seems, aspire to become strippers, and it is worthwhile noting that for the very large proportion of the dancers stripping was at least the second line of work they tried. Prior to stripping, some women worked as waitresses, bar maids, models, entertainers, and hookers, which are somewhat related to dancing; but others worked as secretaries, car hops, tour directors, sales women, factory workers, teachers, and junior executives. A few were university students who hadn't had other full-time jobs, but most held other jobs prior to their involvements in exotic dancing. The girls come in a variety of sizes and shapes, and from a variety of backgrounds. And, while there is considerable consensus in bars that some dancers are "ugly," those unfamiliar with "exotic dancers" might be surprised at the extent to which these girls would be viewed as unexceptional in their "off stage" attire: The agents are very much aware of the lack of necessity for the girl to be beautiful or "well endowed," to work effectively as a dancer:

In terms of looks, what you want is a good looking girl, but not a really beautiful girl, because beautiful girls think often that it is enough just to look beautiful and it isn't. The same with girls who have very large busts. They seem to think that's all they need to get by. You'd like her to have sort of a variety of costumes and be able to do some different things, not just go there and take her clothes off. So that's what you look for, sexiness, eye contact, rapport with the audience, a smile. (agent)

A big thing is reliability. You need a girl who's going to be there regularly, a girl that they can depend upon. So in that regard, I'd rather have a reliable girl than a girl who is a fantastic dancer or really beautiful. Like I have met some very good dancers, but they are so unreliable that you don't want to work with them because Monday morning they might call you and say, "Well I can't go here" or "I'm not feeling well" or whatever, and you know that they are lying most of the time. And that puts you in a bad spot because then you have to run around trying to scrounge up somebody else for that time period. . . . Sometimes you get calls from the club and they say, "Where's the girl?" and you know your girls pretty well and if she's a good girl, you'll say, "Well she's probably just going to be a little late, she may be having some problems." You assure them that she is basically a reliable person, but some other ones you think, "Oh, oh, here we go again!" So then you say, "I'll get back to you" so you try and call the girl and she's not there and then you have to call the hotel back and they call you back, so your expenses really add up especially for long distance calls. Every time a girl doesn't show up in time, then you have those additional expenses and you may lose your commission as well. Then, of course, the management is not happy with you either. (agent)

INITIAL INVOLVEMENTS

In spite of a wide assortment of initial routes into stripping, one finds some fairly general commonalities across the cases. First, many had worked in occupations which made the transition to "dancer" a little easier (for example, waitressing, modelling). Second, many, through their work roles or night life, had become more accustomed to being with bar people and to being in the sort of bars in which one might find exotic dancers. Third, many knew girls presently involved in dancing or had close contacts who encouraged or supported their involvements in dancing. Fourth, while most were somewhat impressed with the money to be made in dancing, many were also disenchanted with their present situation. Feeling that they needed money, a job, adventure, "a change," and so on, they were a little more open to a new line of action than might have otherwise been the case. While the pay for stripping is more than most of the girls could have earned at their former jobs, one would be mistaken to perceive money as "the great motivator." Money is important but must be seen in the context of "climatized involvements," and "supporting casts":

Trixie said that she got involved in stripping at The Bump. She called them up one day and said she would like to work. She said that she had some friends who had been stripping and she thought that she could do it as well as they could. And, it was a way of making money. (notes)

Hot Chocolate was dealing dope and became acquainted with some strippers and club managers and then considered going into stripping since the money was good and since she felt that she was a good dancer. (notes)

I had been with an all-girl's band and we had had some problems internally and it was breaking up. We were feeling unhappy with the situation. I had been around dancers for a while and I thought, "Well, why don't I do that? I can make fairly good money doing that too." One of the things that I had difficulty with was the idea of me stripping on stage and what would all of the people think of me. But then I was thinking, "Well, you can be a lady, regardless of what you are doing and I figured that I wouldn't let the men touch me or be prostituting myself, or anything like that. That was something that helped me get over this feeling. It comes to the point where you have to make that choice. (dancer)

I was working as a waitress. I was having trouble with the boss bothering me, and I met a lot of dancers, so I figured, "Why should I work for say, $200 a week, when they were making $400, and they didn't have to work half as hard as I did." I thought of it that way. That was the thing that really started me off. (dancer)

Agents occasionally get calls from girls "interested in finding out what all is involved in exotic dancing." While these inquiries may be handled in a variety of ways, not many of the girls pursue the matter much further, and few actually end up on stage:

Out of the twenty girls or so that called me this summer about a job, only about eight showed up, and of those eight, only two are working right now. A lot of them seem to lose interest or do other things, I guess. But I tell them what's involved and some of them are surprised to see that there's work involved in it. I guess they've seen other girls and they think it looks pretty easy on stage. And, of course, sometimes the easier it looks on stage, the more that girl has worked out her routine. Also I tell them that they are going to get propositioned. That doesn't mean that they are a whore or anything. It happened to the girl before them, last week, and it probably will be happening to the girl following after them the next week. It's just something that they should know about if they are going to go into that situation. I tell them that they are going to be making money, but they are going to have to invest some of it in their costumes. I also tell them about the travel involved. And some of them will say, "Oh, I have a boyfriend and he says such and such." And then, if he is already telling them what to do, there is going to be problems. (agent)

GOING ON STAGE

While a good number of interested prospects never make it to the stage, even those who progress to this point may find that "taking it off" in public is considerably more difficult than disrobing at home:

The first time I was on stage, I was very anxious, very nervous; I could hardly move my knees or my feet. I was sweating, my hands were sweating, perspiring, and I didn't know what to do or what to move. It was also difficult just to take the clothes off, even find the hooks or buttons or whatever. I just seemed to be numb. (dancer)

The first time I was dancing I really had problems taking the bottoms off. Like the dress came off, and the bra came off okay, and I'm on the last song and they're yelling. "Take it off. Take it off," kind of thing. and I just couldn't. The manager of the place was getting quite upset about that and he was yelling the loudest, "Take it off, take it off." (dancer)

I couldn't picture myself going into dancing before. It's hard to picture yourself on a stage. It's hard to picture yourself doing things that all your life you've been told not to do. And it's hard to try and find a way of doing it with a certain amount of style and until you actually try it, you don't know if you can do it. . . . The first time I got up on stage, it was horrible. I was really terrified of getting up on stage. The first time, when it was over, I think I just went, "oooh. . ." Then after the first time, I realized I liked it. (dancer)

The first place I danced I was kind of scared and I didn't like the way people were looking at me. I didn't have any problems taking my clothes off — like the top or the bottoms, that came off, but I had problems just moving. I just felt kind of frozen up there. I sort of notice the same thing when I'd go to a new place. I'd feel a little shaky the first time especially, because you don't know what's going to happen or how your show will go over. But afterwards, in each place, it seems to get better as you go along. (dancer)

Stage fright is not confined to the initiate and, although veteran performers may, through the development of acts, props, and routine, reduce the anxieties they experience, each new club offers some uncertainties with which the girls must come to terms:

It took me about four years to sort of get over the nervousness associated with dancing. But even now I find that when I am in a new place or a new environment, that I still get a little apprehensive or nervous at the start. It's mostly the audience, because I have my act and I know what I'll be doing. So whether they like me or not, I'm doing my act. So I'll be trying to relate to the customers, but if they don't like you, they don't like you. So then I'll think in terms of money. I'll think, "Well, so they don't like you, but they're paying you for your time so you might as well operate that way." When you get off the stage you say, "Well, that's one more show. That's done. That's it." When you are at a new place, you feel nervous, especially if they have a juke box and maybe you haven't danced to the music before. You are thinking about the stage, and if the people are going to like you or not. But it is not like the very first time that you dance, it is a different type of nervousness. The second night you are starting to enjoy it more and the third night you are pretty well knowing the people and maybe going to a party the rest of the week. (dancer)

Whenever a girl was going on stage, there is always a problem with nervousness. She has to psych herself up for each new place in each show. Some of them have their little drinky, or their drugs, little pick me ups, to help them overcome the sense of being out there alone, in front of all those people. (agent)

LEARNING THE ROPES

For most of the girls, an apprenticeship, in any structured sense, is non-existent. While this seems essential if the girl has hopes of making the "big time," the mobility the job entails, along with a tendency to assume that one's present act is adequate, deters learning from others. Not only does mobility limit one's opportunities to develop close contact with others who could "teach a novice the ropes," but co-extensive stays at clubs are so limited as to preclude the practice required for developing more elaborate acts. As a consequence, most routines would be best described as "makeshift," with the girls copying ideas from one another and incorporating elements of fashionable dancing into their stereotypes of what exotic dancers do:

> *The first couple of weeks, I'd take my dress off and hang it up between songs. Then a stripper came up to me and told me that if I didn't wear shoes she was going to come and break my leg, and if I didn't stop taking my clothes off between songs she was going to come up there and put them back on me. She was joking around, but doing it for my own good. She really helped me. . . . I also learned a little bit of belly dancing from one girl I worked with. I capitalized on that because I could do it easily. You pick up a few ideas here and a few ideas there. And moves, I don't think there are any original moves. Someone's always done it before you, but it's different with each girl. I think the best compliment is if someone copies you, your show or your moves. Then you know you must be doing something right, if the other girls want to dance like you. A lot of these go-go girls here in Eastville are so bad. They're just bodies that get up on stage.* (dancer)

> *When I first started, I kind of gritted my teeth and went out. I was only doing it for the money and then I was fortunate to see some good girls working in some good shows. From them, I got some ideas of how to improve my own show. What I have picked up from other girls was simply by watching other girls. I really didn't have anybody who sort of took me aside and explained things to me. I was lucky in the sense that I had some dancing experience from years before and had been on the stage before, but my actual first strip show was a bluff because I had never even seen a strip show. I had done some topless go-go dancing before, but when it came time to do the stripping, that was new to me. It was in a theatre, they had four other girls there and I said, "I'll just wait and go last." When I got in the dressing room, they said, "Well, what do you do? Do you do a floor show? Do you do a couch act? Do you do a stocking act?" I didn't know what they were talking about. But I decided I would just watch their shows and that's what I did. Then, when I went on, I did a little bit of everything.* (dancer)

Additionally, while some clubs insist on "accomplished" performers, others are satisfied with "a dancer." Under these latter conditions, the criteria of "being a good dancer" are sufficiently vague that the girls performing in these bars generally experience a little pressure to "develop an act." Thus, they tend to be relatively unreceptive to the work entailed in developing more elaborate routines. Part of the failure to develop professional shows is also related to the idea, shared by many novice and experienced dancers, that stripping will be a temporary activity for them. For many of the girls, then, stripping is viewed not in career terms, but as a means of achieving romance, wealth, and attention:

I'm not going to stay in it all my life, just until I can get enough money saved where I can get myself an apartment and a new car and sort of get my things together. It'll probably take another year. I've got a lot of money saved and have been able to save it along the way, so I figure another year should pretty well do it. (dancer)

My real ambition is to become a singer. Dancing is just something to tide me over until I get my start. (dancer)

When I first started dancing, it was a big thrill. I had always been a little bit unpopular, actually very unpopular during school. I hadn't gone out much. All of a sudden these guys wanted to go out with me. It was great. And for the first month or so I was really going crazy. My agent was furious with me, "You stop that, you're giving everybody a bad reputation. Stop it, stop it." I couldn't help myself, it was almost like a compulsion to go out with the best looking guy in the place every night, just to be seen walking out the door with him! Whether it was for breakfast or to my apartment, it didn't make any difference to me, I just wanted to be seen with him. Then came a whole new set of problems, the very depressing one night stands. That's when I realized that the guys that came into the place were not interested in meeting you as a person, they just wanted to take you home and that's it. (dancer)

I enjoy it, having all the guys look at you. You sort of figure that you're there and they admire you and look at you and I kind of like that attention. (dancer)

STRIPPING AS A WAY OF LIFE

To this point, we have examined what is involved in putting on a show and have indicated the sorts of conditions under which the girls have become involved in exotic dancing. We now turn to a consideration of some of the more "mundane" aspects of stripping, focussing on mobility and the problematics of fitting into the hotel community, concerns of considerable importance in defining the life-style of the dancers.

MOBILITY

Stripping offers one way of "seeing the world," but the travel conditions most dancers experience make this a less than desirable way of becoming familiar with exotic places and famous landmarks. While some girls enjoy the variety the week to week stays provide, for many others travel is a source of inconvenience, discomfiture, and rootlessness. Not only do they leave family and friends behind but, to a very large extent, their sense of personal happiness depends more or less on their continually fitting into new places with groups of relative strangers:

Monday is always the day of apprehension. That's the day you always try to do your best because that is the day that, if the hotel owner decides he doesn't like you, that's the day it happens. The first day. . . . They do it that quickly, because if he's going to get another girl, it has to be early enough in the week. (dancer)

One of the things I find about dancing is that by the time you travel to a new job every week, and try to get settled and work things out, you don't have that much free time to really do anything. Things like shopping and laundry is a problem, because the places are too far away, or you may not have that much time, or you're not familiar with the city. Sunday, if you have a chance to go home, usually you will do that, and it is nice even for one day to be at home. You have your own TV, your own bed, whatever it is. Otherwise you don't have that chance to relax during the week. But going home is going to take extra time for travel. (dancer)

They wouldn't give the best rooms to the dancers, they never do. And they always give the dancers the same room, which I think is really sad, because there'll be one girl that will bring guys up to her room and the next week the dancer doesn't, so she's going to have these guys knocking on the door. Especially in a motel situation like this, you're not protected at all. . . . You'll come in and sometimes the room isn't always clean by the time you get there on Sunday and you'll find an absolute mess. A lot of dancers aren't known for keeping the room tidy and all that. Some of them make a real mess and destroy things. And that's why I think the hotels give the dancers the worst rooms. Because they don't want to have their good rooms ruined. (dancer)

FITTING IN THE HOTEL COMMUNITY

During "working hours," the dancers typically have 45-60 minutes between shows. While some of this time will be consumed changing costumes, arranging music and the like, it is also a time during which they can mix with the patrons, the staff and management, or the other girls. Unlike their off hours, however, their mobility is constrained by time schedules. Some clubs require that the girls mix with the customers, some prohibit "fraternization," but many leave this to the discretion of the entertainers:

When I come into a hotel, I find out the rules right away, the house rules, because every hotel is different, every locality is different, it has different laws; like in Eastville you're allowed to take your G-string off in some parts of the city, but you have to wear a veil, an article of clothing, a feather boa or something. And there's parts of Eastville where you still have to wear your G-string. You're allowed to undo it, and give them a quick flash, something like that, but that's as far as you're allowed to go. . . . There's always the little laws, the little peculiarities you have to know about. Like some hotels will not allow you to sit with the customers, you're allowed to sit at the bar and have a drink if you want to, but you are not allowed to sit with the customers. As far as I'm concerned that's fine with me, you know. Here, a few guys will ask if I'll come down and sit and have a drink with them, and the waitress will come over and tell me, and then I decide whether I want to go over there or not. (dancer)

Staff-Dancer Relations

Having discussed the ways in which dancers relate to customers, and deal with the mobility the job entails, the focus now shifts to the dancer's relationships with the male staff, the female staff, and the management. In part, the girl's reputation is established upon her arrival. Although one finds few staff people enamored at the prospects of entertaining another stripper, the way in which the girl is received reflects the way in which she initially presents herself to them:

If they are going to a second- or third-rate hotel, and the staff isn't very friendly, where they don't treat the girls very well, it's quite easy for the girl to be depressed when she first arrives at a place. Say she's carrying her luggage or struggling with it, and nobody there offers to give her a hand, well she doesn't feel very welcome there. Then a lot of girls travel in jeans and T-shirts too and maybe a garbage bag for luggage and so people don't usually go out of their way to treat these girls as well as they might someone else who is dressed better. . . . I try to tell them, if you arrive like that, then you are not going to get as good a response out of people as you would if you showed a little more respect for yourself or for them. A lot of girls will be partying all weekend and then they'll drag themselves in. And the manager looks at them and thinks, "Oh my God!" It's a two-way street. (agent)

In general, the strippers feel more at ease with the waitresses than with the male staff. Their relationship may, nevertheless, be somewhat strained. Although many of the waitresses have indicated that they ''would never lower themselves to that,'' they tend to be somewhat resentful of the money and attention the dancers receive, ''just for taking off their clothes.'' While the dancers and the waitresses tend to be reasonably pleasant towards one another, the situation can become particularly volatile when the waitresses sense that they are being treated as servants by a ''haughty dancer'' (''Who does she think she is?'') or when a waitress suspects the dancer is making a play for one of the staff or patrons on whom she feels she has ''squatters' rights'':

The waitresses are a guide of what sort of people is going to be in there. How they act toward the people, you kind of take that as a guide on your own behavior. If they've got older waitresses, kind of matronly type people, then you can usually expect older people to be coming into the bar, not always, but usually. And if they act kind of homey and friendly, that's how you ought to act, because that's the only personality that will go over. You have to carry your personality on and off the stage in a place like that. If people don't like you when you're off the stage, then they're going to hate you when you get on the stage, no matter how good you are. Sometimes the waitresses resent your getting attention from the men. It's almost always the younger waitress. They think that you're trying to move in on their stomping grounds, and no matter how much you try to convince them that you're not, they're still a little bit touchy. Like they see these customers every day and they might have a crush on one of the customers. Then, when they see me sitting down and talking to them, and they think ''Oh, oh! The competition. . . .'' The older waitresses are usually pretty nice. You have to be a slob before they're not going to like you, but there are a lot of slobs in the business. (dancer)

While the strippers' primary purpose in working at a bar is to entertain the customers, their entertainment value for the male staff should not be neglected. Not unlike doctors (Emerson, 1970), the male staff do become somewhat situationally desensitized to the dancers as a group, and have other matters to occupy much of their time and thought. Nevertheless, any dancer attracting the attention of one or other of the male staff may find that her work role becomes more complicated. Further, as she is dependent on the staff for their co-operation and/or assistance in time of trouble, she may find that she has more difficulty handling their advances than those of the patrons:

If you can keep a good ten feet between you and the male waiters, you're all right. The waiters at Central, the first time, knew that I was with someone and they didn't bother me. Now this time around, it's, "Oh, hi, how are you?" and they're always trying to put their arms around me and stuff. You just kind of keep a little distance. Usually it's a hello-goodbye relationship with most of the people, because I'm working there mostly for a week at a time. At Central, it's a little different, I've worked there quite a bit, so I know most of the people pretty well. . . . When I first came with my boyfriend, they stayed away from me. Now this time around, the great big waiter, Roger, started pestering me. And you just kind of have to laugh it off, trying to keep him at an arm's distance. Of course, there are some guys I wouldn't mind knowing, but it's not really good to go out with somebody that you're working with. It makes it hard to work. (dancer)

It should be noted, however, that while some girls have no desire to become involved with the bar staff, others may be quite receptive to overtures from the male staff (and the management in particular):

A number of the girls who've come back a second or a third time often get involved with the male staff or management. It's interesting, because although some of the girls get involved the first time they come around, these other girls often have had very little to do with the same people the first time they danced here. Also, of the returning girls, the ones who've gotten involved with staff on earlier trips, the next time, they often get involved with someone else on staff or a friend of the management. (notes)

Gladys falls in love very easily, and it's happened with a couple of the managers at different places already. It's easy to get to liking them if they're at all decent with you because you know they're there to protect you if you have any trouble. Who's going to help you from the audience? They might help the other people. But the managers are there and you can sort of tell them things and they're there to help you. You start to feel a little closer to those people that would help you. Sometimes you'll find that with other staff people too. But sometimes we seem to be on our own, and like we'll help one another out too. If I notice that she's getting hassled by somebody I'll go and kind of pull her away from the person or go and ask somebody to help us. Whereas, alone you have to sort of watch out for yourself. (dancer)

Although the girls work most bars on a weekly basis, it should not be assumed that employee-boss problems are absent. The following extracts, while denoting some dimensions of these conflicts, are also useful in providing further indications of the everyday work situations in which the dancers find themselves. One set of conflicts reflects the work habits of the dancers and the conditions under which they are asked to work:

The complaints that you get from the management is usually in terms of lateness or drinking too much, sometimes not enough variety in the girls' costumes or their shows. The complaints vary by hotel. If I have a hotel that I'm getting a lot of complaints about all the girls, then I start to think there's something wrong with the hotel or the way it's being managed, but if the girls are quite happy with it, and you don't get very many complaints, and then you get the odd complaint, well then you start to wonder about those particular girls. . . . From the girls, well maybe she doesn't like the stage, or the music isn't loud enough, or her room is crummy, or the bathroom is down the hall. Those sorts of things. Maybe they are not getting along with the staff. Usually, though, I try and oblige my girls. If they don't want to go out of town, I try and keep them in the area and if there are certain hotels that they don't want to work, they let me know and I try to avoid booking them into those places. If she's just there for a couple of days and then she's complaining, I ask her to try and stick it out for the rest of the week, telling her that the money is there and she might as well have it, rather than walking out. (agent)

I have walked off the stage, not because of the customers, but because of the management. Like they try to rip you off in different ways. Sometimes they ask you to do more shows than what your contract says, or more songs than what was agreed upon in terms of the specific sets. And like the last place I worked, it was illegal not to wear pasties or to take your g-string off, but the manager wanted me to take the pasties off and he wanted me to flash. He said, "Just do a little flashing." And I'm not going to flash. Like if he wants, I'll take the whole thing off, but I'm not going to flash. Then he'll come and say, "Well, leave it on," and you didn't know where you were with the guy. Like I'm the one who's going to get in trouble. And I took it off because I'm used to dancing with the g-string off. . . . Another time he cut me off. I wasn't even drunk. I had four drinks and he says, "No more for you." He's a real bastard. They have all their little rules. Sometimes a guy might come up to you and he puts his hand on your shoulder. "Bang" somebody hits him, the bouncer hits him. You're not supposed to touch the girls. Well, he wasn't bothering me or anything. All he was doing was talking and here they were throwing him out, beating him up, and that's not right. This one place was very very rough and I just hated it. They were always telling me what to do. It's my show and they were telling me to do this and do that. (dancer)

I found the management usually pretty understanding when I have had problems, but it is different in all the bars. Some of the bars, like Central, there really is no problem if people start getting smart with you, the doorman or the waiters will be there to help you, but some of the smaller places you don't know what to expect. You are on your own quite a bit there. So that can be a problem, where they don't give you any support. (dancer)

Some other problems arise when the managers take a personal interest in the dancers. When the girls encounter these situations, they may have to negotiate their relationships a little more tactfully if they wish to maintain reasonably congenial work conditions:

The male managers or owners. You have two categories. The ones who are in it as a business and treat you as a business person and the ones who are in it to get a little extra on the side and treat you as an object. It makes it very bad for the whole week. It puts both of you in a very bad position, because if you are going out with the owner or the manager, then you feel like, "Oh, if I'm late for a show he won't mind. What's he going to say to me?" And they're afraid to say anything to jeopardize their own relationship, they're kind of caught between, "Well, ordinarily I would fire a girl like this, but I can't fire her. I'm going out with her." It can make it very uncomfortable for a week. . . . Some of them use the position as manager to just walk right into your dressing room and think nothing of it. I don't like that and I tell them, "This is private in here. This is not the stage. This is not the show. The show is out there. This is private!" This makes them a little bit mad, "Who do you think you are? This is my place." But it's not. The dressing room is private. A lot of them will just peek in the dressing room and say something about what time your next show is or something, and they will invite you to sit with them at the table. (dancer)

Getting along with the managers at the different places, that's one of the things I worry about. I don't worry about the staff. If the staff doesn't get along with me, fine, I just avoid them. But the manager, he'll either ruin the whole thing or he'll make it pleasant for you. There's some that won't talk, don't even have anything to do with you, just tell you the hours and leave you alone. And there's the ones that are very friendly and they're not after anything, they just enjoy talking to you. And then there's the ones that are after something, and you tell them "no," and they forget it, but then there's the ones that keep it up. . . . I didn't like The Lemon Tree because it's one of these hotels where the owner bothers the dancers, knocks on their door at night and that. He'll knock on the door and say, "Come on over to my room for a drink," and you know what he wants. (dancer)

Viewing the dancers as temporary and replaceable staff, the managers of bars employing strippers are frequently very casual about dismissing these employees. This is particularly the case where a group of girls are working at the same bar and the manager expects that the other girls can fill in the spaces, making an absence less obvious to the patrons:

I have fired a lot of strippers. They were too mouthy or were thinking that they were better then everybody else in the place, trying to run the place. I tell them, "Just pack your stuff and get out of here." (manager)

Drinking

Without suggesting that strippers will inevitably become heavy drinkers, their situation, like that of other bar workers (staff, entertainers), tends to promote higher personal levels of liquor consumption than would ordinarily be the case. Not only are people in bars expected to drink, but drinking is commonly viewed as a means to having a good time (or at least a method of making a difficult time a little easier to bear). Additionally, while some prestige tends to be associated with persons who can maintain their composure while consuming more liquor, the dancers are particularly likely to find others offering (sometimes very insistently) to buy them drinks:

Drinking, that's another thing that I tell the new girls, "Stay away from the booze." Because, it is very easy for them to get involved in drinking. I say, "If you have to drink, find a drink that you can handle and don't leave your drink on the table unattended because sometimes a guy might pop a pill or something in it. In the hotel business, it's so easy anyways, because you are so close to booze all the time. . . . Another thing that I find kind of amazing is the general attitude of the people there. Like a lot of times, they will say, "Well, will you

*join us for a drink?'', and you stop and they say, "What would you like?''
If you just order a coke or something, they say, "You don't drink?!? What do
you do for fun?'' And really, I'm at kind of a loss as to what to tell them, because it seems in our society that drinking is so ingrained with having a good
time.* (agent)

*I haven't bought one drink myself the whole week we've been working here.
Even like cigarettes, people keep giving me cigarettes. It's not that I mind
buying my own things, it's just that people are sort of pushing it on you. Even
when I come down here after my shows are finished, in the evening, I notice
it's still the same kind of thing, "Hey, can I buy you a drink?''* (dancer)

For some of the girls drinking becomes a way of life. In some cases, it becomes
a much more central activity than dancing:

*I gave up on Mona. She is a good-looking girl and she is quite capable but
she drinks like a fish and after all this time she only has two costumes. I get a
lot of calls for her, I think most of these are debts.* (agent)

*Wet 'N Wild was getting quite drunk and had been getting a number of guys to
buy her drinks. She didn't seem too attuned to the whole situation, and it was
a little awkward because I always had to collect from these guys who often
weren't sure that they were in fact paying for her drinks. When she came down
for her act, she was quite drunk. The girls had apparently gotten her dressed
and ready before and in the first 30 seconds she had already taken off all her
clothes and she only lasted for the first song into her set before she was sort of
stumbling around and the other girls helped get her off the stage.* (notes)

*The customers really treat the strippers good. A lot of times you'll see a girl
will get off the stage and she'll get a lot of offers, "Can I buy you a drink? Gee,
you're a good dancer.'' She could be the world's biggest amateur. She's got two
tits and two legs, "Geez, you're good! Can I buy you a drink?'' And, if she
says, "No,'' he's going to say the same thing to the next one that walks down,
"Goddamn you're good! Buy you a drink?'' A lot of times they'll say, "No,
pass. I'm not into it.'' But the ones that are into it, like Marigold, "Sure, be
down in a second.'' They're so easy to stop. She'd hit everybody for whatever
she could get. If a guy sat down at the bar she'd sit there and drink all day with
this guy.* (bartender)

While the use of marijuana is a very common activity amongst the dancers,
the bar environment also affords the girls contacts with other drugs. Although we
have encountered very few persons in the hotel who are "hooked on heroin," one
does find a variety of other drugs being utilized:

*I think pretty well everyone is into grass. . . . It's the same as booze. Some
girls need a drink. I think it has about the same effect, the same desired
effect.* (dancer)

*I used to be real junkie. Like I'm an ex-addict and I've been off the shit for about
a year now. I got into it a little after I started dancing. I sort of wanted that extra
push to sort of get me going for a show. It's less common now than it used to be,
but where I was before, in this one place, it was like a shooting gallery. I was
broke all the time. Making $25,000 a year and broke. I kicked the habit, and*

I feel I can do things better now that I'm off that. I'm still doing grass and whatnot. . . . Like now I have my little drinky poo and that kind of helps get me up and my little smoke and marijuana. I smoke every day. (dancer)

Two of the dancers, Flower and Foxi helped me get off the shit (speed). They've been through it before themselves. They were the ones who really helped me come down. Some of these girls, though, they've been through a lot, they've been through it all. (desk clerk)

LOVE AND SEXUALITY

In discussing dancing as a way of life, it is important to consider the intimate relations the dancers have with others. One finds these women involved in a variety of relationships, ranging from superficial relationships with fans, to heterosexual romances, lesbian encounters, and prostitution.

AMOROUS FANS AND BAR FRIENDS

One group of men with whom the dancers become acquainted might best be termed "bar fans." They may offer to buy the girls drinks, ask them out on dates, send them postcards, and give them gifts, as well as "follow them around" during their stay at a particular bar or occasionally from bar to bar. While some of these people also become friends, they are generally not viewed as serious prospects for love or romance:

Irene said that she had occasional trouble with fellows wanting to attach themselves to her, specifically mentioning Edgar. He is about 23 years of age and living with his mother. He seems to have become quite attached to Irene and he is always giving her little gifts and wanting to hang around. She says that he is not a bad guy, he seems well intentioned, but she did not care for him. He is overweight, sort of pudgy, and she just seems to feel more sorry for him than anything else, but she says she doesn't have the heart to tell him more forcefully to separate himself from her. She says he has been hanging on for about four months. (notes)

Shortly after Karen returned to the table, John came over. She had been talking about him earlier. Apparently, they had spent a couple of evenings together. He had taken her out for supper, and so forth. The juke box was playing, "Put Your Head on My Shoulder" and he was saying, "Anytime," kind of drooling over her. In the meanwhile, she was trying to avoid eye contact with him, trying not to be intimate with him. He appeared to be wanting to hold her hand, and she was finding the situation rather awkward. She was also saying to me, "Shouldn't we be leaving?" I said, "Yes, I guess it's that time all right," even though it was about two hours too early for her train. On the way, Karen said, "He is a beautiful person, but not the type I would fall in love with." John is not a particularly attractive individual. It seemed that Karen was one of the big things in John's life, but for her it was quite different. She later added that she didn't want to get too involved with John, saying that he was falling in love with her. It was a case of her liking him as a friend, but not wanting other kinds of involvements. (notes)

FLEETING ENCOUNTERS:
PATRONS, STAFF, AND MANAGEMENT

While the dancers are not as promiscuous as some might assume, and while some are "totally loyal," the work conditions and the generally more tolerant bar setting are conducive to the girls finding themselves in a series of casual, intimate relationships. Additionally, not only are most strippers likely to find someone in the bar whom they consider "reasonably good-looking," but they are also apt to find that more of these men are approaching them than in most other settings in which they might find themselves. The very short time (a few days, a week) in which the couple has to become acquainted, in conjunction with the low levels of accountability both parties associate with the dancer status, suggests a situation in which normally operative constraints are inappropriate:[2]

I have to get to know people pretty fast because you just spend maybe a week in one place and a week in another. You can't go through a period of testing people out, you can't play most of the social games that other people play. (dancer)

I know I am going to go out with men, and I am going to be sleeping with them. But I get my choice, and it is not like you are opening your legs to anybody who comes along. And while you are there, you might meet a nice guy who will treat you well. He treats you like a lady and you treat him like a gentleman. You have a good time and you are in bed, it makes it a nicer place to work. Almost every evening you have a chance to go to a party, sometimes a number of parties. But a lot of times I won't go, because you know what is going on there. Other times you will just stay around the bar. You might have a couple of drinks and then around 10 o'clock you go up to do your hair and get things set up for the next day. (dancer)

A number of men that I have gotten to know want to continue the relationship more than I do. Once we get close, the relationship will continue until I have to go, or he may have to go, but usually it is me, because of the job I have. Some of them get really disappointed and so hurt and I end up getting hurt and crying on the bus when I am leaving. . . . You are having a good time with these people and you are liking them a great deal and you know you have to break it off and that is where it hurts. You get along so well, you party, you have good sex, and you have to part. For a few days after you may be trying to get in touch with him, and you are calling him on the phone and crying on the phone. It is quite an emotional problem. If you can somehow resist making that call, or refuse to take a call from him, then it is easier. The relationship is still there in your head but you don't make the effort to continue it any more. (dancer)

STEADY BOYFRIENDS, HUSBANDS,
AND TRAVELLING COMPANIONS

Although fleeting encounters with bar males create a number of problems for the dancers, so do their "old men" (a term used to refer to steady boyfriends,

---

[2] Matza (1964) uses the term "drift" to refer to a situation in which persons are freed from normally operative moral restraints.

husbands, and others with whom they have somewhat stable relationships). Some of the dancers indicated that these men know of the work and accepted it without incident. Most, however, report a variety of difficulties with boyfriends and husbands which they directly attribute to their work. For some dancers, a major problem is that of finding or retaining suitable prospects:

> *With boyfriends, the main thing is that they can't accept my work. We get along for a while and then it's, "Well, I just can't accept the work that you're in." I tell them, "My work is part of me. If you can't accept it, then you can't accept me."* (dancer)

> *I've had problems with every boyfriend I've had as a stripper, and I have just broken up with another man because of this. At first some say, "Well, it's just great, super!" And they think of all the money you can make and so forth, but then afterwards, they want you to drop out. Other guys, they don't like the idea, pretty well from the start."* (dancer)

> *One of the things I wonder about from time to time is if I will ever find a nice understanding man, someone that will treat me well, and respect me and yet who I could tell my past to. Where I wouldn't have to conceal my dancing, someone who would see me for the kind of person I am rather than as a stripper. With this job, the relationships that you have with people are for a week, sometimes two weeks. Most of them are very superficial.* (dancer)

While a number of problems are related to the disrespectability associated with dancing, many of those who are unencumbered by this concern are still troubled by jealousy. Aware of potential competition in the bar, they often become suspicious of any attention (often innocent) the dancer directs towards particular customers:

> *Sometimes, though, a boyfriend will want you to stop and that becomes a real problem because if they want to be with you, they have to accept your job as well. One boyfriend I had, he didn't mind when people were commenting, "Wow, she is a good dancer!", or things like that, but what he objected to was when I would be sitting at different tables and talking to different guys. Then he was more suspicious. But if you just did your show and went up to your room, then there wouldn't be that kind of problem. But if the dancer wants to stay around, she usually has to mix with the people and he has to be willing to put up with that, but sometimes you will see where a couple will get into a fight because of something like that, where she is sitting at another table, and maybe some fellow is touching her, or holding her hand. Later, he will bring that up and they will get into a big argument over that.* (dancer)

Additional problems emerge when the man becomes a full-time travelling companion. This may seem an ideal role to some males, but it tends to have detrimental effects on the overall relationship:

> *Some of the boyfriends or husbands will put restrictions on where the girls can work or how far they can travel, but a lot of them travel with the girls and that's a problem. Also, when they are in the hotels, some of them have big mouths, and they will be telling the managers how to run the place and that doesn't go over too big either.* (agent)

> *I've noticed when men start travelling with women who are strippers, when they start travelling with them on the road, they go through sort of an iden-*

tity crisis. It's funny because at first they think, "Well this is great, I'm travelling with her and she's working and I don't have to do a thing." And then they go through this stage where they're kind of embarrassed because they think, "What are these people thinking of me? I'm living off this dancer. They probably think I'm a real bum, and she's supporting me." The situation is reversed. They're the little stay-at-home housewife, and we're the ones going out and working. I know that this happened with Cliff when we travelled on the road together. And it happened again with Tony. A lot of men just can't take that. They've got to be the one who is on top. And, I don't like somebody to tell me what to do, especially if I'm the one supporting him, like doing the work. And these men, in order to make up for their insecurity over not working, always seem to be really jealous and possessive and they take it out on you. They feel that their masculinity is being insulted, so they have to play big man, and this is where you run into girls who have boyfriends who beat them up all the time. Sometimes the girls put up with it because a lot of times they'll (the men) use this job as kind of like a weapon against you. An emotional, psychological type of weapon, like, "You're doing this type of a job and you're really not good enough for anybody else. You're just lucky you've got me." That sort of thing. Sometimes you fall for it because it's really lonely travelling by yourself, and a lot of girls can't take being by themselves. They've got to have a man with them. And sometimes they figure, well, putting up with him is better than not having him at all. And that's the way I was with Cliff for about six months before I got tired of him yelling at me and telling me what to do and spending my money on other girls, and that sort of thing. I was really stupid. He really put me in the hole. But this is the typical type of man that you meet, and if they're not like that when you meet them, they will be very shortly. It's just something about men who get together with strippers. . . . But taking other girls out when you were working, I guess that's when the shit hits the fan. It does not go over well. It's like a husband coming home and finding his wife in bed with the mailman. "What are you doing?" He's out working his ass off to support this broad and she's having a good old time with the postie. But for some reason very few of the girls meet men who are good for them. And on one side, they're trying to talk you out of it. They're telling you it's no good and you should get out of it and you're degrading yourself and you shouldn't be working in places like that, and you shouldn't be doing this. And the other hand, it's, "Call the agent and see if you can get another job for next week." (dancer)

LESBIANISM AND BISEXUALITY

In addition to romantic involvements with males, exotic dancers (particularly those on the road) are apt to be exposed to lesbian encounters. In discussing the relationship between stripping and gay involvements, McCaghy and Skipper (1969) suggest that the incidence of lesbianism is relatively high with about 50-75% of the girls involved. They also suggest that these involvements to a very large extent reflect (1) the loneliness a mobile life entails, (2) unsatisfactory relationships with males, and (3) a sexually tolerant context. While much of our material is consistent with their analysis, some qualifications are in order. First, while 50% or more of the girls may have had a "lesbian experience" at one point or other in their careers as dancers, we found that relatively few dancers could be termed "dedicated gays." Further, a number of those who are more exclusively gay had developed gay interests and relationships before becoming strippers. Thus, while loneliness, disappointing relations with some males, and a more tolerant atmosphere may make a dancer more susceptible to gay involvements, they also make her more susceptible to "promising" relationships with other males. Additionally, while two women may find themselves feeling especially close on occasion, many of the initial involvements dancers have with one another reflect recruitment on the part of gay-oriented strippers. Dancers disenchanted with males and bar experiences may be more vulnerable to gay involvements, but the role of the more experienced female should not be overlooked. Given shared problems, dancers can more readily empathize with one another, and trust one another. In this respect, gay-oriented females may be somewhat advantaged over interested males, of whom the "target" is more likely to anticipate a sexually oriented encounter:

When you're on the road, you can't really talk to anybody but other strippers. Most other people are always out to get something from a stripper. But, we can be really close, because we understand each other's problems, we understand what it's like to be travelling by yourself, not being able to trust anyone. And I think a lot of relationships, gay relationships start out like that. I don't think many of the strippers are hard-core gay, a lot of them are bi. Another thing that kind of works on you too, is the men. Often you think they're all idiots. Some of them had had pretty bad experiences with men. (dancer)

There is a lot of loneliness on the road and if the girls get along with one another then it is nice to have somebody to sit down with and talk to, in a more relaxed way. And so they might have a few drinks together or smoke a little grass. But one of the main problems you find is that a lot of women in this job just do not trust men anymore. A lot of them will open their feelings only to another woman and they figure that the other dancers understand them and that they can be sympathetic to their feelings. Some of them get very close to the other girls. . . . Sometimes it is an accident, and sometimes it becomes a regular thing with them and whenever there is another dancer where they are working, they will try to get close to that girl. So sometimes you will be with another dancer and then you will start to realize that when she is touching you, or looking at you, or being just friendly, that it means different things to them that it does to you. Sometimes I will come right out and ask them, "Are you a lesbian?" I tell them I don't really care what they do, it makes no difference to me, it is just that I am not. Sometimes they will be touching you and being very friendly towards you and telling you that they like your hair and that they like you, and maybe that they are falling in love with you. Sometimes they will say, "I can't help it, that is just how I am." And then they will ask, "Do you want to get involved with me?" Sometimes it is that forward. I understand their situation, it is just that I am not into that. Sometimes, I wish that I could, because then I wouldn't have the problems I have with men. (dancer)

I ran into some trouble with some gay girls. One of the girls wanted to go out with me and at the time I was very confused and disappointed with Hector, and then Dick, and I started thinking seriously about her, but there was another girl that wanted to go out with this girl at the same time and it was really rough. I never did anything, but I really thought, "Maybe that's the end, maybe I'd be happy with that.'' Then I had friends though, who were gay that kept saying, "You can't get into it. You don't know what you're asking for. It's a really bad life.'' Matter of fact, Cindy was one of them. She said, "Stay away from it, if you can at all.'' (dancer)

HOOKING ON THE SIDE

Of the various sideline activities in which the dancers may become involved, such as "hustling drinks," "working stags," and "topless waitressing," prostitution is one of the most common. Although these activities are generally viewed as a means of supplementing income earned by dancing, they may become full time alternatives to exotic dancing. Even when the girl participates in these activities as a sideline, they have the effect of drawing her more fully into hotel life.

If the dancer is working in hooker bars, she may be able to avoid some prospective "tricks," but if she is working in a bar in which the dancers and/or the waitresses are the only women generally present, she is more likely to be frequently asked if she "does other things." While this suggests that a hooker could use stripping "as a front," it also means that girls involved in stripping will have many opportunities to become involved in prostitution. As with gay involvements, it is difficult to estimate the percentage of dancers involved in hooking. If one is discussing occasional involvements, then a figure of 50-75% seems reasonably accurate, but if one is discussing more frequent involvements, a figure of about 25-35% seems fairly realistic. However, at any given time only about 10% of the women might be decribed as "dedicated" hookers. These figures should also be qualified in reference to race, as the black dancers are much more likely to be involved in prostitution than are the white women:

A lot of the strippers are not into hooking, but some are and they use stripping as a front. With so many people coming up to you and asking you if you do, they probably think that it's easier than stripping all the time. I know a few girls who'll go out in the parking lot between shows. When they're working at a hotel, they'll just take them up to their rooms. I was working at Hi Seas and the girl that worked ahead of me took everybody up to her room between shows. She would do a 10 minute show, grab somebody and run upstairs and spend 20 minutes with them and come down and do another 10 minute show. And her whole show consisted of giving signals to her dates. She was doing a lot of business. The owner was mad. He said that she ruined the reputation of the hotel in a week. It was a nice hotel and here were these drunk men wandering around in the halls with no clothes on and his daughter was working at the desk. But she just didn't care. He said he was sure she'd walk out of there with at least $3,000 extra. And she should've, with that kind of business. Girls like that usually don't care about their shows. They might have beautiful costumes because they can afford them, but as far as their shows are concerned, they don't care. They don't work on them, they don't dance. They just walk around and make advertisements. So that's the difference between a prostitute using stripping as a front, as compared to a stripper. (dancer)

I have some girls who are into hooking. I really can't tell them what to do on their time, but I do tell them, "If you are going to hook, make sure that you take it away from the hotel where you're working." If a girl at one hotel uses a room to hook from, the next week the next girl is going to have all these guys coming around to her room, and it's annoying for that other girl. It's also consideration for the club. . . . Overall, more colored girls hook than white girls. (agent)

Whether the girls are interested in prostitution or not, the patrons frequently assume that she is open to an offer:

You get a lot of guys coming on to you for hooking. And they say like, "How much do you cost?" "Do you want to go out?" Sometimes they ask you things like, "Do you want to go upstairs and make love all afternoon?" You get so many different lines that you just can't remember them all. They're always coming out with different things. (dancer)

A factory guy or an office guy, when they get drunk, both can get rowdy, but they are different too. Office guys will come on to you in a more decent fashion. They want to give you a better impression. The factory guys are much more straight forward. The office guys are more likely to say, "How long have you been dancing?" or "What is your name?", or "Where were you before?", and then say, "Well, would you like to do a trick?", or "Would you like to go for dinner?". And if they ask you out for dinner, you know exactly what the next line will be. . . . The factory guys are more direct. They will say, "I like you. I would like to go to bed with you." They come on too strong, and some of them are really filthy, like, "Do you fuck for money?", "How much you charge for a blow job?" You just say, "Pardon me," or turn your back on them. After you get that kind of question so many times in one night in a place, you just can't be bothered with these people. Factory guys, they don't like to play around, they just ask you what they want to know. If you are a straight girl, they kind of laugh at you. They don't understand that, they just assume that if you are stripping you must be hooking. If they ask you, "Do you do a trick?", and you say, "No I don't", well they sort of laugh at you and say, "You're crazy." But if you tell them, "I do, but not with you," then they seem to accept that more. Then you are okay. Now with the office guys if you tell them that you will not do it, then they are more impressed with you, and they are more apt to want you more. So it depends who you are with. These office people, if you do it you might tell them you don't; and, if you are with the factory people if you don't, you will still tell them, "I do, but not with you." (dancer)

Encouragement does not come from the patrons alone. Some bar managers, usually those void of regular hookers, will suggest that the dancers do some business on the side:

At a lot of the clubs that you work at, the owner or the manager will come up to you about prostitution and say, "Well, do you go for money, because if you do, you can make good money here." Usually, all you have to say is, "I'm not into that." They get the message and leave you alone. (dancer)

Oh, the manager of this hotel was really infatuated with FiFi. She had had a sex change, but he didn't know that. But all he kept talking about was how, if I was smart, I could really make a lot of money too. He told me how she had walked out with probably half of the city in her suitcases when she left. She was bringing guys up and he'd be renting out rooms for her and he was probably making an extra hundred or two hundred dollars a day just on the rooms. So he was trying to introduce me to all his friends, and I didn't want anything to do with his fat old friends. I don't want to be with them. That's all there is to it. No amount of money is going to make me want to be with them. I can't turn my mind off, it's all gotta be there or it's not worth it. But, he was just so pushy, and when I told him that FiFi was a sex change, I told him in a very snide way, "That's about a million dollars worth of girl you've got there. And it was probably for the sex change alone, not counting the nose job and the false teeth." (dancer)

Dancer-Hooker Relations

Given the relatively easy transition of girls from dancer to hooker, or vice versa, and a somewhat shared sense of disrespectability, the relationships between the dancers and the hookers are rather interesting. As "the entertainment stars," the dancers would seem to have more prestige, but any differences in the relative "status" of the two sets of hotel women are less than might first be assumed. Thus, while the dancers are often seen as more exotic (this will vary somewhat across performers by costumes, drinking habits, and the like), and are accorded much more licence in sexually arousing patrons than are the hookers, the regular hookers offer a sense of continuity many staff people and patrons prefer. Further, while both the dancers and the hookers may feel that they are somewhat "above each other," these distinctions become more irrelevant when the strippers are also involved in hooking. If the hooker-strippers operate more discretely, they tend to be viewed as dancers. However, if they operate more openly in bars in which hookers are already present, they tend to be resented by the hookers:

I know a few of the hookers at Main and Central, "Hello. How are you?" kind of thing. The older hookers will often appreciate the strippers because they figure they are stimulating the guys and they figure that there's going to be more business for them. If a stripper is cutting into the hookers' business, they are not going to like it, but if she is sexy, then they are probably going to appreciate that aspect of her. (dancer)

The dancers and the hookers don't have very much in common. Part of it is that there are guys who just go out with the dancers. That way there isn't that much resentment between the two unless the hookers feel that the strippers are really moving in on their territory, then the girls will get a little hot, saying that this girl is just using stripping as a front for hooking. (hooker)

Lest readers assume that the transition from dancer to hooker or vice versa is an automatic one, the following may be informative in indicating how selectively sexual morality may be viewed. For girls becoming career stripper-hookers two sets of reservations have to be overcome:

Irene mentioned a conversation she had had with one of the hookers. She said that the hooker asked her how she had the nerve to get up there and take off her clothes in front of all these guys. Irene said she sort of wondered how the hooker had the nerve to go to bed with all of these different guys. It seemed more of an intimate relationship to her than what was involved in stripping. . . . About two weeks later, I chanced upon a conversation between two hookers, Lisa and Doreen. They were discussing strippers, saying how they thought it was very

*bold for a girl to reveal herself to so many people in a public place, where
anyone could walk in. They felt that they were much more discreet and selective
in their work. They did not seem to be condemning the strippers, but rather
seemed curious about this form of openness.* (notes)

Pimps

Given their prominence in the hotel community, the dancers are also likely to
encounter yet other encouragements to become part of the hooker world. Although
the players are not highly successful in involving dancers in prostitution, they
do view these women as prospects for their "stables," and many women have
indicated that they have been approached in this capacity. It should be noted,
however, as persons somewhat familiar with bar life, the dancers may be less naive
in this respect than are some other women:[3]

> *In a few places, the pimps will come up to you and bother you. They'll say
> things like, "You know, you could be making better money. You don't have
> to do this for a living. I can set you up and help you make lots of money."
> I just ignore them and smile and walk away from them. That's the only thing
> you can do. And there's nothing they can say. I just can't cut through their
> phoney exterior.* (dancer)

> *You do get pimps coming on to you, lots of times. I just stay away from them. It's
> hard to tell until they let it come out, but a dancer warned me, "Stay away from
> those blacks." She was black herself. She said, "Stay away from most of the
> black guys." And Eastville, it's just like any place else. And most of them, they
> always let it be known by saying, "You don't travel around with anybody? You
> don't have a boyfriend?" Usually, you can pretty well figure it out for yourself.
> I'll talk to them, just to see, because I'm curious. I like learning about things
> like that, "Oh yeah, you need someone to protect you, you know. You'll never
> find anybody like me. I'm the best."* (dancer)

STRIPPER COMMUNITY

In spite of the extensive mobility stripping entails and the somewhat haphazard
arrangements under which two or more dancers find themselves at the same club,
one does find a sense of community emerging among the dancers. Thus, although
opportunities for sustained encounters are rather limited, the dancers as a group
share a number of concerns, such as those related to costuming and preparations,
handling customers, dealing with management, and coming to terms with love and
sexuality. These conditions promote a sense of community and, as with persons in
other groupings, one finds concerns with friendship and understanding, competition and conflict, and reputations and respectability.

---

[3] Nevertheless, while seemingly more wary of "black pimps," many dancers do find themselves at
one time or another supporting a man.

FRIENDSHIP AND UNDERSTANDING

While a girl is apt to feel "more alone" when she is the only dancer at a bar, situations involving two or more dancers may be viewed with some apprehension. Reunions with dancers with whom one has been friendly can be a very pleasant experience, but encounters with other dancers are more unpredictable. Generally speaking, the dancers do make an effort to get along with one another, and will frequently turn to one another for advice and companionship. The extent to which these latter elements develop, however, is contingent on the dancers defining themselves as having somewhat similar interests in the particular bar in which they are working:

There's one girl that nobody can stand to work with. She has to have her own private dressing room. And she lets everyone, especially the audience, know it. She will go out and sit with the audience and you hear her saying, "I have my own dressing room.". . . . Most of the girls get along pretty well. A lot of friendships are started at work. I get along pretty well with most of the girls. But there are a few girls I just don't want to have anything to do with, so I just don't talk to them. Like, girls that are always high, always doped up, or drunk constantly. (dancer)

While many of these relationships, like those the dancers have with the patrons and staff, have a transitory quality to them, others have some duration:

That's why I like travelling with Gladys, because we're together a lot and if we want to party with some people we can discuss it over and we sort of go together. Like I've got this offer and they're asking me to go here and there. We sort of go together so we can sort of watch out for one another. (dancer)

Even when dancers do not feel particularly close to one another, they are likely to watch the other dancers perform and will often express approval (clapping, shouting encouragement) whether or not they believe it is well-deserved.

COMPETITION AND CONFLICT

While the presence of other dancers can be comforting to a dancer, suggesting someone with whom to discuss a variety of problems, or perhaps someone to divert the attention of bothersome staff and partrons, one also finds some animosity and hostility between the dancers. "The competition" may encourage the girls to do better shows, but the dancers may also find themselves resenting other performers who seem better received by the patrons:

There's quite a bit of competition between the girls, like there are girls who are always trying to knock me down because their name doesn't mean anything compared to mine. The billing, this is a big thing, like do you get top billing or not. Personally, I don't care if I get top billing so much, what's more important is if I get more money. Also, if you are the last one to finish the show, then that's more prestigious. (dancer)

You're going to get competition. I find dancers very competitive against each other. And there's jealousy. I've seen girls that have gotten so depressed be-

cause there'd be one dancer there and she'd do it all, "So, well, I'm not even going to try. She does it all." And they make it bad for themselves when they do that. And then there's the other ones that will try to outdo you. If you do something, then they try to outdo you. Or they'll sit in the audience with a customer, and they'll laugh at you, and say little things, and get the guy to agree with her and all this. You're going to get that. I take it for what it's worth. If a girl is obviously giving me a hard time, that's a little bit different. Most of them are very subtle, but it's there, it's always there. . . . They'll be close together when they talk to each other, but there is the ones that will talk behind your back and you see it sooner or later. (dancer)

REPUTATIONS

Given the lack of opportunities for the dancers to interact with one another on a sustained basis, reputations tend to be more tenuous in this work setting than in many others. It should not, however, be assumed that dancers do not acquire reputations as they go about their work. Such things as the intricacy or explicitness of a dancer's show, her popularity, her drinking, and her style of relating to the customers, will not only become known to the staff, the patrons, and the other girls with whom she is working in a particular bar, but the longer she works in a particular area, or for a given agent, the more likely she will become known to the other dancers:

It doesn't take too long to acquire a reputation in a bar, even though you are there for only a week. You might get fairly well-known by the staff and by some of the regulars. Like even weeks later, they might still be talking about this one or that one, who was here three or four weeks ago, and how loose she was or whatever. So you will hear about a lot of other girls, even though you haven't met them. . . . Usually the first people I will be talking to about the other girls will be the waitresses. Then, if the bartender says the same thing, and later the manager says the same thing, where everybody is saying the same thing, you can start to believe it. The waitresses, though, they will get jealous, and make up stories about the girls, so you have to watch that you don't rely on their word alone. (dancer)

RESPECTABILITY

Another element promoting a sense of community among the dancers is the shared knowledge that they are considered social undesirables by straight society:

At different times, when people learn what you do, they say, "Oh, you're putting on a show for all those dirty old men." Like this one time I was talking with this guy and we seemed to be getting along pretty well. Then when he found out what I was doing, he said something like, "You don't work in those kinds of places, do you?" and I thought, "Well, I should tell him I'm just a waitress," but then I said, "No, I strip there." After, he couldn't apologize enough for it, but it's something you have to overcome with each person. (dancer)

One of the most difficult things of being a stripper for me is when I meet nice people. It is always difficult to tell them what I do for a living, because they will think that I am just that kind of person. There is the problem of them accepting you. Most of the people will think that you are a loose woman and that you have no responsibility, no respect. Like you would think close friends, they should accept you for whatever you are. Some of my close friends, I tell them that I work in a restaurant, in a bar, as a waitress, something like that, because I don't think that they would accept me if they knew what I was doing for a living. . . . My friends at home, they respect me and if I tell them that I am a stripper, well, I am sure that they would think I was sort of cheap or no good. (dancer)

While disrespectability generates affinity among bar people beyond those involved in dancing, it does represent one of the more effective elements promoting cohesion among this group of people. The girls assume that other dancers have similar experiences and place some value on being around other (tolerant) women.

FAMILIES AND CHILDREN

The relationships the dancers have with their families and children are affected not only by the mobility dancing typically entails, but also by the disrespectability associated with bar life in general, and by their activities in particular. Like the hookers, most of the strippers endeavor to conceal their work roles from their families. While their "old men" are aware of their bar work, few of the dancers willingly disclose their activities to their families:

Most of the parents don't know what the girls are doing, at least according to the girls. I don't know exactly what they tell them and I think maybe a lot of the parents suspect that the girls might be doing something like this, but they don't really know, at least the girls haven't told them what they are doing. A number of the parents know though, because at different times I will get calls from mothers or grandmothers, wanting to know where they can reach the daughter. . . . Usually, I will just take messages and pass them along, rather than tell the people where the girls are working. Some of the girls seem to have people chasing them, or people that they are tangled up with. They don't want other people to get a hold of them easily. (agent)

My mom and dad would disown me if they ever found out what I was doing. They think I'm a waitress in a restaurant. My sisters know, but they won't tell. (dancer)

Jubilee was lamenting her lack of costumes and I commented that I was surprised she didn't have more. She said that when her mother found out what she was doing, they had a series of heated confrontations over her stripping, and that her mother had eventually burned all her costumes in an attempt to dissuade Jubilee from dancing. (notes)

Most of the dancers have children. In some cases these arrivals reflected "carelessness" on the part of the dancer. In other instances these were children who either preceded dancing involvement or who were born as part of a family situation in which the mother was dancing. For the most part, however, regardless of the routing, these women (and their parents) tended to be the major source of support for these youngsters. While the rearing of children can be frustrating under any circumstances, the conditions of travel and work dancing entails make the situation even more tenuous for these (often) "one-parent" families. Most of the dancers, it seems, do want children, and although some of them rely very heavily on their parents, sisters, and other close relatives, for the general well-being of their children, their frequent and often long-term separation from their children adds another element of frustration to their lives:

> Almost every girl I know, with the exception of maybe 10 girls, has kids. And the girls from out of town, usually they either leave their kids with their parents, with sisters, that sort of thing, or a baby sitter family. They're gone for maybe a month at a time, they'll go back for maybe two weeks, and leave for another month. It's really hard to be away from your kids for that long. I'm glad that at least George is in Eastville. I might not see him too often, but at least I know he's here. Just in case something happens, I'm right here. That's why I really don't like to travel much out of Eastville. (dancer)

> I have a girl right now who is, I think, getting her fourth abortion in three or four years. Why they make love when they are off the pill, I don't know, but it is something of a problem. Some of them are married and they will work as long as they can when they are pregnant or when they want to have the child. You run across some who aren't married and get into that emotional thing where, "I want to keep my baby." And there's no way that she can give the child a decent home or be fair to herself when she's on the road like that. Because it's travelling all the time and working these hours and unless the girl has a strong family behind her, it would be very difficult for her to manage that. And sitters are very expensive and then you can't really find a sitter who's going to be like a family to the child. When a girl gets pregnant, I would typically advise her to have an abortion, for her sake and the baby's, because you just can't function that way. . . . Irene had a baby and she went through that whole emotional thing. She wanted to travel and dance and here's this child and she was spending a lot of money on babysitting and never seeing him. Finally, she did put him up for adoption because it's almost impossible to manage it, with this type of job. (agent)

STRIPPING IN OTHER SETTINGS

Although our analysis of stripping has been largely oriented towards the hotel setting, exotic dancers also represent links between the hotel community and other forms of community entertainment. While the "burlesque theatre" is one setting linked to the hotel vis-à-vis exotic dancers, the participation of dancers and hookers in "stags" represents yet another bond.

BURLESQUE THEATRES

"Burlesque theatres" differ from stripper clubs or bars not only in terms of providing more of a theatre setting, but also in terms of liquor restrictions. Patrons pay an entrance fee at the door and can usually remain for a series of more or less continuous floor shows by a set of dancers. The patrons may avail themselves of a "snack bar" generally located at the theatre, but their central financial contribution is likely to be that made on entry.

The dancers typically have access to a dressing room connected to the stage. Under these conditions, communication among the performers is encouraged to a greater extent than that taking place within bars. At the same time, however, communication with patrons is diminished. Patrons may talk with the girls during their performance, but even here, the volume of the musical accompaniment may make this impossible. The following extracts provide further indication of the burlesque theatre atmosphere:

> *Dance Garden features 6 strippers working continuously from 6 p.m. to 1 a.m. Each girl does a 15 minute show, contributing to a 90 minute review. The setting is that of a theatre, with participants able to view the show from both sides of an elongated rectangular stage. The costumes and the music vary from broadway hits to disco to the more stereotyped "bump and grind." In general, the performances become more relaxed and the show more explicit as the evening progresses. Most of the patrons, however, remain for only one show (90 minutes). There is relatively little interaction between the audience and the performers, despite the M.C. (non-visible) inviting the men to feel free to talk to the girls. A notable exception was an elderly male who occupied a central front seat and would make comments throughout his stay to the effect, "Mmm, nice pussy!" He seemed innocuous and the girls reacted in a friendly manner. At another point in time, one of the dancers caught her gown as she was coming off the stage and one of the nearby patrons went to assist her. Also, unless patrons come together, they tended not to talk or otherwise acknowledge one another, although they seem fully aware of one another's presence.* (notes)

> *The Revue is a rather small theatre, seating about 120 people. As we were going in, two young couples also entered, separately, but at the same time. One couple watched one stripper and then they left. The girl seemed embarrassed. The other couple stayed longer than we did, remaining when we left. The music was toned down where it was easier to talk to the girls on the stage. One fellow, about 35 or 40 years old, kept saying, "Hey, baby, you are beautiful! You are beautiful!" Regardless of what the girls might do, or look like, he would say, "You are beautiful! I love you!" sort of thing. Most of the other people were quiet.* (notes)

> *Usually we'd go at the theatre from 12 in the afternoon to 12 at night and you'd have 6 or 7 girls providing a continuous show. Usually the girls would do about 5 shows each per day. . . . Sometimes when you're managing the place you would have a bit of a problem with the girls not showing up or being late, and then you simply grab someone else and she goes out and does the show. You just move people around. You keep those time spots busy. So then I would go on or somebody else would go on. Like, one monkey's not going to stop the show! Or if she's just being a little slow, well you bullshit on the mike with the customers, or if she's really late, get another girl to come in.* (dancer)

The Patrons

In general, unless patrons come together in a group they exhibit what Goffman (1959; 1963) calls "civil inattention." Thus, although they may enjoy the show, direct comments towards the dancers, and the like, they tend to avoid associating with the other patrons.[4] While part of the level of anonymity among theatre patrons may be attributed to the presence of tourists, other patrons could be defined as regulars:

> *At one point the M.C. was asking the audience if they had any questions about the show and a couple of men closer to him asked if certain strippers would be returning. From their conversations, it appeared that these people were regulars at The Bump. They were not only able to recognize different acts that the M.C. mentioned, but also recognized different names quite readily.* (notes)

> *Samuel, a graduate student, has gone to the Dance Gardens several times in the last few months and had taken other people with him at different times. He was immediately recognized by the cashier and the food vendor, although neither, it seemed, knew his name. Samuel took us to the far end of the stage, explaining that this was the best place to sit as the dancers passed by this point as they went off and on the stage. Samuel indicates that although he is "too shy" to talk to the dancers, he has been to quite a number of strip theatres.* (notes)

Putting On a Show

Generally speaking, the acts at burlesque theatres differed little from those of the bars we studied. The stages were larger, the lighting was better, and the performers were routinely announced, but the performances were not noticeably different. Like the girls dancing in bars, those working in theatres exhibit considerable diversity in costuming, preparations and audience orientation. Further, while some of the dancers exclusively worked the theatre circuit, others had previously been, or were currently, working in bars ("doing doubles"). While out-of-town performers are generally better paid than local dancers, the dancers working in theatres, overall, tend to be paid less than those touring bars. At the same time, however, the theatre performers are less likely to be "hassled" by the patrons. Not only does the general structure of the burlesque theatre inhibit intimate exchanges between the performer and the audience, but performers working in theatres can more readily establish higher levels of social distance by making more use of the facilities available to them.

Community

In contrast to the hotel setting, which may represent a 24 hour situation for both the staff and the dancers, the theatre setting is defined more as a specific work context. The 45 or so minutes between shows afford performers some time to become acquainted with one another and the (small) staff, amidst preparations for the next show. The girls may "socialize" with one another after work, but their opportunities for sustained involvement are less than they are likely to encounter in the hotel setting where their rooms are apt to be in close proximity:

> *A lot of times, the girls don't really know what to do with themselves between shows, for the half hour or so before they get ready for the next one. It's too short to do some things, too long to just wait around. Sometimes they go out*

---

[4] These observations correspond with those of Karp (1973) and Sundholm (1973) in their discussions of patrons in "pornographic" bookstores and arcades respectively.

and get a coffee or a snack. Other times, they'll maybe come and talk to you, or just wait around in the dressing room. (cashier)

While it might be argued that dancers in theatres have more opportunity to become acquainted with one another than those working bars, it appears that the closer working conditions characterizing theatres also tend to sharpen awareness of competition and intensify conflict. Whereas girls working bars can almost totally avoid one another if they so wish, electing instead to spend their time in their rooms or with staff and patrons, theatre dancers have fewer options available to them:

My relationships with the other strippers are very superficial. I have very little or nothing to do with them on the outside. I have my circle of friends and I just don't associate with these other people very much. . . . But, things can get heavy in the dressing room, that's a place where things can get pretty heavy. Sometimes there will be arguments, where one stripper accuses another of copying her act or something. I really don't pay too much attention to the other strippers. But when I first started stripping, the most difficult thing I found was that of being accepted by the other strippers. A lot of beginners break down because they don't get any support from the other strippers, or they get hassled about their acts when they come back to the dressing room. If a stripper can break away from that initial testing of the other strippers, then she can build some confidence, some strength in herself to be as good as they are. . . . A new stripper represents a threat to the other girls, particularly if she is attractive and has a good act, so there is a little bit of hostility there. So the head games in the dressing room can get pretty rough sometimes, like last Saturday, we had had some problems between a couple of the girls. The dressing room is very small, and if you did get four or five or six girls in there at once dressing, and eating, and just killing time, then it would be easy for something to get started. (dancer)

WORKING STAGS

As a means of supplementing income derived from regular theatre and/or work some strippers (and some hookers) become involved in working stags. As semi-private, "one-shot" occasions, these male-oriented events represent some of the more lucrative, but unpredictable settings in which to work:

At stags, you usually get paid $150 or $200 just for a few shows. Then afterward, what I will usually do, is join the guys and they are drinking and you are friendly towards them a little bit. A lot of times, some guy is getting married and they will try to set you up with that guy. . . . If you are an easy going dancer, a lot of times you will end up sleeping with that guy. But it doesn't always end up there. A lot of times I end up laughing and drinking with the other guys and partying, it is kind of fun. I have never had any problems. You are treated as one of the guests, and the next day they might come where you are dancing and they treat you pretty well. (dancer)

I didn't like working stags because they're always disorganized and you never know what the arrangements are. Usually, they'll get two girls and it's $200 for two of you, then it's maybe $40 for each guy, or $30 for each guy. That's not bad *if you've got like five guys, but you have to figure that it takes the whole evening, and so there is that. But stags always seem to be something of a mix-up and at first the guys are shy and you say, "Well, I have to go." Then it's "Oh, no, we want you to stay." Then there's a lot of drinking going on, and you don't really have anybody that you can depend on to help you if something happens. It's very exhausting mentally, and I never liked working stags much.* (hooker)

These events may be arranged through the dancer's agent, a middleman, or interested parties may approach the girl themselves:

The bartender at the Corral came over to our table and asked Lovely Lady if she would like to do a stag next week. She said that she really would have liked to, but wouldn't be able to get into town, that she was working too far away from Eastville next week. . . . When he left, she explained that that was a really good way to make some fast money, and that she probably would have been able to turn a couple of tricks as well. (notes)

Typically, the arrangement is that the girl will spend 20-60 minutes putting on a show for a prearranged fee. In contrast to bar or theatre settings, the patrons at stags are less apt to feel constrained in approaching the performers. While these encounters are often viewed as harmless fun, they can become particularly awkward when the dancer has no one from whom to obtain protection. The sponsors are expected to provide protection, but this may not be effective:

Stags were pretty good for us. The lesbian shows pay pretty well, $300 for 20 minutes. Then you can get all the business you want afterwards. . . . I only had one aggravation out of all the shows I did and I did a hell of a lot of shows. The working conditions were very good, the lighting and the atmosphere, it was a very nice place to work. The audience was good. They are mostly businessmen and they had a rule that there was no touching or no talking with the girls. You had to keep your distance, so that was good too. There is no touching or talking, well a little talking, I guess. Then this one time they had a football team that was the audience. The show lasted about three minutes and then we quit. What they were trying to do was crawl on top of us and touch us and everything like that. This is a young football team and we presumed that since we did shows for so long, at that same club, that we wouldn't have any problems. (hooker)

You get stags that are really poorly organized, where like things are just falling apart all around, the bodyguard is the first one to try to get through the door, an unruly, unmanageable audience, and yet, on the other hand, you can have a stag that'll make up for all of that. Usually, the bigger they are, the better they are. Like one I did the other week, they were a very appreciative audience. It was really great. I had absolutely no problems, because it was a well organized stag and that can make all the difference in the world. But I went to one where the oldest I think was 21 years old, and they were raffling off things like a pound of grass for a door prize, and throwing tennis balls at you. (dancer)

DISENCHANTMENT AND CONTINUITY

Having reviewed many of the features defining the day to day routines experienced by the dancers, the readers are unlikely to be surprised to find that most of the dancers, at one time or another, find themselves extensively disenchanted with their situation:

> *Sometimes, if the girls are having problems in their personal lives they are anxious and nervous about that, and then they run across an audience and some of them become unhappy at that point. If you're not in a good frame of mind, it is hard to do a good job as a dancer. . . . For some of them, travelling is a problem, because if they start to settle down in any kind of way, then they are not going to want to get up and leave that, travelling on the road for weeks on end. Or maybe you'll have a number of shabby rooms in a row, and you'll think, "Well, what am I doing here?"* (agent)

While high levels of dissatisfaction tend to be sporadic rather than continual one finds much less correspondence between expressed dissatisfaction and disinvolvement than might be expected:

> *When it's been a bad week, you think of quitting. A really bad week and you cannot get anything across, then you wonder, "What am I doing this for?" Like you're having this impossible audience, and it doesn't seem to matter what you do, you can't get the show across, people are just sitting there going, "Is that all there is?" and there's no more to give. Then you really wonder, "What are you doing this for?". . . . But then, there's the freedom, the money. There's no other job in the world that you can do what you want basically. The only stipulations are, "These are the rules that we have for the hotel, the local by-laws of what you can and cannot do. These are the show times and after that it's up to you." There's no other job that'll give me that. . . . It sort of spoils you for a regular job. I have a lot of qualifications, I could do other things, but I'm young right now and I enjoy the job. It spoils me for a 9 to 5 job, the same thing every day of the week.* (dancer)

Although it is difficult to accurately estimate proportions, it appears that the number of girls who become regular (''career'') dancers for six months or more is relatively small compared to all those venturing on stage. Thus, while certain aspects of the job, such as travel, the bar environment, and pressure from parents and boyfriends promote disinvolvement, some do get ''caught up'' in stripping as a way of life. And while compliments, gifts, proposals and the like, may define a ''better than routine job'' situation for those seeking stardom, these acknowledgements also seem important in promoting continuity in stripping careers more generally:

> *If they quit after a week, that's fine, but if they're there for at least three months, they usually stay. You don't punch a time clock, you're not committed if you don't want to work a week or if you do. If you want to pick up a nice guy, you pick up a nice guy. There's a lot of freedom in this job.* (agent)

> *You have an audience and all eyes are on you. You're "it!" And, if you have a real good audience, and they're really with you, you just carry on and really get them going. It can be a lot of fun. And people come up to you and they want to shake your hand or give you a kiss, or say they'll be back tomorrow with their friends. Where else do you get that kind of idolation?* (dancer)

Contingencies, such as agency-arranged bookings, fanfare, commitment to dancing by building up costumes, acts, and music collections, as well as becoming

more comfortable with the other dancers, and the hotel community more generally, promote continuity, but the significance of the money to be made in dancing
should not be neglected. Given the girl's training and experience, the money
attainable through stripping is excellent compared, for example, to general office
work. A girl working steadily throughout the year can make more money than
many office managers, executives, and academics. Accordingly, one may be
somewhat surprised by the relative day-to-day "poverty" of many of the dancers.
Some of their salary will go for costumes and other stage requirements, but
strippers generally do not dress or eat well. Some money is used in travel, and
some may be spent on child support (although this tends to be erratic, especially
when relatives are involved). Few girls utilize budgets and, overall, a considerable
amount of money is spent with little planning or in some cases is absorbed by
expensive habits (drinking, drugs). Some girls also work irregularly (usually by
choice), making any systematic accumulation of funds more problematic. Thus,
although part of the attraction of dancing reflects the money one earns, in few
instances do the dancers achieve financial success. The spending habits they
develop, however, along with the prospects of making good money, tend to keep
them dancing "just a little longer":

> *I really don't know what they do with all their money because they are making*
> *pretty good money and yet you find that after a number of years, 85% won't*
> *have anything to show for all the time they have been working. I'm not speaking*
> *of costumes, but rather having a home or having a car, having something more*
> *concrete, where you could see them making financial progress in their job.*
> *Plans, oh yeah, they have a lot of plans, but they don't seem to materialize.*
> *They run into this guy or that guy and you come back a couple of years later and*
> *they still have the same plans, but they haven't made any progress.* (agent)

> *Here, it's easy money and it goes easy. If I worked in a factory then I'd be penny*
> *pinching. You figure, twenty dollars it has to last you this long or that long. But*
> *when it comes this easy, then you figure you are entitled to this or that. When*
> *you make this sort of money, you figure, "I'm going to get this coat", or go*
> *here or there and you figure, "Well, why not? I'm not always going to be*
> *young."* (dancer)

Another related element, also promoting dependency on stripping, is the un-
willingness or inability of the dancers to seriously pursue other jobs:

> *I wouldn't be happy with another job, maybe being in the band wouldn't be*
> *so bad, but most other jobs, I wouldn't be happy there. I am basically a*
> *lazy person. This way, you only have to work 15 minutes every hour or hour*
> *and a half, it's not so bad. If I was just to quit and just keep house, I don't know*
> *what I would do with myself in all that time. Dancing gives me something to*
> *do too.* (dancer)

> *One of the saddest things to see is when the girls have gotten past their prime*
> *and they're sort of on the way out and yet they haven't put any money aside, or*
> *they haven't developed other talents. They keep scrounging for jobs and it*
> *becomes very difficult to place them. And it's hard for them to get out of it. I*
> *know girls who have sold all their costumes and then you see them and they are*
> *back again. Some of them have tried straight jobs, nine to five, and they just*

can't hack it. They miss the travel and they miss the people, and they miss the limelight. And they'll come back, and they'll buy costumes again, and there they are. . . . It's show business, and if you've done it long enough, that sort of gets into you and even if it's only stripping, when you've had that whiff of the stage and the applause, it stays with you. It's a very common thing for them to be hoping for their screen test, their big chance, that something nice will happen to them and they won't be stripping any longer, but I haven't heard of that happening to anybody that I know. (agent)

The following extract portrays in sequence the sorts of concerns affecting both disinvolvement from, and reinvolvement in, dancing:

Several times, I've tried to quit, leave the business. It's kind of hard to quit. Like after this bad experience with Sherman, I just couldn't take it anymore. I was scared to death. I was a nervous wreck. I called my parents up and told them I just had to come home, I couldn't take it anymore. That's the first time. And they were great about it. They sent me a bus ticket and money to get back home. So I worked in this donut place because my sister had worked there for a summer between college years. But I just had the manager in tears every day. I was always doing something wrong. I was not cut out to do that kind of work, and I hated it. It was just something to make money. . . . I was so confused when I went back home. And Sherman came back. He was going to turn himself in, so he came back to my home town, where I was staying with my parents, and he called me up and asked me to come out and see him and he was going to turn himself in. He did turn himself in, which got me started all over with him again, because I felt if he turned himself in he must really care. You know, that's a big thing for him. . . . Then Sherman got out because he turned his brother in and he made a deal to get out. I got dragged right down to the bottom of that. And we started living together. Then I went on the road. The first week he stayed home, then he came on the road with me. In March, I split up with him and went back to live with my parents and I got a job bookkeeping. I didn't hear from him, didn't call him or anything else. I stayed at home for six months, tried to do bookkeeping. I was getting into a new type of job, getting back to school a bit, taking courses at night. I made a big deal of throwing all my costumes out and my parents were sure that I was serious at the time. I was not going back into it. I was going to stay out of it. And then one of my friends called just to see how I was coming along, ''I'm so happy you got out of it.'' And she was, because she loves to dance, but she hates the life. She really hates it. She's married now, but she dances when the bills are too heavy. And she wanted me to come up to her house and visit. She came down to pick me up, but before we went up to her house she worked that night, so I went with her and I watched. I sat and watched, and started thinking, ''It would be so nice to get up there and do it again.'' And so I did, I got up and did this act. And everybody was clapping. And it hit me again, just like that! I can still remember saying to the owner, ''No I've got a good job, I'm not going to go back into dancing.'' This has security for me. If I break a leg, they'll still want me to do bookkeeping. If I break my leg, there's nobody to take care of me when I go into dancing. So I went back to bookkeeping, and I saved enough for a car. . . . Then, one day, I went to visit a friend and heard where Sherman was working and thought I'd go and see him, see if he had changed. I went and saw him again, and we decided that we were going to do everything right this time. I was going to go back and work at my bookkeeping job and he was going to continue working. He had another manager's job, believe it or not, in another bar, after all that trouble! He was saving some money. We both had nice cars, it was really nice, we both had improved so much since we had split up. And so I went back to my parents and I tried to work that week and I just couldn't hack the routine. The dancing was going through my head and seeing him again. At the end of the week I told my boss, "I don't think I'm going back on Monday. I've got to go back to my old boyfriend." I explained a little and said I've got to go. Then I drove back to Sherman and I called my parents the next morning, "Where are you? Are you all right? What happened to you? Where are you? You can't stay out all night like that." "I'm sorry, very much, and I really appreciate what you were trying to do for me, but I can't do it anymore. I've just changed too much to try and go back and live like that. I'm back with Sherman." As soon as I said, "Sherman," my mother started screaming and threw the phone on the floor. My little sister picked up the phone and said, "You can go to hell! You can just go to hell!" And that was the last I had talked to them until about a year later. I stayed with Sherman for about three days and I realized that he hadn't changed. It wouldn't work. Then, I went to stay with a friend of mine and she loaned me some of her costumes and I was back into it. (dancer)

OTHER ENTERTAINERS

As individuals, the dancers tend to live rather unsettled lives. Not only are they continuously faced with the problems of adjusting to new people and new places, but they lack the supporting cast that regular bar staff typically have behind them. Lest it be assumed, however, that these problems are unique to dancers, it may be instructive to briefly compare the situations in which dancers find themselves with those experienced by other entertainers, referring here to comedians, singers, and band musicians.[5]

Most entertainers anticipate success in show business:

Bobby Joe said that this place is kind of the stepping stone for him and for most people that work there. He says that even if you don't put on a terrific act you won't get fired, and you can also try out new material in this place. He said that sometimes the audience here is not so good, but he really enjoyed them when things clicked. . . . Bobby Joe has been expecting a call, supposed to be his big break. (notes)

When I finished high school, a guy gave me a chance to play in a band. At first, I was all impressed with this and I thought, "Oh wow, I got it made!" I was working in a bar, but after a few months I started to become quite disillusioned with that idea. I thought, "Once you got into a bar where they pay you money, you just have a few steps to go and that's big time." I remember the first night. I was very nervous and I expected to read about my performance in the newspaper, but then you start to realize that the newspaper doesn't carry stories

---

[5] Readers are also referred to Becker (1963) for some highly insightful material on the work styles and social networks of jazz musicians.

about Harry Schmoe and the dime tavern down the street, you only hear about the big times. It was also occurring to me that the people could dislike your show, that they could dislike what you're playing and how you played things. That was something I hadn't anticipated. The idea is that you have to sell yourself. But you have this idea, this myth, that musicians are above that and shouldn't have to go and sell yourself the same way that somebody selling brushes would. (musician)

A lot of musicians have that hope. I meet very few that don't. Like there's no other reason that they would be doing it, it's not worth it for the money they're getting paid. I know musicians that are living on $100 a week and they're putting up with so much. They'll be working six nights a week and then you usually don't sleep on Sunday because you're going to be driving, driving somewhere where your agent has sent you, and you get to see home five or six times a year for a couple of days, and you have to eat at restaurants and motels all the time, so you're living off hamburgers and fried onions, and it's not worth the money for sure. It's just the hope of actually doing something. Not that it gets any better, that's the crazy thing. (musician)

Like the dancers, the other entertainers face the problems of relating to and managing the audience, as well as maintaining enthusiasm in their performance in spite of minimal or critical audience response:

Another thing you'll notice is that sometimes there's nobody paying much attention. I'll either get bored or else I'll try to entertain myself and try some new things to help you keep going. . . . The problem is getting that sense of immediacy in your music. Sometimes the audience picks you up. Like this guy who was in last night singing along with us. Now he's very good. He came in this morning, still corked, but he sat down at the piano and played some of the hippest jazz around. In a way, that's kind of scarey for me to see, someone with all that talent just hangs around hotels and becomes a lush, because I'm not that set in my ways yet. I'm just young. I haven't been doing it long enough to find a nitch that I can settle into. I want to play and once the music gets in your blood it's difficult, almost impossible, to get away from it. So I know I want to do that, but then you wonder, "Well, will I end up like this guy, more successful, or like this guy, who's a loser?" (musician)

You also get some trouble from some of the bar regulars. If there are a couple there that don't like you, they may go to the management. Some places, he'll tell them, "Well, they'll be here all week and then they're going," or whatever, but other places, they'll come to you and say, "A couple of people don't like the way you did that song," or "They don't like the way you do country music," or whatever it is. (musician)

It's probably easier for a band to accept criticism from an audience than dancers. . . . There's also power in numbers and also you've got a microphone, so you can be really nasty right back at them. I don't really know much about dancers, but I can see how if you're hiding behind your piano, you can sit there and it's easier. But if you're just standing there with half your clothes off, there's not much you can really do. (musician)

Other audience-related problems revolve around intimacy and distancing. Most entertainers find it difficult to maintain desired "public-private self" distinctions, and achieve comfortable levels of closeness with persons of the opposite sex:

When you're on stage you entertain people, you joke with them. I'm an entertainer, not a jazz musician. If I was a jazz musician, I would just tell them, "Fuck you! Sit down or leave." But here, it's a different kind of situation and yet you'll find people approaching you afterwards. They want to buy you a drink or they'll come banging on your door at 2 o'clock in the morning or something, and you have to tell them, "Look, I'm an entertainer when I'm there. When I'm not, I'm me and I'm not entertaining 24 hours a day." But it's the same with the women, they think you should be the same way off stage as you are when you're on the stage. When you're on the stage and you're trying to entertain them. They make a line, "What is that? A machine gun or a guitar? Ha ha ha." "Where's your fedora? Ha ha ha." You're there, "That's funny." You have to compromise with the people because that's what sells, otherwise I won't be working. (musician)

I found that it was difficult for me to relate to girls, because before, you would get to know a girl a fair bit before you would have sex with them. Now you would say, "Well, I am only going to be here for a week or two weeks," and you would think in terms of those very short relationships. So you would have these one night stands, that you really don't know the people. And you realize also that the relationships are not because of you, but because of what you do, that you're an entertainer. At first I thought, "Wow, this is really great!", but after it just seemed like it was much too superficial. Some woman takes you home and goes to bed with you because you're a musician and then in the morning, "Well, what's your name?" and, "See you around one of these days." (musician)

It's a game I play because I'm an entertainer. I'm really close inside, but I know all the right lines to say, it's a matter of the right lines. I can be whatever I want. I come in a new club, nobody's ever seen me before, I can be whatever person I decide I want to be. And I have a pseudonym, I don't go under my real name a lot of the times. I make up names wherever I go, I play at being whatever I want to be, I do whatever I want. And yet it's very perverse in a lot of other ways because I'm losing myself, losing my own self-identity and playing roles. Like every night, it doesn't matter how I feel, my job as a professional entertainer is to be happy and be cheerful and get up there and please those people. I've got to sing it because those people, they're paying my salary. And whether I feel like a piece of shit, or I don't, or I feel great, I still have to get up there and put out, because I'm getting paid money by the hotel manager and those people are paying me. And every night, six nights a week, no matter where I am, no matter what I'm doing, I have to be up every night. (musician)

By no means is the similarity between dancers and other entertainers limited to stage performances and audience receptivity. Hotel life, and the mobility their work entails tends to color the experiences and images of all entertainers:

At one point I was on the road with the band for five weeks straight without a break, because we'd been working six nights a week and Sunday you'd get in

*the car and drive off to the next place so you really didn't have a break. . . .
And some of the groups that you might be playing after, they might not be very
responsible people. Like a lot of the rock bands, following after them, if you
get the same suite or rooms, the place is often a real mess. They'll mess up
the furniture and the pictures and a lot of places they'll only let the bands stay in
the basement rooms, or sometimes in a lot of the better hotels, they won't even
let the band stay in that hotel. They have to stay in another motel where the
management pay for the rooms in these other motels for them. It's that bad. It
doesn't take too many, one or two bands can ruin it for the rest of them.*
(musician)

*Probably the most difficult thing for me was being alone. Being by yourself, and
knowing that you are by yourself. Now, I am very used to being alone, and I feel
more comfortable alone than I do with people. Another thing about being a
musician is that you will spend a lot of time alone just practising, I mean if you
are serious about it. . . . So, you will have a lot of people around you, but there
is nobody that you feel close to. I spend a lot of time feeling kind of despondent
and just walking around, reading papers, and such things.* (musician)

Just like the dancers, these entertainers also find that fitting into the hotel
community is a more totally involving experience than they originally anticipated.
Not only are they likely to encounter extensive variations in the expectations the
management holds for them, but they are likely to find that the hours and other
conditions of their work setting facilitate more extensive participation in other
bar-related activities:

*You get to know the people in the bar very quickly. Yeah, you get to know the
staff and also the regulars fairly easily, especially in the smaller bars. . . . It
varies a lot with the management. Like some places, they're, "Hello, how are
you? If you need anything let us know," and it's really nice to work in that sort
of atmosphere. Other places, they'll say, "Well, we want you to do this, this,
and this, and these are the rules, and don't do this and don't do that," and
already they've created a barrier between you and them. . . . But, with the
management, there's one thing that tells them whether or not you're good and
that's the "ding ding" of the cash register. Their business is to sell booze and if
you're selling booze, well then, "You're good!", and they're happy with you
and if you're not, then they're going to be looking for somebody else to come in.
Like they won't think of it in terms of how the bar's being run, but in terms of,
"Is the band bringing in the customers or not?"* (musician)

*Whenever I go into a club, the first thing I do is I try to get friendly with the
manager. You have to. It's a must. If you don't get along with the manager,
forget it. And after that, it's trying to keep the staff happy too, because you've
got to be there with them every night. Say if you do an encore for a night, and if
you're kind of late, well they won't mind slipping you a beer. It's against the
law, but they'll sort of pretend they had that out before. You're doing a job for
them and they'll do a job for you. You've got to work together. And like some
places, the staff isn't happy, it rubs off. . . . Generally Monday is the worst
day, because Monday there isn't a crowd, like it's a lot easier for musicians to
play to people, rather than playing to four people in a lot of empty rooms.
Monday night also, the manager's looking at you, going, "Well, who did I get*

this week?'' He's sort of watching you, seeing what you're doing. And Monday night, you've just set up, usually the band isn't very sharp, because they haven't slept and they haven't eaten properly, or they haven't had time to take a shower. Just set up their equipment and they're pretty groggy. Monday night I would say is the hardest. (musician)

Most of my post-educated life has been spent in taverns, either as a bar fly, either as a person that's sitting in bars, watching entertainers so I could pick up what they're doing, talking to entertainers, or entertaining myself. If I have more time, where do I go? I go to a bar. If I go on holidays, I don't go skiing, I go to the bar, go sit in the bloody bar. What do I do? I go talk to the regulars, I go sit in the bar. I'm a bar person. I live there, I study it, it's my whole life. And if I don't do a good job of knowing the bar, I can't make a living. Like I hope not to be in a bar all my life, I'd like to get out of it, to try something else, but right now, like I can see a few more years ahead of me, just in bar rooms. I'm getting an understanding of it. Like I even get to believe my songs, I can get to believe ''The Girls All Get Prettier At Closing Time.'' I even do it myself, if I'm stuck in a hotel room and a bar far away, and my woman's not there with me and some broad's over there, and, ''Let's go,'' ''Hey honey, you want to go for a drink. Come rub my back.'' (musician)

Entertainers find themselves coming to terms with other aspects of bar life, such as violence, prostitution, and drinking. And, like the dancers, the musicians usually try to avoid physical confrontations lest these result in personal injury or damage to their equipment:

If there's a fight in the bar, basically you try to remain away from it because you don't want to get messed up in any way. Occasionally you'll find yourself helping to break up something, maybe helping to quiet somebody down, but it's not like it's your bar so if something does happen, you sort of look for a back way out. (musician)

While relatively few of the bars in which the musicians work are ''hooker bars,'' they are also likely to have some contact with the working girls or those interested in their services:

I've run across hookers at a few bars where I've worked. One of the ways you can tell is their dress, or the way that they walk through the bar, but another one of the ways I sort of pick them out is if they go to the bar alone, because I've found it's very unusual for girls to go to the bar by themselves. Usually they have another girl with them. . . . I think bar managers are absolutely stupid if they throw the hookers out of the bar, because it's so good for business. They have to be able to keep it looking not obvious, but guys'll be looking for hookers all the time. . . . A lot of times you'll have guys coming up to you because they figure, well, if you're an entertainer in a bar, then you should know what's happening. And a lot of times you do. They'll come up to you, ''Hey, where can you find some action?'' and so you maybe direct them towards a couple of girls you think might be doing business. (musician)

Drinking represents an ''occupational hazard'' for most entertainers:

I get sometimes caught in a web of alcohol, being around alcohol all the time. Even if I don't want to drink, somebody's always going to buy you a beer, and if you say, "No," that's insulting them, because you've pleased them and their way of paying you back is buying you a beer. And if you don't accept the beer, it's like a slap in the face to them. And you're also turning business away from the club owner, and what you're trying to do is get business. To not accept it, it's like cutting your own throat. So I just have to put up with it, let's say. And sometimes I say, "Monday, I'm not going to have a beer," and everyday, like I may have four or five beers. It may not be that much, but I wonder what's going to happen to me after. . . . So I get worried about it sometimes. But then when a guy turns to me and says, "You won't take my beer, how dare you?" So I'll say, "Glass of draft." (musician)

Everybody falls in love with Edna, she's a good-looking girl. All the guys are always falling in love with her and buying her drinks. She's sitting up there at the piano, she's smiling and talking to everybody, and she has all these people drooling, and they buy her drinks and they line them up on the piano. She gets very tipsy by the end of the night. . . . People will be buying her drinks all night and she feels obliged to drink them, and as a result she'd be weaving back and forth, knocking her tooth on the microphone and dropping her tambourine, but she tries not to do that. Well, it's one of those things, when you work in a bar and people buy you drinks. (musician)

Although the band entertainers' lives are apt to be less complicated than those of the dancers, their lives are strikingly parallel. One gains a further sense of their affinity from the ways in which they associate with one another:

You run into strippers some places that you work. Usually what happens is that they'll be working in the afternoons and you'll be working in the evenings and you don't have that much to do with them. Perhaps you become good friends, because you do have things in common, both working in the entertainment business and discussing the audience or why there aren't more people there and things like that. . . . You will get the occasional guy in the band who says, "Wow, a stripper, got to make out with her," but you get used to them and become more or less friends over that week. You might be down between her shows, maybe have a drink with her in the afternoon, or invite her to your show in the evening, or she might be by and you start talking. Mostly you sort of think of her as one of the guys. (musician)

I had some difficulty carrying on a sustained conversation with Linda Lou. Her boyfriend, a musician, kept wanting to keep her alone with him, resulting in a somewhat abbreviated interview. Apparently they met when they were working at two bars across the street from one another. He came over and they started talking. They indicated that they could understand a lot of one another's life-style, whereas they thought that outsiders couldn't. She tries to work in the same town, but they're not always successful. . . . (notes)

There are, of course, some differences among dancers and musicians, and especially noteworthy is the concern on the part of bands to present a synchronized group act:

When you work as a jobbing musician, what you end up doing is building up a basic stock of tunes, so that when you play with different people, you may not have played with them before, but you'll have things that you can play with them in common. (musician)

That's a place we're different. Few dancers have co-ordinated routines. It's pretty well all solos. . . . Some places, they'll have three or four girls dancing at once, but in different parts of the bar, where they can do their own thing. A little view for everybody, but mostly, it's one girl at a time. She does her thing, and then it's either another dancer following her, or in a smaller place, there's nobody for forty minutes or so, and then she's back again. (dancer)

"Community ties" among group entertainers are also likely to be stronger and more extensive than those the dancers experience. The "groupness" aspect of band entertainment not only provides immediate support for these performers within the hotel setting, but also fosters contacts across groups and performers:

You're very much aware of other groups in town. Like, if we have time, we'll go over and hear a group, like a new group or maybe one that's breaking up. You or somebody in the group often knows somebody in the other group, and you'll get talking to them or sometimes you just introduce yourselves. (musician)

Bands, musicians, they're a whole little community to themselves. Most musicians who've been playing professionally for a number of years, know each other around the area. If they don't, they all know somebody. Like they've all played with somebody before, and because bands break up so often and re-form, they play with people who are playing with other people. . . . And they've all got reputations. Some people, everybody just knows, it's like the best bass player in Eastville, and he's got quite a reputation, and the best guitarist, then there's other people, song writers. I don't think this reputation thing goes outside of music. If you're a good musician, not many people care whether you're a nice guy or an asshole. Not many people will say, "That guy is really a terrible person," or, "That guy beats his wife," or "That guy kicks his dog out at night." The only reputation that really spreads around is talentwise. . . . You might learn a little about his reliability or drinking habits, but it's generally the leader that really has to worry about those kind of things. . . . Most musicians are very forgiving in that way. If he could actually get up there and play, then it wouldn't bother them. (musician)

Other hotel entertainers are also apt to share with the dancers a sense of disrespectability that pervades the hotel community more generally:

Respectability is quite a problem. First of all, there's very little status for musicians. Often the bar people, or the management, they even think, "Oh, it's just a band. Stick them in a little hut somewhere outside of town,". . . . With the family, relatives, most people, "Well, he's going through a stage. Soon he'll be out of it, soon he'll settle down and get a respectable job." I suppose you get to a point, when you get to be about 30, your parents start to realize that you're in this pretty much for good, and so they accept it, most times. A lot of parents don't really know anything about music, professional bands or whatever, so they don't really understand what their son or daughter is doing. (musician)

My father's a dentist and my mother's a psychologist. It's pretty difficult for them to accept the idea of me working in bars and saloons and strip joints. They say, well, "I've worked hard, tried to make something of you and you've become a musician," so it is a problem there. But it's more general. I find that people have these stereotypes. A musician is a drifter, he's having a good time all the time, a real party goer. Someone who's into sex and booze all the time and has a way with the women, and leads such an easy life. They'll say, "Well, look, you just play for a couple of hours a day and look at all the money you make, and you get to stay in hotels, and all the girls are running after you." They should live in some of these places that I've stayed, sort of a hole in the wall, raunchy places. But that's the stereotype.

Finally, most entertainers (musicians, comedians, dancers) find that disinvolvement is not as simple as it might appear:

Oh yeah, a couple of times I've thought of quitting, but then, there are times when I've made great decisions, like, "I'm never going to do that again. Awful, stupid job," or whatever, but then I'll know it's just a matter of time before I get in with another band. Right now, I've got this duo thing, but I sort of hope that these people get into a band again, because I'd like to work with them. But I know that I'll be doing this again and probably for an awful long time. I like it and I hate it. . . . I guess the same is true with strippers. Like we got paid on Saturday night and they paid the strippers at the same time. . . . I can see how it would be difficult to turn that down to work as a secretary with a boss that yells at you and you take home like a $200 pay cheque, I can see how it would be difficult to get out of that when you're in it. . . . Something else they'd miss is the show biz thing. There's something about being on stage. (musician)

Unlike the regular bar staff and the management, who are apt to view their bar as "special," the jobbing entertainers view each new place as another spot to work and live out part of their lives:

One thing I found, when I work lounges, your higher class lounges, with the doctors, lawyers, the cheating crowd. I found their tastes and their class, even though they were drinking Regal rather than bar scotch, they're basically the same people, except that they have a higher bank roll, they pretend more. There are more games. I prefer the down-and-outer bars because there people say, "Fuck," and they call a spade a spade, and they call a nigger a nigger. (musician)

After a while, the bars, the patrons, they all look the same. The bars always look the same to me, generally the same. What makes a difference is whether the patrons took to the band or not. If they like you, it's a better week. If not, we just try to ignore them. We play for ourselves. (musician)

While their individual stays within particular bars are generally short-lived, collectively the entertainers shape ongoing group life and provide diversion and meaning in the lives of those with whom they have contact. In subsequent chapters, as we examine the "work world" of the staff and the "recreational world" of the patrons, yet other aspects of the entertainers' links to the hotel community will become evident.

Chapter 5

Working the Bar

Having considered the activities of hookers, desk clerks, and entertainers, the focus now shifts to the staff, looking at their work roles, their relationships with hookers and strippers, and how they fit in the hotel community more generally. Especially noteworthy are the ways in which the bar staff work out activities in conjunction with one another in both short-run (for instance, hustles, handling disruptions) and long-run (such as, career contingencies, maintenance of community) instances. In depicting the relations of staff with one another and with the patrons, it is suggested that the activities of the staff are of paramount importance in creating and maintaining the hotel community.

In order to ascertain the representativeness of staff work beyond that encountered in hooker bars, we talked with staff people from a wide variety of bars, ranging from some of the most prestigious bars in the area to bars considerably rougher than Main and Central. As the following considerations of "providing service," "managing customers," "fitting into the staff community," and "continuity in bar work" suggest, bar work is a great deal more similar across bars than one might infer from the decor or the entertainment.

PROVIDING SERVICE

When discussing bar work, it is first important to note the relatively easy transition of persons from one staff-role to another. Thus, although the positions of bar staff persons seem readily distinguishable at any given point in time, many people have held a variety of positions in the bar or hotel more generally, at various times in their careers. A "bouncer" may have been a barboy, a waiter, and an assistant manager. A "waiter" may have been a bartender, a desk clerk, and a janitor. Further, as these transitions may occur overnight, or within the same shift, depending on staff fluctuations and work demands, it would be misleading to present an analytical discussion exclusively based on "occupational categories." While the various bar positions make somewhat different demands on the involved actors and may offer differential opportunities for hustles and the like, the more general notion of "staff people" is the more feasible concept. Accordingly, in developing this discussion, we will be sensitive to both positional and generic aspects of bar work. Thus, while we begin with a discussion of service, tips, and hustles as these pertain to bartenders, waiters, and waitresses, it will become apparent that there is much more to bar work than the serving of liquor.

TENDING BAR

Allegedly skilled in mixing drinks and controlling access to hard liquor (and frequently beer as well), the bartender is a central figure among the bar staff. Given his position as the "banker" in the bar, he also tends to have more responsibility than other staff people. Practices vary across bars, but two bartending roles are noteworthy. "Service bartenders" spend most of their time mixing drinks for the waiters and waitresses, while "stool bartenders" mainly serve the patrons seated at the bar. The job activities of the service and stool bartenders at times overlap, however, and distinctions often become blurred, particularly in small bars or on those occasions when only one bartender is on duty. In general, stool bartenders have much greater contact with the patrons and are expected to be more sociable than either the service bartenders or the waiters:

> *Felix was saying that being a stool bartender was different than being a waiter since the bartender made his tips by talking to people whereas the waiter pushed liquor and did very little talking. He also added that it was a more difficult job and required more finesse.* (notes)

Regardless of whether he works the service bar or the stool bar, the bartender also has the task of maintaining service under pressure:

> *You're serving people, serving the waiters, serving the customers. . . . You have customers coming to the bar and you give them what they want. The waiters come up to the service bar and you serve them. . . . it gets more difficult when it gets busy. You've got a certain number of people that expect a little more of you than what you can give. You get all of these people around, "Let's have it over here," "Let's have it over here." I worked at places myself, without another bartender on a busy night, without even a barboy. It's hell. You run back and forth, you don't know where you're going. You lose a lot of money that way, the hotel loses a lot of money that way. They have got you running your ass off. They say, "Come on, these people want this." Then you say, "Hang on!" I used to get uptight sometimes, get really mad. That is why you get mad at customers. I think everybody hates that. And if the guy doesn't get served, ten or fifteen minutes go by and he walks out.* (bartender)

While typically paid an hourly wage, tips and hustles represent a significant aspect of the bartender's take-home pay. A stool bartender will be tipped for service, friendliness, and the like, but he may also implement measures intended to promote further generosity on part of the patrons:

> *Lucky came in and ordered a Coke. I gave him one free and he left me a dollar tip. . . . Beyond the tipping thing, it's very easy to sell sodas to customers and pocket the money. Pop is not metered so they really can't keep track of it.* (notes)

Service bartenders are also likely to receive tips, but these come from the other staff whom they serve. These bartenders usually are given 10% (sometimes 20%) of the tips waiters and waitresses report receiving.

Having access to the liquor, bartenders also have opportunities to engage in some position-specific hustles:

Greg said that when you are mixing many drinks such as Johnny Walker and Coke or another kind of brand name liquor and a soft drink, you typically put the cheapest kind of liquor and charge the higher price. He also said that when preparing cocktail drinks such as Tequilla Sunrise, Singapore Slings, or Zombies, which have a great deal of soda drink and fruit juices in them, you can cut short on the liquor and thus have a surplus of liquor over the evening. He said when someone comes in and orders a Singapore Sling or a Zombie that just sort of tells him that this person is a real sucker. The surplus can be sold without ringing up the cash, so this won't show up in the percentage. He also said that you can also shortchange customers and that people may leave some money on the bar and different times you can pick it up as if it were a tip. You might also drain some liquor off a new bottle and pour some water back in and mix it — cutting it with water. That way, you gain an ounce here and there. (notes)

There's great ways of stealing, I'll tell you. Like I might steal forty or fifty bucks a night. A lot of times, it is just flat out stealing, that's all. You pour a shot and you put the bread in your pocket. Free pouring, right out of the bottle, right, it's great. Say you get somebody sitting down and they'll drink and drink, a lot of times you don't pour an ounce. You got friends coming in, you pour an ounce and a half, or maybe you give them a shot on the house. Otherwise you just pocket the money. I've walked out of there nights with over a hundred bucks, and nobody knew it. (bartender)

When you're keeping tabs and the person has had 4 or 5 drinks and is buying more, it's easy to add another drink on his tab without him becoming suspicious. (bartender)

Barboys

As the bartender's assistant, the barboy's position requires little expertise and typically no prior experience is required to obtain this job. As such, it should be noted that this position not only facilitates entry into other staff positions, such as waiting on tables and tending bar, but as he spends more time in the bar, he is apt to be considered "regular staff" and will likely become more immersed in the hotel community.

Seldom serving patrons directly, the barboy's hustling opportunities are restricted. His major supplementary income comes from tips received from other staff people:

The barboy usually gets tipped by the waiters at the end of the evening. They will often give him a couple of dollars apiece. All the barboy gets is the basic salary. He wouldn't get any tips from the bar and this is where the waiters pay him for helping them with the service. (barboy)

WAITING ON TABLES

Regardless of whether one is discussing waiters or waitresses, their duties are fairly standard across bars: on being assigned a "station" (a designated area of tables or booths), waiters/waitresses are expected to take and deliver patrons' orders in a somewhat efficient manner, keep tables and ashtrays free from clutter, promote business, and ensure that the customers' behavior is acceptable within the bar setting. Their ability to perform these tasks requires manual dexterity, short-term memory, and social skills. While outsiders frequently assume that "anyone could wait on tables," other staff people and management appreciate experienced personnel. In addition to coming to terms with the physical aspects of bar work (walking in crowded spaces, balancing trays, and so on) bar staff must possess a basic knowledge of alcoholic beverages and some social skills as well:

It's the kind of thing that most people can't do. They really can't. It takes a certain person to be a waitress. . . . You always have to be pleasant, no matter what is happening in your own life, you always have to be pleasant and courteous. You have to always be alert and knowing what you're doing all the time, because you're handling money constantly. And you're giving the customers the impression of the establishment that they're in. Not only the walls and what the place looks like, but by the kind of service they get and how pleasant the people are that work within the establishment. . . . Everybody has their bad days occasionally. But you have to put on a face or a facade when you're serving the tables. . . . There's much more involved than just serving drinks and taking orders. . . . And you can't be stupid, because if you forget your orders or forget what you're doing, you're not giving good service. (waitress)

As bar work is often dependent on teamwork, staff members failing to maintain desired levels of competence in the execution of their duties will encounter criticism from their co-workers as well as from the management:

This one girl is very slow, she's always very chatty and very stupid, so when she's emptying her tray, if you're caught behind her, you end up shoving her aside and say, "Here, let me do it quickly, while you just take your time." And when she's up at the bar ordering, she's always going, "Er, well, I'll have, er, 2 Singapore Slings, 1 draft, 2 rye," she's going on, and you're going, "Oh, God!" And the bartenders hate it and you hate it, and the bartender likes to go, "snap, snap, snap," and the same thing with the cashier. The cashier likes to hear it snapped off, like "2 draft, 2 shots, 1 mix." That's how they want to hear it, and if you go, "2 draft; no, 3 draft; no, 5 draft," or when you're getting change from the cashier, you're going, "Well, give me two 2's, three 1's," and whatever else might happen, and you're going, "No, give me. . . ." They're going to wipe out. (waitress)

While some skills reflect direct tutelage, much of the learning comes about incidentally, as the novice observes and interacts with more experienced bar workers. It should also be noted that in waiting on tables, staff people may not only work for the bar, but also for themselves, in terms of facilitating work routines, avoiding fatigue, promoting tips, and capitalizing on hustles:

After working as a waiter for a while I found out that I save myself time and effort by making tables pay in rounds rather than have each person pay separately. When I brought the drinks over to the table I'd say, "This is all together, right?" and usually the people would look at each other and someone would say, "Yeah, this round is on me." Once you do that, those people will probably pay in rounds for the rest of the night. (notes)

Here we get paid, like minimum wage, so that's nothing, right? So, it's up to you, how much you can make in other ways, through tips or like these little hustles I was telling you about. Tips and hustles, that's where the real money is. (waiter)

Tips

While persons working in some bars will be tipped better than others, seemingly regardless of the service they provide, attempts on the part of the staff to promote tips are very commonplace, particularly among regular bar staff. Newcomers often seem unaware of their ability to "shoot up the tips," but long-term workers are apt to be very tip conscious and orient their service accordingly:

When I started, I didn't really understand what all was involved in barwork. This owner was really helpful in telling me, well, how to make money in a sense. "You have to hustle drinks, you have to be friendly," and she said, "Don't worry about being too friendly with people, because that's what makes the money. You can't make it otherwise. . . ." You have to be able to just hustle a little bit, and learn little tricks of the trade, like when you're giving back the money, do it very slowly, you put the bills down and slowly count the change. (waitress)

Generally speaking, tipping practices in bars tend to be preferentially skewed in the direction of the waitresses, who may find that "looking good," is both an advantage and an inconvenience. Representing elements of entertainment, romance, or merely diversity in a more extensively male populated bar, waitresses are particularly advantaged in dealing with male customers. Wearing "provocative attire," (of which the girls may or may not personally approve), and appearing to be interested in the customers through sexual bantering or flirting can further promote tips:

To get bigger tips, you have to be polite and it's useful if you joke around with the people as well. If you have a pleasant disposition and you like your job, that will help out as well. It's also good if you wear low cut dresses and short skirts, so you look sexy. That helps in tips. Flirting with customers also helps. (waitress)

While promoting tips by appearing to be friendly, the waitress may find that customers demand more attention or take more liberties with her than she considers appropriate. Although any waitress may encounter difficulties with patrons, "topless waitresses" are particularly likely to have difficulties managing males in the bar:

Melissa said that she was becoming very upset with all the "come-ons" she was getting. "As soon as I get in to work, everybody is trying to get into my pants. The customers, the management, the staff, everybody. . . ." Melissa says that she is occasionally grabbed when she is serving tables, but usually tries to ignore it. . . . Wanda, however, is much more vocal, "Get your fucking hands off me!" She has hit customers who get a little fresh with her. (notes)

Lacking the "sex appeal" of the waitresses, and often sensing a greater need for money, it is instructive to examine some of the ways in which waiters may pursue tips:

They're expecting tips. These guys do expect it. They'll wait. They'll go up to you, they'll drop your change and then they'll wait around. They'll stand right in front of you with the tray down here. So you've more or less gotta give him something. This guy wants it, right! I've seen these guys, like if somebody leaves a nickel or something, these guys will get up and literally throw it at them on the way out. Clyde will do it, "Hey, you son of a bitch, cocksucker, you left your nickel here." He will chase the guy right out the door. The guy feels like shit going out. Here's a waiter chasing you out because you didn't tip him. . . . The waiter expects a tip, especially down there. You don't tip, you don't get served. That's the way it goes. Like Clyde, if somebody doesn't tip him the first time he serves them, he don't serve them no more. If the guy goes to another section, Clyde will just pass on to Ray, "Don't serve him, he doesn't tip." So the waiters are not going to go over, and after sitting there, waiting ten or fifteen minutes, the guy walks out. What are you going to do? Walk up to the waiters and say, "Where's the boss?" The waiter's going to say, "He ain't in. Speak to me." That's it! (bartender)

After I serve a person, I usually stand around, waiting for him to tip me. Even if he did not intend to tip me, this often makes him feel awkward and embarrassed, to where he ends up tipping me. (waiter)

If someone orders drinks and the change could be given in bills only, it is a good idea to break one of the bills into change as you give it to him. Some people might not tip you a buck, but they may be good for 50 cents if they have a dollar in quarters. (waiter)

Staff people will occasionally encounter patrons who, regardless of the service offered, seem likely to either tip very little or not at all. Although female customers appear particularly problematic in this regard, other patrons such as regulars, or friends of management can also be sources of tip concerns. While most staff persons seem more or less to accept this state of affairs and continue to serve these patrons, other bar staff will confront them, occasionally "intimidating" these persons into tipping more generously:

If you get a table of people that haven't tipped at all, they're really rude, they demand instant service, you have a tendency to forget that table, because you find them really obnoxious. And I've told people, "Don't mind if I don't come around for another hour, because you won't see me for an hour," and they'll look and say, "Why?" and I'll say, "Well, I don't think you guys deserve service any faster than in an hour," and I've given them shit. You have to let them know that it's a good policy to tip. (waitress)

Say you've got a table that's not drinking, where you're not making your tips, you get rid of them. Maybe they'll be up dancing and you just clear off the table and get somebody else down there. If there's any trouble, you've got the doorman, right? Sometimes, you'll just tell them, "I'm sorry, but you're not drinking, I'll have to ask you to leave. That's what we're here for, you know." (waitress)

Pushing Drinks

While it may also be viewed as a "hustle," a noteworthy strategy for increasing tips in many other bars is that of "pushing drinks." Assuming that tips increase with the volume of liquor sold, many staff people have developed a variety of techniques to encourage patrons to increase their liquor consumption. While some staff will bring unrequested drinks to patrons, others will attempt to persuade patrons into purchasing additional rounds and staying longer than anticipated:

> *I'm a hustler, but I don't rip people off for their drinks. I make my money on volume and so, if you sell, for example, $400 then you should be getting at least 10% or say $40 in tips at the end of the evening. Unlike the waitresses, who make a lot of money just with their tits, I have to move around and volume is a big thing. . . . I can't rip off the customers because here I'm too dependent on the regulars. We don't have much of a tourist trade and so if it gets known that you're stealing from the people, then it's going to be really hard to make money here. And I can make good money as a waiter. Now you take Vanessa over there, she doesn't work anywhere near as hard as I do, and you saw how when she came to the table she really didn't push drinks. Well, I have to do that, because that's where my money is, it's in the volume. . . . Friendliness, that's a big thing too, both in terms of getting tips, and pushing drinks, like call people. "Sir," and I try to get along with them. If you see someone who's lonely, maybe you talk to them a little more. But I'm always friendly and I find that when I'm walking around, when I'm at work, maybe things are bothering me, but at the same time, I have to try and put on that front for the people. . . . In terms of pushing drinks, say somebody's sitting there with half a glass of beer, I'll take the bottle and pour the rest into the glass to where it's the same amount of beer, but it looks as if there isn't much left. Also, I really won't wait around for people to order so much. I'll take more initiative in delivering drinks to them, but, of course, you have to be careful that you don't seem pushy. That's the real secret to it. You want to appear efficient and you're trying to help them out, but you really can't appear too pushy. Also, if there's a bottle around, I'll pick that up, just where you're always sort of clearing the table away and you're always around, and you ask them, "Can I get them this or that." And it also helps if you remember what they drink. They sort of notice that, "Hey, he remembered what I'm drinking." It seems to make them feel more important. . . . Another thing, if you buy them a free round of drinks and there you'd be surprised how people start to show their gratitude after that and will start to leave you larger tips. . . . So, if you're a male you have to work harder to make the same amount of money as a woman. That is unless, of course, you're ripping people off, and even there you find that it's easier for the girls to get away with, say, overcharging people with a round of drinks, than it is for a guy. And the people, the men, they will accuse you rather than accuse some girl. A girl can get away with a lot more because they figure that you're the one who has to beat them for the money. She just made a mistake, right?* (waiter)

> *The amount of liquor people drink, that can make or break you. You've got a lot of influence on people, on how much they drink and how much of a good time they have. A lot more than most people would think. Because I know when I'm in a bad mood, pushing has gone down to nil, and I don't hustle for booze, I just sort of ignore them, and it sort of generates that same attitude to the crowd, like, "Well, I think we might have a good time, but maybe not," and "I don't think I'll drink that much." But if you're really going, if you're really happy, you're swinging, moving around with the tray, and you're walking up to*

*everybody saying, "Hi," you can con them into drinking so much, just your
whole attitude.* (waitress)

Hustles

In contrast to the preceding material on "promoting tips" and "pushing drinks,"
the following extract denotes more direct versions of "theft":

> *At the bar, the hookers had to order doubles and it had to be a cocktail, like
> Scarlet O'Hara, Grasshopper, some kind of cocktail. So a waiter would walk
> up and order a double Singapore Sling, so you would give it to him and he
> would walk over and put it on the girl's table, that's $4.00. Now if this girl
> happened to get picked up in a few minutes or even if she just lets it sit there,
> they are not going to gun a drink down or they will have to order another
> double. So they will often just let it sit there and if they happen to get picked up,
> the drink would still be there. Then the waiter would walk by and pick it up, as if
> he was going to drop it in the sink or throw it away. Instead, he would put it
> under the bar and take the ice out. Then if somebody ordered a Singapore Sling
> again, whether a girl ordered another double or some customer orders one, the
> waiter will just throw a little ice in, sweeten it up and give it back. You can see
> one drink go around ten times, fifteen times. . . . These waiters have these
> service bars, and they've got their own bar. They may have Martinis, Black
> Russians, whatever. They just take the ice out and if somebody sits down and
> says, "I'll have a Black Russian," and they've got one there, they just throw
> some ice in and, "There, a Black Russian." . . . . There were four waiters and
> they would buy drinks off each other, "You got a Martini there? I'll pay you for
> that." Then he'd take it and sell it as a double. He just bought it off this other
> waiter as a single, "Here is a buck for yourself." They just do it as many times
> as possible. . . . That was where I got a lot of shit, from working there, right? I
> let them do it, where I shouldn't have let them do it. I should have told, but if I
> told the boss, I would have been in shit with all the waiters, and I have to work
> with the waiters rather than the boss!. . . . The waiters always hated to see the
> owner there. Everybody has to be on the cool, walking around doing their job.
> You would yell at somebody and say, "Sit down there, come on now," making it
> look totally unreal. The owner doesn't know what is going on, "Nice night, eh?
> Looks busy." No money coming in. All these waiters make $100-$120 a night,
> something like that. Which is a hell of a lot of money to make. One waiter, I was
> at his place on Sunday and he was adding up what he made all week, $840. He
> made $840, that is without his pay, right? "Oh yeah, then I got paid." . . . . A
> waiter's pay isn't very much anyhow, minimum wage, right? $840, that's a hell
> of a lot of money for a waiter to make, in a dingy hotel. . . . You go over to
> Central, they also make minimum wage and one of the waiters drives around in
> a new Cadillac. . . . I don't know what his home looks like, but when I last saw
> him, he had just gotten back from two weeks in Bermuda.* (bartender)

Many of the hustles may be employed by either waiters or waitresses. Generally
speaking, the waitresses tend to fare better on tips alone, and so feel less compelled
to hustle in other ways. It should not be assumed, however, that waitresses do not
hustle the patrons:

> *With a group of people, if they're buying drinks in rounds, you might charge*

them a dollar or two more than the cost of their order. Anything more gets a little risky, but you can usually get away with that. (waitress)

You can serve bar liquor when someone orders a special liquor and pocket the difference. The customers can't tell the difference anyway. (waitress)

Some of these hustles work better for larger, tougher looking waiters than for smaller persons. However, as long as one assumes the backing of the other staff people, the effects of physical prowess diminish:

Say a guy drops a twenty, the waiter steps on it. The guy says, "I just gave you a twenty." "No, you didn't!" If they had a chance to grab a buck, they would take it and would get it. I have seen them put their foot on it, then bend over to tie his shoe and take the twenty. . . . or, if the guy had given him some money, he might give him change for the wrong bill. If they see a guy drunk or something, there they go, they'll take their chance. Like many times the manager has been called over by a customer and he says, "This guy ripped me off." The manager always says, "Well, I work with him, I know him." He always does this. The waiter is protected in some way. Nobody really worries about, "Gee, what is a customer going to say?" If he did make a fuss, the waiter is going to punch him out! . . . Central is about the same, they have other little ways too. Say a guy goes to get a girl. He orders a shot and the girl orders a shot too. He may get his rye and coke, but the waiter may bring a shot glass with ginger ale in it for the girl. The waiter will just walk up and dump it in her glass himself. Or if she orders a vodka, then it's just water, that's all. That place is similar. (bartender)

Sometimes, when you are giving change for a twenty, you give back let's say, change amounting to $10, telling the guy that you have to get more change at the bar. Then you hang around the bar, or if it's busy, you wait on tables. If they're drinking, they'll often forget about it. If there is any trouble, you call the bouncer or the manager, and they will usually stand behind you. (waitress)

Dick, a barboy at Central, was saying that the waiters there frequently short-change the customers and straight out steal from them as well. And, he said, "Who would challenge them? The waiters stand behind one another. . . . It's a real mistake to go and challenge anyone in the bar. I've only seen a couple of times when it's happened. What's happened is that the waiters have all ganged together. A number of them have been there for several years, so that they know each other well and do not like to see anybody take a slug at any of the other waiters." (notes)

Although our research suggests that persons working in "straight" bars were less likely to be involved in systematic bar hustles than those working in "action bars," there appear to be some hustles, such as "overcharging on rounds," "short shotting," "watering (juicing) down of cocktails," "substituting bar liquor for premium brands," and "adding an extra drink on a tab" in effect at most bars, including those considered to be the "high line" or "prestige" places within the community. Practices may vary extensively from place to place, but some hustling promoted by the bar itself or some of its employees seems present in most places:[1]

---

[1] We do not intend to alarm or discourage bar patrons, only to indicate that they will not always receive that for which they believe they are paying, even in "the best bars."

Where I'm working, the Lamplighter, it's one of the elite places in town, right? But things go on there too. . . . If somebody orders a straight shot, they get an ounce and a quarter, like all drinks should be at least that. Once you get into the cocktails, things like Screwdrivers, Black Russians, Gimlets, that's just maybe a shot of booze and the fruit juice. They'll cut back an ounce and a quarter to maybe an ounce. . . . The bartender at the Highliner, he used to bartend at our place and now he's the full-time bar manager both upstairs and downstairs. We get together on occasions and when we do, we sit there and talk shop for a while. He was telling us that for their bar liquor, like maybe their gin, before they crack a bottle open, they'll dump some out, and put some water in. So if you go in there, and you order, maybe, a Tom Collins and they're going to cut back their liquor, by the time you get that drink, hardly any booze at all. It's been cut twice, they've watered it down and they've short shot. . . . Adding ice also brings up the volume. What they'll do, when you're making cocktails with any of the juices, like there's a special bar mix that foams when you shake it. If you're not busy and the waitresses are waiting for drinks, you really shake it well and the more you shake it, the more foam you get, and if you're making like three slings, you can really cut back on the booze and just make lots of foam. . . . The Highliner also substitutes liqueurs. We do that too. We have a coffee cart that goes around if anybody wants a Spanish, French, or Irish coffee. On the cart you have all these liqueurs that go into a certain coffee, and for example, you'll have Kahlua on the cart, but that's not really Kahlua, it's Aloha Coffee which is a cheaper liqueur. What they do is, they have all the bottles on the cart, they keep refilling it with all the cheaper liqueurs. We do that for sure and I know the Highliner does it for sure. (waitress)

Here at JoJo's, the liquor is cut, and the bartender will sometimes give you a short shot. You really can't complain to the bartender, so what you do is cover the glass with your fingers. That way, the customer can't really see how much liquor is in the glass. (waitress)

The manager would have his friends in. Free drinks, right? Then he'd say, "Okay, Grover, I have to make up for 8 drinks," or whatever. He'd give out drinks to friends of his and he'd say, "I want it made up." So we'd short shot the customers. (waitress)

Percy said that he likes the Blue Grass because it's a great place to hustle. Rarely does he give patrons the correct change. The price of drinks there is pretty low, so he finds it easy to overcharge people without them becoming aware. He may, for example, charge a table 75 cents per draught for a round when draughts really cost 50 cents. If he does this all night, it can really add up. He also said that he will also mix up orders on purpose, so that patrons become confused about the actual charges. He did this with Rocky several times as a joke and it worked everytime. I was surprised to see how good he was at it. Later Percy put on a show for me, showing me how he hustled patrons. There was an old drunk sitting a few tables down and he had a $5 bill lying on his table. Percy went over and greeted him, shaking his hand and putting his tray in front of the bill. While patting the man on the back, Percy reached over and took the bill and walked away. . . . Percy said that at the Blue Grass, the management allowed patrons to become quite drunk. This gave the waiters a greater opportunity to steal from the patrons. . . . Also the waiters were *allowed to drink and smoke pot on the job. He said that he enjoyed working at the Blue Grass because he could enjoy himself in this way and because of the hustling opportunities. He also said that he had made several dope connections at this bar and was making extra money selling grass.* (notes)

SERVICE, TIPS, AND HUSTLES

As the preceding discussion suggests, service, tips, and hustles are highly inter-related. Staff members are expected to display reliability, efficiency, honesty, discretion, and reasonable friendliness in their relations with patrons. As Goffman (1959) in his discussion of teamwork would suggest, the staff are there to serve the patrons, but they are also obligated to sustain a definition of the bar as a viable drinking establishment. At the same time, however, the staff people may be expected to "work for themselves," as they endeavor to supplement the normally low staff wages through tips and hustles.

In discussing tipping practices, it is important to recognize that there are certain skills involved in securing larger tips, and that tipping practices may reflect underlying hustles.[2] Tipping is an important element in bar work and although tips in some bars are very meagre, an efficient, courteous waitress (she need not be provocative) or waiter can make $30-60 in tips in an evening in many bars:

Weekends are our busiest time. On Saturday night any girl should be able to make between $50 and $60, no problem, and that's without hustling, because we're busy. On Friday night when it's not as busy, if you hustle and talk to your customers you can make just as much. (waitress)

Here, the bartender can't sell anything off the bar simply because he can't access the till and he can't punch it in, so the customer has to buy from a waitress. . . . The girls overall can make better money than the bartender, and even better money than the management. As the manager, I work 60 to 65 hours a week and I have waitresses who take home more money than I do and only working 25 hours a week. You know they'd work 4, six hour shifts. . . . If only I had nice legs and big tits, I'd be dynamite. But, that's the way it works. (manager)

Not unlike the desk clerk hustles we discussed earlier, bar hustles are tolerated and may be emulated by other staff people, provided they do not interfere with work situations:

I was working with this one waiter and he told me that he made $30 in 2 hours. I asked him how he did it, because I wasn't making anywhere near that much. He told me a few things about different hustles he was into. Learning about these little hustles are part of your job training. (waitress)

As bar hustles are built around the existing systems of particular bars and the duties of the specific staff people involved, someone who engages in bar hustles will have to adjust accordingly. Experiencing a variety of hustles through working in different bar settings or in different positions, staff people may develop personal

---

[2] Fred Davis (1959), discussing cab drivers and their fares, provides another illustration of both the relationship of tips to hustles, and the significance of tips and hustles to service people.

qualities and attributes conducive to hustling in other fields. The simple knowledge, for example, that one's "take home pay" is not dependent on one's salary, or the kindness of patrons, may lead persons to contemplate and seek out other money-making enterprises:

We get some staff people that come in and just naturally do it. I guess anybody could do it. Anybody could walk in a hotel and if they figure there was a chance to make an extra dollar, they do it. I have done it myself. I haven't done it all that much, because I am not good at it. Also, I had a lot of friends who sat at the bar. You don't rip off your friends. But you do have the opportunity. Like, say a drunk walks up and orders a beer. The guy gives me a twenty dollar bill for a dollar. I say, "You still owe me a quarter." Now he gives me a dollar and says, "Keep the change," so twenty-one dollars you know. And he is still going on, "Oh, you are a good guy, a great bartender." What the hell does he know? I just ripped him off for $20! He doesn't know where the hell it went. Later he is looking in his wallet and says, "Gee, I was sure I had more than that in here." And I say, "No, you just gave me two dollars." (bartender)

Much like prospective card hustlers (Prus and Sharper, 1977), staff people face the problem of whom to hustle. It may be easier and safer to hustle friends since they are less likely to be suspicious than are strangers, however "beating a friend" is contrary to the prevailing norms (in-group loyalties are no less significant in "deviant subcultures" than in more conventional groupings). Furthermore, hustling a "rounder" or "regular" may also become problematic, given that person's affiliations within the hotel community. A staff member may find his reputation damaged (and even have retributory action taken against him) if he is caught "ripping off the wrong guy."

Not all hustles are directed towards patrons. While the staff develop hustles around existing routines, some hustles are directed towards the bar itself:

It's really easy to rip the place off during the day. You're left all by yourself, you just don't ring it in when you collect the money. (waitress)

On the old system, when we were on keys, you could just not ring something in and hope that they didn't notice. If they did notice, it was just considered a mistake. . . . Then when we went on a cashier system, if the cashier wasn't watching close enough, like you have to be busy, and you have a trayful, you could do it, you could have 15 beers on your tray, and tell the cashier, "I've got 13 beers." (waitress)

Hustles directed towards the hotel are "less personal," but are also apt to be less tolerated by other staff people and/or the management. Co-workers may be concerned that they not be blamed for any shortages. Likewise, while a manager may tolerate some loss of hotel income or property, he may want to keep it hidden from the owner, lest it appear that he is mismanaging the bar. Word of various hustles particular staff employ does circulate among other staff people, but the individuals are not usually challenged unless the theft is thought to be quite extensive or their hustle becomes more obvious:

There was one guy that was ripping them off for cases of beer and stuff like that, and you can't snitch. You want to be friends with the people you work with, so you don't want to go snitching on them. But if somebody is stealing, it makes the whole staff look bad, so one of the waitresses finally snitched on the guy, and said, "Look, if you're worrying about your losses and blaming the rest of us, it's the person you least suspect." The guy that was doing it was coming in everyday, and he'd run the errands for the boss and the boss just thought he was great. And Mabel's going, "It's the person you least suspect." And when you say that, all of a sudden everybody's suspect, so she finally said, "It's him, he's doing it." (waitress)

Another girl I was working with in this cocktail lounge, she was doing all these hustles, and I wasn't aware of it until she finally got laid off. The owners were afraid it was them she was ripping off too. There was no proof there of how she was doing it, but she was making too much money, and since they were afraid it was them, they wanted to get rid of her. (waitress)

Whether or not the employee suspected or found stealing from the bar will be dismissed or otherwise reprimanded will in part depend on how much the person detecting the theft has at stake. Some employee theft may be tolerated when the management deems that the losses are inconsequential, or it is not worth trying to replace an otherwise acceptable employee:

There is a lot of ways of stealing, if you have the guts to do it. I think once you start it's easy, it's just the starting that takes guts. And if you get fired from the place, it's not like it's so hard to get another job, you can always work in a bar. Bar jobs are just so easy to get, you can just snap them right up. Experienced people though. They don't want to go through all the bother of training a new girl. (waitress)

These guys are not angels. They're going to take a little now and then. But I don't want it getting out of hand, where it's costing the bar too much, or where you're having a lot of problems with the patrons. Then you've got to get rid of the guy. (manager)

In attempting to account for variations in hustling across bars, and amongst individual staff members, the notions of "differential association" (Sutherland, 1947) and "drift" (Matza, 1964) seem especially prominent. As one moves from bar to bar, one not only finds varying degrees of awareness of hustling practices, but one also finds varying degrees of support for hustling practices. Thus, in few other bars have we encountered staff persons being generally as aware (and tolerant) of bar hustles as those at "action bars." Staff people at action bars are more likely not only to have been exposed to rounder life-styles before beginning work there but, as staff people, they also have greater opportunities to become exposed to, and absorbed into, a larger hustling culture. These contacts not only sensitize staff to hustling as a lucrative sideline, but they also provide a level of social (and if need be, physical) support for hustling. Not all staff at action bars hustle extensively and/or systematically, but overall they are more likely to be attuned to hustling opportunities than those working in "straight" bars:

The people here, they're really not aware of many hustles. They all pretty well started here as their first job, and they're not really aware of all the ways people can make money in a bar. (bartender)

I counted my money and I realized I had not charged the guy enough for his drinks, but by this time, he'd already left. So I got even on the next guy who was drinking a little more. I figured, well, a customer ripped me off, I'll rip off a customer. Why should I pay the bill. (waitress)

Once one puts aside naivete, concerns with "trust violation" and "the fear of being caught" become more prominent in accounting for differential involvements in hustling. Also, these concerns seem most pronounced in "straight" bars in which the staff has minimal contact with persons involved in rounder or hustler life-styles. In general, however, persons seemed more willing to steal from others when they were displeased with them and/or felt a greater sense of distance from those targets (be they patrons or the bar).

MANAGING CUSTOMERS

Defined somewhat by concerns with providing smooth, efficient service, acquiring tips, and to a lesser degree by hustles directed towards the patrons and/or the staff, the work role of the bar staff is considerably more demanding than these activities suggest. In addition to "serving drinks," bar staff, regardless of position, can expect to routinely encounter a variety of troublesome customers. As agents of the bar, they are apt to find themselves somewhat more obligated to deal with these persons than they might otherwise desire. Although the sorts of problems the staff encounter vary somewhat by their bar roles, the role of the waitress is particularly interesting. As the "front line" in most bars, waitresses are obligated to be "public relations" people and "peacekeepers"; but they are also likely to be viewed as the "entertainment."

PROVIDING ENTERTAINMENT

Although indications of intimacy, be these in terms of "provocative attire," "flirting" and the like, or "just being friendly and courteous," may promote tips from a predominately male audience, it is likely that a waitress will have an entertainment function her male counterpart lacks. It should not be assumed that all males find her attractive or are interested in her company, but most waitresses will find that they are the recipients of amorous attention and are subject to some sexual advances, regardless of whether these are desired or not. Insofar as the waitress's tips (or her job in some cases) may depend on how she handles this attention, her situation, not unlike that of the stripper, lends itself to concerns with managing intimacy and distancing:

> *I was working Saturday night and I walked right into it. He sat at the bar, and I said, "Do you want anything?" and he says, "Yeah, but you're working," and I go, "Hmm, hmm, here we go again." Like you walk out and say, "Would you like anything here?" "Yeah, but it's not on the menu." Why do people say things like that? Don't they know that we've heard it 10 times, if not 200? "What would you like here?" "Oh, I'll have one waitress, no dressing." "Oh ho, funny! Can't you come up with anything more original than that?" But you walk right into it and you don't even realize it.* (waitress)

> *I don't like to socialize where I work. The management wants me to spend more time socializing with the people in the bar. But when I mix with people at work, then too many people come on to me. You're friendly with them when you're*

working, and then after they figure that they're somebody special to you. No, I don't need that. You get too many hassles that way. (waitress)

Although the waitresses seem to receive a lot of offers for dates and the like, they, like the dancers and the hookers, tend to dismiss many of their customers as ineligible prospects for futher intimacies:

Well I've had people who've asked me out while I'm working, but I just make it a policy never to say, "Yes," because it's in a bar setting and you can't take anything seriously in the bar setting, so I usually say, "No, I've got a boyfriend," or "No, I don't like you." (waitress)

The customers, they're jerks. No, not all of them, but you don't think of them as eligible. When I was single, I went out with a couple of them, and I imagine if I was single now, I would go out with customers, but it would come to a point where I was very selective, about which ones. (waitress)

"Regular customers" and "friends of the management" represent special difficulties for the waitresses. Given their bar business value or privileged position, these people create particular problems in distancing for the waitresses. Not only is a waitress expected to be tolerant and attentive to these individuals, but she is likely to find that she cannot readily turn to other staff people for help in resolving any difficulties she has with these people. Realizing that these customers may feel more "entitled" to her affection and could get her into trouble with the management, she is, nevertheless, left much to her own devices in dealing with these people. Regulars and friends of the management are not the only persons making plays for her, and customer "come-ons" represent an element of bar work which waitresses routinely encounter. Any female unable to "maintain her cool" (Lyman and Scott, 1970) would not likely be tolerated for long in this setting.

Patron interest has other implications for the waitresses as well. Although other bar staff tend to be more understanding, given the relative proportion of males to females in the setting and the need for the waitresses to be reasonably congenial with their patrons, the waitresses may find boyfriends or husbands becoming "overly concerned" about their relationships with patrons:

Jealousy is really not much of a problem if the boyfriend has worked in a bar before, because then he will usually understand your routine. But my husband didn't know the patrons or like them, so when I was working, he was always suspicious that something was going on. It caused a few hassles. Eventually, the manager had to sit Geof down and talk to him. We decided that he shouldn't be in the bar before closing time, because in this line of work, you have to give guys half come-ons to promote tips. You've got to pretend that you're available. Some girls don't wear wedding rings to work for this reason. (waitress)

The biggest problem with boyfriends or husbands or whatever is the hours. Because most men are not working nights and weekends and they want the little woman home with them sort of thing. I personally have never had that problem. But I know that a lot of guys get really uptight if you have to kiss ass, if you'll excuse the expression, to some customers, and play their little game. And, if they're tipping really well, then you sort of play along with their little thing, "Oh yeah, yeah, I'll come to the party after work," and then you sort of disappear at the end of the night. You've made five bucks off the table. Some guys get really uptight about that sort of thing. They don't realize that that's part of your job. (waitress)

PUBLIC RELATIONS WORK

Although most bar work may be perceived as public relations work, this aspect of the staff role becomes particularly prominent when customers complain about some aspect of the service they have received.

On encountering complaints, the staff will often disclaim responsibility, and generally try to handle the event informally with the least inconvenience to the other staff or the management:

What we did, if somebody would bring a Martini or a Manhattan on the rocks back, saying it was too dry or whatever, we would take if off the bar and drop it into another glass and take it back. The customers never returned it a second time. I don't know why, it was the same drink. But it was just that they didn't send it back, or whatever, and I guess they figured they were getting a different drink. (waiter)

Most hustles are easy to get out of if the customers complain, because you can always return the money and say that you made a mistake and apologize. (waitress)

Our manager was making drinks, and one of our waitresses refuses to serve his drinks if she doesn't think they're good enough. And this one night, he told her to go and serve this Martini. It was straight up and just barely an ounce. The guy she served it to was a bartender and he said, "Bring me a shot glass and bring me the guy who made this drink." There was no way our manager was going to that table because he knew damn well it wasn't the proper amount. He just made him another one and that was it, hoping he wouldn't say anything. She took the drink over, said, "You know how these things happen. We're busy tonight," and so on. (waitress)

The general significance of any complaint, however, tends to be qualified by the conditions of bar work at the time, the status of the complainant, and the reputation of the staff person about whom the complaint is made:

Female patrons, they are generally more bitchy and more demanding and this, that and the other thing. . . . You get a bunch of women together and nothing goes right, they'll always complain. (waitress)

If some drunk is complaining, it's not so bad, but if it's like a regular who's a good customer, then they get more concerned. (waitress)

When you're a customer, the other waitresses treat you very well, even if they don't like you. They don't want you to complain that you're getting poor service. It means a lot more if it's coming from one of the staff than say, some customer. (waitress)

Providing Support

In an attempt to maintain conditions conducive to the smooth functioning of the bar many places employ "doormen" and "bouncers." Generally speaking, these people are expected to act as "traffic directors" and "peacekeepers" rather than "heavies," and their activities in many ways parallel those of the police (Skolnick, 1966; Bittner, 1967; Parnas, 1967). They are expected to use discretion in dealing with troublesome situations.

Part of the doorman's (sometimes hostess's) job is that of controlling access to the bar, discouraging the underaged, the intoxicated, and other "misfits" from entry. They may also collect cover charges and direct or personally escort persons to what they consider appropriate sections of the bar. In this respect, doormen function as hosts and as they are better received by the patrons their value to the bar increases:

> *Mitchell said that James was the best person he could ever hope to have at the door. He is quite a character and is considered a "celebrity" in underlife circles, so he attracts a lot of people to the bar, just by being there. He is also very comical and is entertaining for anyone there.* (notes)

"Public relations" work suggests, but often does not adequately define the doorman's role. In the event trouble arises, he may be expected to either double as, or assist, the bouncer.

In contrast to the doorman, who may work out routines for the more efficient direction of traffic, the bouncer is apt to find that more of his work involves unpredictable elements. He is expected to quickly interpret a scuffle or a call for help, and to devise a plan of action affording adequate protection to the staff, the hotel, and innocent patrons. The bouncer does not have the legal authority of the police, but his use of force can often be more readily justified, given the problematics of managing a group of intoxicated persons in the bar setting.

Although it is important for a bouncer to be viewed as someone "to be taken seriously," one finds a wide variety of operating styles:

> *This one bouncer, Frank, he would gladly punch anybody out. And many times he could've avoided fights, but oh no, he just wanted to show everybody how hard he could hit him, "Hey, did you see how I hit this guy? Did you see what I did to this guy? I really wrung his bell, didn't I!" He has literally pounded a guy to a pulp, where the ambulance has to come and take the guy away because the guy could not walk out. He's out! Then when the police would come, he'd say, "Well, the guy was causing a lot of shit." Everybody goes, "Yeah, yeah." Like at one point, these two guys got a little rowdy and they hit somebody and then all the waiters got into it. There were like 8 guys punching the living shit out of these two people. . . . Like this bouncer, he always thinks he's "Mr. Body Beautiful," he stands up in front of the mirror and does a little shadow boxing kind of thing. It doesn't matter if the guy's small or whatever, Frank just whales in and beats the hell out of him, "Hey did you see me do it!" "Yeah, Frank, we all saw you do it, it was on the stage, right?"* (bartender)

> *All the bouncers are separate characters, so there has to be differences in how they handle it. I know this one bouncer who's very diplomatic, he could talk down any trouble that could ever possibly happen, it's like he just argues it out and just simply tells them, "Why don't you sit down." And then there's bouncers who are very macho looking and guys immediately take offense to him, even if he hasn't done anything. He'll maybe try to handle it diplomatically, but he can't get away with it, because he looks really macho. Guys*

immediately want to pick a fight with him. If he's in the area where they're upset, and he's trying to straighten them out, they'll fight him. . . . And I've seen instances where the bouncer's a coward, a fight happens and he runs the other way. I've seen that happen too. One man that works here, when there's a fight, he'll look and he'll wait for somebody to tell him to get involved. So by the time he gets around to getting involved in it, it's all over. (waitress)

As the following extracts indicate, however, even where doormen and bouncers are hired, a major concern is that the bouncers not become excessively physical in dealing with troublesome patrons. The use of force can be an important element in establishing the reputation of a bouncer, but those who are more zealous in the use of force may find that their efforts are not appreciated by either the witnessing patrons or the management. Like a "good policeman" (Werthman and Pilivian, 1967) or a "good muscle man" in a hustling crew (Prus and Sharper, 1977), a "good bouncer" is one who relies more extensively on social skills:[3]

When you hire those people, you're looking for an entirely different person again. I had a guy come in to me and all he could do was talk about how he was a black belt in karate and how many fights he'd been in. Well that wasn't important to me, I just said, "Sorry I can't use you." All the guys that work here can handle themselves in a scrap, if they have to. They're all big and they're athletic. Most of them have had experience in wrestling or karate or boxing, a lot of them are boxers. But these guys are hired for their ability to talk with people. . . their diplomacy. Their size was impressive, and was definitely a deterrent for anybody wanting to cause trouble, but it was secondary. The main reason for them being here is that they didn't have to fight. They could use their mouths as well as their fists. But if they had to use their fists, they could do quite well in that area as well. These guys, they were trained just like waitresses, to wait on tables. How to handle being at tables, and empty ashtrays, everything else, because that was part of their job. They were hosts and they were security as well. They checked out the parking lot, just making sure everything ran smooth. (manager)

I don't like using bouncers, they're more trouble than what they're worth. . . . I don't want bouncers around the place. No, I definitely try to avoid using bouncers because what I found is that it scares more customers away than what it's worth and some of them get pretty rough with the customers and it's just not worth it. (manager)

The bouncers, they all had their own way of doing things, but the life expectancy of the bouncer in here was about 6 to 8 months. After that time, he had been in enough scuffles, and he'd had enough trouble that he sort of got jumpy, because he had enough guys try to hit him, enough guys try to come on to him, that he got jumpy and I had to get rid of him. But, for the guy, up until that time, all the guys who worked for me were, they had their own style, but they were talkers. They'd rather talk than fight and they'd talk, and they'd talk, and they'd talk, and they'd try to convince the guy of leaving, of calming down or doing whatever he had to do to maintain the rules of the business. They would talk,

---

[3] Roebuck and Frese (1976: 248) note that bouncers at the Rendezvous were also expected to handle trouble with a minimum of physical force and intimidation.

and finally they got the guy to leave, or they used force to eject him. But, really the work expectancy was 6 to 8 months when it was rough. . . . . I was likely in more scraps in the last year than any one of the doormen, but even I got jumpy after a while. (manager)

HANDLING DEVIANCE

"Troublesome behavior" in bars assumes a variety of forms; from attempts of underage people to obtain service, people stealing glasses and ashtrays from the tables, and patrons bringing their own liquor into the bar, to the illicit usage of drugs on the premises and large scale bar-room brawls. One of the easiest ways of handling deviance, generally, is to overlook it. Not only may the offenders leave the bar on their own, but they may spontaneously desist from an activity, perhaps wearying themselves of their own actions. More importantly, however, "doing nothing" avoids the likelihood of a scene, and unless other customers complain, staff people may attempt to ignore behavior that is not quite in keeping with bar norms. However, if the behavior seems more troublesome or persistent, the customer(s) may be "cut off" or asked to leave, typically with the assumed support of other staff people:

You'd hate to get in a fight there because all these guys stick together. It's much like at Main, where if somebody jumps a waiter, well, you can pretty well bet that all the others will be right on top of him, "Let's kill the bugger" kind of thing. It may start out one on one, but pretty soon everybody jumps in. (waiter)

When we were leaving Central, Dick pulled me across the street, through moving traffic, with him to avoid meeting a fellow standing on the corner. Then he explained that he had earlier told this man to, "Fuck off," to get out of Central. He said that while he could do that in the bar, he was afraid of this fellow on the outside. . . . . This coincides with what different people have mentioned about having confidence in a bar where you have all those people to stand behind you in the event that anything goes wrong. (notes)

Patrons sometimes become indignant when asked to leave and will confront the staff. However, perceiving themselves as rule enforcers, who may also be suffering some personal indignity in their home arena, staff people generally do not appreciate these responses:

A drunk got into an argument with the doorman and the doorman told him to leave. The guy turned to him and said, "Do you know what you are, you're a fucking pimp!" The doorman hit him and knocked him out cold, saying he didn't have to take that from anybody. (notes)

Four young Mexicans were very noisy and were told to leave. As they were leaving, one of the hookers was using the pay phone in the lobby and one of these guys grabbed her hair. She started screaming. Then the bouncer came up and started fighting with these guys. As the fight progressed, it went back into the bar and at this point a number of staff members became involved. Eventually, they threw these four guys out. They were beaten up pretty badly and were covered with blood. But once outside, they then started yelling and kicking at the door from the outside, and one came rushing back in. The bar people were just waiting, and when he came in, one of the waiters grabbed him and started hitting him in the face. The manager started hitting him in the back. The man went limp, but they just kept kicking him. At this point, I called the cops. A few minutes later, the manager came up and told me that I had better call the cops, to get this guy out of here. The police arrived, and by then the four guys were all outside, in very bad shape, bleeding extensively. The police called the ambulance and it took them away. The police talked to the manager a little. The manager was quite upset because the door had been battered. (notes)

The staff in most bars also indicated that they could expect some assistance from their regular patrons when trouble arose. It should be noted, however, that while certain persons may be counted upon to help out in troublesome situations, their presence, like that of the bouncer, is not always guaranteed:

One of the waitresses was saying that if there is any trouble, the staff usually sticks together and helps one another out. She also said that the regulars were pretty helpful in that sense too. They would pitch in and help out if you got into trouble. She added that the reason she thought the regulars got involved was because it was their bar and they felt that things like that didn't belong in the place, which is in a sense like their home. (notes)

A lot of times a regular customer will be there, maybe ready to help, but we try to keep them out of it because we don't want things to get out of control. Also, you really can't tell whose side they're on a lot of times because it may be their friends that you're fighting with. So we try to keep them out of it as much as possible. But if one of our guys got into trouble, well, then the other staff, they pretty well have to be there, to back him up. It's good that way, because like one night a group of people might come on to you, and may be ready to jump you, and then, if your guys are around, they're going to think twice before they do that. (manager)

In actuality, there seems no limit to the range of troublesome behavior staff may encounter, but particularly significant, given their frequency and/or disruptive potential, are drunkenness, insults, and fights.

Drunkenness

While patrons may be out "to get drunk" or may inadvertently overindulge themselves and thus create problems for the staff, higher levels of consumption are also associated with bar profits and individual tips. The management and staff generally dislike having to deal with drunks, but they tend, by "pushing drinks," to contribute to this phenomenon, and may tolerate drunkenness in anticipation of further individual and bar profits. Drunks represent particularly viable targets for hustles, but even when these are minimal, heavy drinking is often tolerated. This is in spite of the fact that most of the bar staff with whom we talked mentioned "drunkenness," or "having to deal with drunks," as one of the aspects of bar work they most disliked:

The way we look at it is that getting drunk is their business. We just serve them. They're adults. We run a bar, not a babysitting service. . . . No, the management don't hold us responsible for anybody getting drunk. (waiter)

If I see that they're getting too drunk, then I'll start slowing down the drinks on the table, without saying anything to them. I always try to watch to see who can use another drink and who doesn't really need one. Then I'll slow down their service and let them sit on a drink before I serve them again. Give them time to sober up. (waitress)

As long as they didn't start to get abusive, they could get as drunk as they wanted. As I said, the morality squad had an understanding that they don't bother us. We had people falling asleep at tables and we'd give them a nudge and wake them up, to see if they wanted another round. . . . They were pretty tolerant with that because the place wasn't rowdy. (waitress)

While the staff and management may become liable for injuries arising as a consequence of bars serving persons to the point of intoxication, few staff people seemed concerned about this on a day-to-day basis. It should also be noted, however, that it is somewhat difficult for staff serving liquor to know at what point persons "become intoxicated"; thus, intoxication associated with "obnoxious" or "rowdy" behavior tends to be a more commonly applied benchmark:

How do I determine if a person's had too much? When they can no longer speak and no longer walk and then they stick up their finger for another one, and I say, "Sorry, I can't serve you any longer." I tell people that, I'll say, "I'm going to cut you off now and I advise you to leave because I'm now going to inform the manager," and you cut them off. But it's usually because their behavior's a little bit more rowdy than it should be. People who are getting really obnoxious. . . . (waitress)

You can tell by the way he talks, or by the way they're sitting in their chair. It's something that you kind of develop a sixth sense for. Or maybe they're just sort of rocking in their chair, or wavering a little, or when they talk, you tend to be able to pick up a bit of a slur. You're the only sober person at the table, so you can pick it up a lot faster than the person or somebody else at the table. . . . They see it develop over the night, slowly, whereas the waitress comes to the table about every fifteen or thirty minutes, so you can see it. But some people can really handle their drinks, like Toby, he comes in the afternoon and he spends. Last Thursday, he spent $70 in here. He was in here from 2:00 in the afternoon until it closed, and he spent $70 on booze and he's not a big tipper. . . . But he walked out of here. (waitress)

Insults

Insolence is to some extent associated with drunkenness, but bars also represent settings in which reasonably sober individuals may feel less obligated to be civil to persons than they do in other settings. At the same time, however, behaviors or expressions are "insulting" (regardless of their intention) only to the extent to which they are perceived as such. For example, a waitress may dismiss as inconsequential a remark made in the bar that she might find offensive had it been uttered in a grocery store, in her house, or on the street. Staff persons, nevertheless, find patrons particularly insulting on occasion. "Insults" are taken personally, but in addition to their potential significance for the worker's self esteem, they may also affect his/her ability to provide service, and maintain order within that bar setting. The way in which a staff member reacts may depend on ''what has happened previously'' with other patrons or the one(s) defined as insulting, as well as ''whether or not the culprit is a regular, and a good tipper.'' The major ways of handling insults are: ignoring the comments (and possibly neglecting to serve the offender), asking the customer to alter his behavior, and ''cutting patrons off'' (refusing service). Staff persons will occasionally become involved in verbal and/or physical exchanges stemming from a perceived insult, but the other options seem more common. Bar workers seem to define ''cutting a person or a table off'' as a fairly serious sanction. The implication is that not being served, the problem individual or group, being deprived of a central activity, will soon depart:

> *If somebody says something about me and they don't say it to my face, then I just pretend I didn't hear it at all. Like if you serve a table, and you turn around and somebody goes, "What a sleazy bitch," or something like that, which is grounds for getting them kicked out. Because I want to be respected too, but if they don't say it to my face, they can say whatever they want. But if I'm standing at the table and they're going, "You're a sleazy bitch," I go, "You're out. That's it. I'm not going to put up with that."* (waitress)

> *I had one guy, the first guy I ever kicked out myself, I walked past him and he goes, "Hey, Tits. Get me a beer." I was really mad that night, because I usually, if I have to throw somebody out, I go to the bouncer and I say, "See that table, I want them out," but I was really mad and I walked right up to him and I said, "You are going out, right now!"* (waitress)

> *If they were just being a little overexuberant, you would just walk up and say, "Keep it down, you're disturbing the other people." Try to joke around with them, and from then on, it would just depend upon their attitude toward you. If the guy turns around and tells you to, "Fuck off," that was my magic two words. Anybody in here told me that, then they were gone. That was it! I would pretty well take anything else said to me with a grain of salt, but those two words meant they were out. Then, you'd just ask them to leave. If they didn't leave, you'd take them out, and if they seemed that they were going to fight back, and say their numbers were too large, just call the police.* (manager)

Fights

Bars vary greatly in terms of roughness. In general, the posh middle-upper class bars evidence very few fights, but action bars, bars catering to younger males, and those situated in factory and downtown areas, tend to evidence a higher level of violent exchanges both among patrons and between staff and patrons. Thus, while there are more fights in Main and Central than in perhaps threequarters of the bars, there are many other bars in which the staff members are more likely to find themselves involved in violent exchanges.

While management policies on handling physical violence may vary extensively from bar to bar, the exact form any violent encounter will assume is difficult to predict. Further, as these incidents may take place very quickly or only come to the attention of the staff at a particular point in time, actual responses may be somewhat at variance from stated policy. In general, however, while the staff may attempt to ''cool out'' angered parties prior to any physical exchanges, once blows have been thrown, most waitresses and some male staff attempt to become disinvolved:

Usually, if there's trouble I find that I almost automatically get involved in it, and I'm in there trying to break things up. I've also got punched, when one of the fellows went to hit somebody else and hit me. I came home with a black eye. But mostly, what I try and do is sort of get to things before they develop and then try and settle the people down. Sometimes I'll say, "Come on, come on sit down, I'll buy you a beer," anything to sort of settle things down. Usually we try not to call the police unless we have to. They're pretty good in getting there, but if you have too many calls to the police then that's apt to look bad for you too, because they keep a record of all the different calls that they go to at different places and after a while they might investigate you just to see why you're having so many complaints. Usually though, we really don't have that many fights. (female bartender)

Fights we can't do anything about. The first thing I do when I see a fight is I leave. I don't even want to get involved, right? And that's what they tell you to do, they say, "Leave. Take your tray away and just wait till the fight's over with." (waitress)

When there's a fight, I just stand back and let them go at it. I'm getting paid to wait on tables, not to get punched out. No sir, a fight starts here, and I get the hell out of the way. (waiter)

Although some male staff are reluctant to become involved in physical exchanges with patrons, the task of policing troublesome patrons is by no means limited to the bouncers, even where they are employed:

Melissa was having difficulty with one of the customers. He came in drunk, sat in her section and started insulting the other patrons. She became annoyed and told the man to leave. He then picked up a glass and started running towards Melissa, who was at the service bar at the time. He threw the glass, narrowly missing her, but striking a tray of glasses. He almost reached the bar when Hank, a waiter, grabbed and punched him. He fell with the first punch and was thrown out. (notes)

If it's in the afternoon, there's no bouncers around and things get really rough, well, I'll just call the cops and here it takes about 3 minutes for them to come because we're in the downtown area. But if it's just some punk, well fine, I'll tell him, "Get the fuck out of here," whatever, and handle it by myself. In the evening, we have the bouncers. But you know them, they're into the macho trip and they think you have to pound up on everybody. So that can be a problem sometimes too. (waiter)

You try to get them out without hurting them. . . . A lot of fights that occur were fights between customers, and you're just the referee, which is a bad place to be in, too, because then they might both turn on you. But it was pretty easy sometimes to break up these fights, because sometimes the people got themselves into trouble and they were very happy to have somebody come along and get them out of it. Well, they thought they wanted it, but once they get a bloody lip or a cut on the nose, they soon decide that they made a mistake. Once you get them spread apart, they usually calm down pretty fast. We always just took one guy out the back door and one guy out the front door. (manager)

Although most of the patron-trouble vanishes with the removal of the troublesome people from the premises, it should not be assumed that its significance for the bar or the staff always ends this abruptly:

Sometimes, a guy gets roughed up and he presses charges of assult. Often he doesn't remember exactly what happened until it comes up in court. Like the guy finds out that he was hit 3 times in the head, but only after he threw a beer bottle at the doorman. This sort of thing occurs quite often. Often I go to court as a witness and the guy pressing charges doesn't even show up because after he's sobered up a couple days later, he wouldn't remember what he had done. He couldn't remember the situation. He knew he'd gotten hit, he knew who'd hit him, sometimes they couldn't even remember who hit them, and he just wouldn't show up. . . . Now, if he's been drinking, he pretty well automatically loses in court. Because he's been drinking and you haven't. . . . It used to be common practice around here that if you had to hit somebody, you'd hit them in the body and not in the face where there's going to be marks. You hit a guy who's been drinking in the stomach and the trick is to see how fast you can move out of the way, because the first thing he's going to do is bend over and throw up. The worst part was that sometimes, it'd end up on your leg. It's the easiest way to end things. Just give him a whack in the stomach and no serious injury to him, whereas if you start hitting guys in the face, you can knock out teeth or break noses. . . . There's a lot of people in this town that over the years I've kicked out of here and I've been in scuffles with, had hard feelings with, and I don't care, but I sure wouldn't want to meet some of them by myself in another bar. I know they still hold hard feelings against me, and it can be rough. It's a rough business. You can get hurt working in bars. Like now, I'll only drink in certain bars I know are safe. (manager)

Police In The Bar

Generally speaking, "calling the police" tends to be viewed as a last resort. The police, it seems, are generally not fond of answering trouble calls from the bar and may become somewhat annoyed at bar management and staff who seem unwilling or unable to handle minor problems themselves. At the same time, however, they would rather be called to the scene of a bar fight before "it gets out of hand." The issue may become more complicated in "action bars" wherein no one may want the police around, or when the managers become concerned with an image they associate with the frequent presence of the police. Nevertheless, calling the police does afford a level of protection to hotel property, personnel and patrons:

You don't like to call police anymore than you have to, because that's all we need is a squad car sitting out in front of the place or one in the back, because you'll see people just walk up and walk by. I'll call them if things really get out of hand, because why should my staff get banged up. (manager)

As the preceding material suggests, bar people are reluctant to call the police for assistance in handling trouble. Even more unwelcome, in hotels such as Main and

Central which feature strippers and hookers, are police officers who drop by uninvited:

> *This cop would come and watch you at the bar, and you sort of wonder, "Well, gee am I doing everything right?" You look in the mirror, "Is my face on right? Is everything okay?" They figure, "Well, I'm getting paid for this, I've got nothing better to do, might as well watch the whorehouse." You hear a little "Pssst" going around the bar, "Cops at the bar, cops at the bar." Everybody lets everybody know they're there, so it's no big surprise to anybody after a while. But nothing will happen. Like the guy sits down to buy a girl a drink, fine, she drinks the drink. She tells him she has to wait because the police are in there. . . . If the guy really wants it, then he'll wait. He'll wait the whole day if he has to.* (bartender)

The relative popularity of uninvited police officers varies considerably from bar to bar, and although these men are treated fairly well by the management in most bars, some bars "appreciate" their presence:

> *If there's any major trouble we call the police immediately. We have a very good rapport with the police. In fact, a lot of the policemen come and drink in our hotel when they're off duty, and because of that they're always around anyway, they're always in our hotel anyway. That's where they sit for 20 minutes or whatever the case may be when they're bored with walking the beat, or whatever they're doing. They'll come into the hotel. They know that three quarters of the people in our place are underage and they still haven't done anything about it. They'll never charge the hotel or us for having so many in our sections that's underage.* (waitress)

> *We like to see them come by. This is a rough bar, like a couple of people have been killed here in the last little while. Actually, we'd like to have full-time policemen here all the time. On the weekends, we pay an off-duty cop to come and hang around, in his uniform. It keeps things under control, a lot better than a bouncer, because here's the heat, right in the bar.* (waiter)

FITTING IN THE STAFF COMMUNITY

Having discussed the ways in which staff-related activities are worked out within bar settings, we will now consider how employees adjust to their work situations more generally. As will be seen, "fitting in" is highly dependent on the efforts of both newcomers and "resident" staff members.

GETTING STARTED

Insofar as bars represent somewhat unique and disrespectable aspects of social life (higher levels of drinking, fighting, and sexual tolerances), one finds that many persons in our society are opposed to the idea of themselves working in bars generally, and some "ill-reputed" bars in particular. Bar work is seldom a first choice for persons in our society and clearly not all those "who need a job" will consider bar work:

A lot of people are not interested in bar work, and a lot of people couldn't fit into a bar routine. We'll sometimes suggest bar work to people, but only if they seem receptive to it. (employment placement officer)

While those who apply for bar work tend to be among the less "squeamish," many applicants remain apprehensive:

At first, I was really nervous about actually serving customers. Like I've gone to bars, but I'd never waitressed or anything, and I just didn't like having to tolerate hassles. I thought that if I started working in a bar, that a lot of people would come on to me, which is a general conception. Generally what you hear happens, and a lot of people would be rude and obnoxious, and things like that. And I didn't know my tolerance level of people. I'd never had it really tested, so I didn't really know what it would be and how I would react. (waitress)

Initial apprehensions in part reflect, or at least are complicated by, concerns with respectability. While these concerns may be dissipated somewhat if persons are considering working in a "high-class establishment," a general aura of disrespectability seems to surround bar work and particularly those dealing most closely with the patrons of drinking places. Thus, not only may prospective workers be sensitive to their own concerns with respectability, but they are unlikely to get encouragement from (outsider) family and friends for their "choice" of work:

My parents don't know I'm waitressing. If they knew, they'd be really hard on me. I come from a very moralistic unbringing, staunch Catholic, the whole works. It's not done. Like my mother doesn't know I can get into a lot of drinking situations. (waitress)

Some went to another bar, some left the business altogether. Especially girls who left because boyfriends didn't want them working nights. That was a big thing, too. A girl would start and her boyfriend would say, "No way." A girl would come in and she'd try it out, mostly these were university students. They'd try it out and decide they didn't like it, and then leave. They didn't really have to work. They were just working to make a couple of extra bucks. . . . They just didn't like it. When we were going through such a large staff, such a big turnover, it was a pretty rough place. It was very hot, and it was always crowded, and the clientele was a young, working class clientele and they were rough and they were noisy. Sometimes they'd get rather vulgar in their speech and what not, and a lot of the girls were totally turned off. (manager)

If people ask where you're working and you tell them, they kind of, "Ho, ho, ho! Making lots of money?" (waitress)

While persons occasionally become involved in hotel work by answering newspaper advertisements or through employment agencies, three other routes are especially noteworthy: family connections; friendship networks; and regular bar patronage.

Family members are not only aware of the financial opportunities bar work entails but also, through association with bar people, tend to be desensitized to other elements of bar life (violence, drunkeness, and disrespectability). They may also anticipate some preferential treatment from the employer, feeling that family ties obligate him to them. Family ties are by no means limited to owners, but extend to managers and other staff people as well:

> *When the new manager came, he brought a lot of people with him from the Bluegrass. It's a real family thing. Metro, Alfred, and Perry are his brothers-in-law. Edgar also has a couple of his brothers, Melvin and Max, waiting there. Vito also had his brother Carl working in the hotel, along with his sister Harriet. Mitchell, likewise, has found his son work in the hotel.* (notes)

Pre-existing friendship bonds operate in ways similar to kinship ties. Many staff people are in a position to learn of forthcoming vacancies, and they may promote particular applicants:

> *Ted said that he got his maintenance job through Talcott, the manager's son. . . . Otis said that he was instrumental in getting Erving his bartending job since he recommended him to Ray.* (notes)

Another method of obtaining employment in a bar is through regular patronage. Being familiar with staff and management, bar regulars often become aware of job openings and, as insiders of sorts, may be in a favorable position to take advantage of these:[4]

> *Dick was saying that he got the job as barboy through one of the staff people. He is something of a regular at Central and was telling Kathy that he planned to go to a technical school in the fall, but needed a job desperately.* (notes)

"FITTING IN"

Regardless of the routings, once employment is obtained, the incumbent faces the problem of coming to terms with the work setting, for, as Roebuck and Frese (1976:220) note, anyone not able to adjust to bar life is likely to have a short career. Although "novices" are differentially prepared, the essential elements involved are: (1) coming to terms with the bar environment; (2) learning to become comfortable with one's duties; and (3) developing a working relationship with staff and management. It should be emphasized, however, that "fitting in" is a two-way phenomenon. Although few persons seem to realize this en route, as they become more a part of the hotel community, it becomes more a part of them. Further, as persons endeavor to expedite work routines or maximize payoffs in the bar setting, they are apt to be drawn further into the webs of the hotel community.

In contrast to other newcomers, applicants with pre-existing contacts at the bar at which they're working generally indicate that initial adjustments are less demanding. They have to contend with the service aspects of their job, but are less burdened with the problems of feeling comfortable with bar life:

> *Most of the people who get jobs here were people who knew somebody and it is very common for friends to bring friends around. I guess they'd be telling them about the bar and what sort of money they made there and it's very common. . . . They'll often suggest people or send people around; you take their*

---

[4] Roebuck and Frese (1976:219) mention "bar regularity" and friendship networks, as commonly operative in obtaining employment in the Rendevous.

names and if they look good, you can try them out. Otherwise you have to think of them like anybody else. (manager)

I used to come here all the time when I was underage. . . . I lived with a girl who had worked here, but when I started she had quit. She used to tell me all about it. So it wasn't a shock. (waitress)

Although management frequently hire family and friends available for work, when outsiders are involved, the management generally prefers more experienced workers. Experienced workers may be inclined to be more relaxed in doing their work than novices, and they may be more hustle-wise, but their greater familiarity with the drinks, their greater dexterity in handling trays, counting money and the like, as well as the knowledge that they can "take the pressure of bar work" are valued considerations. They are not only seen as providing more knowledgeable service, and being able to handle drunks, fights, and so on, but are also thought more likely to return to work the next day:

In hiring somebody new, I'm interested in their record, what sort of work experience they've had before in bars and also what class of people they are, and what about the people they hang around with, because if you get somebody who's with a rough crowd then probably he's going to bring his friends around. . . . I've broke in a few people and I find that it's better to have somebody who knows what they're doing than someone that you have to start from scratch with all the time. (manager)

When I applied for a job at the Double Inn, the manager rather pointedly asked me if I would be able to cope with a number of situations such as carrying a full tray of draft, managing a large section by myself, dealing with drunken patrons, and manoeuvering around a crowded dance floor. She said that if I was not positive of my ability to do so, that I need not apply. (notes)

As it is time-consuming and costly to locate and train persons for bar work, bar managers also tend to be concerned that they hire people whose orientations are reasonably compatible with life in their bars:

The first thing is appearance, not particularly looks. My waitresses were never the best-looking girls around. Basically because it's very hard to find an extremely good-looking girl who had the personality to go along with it. . . . If a girl walked in in a pair of grubby old blue jeans, and a not very nice top and her hair was disarrayed, she has a much poorer chance than a girl coming with nice clothes on and a neat appearance. The next thing that is important is her being able to sit and talk to me and not be nervous. She never met me before and she's applying for a job and she might be nervous as hell inside, but she's got to be able to control it, because she's got to deal with people every night. Every time she comes in here. . . . General politeness, speech characteristics. A girl who talks in a very soft voice is not going to make a good waitress because the customers are always going to be asking her to repeat herself, and for her not to be that way, she almost has to yell and then she doesn't come across naturally. A girl with a very strong, raspy voice. You don't want that either. So, aspects like that. Just the general speech pattern, whether she used good English or whether she threw in a swear word once in a while. That used to really turn me off. Not that the people who worked here didn't swear, but they weren't going to sit there and curse just for the sake of it. . . . Another important thing I've always looked for was how well I thought the girl would get along with the rest of the staff. How well she'd fit in. Most of the girls who work are kind of down to earth people and they're friendly, they aren't snobby or anything. You get a girl coming in who has her nose stuck up in the air and you know that she's not going to stimulate interest in the people who work here. (manager)

Bars vary greatly in terms of their unconventionality, drunkenness, violence, and sexuality, but unless novices are able to define these potentially disturbing elements as "relatively non-threatening" they are unlikely to remain on the job:

Frances, the new kitchen girl, seems a little terrified of the place. She won't even go in the other section where the hookers are. She sticks to the dining room section. She's afraid to go any other place in the bar. She's been working there a couple of weeks, but she's afraid to go to the bar and get a drink. She's also afraid to wait for a streetcar, and when she goes out for a cab, she wants me to stay with her till she gets one. Dave got her the job there, and she's really dependent on him. . . . (P.S.) Frances quit today, she said she couldn't stand the place any longer. (notes)

Mahogany, a topless waitress, was telling me that she has gotten used to almost all aspects of bar life. She feels that there is little that could happen that could shock her. She said she has gotten used to people talking about her tits, her ass and her pussy in front of her and she has gotten used to going around naked in the hotel. (notes)

Acceptance of the bar setting may be facilitated by desensitization through prior involvements or by having insiders explaining, qualifying, and sometimes protecting the new person from incidents. At the same time, novices may pick up cues from the staff. However, both new and regular staff, cannot readily run away from unpleasant situations. The social life of the bar is contingent upon the staff: they maintain continuity in the bar in the context of transiency and disruption.

Fitting into the staff community also involves becoming competent in one's duties. Not only is there a concern that the boss might become disenchanted with poor performances but, given their interdependencies, other workers are also likely to be critical of one's work. Anyone not seen to meet staff standards (given some allowance for experience) is likely to find that animosities generated in this area make it more difficult for the newcomer to fit in in other ways.

"Fitting in" is also contingent on the resident staff's accepting a newcomer. Although seldom a highly homogeneous group, the bar staff tend to develop a sense of solidarity with which newcomers may have difficulty dealing. Much like new patrons, new staff members may be subject to some distrust and distancing:

It's almost like you have a glass cage around you. The staff is almost unfriendly to outsiders, but not really unfriendly. You're not ugly to the outsiders, or anything like that. But there's an aura, like we all know what's going on and they don't, sort of thing. When people start, there is often that outsiderness. (waitress)

I never had a chance. It wasn't a personality clash so much as just being spotted as different. But from what I've seen they hire people all the time, and very few people stay on. Those that do are people that fit in with the other girls,

*and those who don't fit in just never get any hours and finally quit. That's what
I did.* (waitress)

*The people at the Driftwood are very, very close and a new girl comes in,
probably her biggest problem adjusting to the work is whether or not she's
going to be accepted by us because if she isn't somebody that we all like, then
she's really going to have trouble getting along. The group's very close. After
work we'll go to a restaurant together or maybe stay around the bar and have a
few drinks afterwards, but we've been together for about two years now and it's
a very close-knit group. If we don't like her, she's going to have trouble, we'll
get rid of her. It's not as if we sort of conspire against her, but what we'll do, if
she makes mistakes, and everybody's going to make mistakes, when she does
something wrong, we'll just say, "What the hell is going on here? What's
the matter with you? Can't you get anything right? What the fuck are you
doing here?", and so forth, to her. After a while she really doesn't want to stay,
but it's not like we go out of our way to mess her up or anything, it's just that
when she makes the average routine kind of mistakes, we just pick up on that
and really don't let her forget that we're not that fond of her. With other people,
we'd be more inclined to overlook things and maybe help them out, but here,
you sort of blast her. If we don't like her, she just doesn't stay very long.*
(female bartender)

The notion of "fitting in" also has significance for related concepts such as
"secondary deviation" (Lemert, 1951, 1967), "career contingencies" (Becker,
1963; Prus and Sharper, 1977) and "continuance commitments" (Stebbins, 1970;
Hearn and Stoll, 1975). It should be noted, however, that while "fitting in" can be
a highly situated phenomenon, bar work also involves persons in a more general
hotel community than that represented by the particular bar. As newcomers go
about their bar work, working evening hours in a "disrespectable" setting,
especially in the company of others who are not fond of "straight people," they
tend to find themselves feeling more isolated from former acquaintances:

*What happens is that you lose contact with a lot of your straight friends,
because you work different hours. And then you realize that they just wouldn't
understand what's happening in your life if you tried to explain it to them. And
I've tried, but it takes too long, and after you just realize that they're just not like
you anymore.* (waitress)

Although a sense of rejection does not constitute the basis of the staff community,
other staff people clearly represent an important community element. They are
people with whom bar workers can meaningfully discuss work and work-related
problems. Not only might their co-workers indicate ways in which to facilitate
work, and ease the "sting" of conventional morality, but they also represent links
to other aspects of the hotel community. To the extent they are supportive of the
newcomer, bar staff promote continuity in his bar involvements in dealing with
both outsiders and troublesome incidents within the bar itself. Further, as bar
people show newcomers how to increase their tips or how to hustle, they indicate
that bar jobs can be profitable, perhaps more profitable than any "straight" job
they may be able to obtain.

On becoming more accepted by the other staff newcomers are also drawn more
fully into the staff community. While work relations in many other contexts (such

as hospitals, businesses, universities) tend to overlap off-hours activities this seems particularly true for the bar staff. Not only do they work somewhat unusual hours, and experience a somewhat shared sense of disrespectability, but their work place is also commonly viewed as a recreational area by most people they encounter. Recreational facilities are much more readily available to them as a group than most other work groups. Thus, the off-hours lives of bar workers more often become melded with their bar lives:

> *Some of the staff never come in. They work, then go home. But you find that when people start, maybe the first few months, they won't come in here at all, but then they'll get to know everybody and they'll come in. . . . But if you didn't have anything to do, you'd stand at the bar and everybody would chit-chat. It's a social thing. You know about everybody in the place, like this girl is fighting with her husband, whatever, or this girl, who she went to bed with last night. You know everything about everybody, sort of thing. But there were some that kept it pretty quiet.* (waitress)

> *I would come in on my off days and sit around and drink with the boys. Sometimes I would be there three or four hours. I might ask them if they wanted to have a break or lunch. You didn't have to do that, but they normally do that. There were lots of other things I could do, but it was go there and talk, shoot the breeze. That's how you spent your days off.* (waiter)

Drinking Involvements

Having relatively easy access to liquor and being in a setting in which the consumption of liquor is a central and generally accepted activity, drinking tends to be one of the more common activities in which staff members at both individual and group levels become involved. Some bar staff drink very little alcohol, but newcomers wishing to become part of the bar staff may find it difficult to fit in without drinking with other staff persons, and many, it seems, find themselves drinking more extensively than otherwise would be the case:

> *Most of the people who work here can certainly down their fair share of spirits. Doesn't matter which type they were, they can handle a good volume. . . . Alcohol is a big problem in this industry because you do handle it all the time and a lot of people I know who have worked in bars, myself included, have had drinking problems. I went to A.A. for nine months. I was just drinking too much. I was drinking all the time. The industry has the highest rate of alcoholism of any industry. If you're the manager of a bar, you have to pay a rate of life insurance higher than what a heavy construction worker has to pay. . . . For a bar manager to buy life insurance will cost about $2.00 per thousand more than the average person, because he's a pretty high risk. . . . A lot of people in the industry have a drinking problem. Just because it's too easy to get. It's always at your fingertips.* (manager)

Generally speaking, there is little managerial support for staff people drinking on the job, but most of the drinking in which staff people engage cannot be understood apart from a group perspective. Thus, some after-work drinking may be encouraged by the management, but even when this is not the case, after-work drinking allows the staff, as a group, to unwind and to discuss and negotiate work-related problems:

After work you might have a drink or two together. It was a time to relax and straighten out things. Like a couple of girls might have had a fight during the night. They were upset, tense, it was busy and they were pushing around and they got into an argument. Well, they didn't have the time to straighten it out then, and after work, over a couple beers, they could get it all straightened out and they were friends again before they leave. That happened quite a bit and quite often I found that the people who did become problems, were people who, for one reason or another, got away from the system, and weren't accepted by everybody. The people who were always getting into arguments and hassles with other employees were the people who never stuck around after work, they were always the ones that'd scoot right home. That sitting down after work, that socializing, it's really important to keep the natural harmony of the place going. You can't work in a high tension job with a person night after night without developing hard feelings and if you don't have some time when you can sit down in a relaxed atmosphere and get rid of those hard feelings, they will just continue to build up. (manager)

In addition to drinking opportunities afforded staff during or after work, another form of staff drinking, albeit easily overlooked, should be noted. Although some bars explicitly prohibit staff patronage, in other bars, when staff people return to their bar to drink while off duty, they tend to be treated exceptionally well by the staff on duty. Not only are they likely to get preferential service, but their bar liberties are also apt to be greater than those of other patrons, thus making drinking an even more attractive activity:

Who doesn't want a staff person in their section? They're the best tippers, staff people, they always tip. Anybody who's ever worked in a hotel, any waitressing job, they're great tippers because they know. The staff, they're the hardest ones to get rid of, last ones to go at night, usually two o'clock before they leave, they're the ones that drink the most, you're always conscious of that table the whole time they're in your section. They're joking around, they're a little bit more rowdy than most of them, you don't cut them off, you don't! You have to tolerate it, but you don't mind it because it's worth your while. . . . We can also table hop, and we can get in any time we want. It doesn't matter how many people are in there, you're always in there. And we sit where we want and usually if there's no tables available, somebody in somebody's section who's not drinking, that table's cleared for us. (waitress)

Here, it's great. You know most of the people here, so there's that security, and then it doesn't matter if you come in alone or whatever. You just pop in and you have a good time. . . . Then there's the staff people who live upstairs, and generally most of the staff party there. So you can go in and drink for a few hours, and then after you can go up with the staff that was there and party with them. (waitress)

Heavier drinking seems indicative of a more general life-style characterizing barwork. Staff are thus likely to find that not only do they tend to smoke more heavily as a result of working in a bar setting, but also that their orientations towards money are also likely to undergo some change:

When I started there, I had just quit smoking for three months. But at the waitress stations, everybody smokes. I think it goes with the job, and I started smoking again. Now I'm on a pack a day. . . . It's getting bad again. (waitress)

Everything is day by day, not a long-term thing. And for me, that's really hard because I always wanted to save, save, save, and then buy something; but they see something, they'll go out and buy it, and a lot of their habits cannot be supported by their salary. . . . When I first started there I couldn't believe the tips we were making. Where I'm working now, I can make anywhere from $30 to $60 in a night and one of the waitresses was telling me, "You'll get spoiled," and I said, "Oh, I'll never get spoiled, I can't believe the money I'm making." One night I made $15 when I'd finished. . . . At the old place it would have been an average night, but here I went, "Oh, I only made $15!" and I'd just started there. So it's very easy to be spoiled. (waitress)

Humor and Animosity

One of the ways in which persons participate in the hotel community is through involvement in bar humor. While providing diversion and entertainment, active involvement in staff joking is a noteworthy means of acceptance. Being perspectival, humor incorporates an element of "insiderness," thus providing both an indication of one's acceptance within the community and a route to one's acceptance. In a more Durkheimian sense, not only does joking behavior reflect (and define) community boundaries, but it also represents a means of permeating those boundaries. Hence, one finds that newcomers who are more willing to interpret pranks, insults, lewd remarks, flirtations, and the like in a humorous vein (thus sustaining joking activity), are more readily accepted by their co-workers:

One of the topless waitresses, Fuisha, was saying that she was very shocked by some of the things going on at Main. She'd never been around that sort of environment before, but said she was getting used to it and started to like it, and was joking around with the people there. . . . I've noticed similar things with some of the other new staff. If they've been able to joke around, the staff seem to be more accepting of them. (notes)

Not all exchanges between the staff are congenial. While less common than those involving patrons, confrontations represent an important element in the staff community:

Two of the topless waitresses, Gerda and Wanda became involved in a dispute over some costumes (both are also strippers). I had dropped by to pick up Wanda for an interview, but found all the waitresses yelling and screaming at one another. Wanda had apparently threatened to have Gerda's apartment blown up and Gerda had called the police. Wanda, as a result, had gotten fired, and was being investigated, but Gerda had also been warned. (notes)

While many of the confrontations are readily dismissed, being attributed to the patrons, late hours, and the like, other conflicts revolving around issues such as incompetent service, laziness, improper attitudes, sexual promiscuity, and unfair treatments tend to persist:

Almost in any bar you work in, the management has got to be the pits. They don't know what's happening. . . . Like in the old place, we had two owners, and then you have one owner's wife and the other owner's girlfriend, so there's four people you've got to listen to, and then there's the manager on top of that, they have a manager. . . . There's a lot of this, like the owner goes out with one of the waitresses or a waitress goes out with the manager or the assistant manager, and there's a lot of back stabbing. You've got to watch who you say what to and things like that. And almost in any place you work, there's always a social situation where somebody's going out with somebody else, like in the higher echelon sort of thing. (waitress)

These conflicts could be over anything. One girl might consider that the other girl is tip hungry, she's only waiting on the tables that are tipping well and leaving the bad tables for the other girls. It might be a problem over a boyfriend or it could be any one of many things. It could be something that happened outside of this place. Maybe they knew each other from before they started working here, and didn't like each other. Or maybe just a snide comment made at the wrong time can fire off a really bad conflict. (manager)

As the preceding suggests, staff conflicts may arise in almost any area. There seems, however, some effort on the part of most staff people to maintain reasonably good working relationships with one another. In part, this seems predicated on the problems of finding replacements who would be more adequate, but also seems based on the recognition that most staff persons are ''part of the staff community'':

All the workers are different people and they have different skills. Some of them might be very good workers in some ways, say in terms of being very pleasant with the customers, but they might not be very good in terms of cleaning tables and ashtrays and such things, and so you try and balance them out with somebody else who is good in the other ways. You set up your schedule putting people who are weak and strong together so that things might work out better. . . . One girl who comes to mind was not at all what we call a good waitress, and yet she stayed for quite a long time with us. But she was willing to work. Whatever jobs we wanted done, she's willing to do that and she's also willing to work whatever hours she was needed on very short notice. She realized that she wasn't the best waitress around, but we could call her in 10 minutes' notice and she'd be down, very reliable, and so she was worth something to the bar. (manager)

When you're working in a place like that, you have to maintain a fairly good relationship with most of the people that you're working with, especially the important people. The ones that mean something, like the manager, the bar manager, the one perhaps second to the bar manager, and the good waitresses. Those people I've taken time out to make sure I'm good friends with. The rest I couldn't care less about. And I find that really important because I have their friendship and they're always behind me. . . . I've made a point of doing every one of those people favors, so that they owe me something. Like Helen and I have heart to heart talks now and everything and she says, ''You really are a daughter to me. You're just like my daughter.'' A mum-daughter relationship. I really worked myself right in there. (waitress)

Dating and Sexuality

Further indications of the extent to which bar work roles become entangled with other aspects of staff people's lives may be noted in reference to sexuality and dating. While some playful flirting between staff may be found in a variety of work settings (see Roy, 1974), that occurring in bar settings tends to be more physical and more overt than that occurring in other semi-public settings. In part, this seems attributable to the more relaxed, tolerant atmosphere of the bar, but also seems to reflect the interpretations by those involved; that these activities are to be viewed in the spirit of fun, as constituting a playful diversion:

> *The bartenders, they'll come up and give me a kiss and hug when I come into work and stuff like that. Or we'll be fooling around and he'll drag me off downstairs or something like that. It's all in joking, these are friends of mine that I let get that close to me, that they can do things like that with me. And a guy you're going out with, he doesn't understand that. . . . The bar manager, his girlfriend, the first time she ever saw us, like he grabs every girl that he sees, and gives her a hug and kiss, and holds her really tight, and nibbling on her ear and stuff like that, all on a joking level. And she saw this and she just freaked out on him.* (waitress)

While the targets (typically female) might become very upset with bar patrons were they to assume similar liberties, there is a sense of familiarity, trust, and interdependency which makes these activities generally more acceptable when initiated by "staff people":

> *I found that I was like a brother to a lot of the girls who worked here and you just start to feel close to them because different times they'll be having problems with people on the floor, like, maybe some one's grabbing their tits or their crotch while they're serving people. Well, then they'll be crying in the back-room and you go and comfort them, maybe give them a shot of scotch or something, try to pick them up, because they have to get back there on that floor and work, and so you develop a closeness with them.* (bartender)

> *There's a lot of camaraderie involved, but if the customer saw it being done, then he thought he could get away with it. There was a lot of that in the back behind the bar, in the kitchen, to cheer somebody up. You'd walk up and put your arm around them and start kibitzing, but that was us and that was our private little thing. It had nothing to do with anybody who came in here and we kept it that way because we didn't want other people involved. Those people were the customers and sure, we might see them off work, but when we were at work we were our own little family and they had no business being part of it. . . . Like the patrons probably wouldn't object, but if some of our customers ever had of seen one or two of the staff fooling around, a guy pinching a girl's bum, that girl'd be black and blue before the night was over. . . . But say you're the bartender, like in the kitchen, you might walk up to and drop an ice-cube down somebody's back, or pinch a girl's bum, or she'd bend over tying her shoe and you'd give her a whack and run. Come out here and have a customer do it and he'll get his arm broken and thrown out. . . . It's strange, but it's like it's all right for you to smack your wife on the rump, but it's not all right for your neighbor to do it. Well, that's the way it is in here. It's all right for*

us to goof around amongst ourselves, but let an outsider try to get in on that, forget it. He's out. (manager)

Some of these encounters are clearly not desired by the recipients, but their significance does not end here. Not only may persons change their ideas of "acceptable levels of familiarity" among bar staff over time, but some of this playfulness may be linked to past, present, or future romantic involvements. The extent to which staff persons in bars become romantically involved with one another will depend on staff alignments (for example, male/female, age), but a considerable amount of staff dating may involve partners who work at the same bars. Dating other staff people can be a means of consolidating oneself in the bar setting, but it is facilitated by the hours bar people work, and by their tendency to spend large amounts of non-work time in that setting:

There's a lot of dating among the staff. Most of the time staff works nights, the bartenders work nights, male members work nights, so your social life tends to be restricted to those hours, so who else better than fellow bar members to get involved with. So there's a lot of that going on. The staff at the Crossroads was almost all going out with each other. Darcy and I got married. Pearl broke up with her husband and started going out with one of the doormen who she lives with now. Magda is going out with one of the doormen. Mae who is our waitress today, is going out with a guy who used to work here, she met him in here as a customer, he worked here on and off for over four years sort of thing. Actually, it was really funny because I met Darcy and started going out with him. Then we broke up, and Mae had been going out with the only waiter that we had at the time, Edmund, Mae was going out with him, not seriously, she just wanted to go out. Then, when Darcy and I broke up, Mae started going out with Darcy, and I started going out with Edmund. Then I started going out with Darcy again. (waitress)

You're there working together, and you're around one another a lot. You get to know one another really well, because you're working long hours and you'll be drinking together after. Dating, that's just another part of it. (waitress)

IN "THE LIFE"

To this point, in discussing service, income, and keeping order, and the problematics of "fitting in" the staff community, we have introduced concerns strikingly common across bars. However, we would be remiss were we not to consider staff contacts with "the life." While bars (and individual staff members therein) vary greatly in the extent to which they become involved in "the life," the regular presence of a few hustlers introduces significant undercurrents in any bar, and a larger number of "action people" can dramatically color the atmosphere of a bar. We will be discussing staff/rounder relations in the next chapter in more detail, but at present we will focus on the impact of hookers and strippers on the work and social life routines of the staff.

While staff people at most bars áre likely to have some contact (desired or otherwise) with hustlers, drug dealers, and so on, chance encounters of staff (in "straight bars" or at after-hours settings) with hookers and strippers may also afford staff people levels of familiarity with "the life." These opportunities are especially pronounced in action bars, wherein frequent casual contact with hustlers enables staff people to more readily overcome the "mystique" commonly associated with prostitution, for example. Newcomers in action bars are also more likely to encounter other staff involved in "the life." Further, insofar as regular staff members are considered "cool" people and receptive to their overtures, hookers (and other hustlers) may envision in a new staff member a willingness to become involved in aspects of "the life." These opportunities do not replace other bar roles. The earlier mentioned concerns with service, income, control and the staff community remain. Nevertheless, people working in action bars may find themselves further embedded in the hotel community as a result of these contacts.

STAFF-HOOKER RELATIONSHIPS

The bar staff-hooker relationships in many ways parallel those of the desk clerk and the hooker. In general, the presence of the working girls promotes the liquor trade (and tipping), helps create an atmosphere conducive to other hustles, and provides a source of entertainment in varying degrees for the staff people. At the same time, the hookers may occasionally become belligerent or otherwise difficult to handle, and may involve the staff in disputes with the patrons. They also represent a legal liability to both staff and management.

To the extent the hookers "solicit" largely on their own, the staff's major utility to the working girls is to provide assistance in the event the girls are having difficulties with patrons. The staff will also endeavor to cover-up hooking activities should they suspect legal complications, but this activity stems more from concerns with their own safety than that of the "hookers." While it would be considered extremely bad form to draw undue attention to the girls, it is expected that anyone "on the hustle" would be responsible for being reasonably discreet and alert, thus "protecting their own tails."

While most of the hookers at Main and Central "work for pimps," it is important to recognize that these individuals are unlikely to be of any assistance in the hotel setting. Thus, in handling any difficulties a girl experiences in the bar or in the rooms with her "dates," she is dependent almost entirely on her own resources and the good will of the staff. Another hooker may help out, as might the occasional bar regular or rounder, but the staff people do have an opportunity to consolidate themselves with her in times of trouble. And, once a girl believes that she has the support of the staff, she can be a more effective hustler. As the following material on tips and hustles, entertainment and romance, legal entanglements, and hooker involvements, indicates, a number of themes are significant in depicting aspects of staff-hooker relations.

Tips and Hustles

Not only are the hookers typically generous tippers, but through them, staff people may be able to generate better tips from the patrons, and may on occasion hustle the hookers as well:

> On the floor, waiters get tipped very well because of the protection thing. The hookers always try to stay on your good side and tip you well in case there is trouble at the bar with a customer. (waiter)

The hookers take care of you. If you work there, you don't have any problems. They take care of everybody. Same with the rounders, if they like you, you have absolutely no problems, they take care of you. You're like everybody's daughter, or everybody's baby or something. (waitress)

Sometimes the waiters will lean on the girls for money. A lot of times a girl is sitting there all day and she's not ordering drinks or nothing, so sometimes they'll sort of, "Hey, come on, pack it up." See, if the girl is a prick about it, he'll just take her drink away. Or next time she orders, she's got to order a double anyhow, he won't give her money back, he'll just walk away, "Thanks." (waiter)

Entertainment and Romance

Viewing staff people as both more tolerant and more "hip" than their tricks, friendship and the occasional serious romance will develop between staff people and the hookers.[5] Many of the exchanges are, however, of a fleeting, playful variety, providing a break from the routine elements of their respective jobs:

The last manager was always in for the girls, always on the impress with the girls. But he was strict too, he'd bar them when they needed to be barred, right? But he tried to get his little pieces of ass, little parties, upstairs, or in the office, right? At these manager's parties, maybe some friend of the boss would come down, some friend that he knows has a lot of money. Usually, they'd start out drinking downstairs and call a few girls over. Some little remark, and the girl would turn around, and naturally the boss was there and, "Oh, ha ha ha, you've got such nice friends." They'd sit down and start having a couple of drinks, a couple more girls might come over, maybe more, depending on how many people were there. Then they'd just sort of adjourn it and go in the office. These girls were hookers. I imagine they got paid, I don't really know. The odd time they'd just go up and have a little fling, for nothing. (bartender)

Legal Entanglements and Precautions

As indicated in the extract following, staff members may become concerned about the extent to which they become close to the hookers, creating yet another instance of "restrained involvement":

I never did get too friendly with the girls. I was doing it for their good as well as mine. You'd have a cop sitting at the bar. They don't know this and they come up and start moving in on this guy right in front of you. You can't say, "Don't do that, there's a cop here." The cop will grab you just as fast. So I got a few of them privately and I say, "Listen, I don't want you at the bar. If you want a drink, and you're not going to hustle, come on up to the bar and have a drink, it doesn't matter to me. Just don't hustle at the bar!" You have to watch them all the time, because the minute they sit at the bar it's, "Hi, there!" They'd start

---

[5] While hookers and strippers tend to find male bar workers more socially compatible than most men they encounter, it should also be noted that male staff people also find these same women more understanding of their work than are most "straight women."

rapping about prices and everything, and they might have a cop sitting in the next stool, taking it all in. If I allowed it to happen, I'm going to be in just as much shit as she is. That cop will take you right off the bar in no time. (bartender)

Hooking Involvements

Because of their opportunities to become intimate with the hookers, to where the girls might define them as lovers, some male staff also become involved in "pimping." Since hookers are typically accustomed to helping out "their men" financially, male staff may have their income supplemented on a long-term or occasional basis:

Pimping, I had a chance to do it. I thought about it a lot because I had three chances that I could've got money like off these girls. . . . I don't know what came over me, but I'd say, "No, listen, try and put it away for yourself. Maybe you can put some money away for yourself in the bank. I don't want your money. . . . It was the same with Jack. There was a lot of nice chicks. He has gotten bread off these chicks, a few hundred, a thousand bucks every now and then. But he literally falls in love with her, "Oh, I love you and I'm not going to take your money, because I love you so much." After she'd turn him off, or something else would happen. (bartender)

When I became involved with Maggie on a more serious level, she told me that she was willing to help me out with my expenses. She said that she would very much like to do this. (waiter)

Although only some female staff members become involved in prostitution, it is not uncommon for cocktail waitresses, barmaids, hat-check girls, or maids, particularly in action bars, to get propositioned. Finding themselves in an environment in which sexual exchanges are fairly common, persons working at hooker bars are apt to feel less constrained than they might in other settings. Additionally, their own past involvements and/or present circumstances may be such that certain aspects of sexual exchange do not seem as disrespectful as it might to some others. Among staff members in these environments, there is a certain casualness associated with hooking. Although individual staff females will, at different times, say that they dislike working with hookers, one occasionally finds some of these same women "turning a trick." The other staff members generally do not encourage this sort of arrangement, but as long as the woman's activities remain reasonably discreet, they are likely to tolerate them:

One of the waitresses, she used to be a hooker, does a couple of tricks on an off-and-on basis. Lisa was doing a trick with this guy after work and we had a kind of special arrangement with her for the rooms, so he didn't have to pay. I got $10 for myself and didn't make out a card on it. (clerk)

STAFF-DANCER RELATIONSHIPS

Generally speaking, relationships with the dancers are less financially rewarding, but are more apt to have an entertainment value than those with hookers. At the same time, however, the dancers represent a frequent source of aggravation for the staff as they often request special privileges (for instance, paying for drinks later, running a tab, leaving a drink on a table during a show):

Some of them are okay. They pay for their drinks and leave you a tip, or only drink when some guy offers them a drink, but some, like Seattle Sheila, are a problem, because they want to run a tab, or you always have to chase some guy down to pay for her drinks. (bartender)

The strippers don't really do anything for them. They don't really like the strippers that much. Maybe some of them will do something for a waiter, but usually they don't do that much. It's maybe, "Give the guy a tip, shoot him a buck, or something." (waiter)

Melissa was saying that that she did not get along with Bunny at all. She said Bunny was "spreading her legs" for the management and their friends and felt she could do whatever she wanted in the bar. She said that Bunny was acting really bitchy towards her, snapping her fingers for service. (notes)

Additionally, while some dancers create very little difficulty for the staff, any disruptions involving the dancer may be blamed on her, whether these are attributed to her "haughtiness," the boisterousness of her fans or critics, or her involvements in hooking. She is more transient, and it is easier to define her as the "troublesome party." Where these incidents involve regulars, friends of the management, or other staff people, the staff may provide little support for her. Further, we have noted that to the extent dancers align themselves with particular customers rather than staff people, they may treat staff members much more casually than desired. For example, special concessions may be demanded and the friend may be told that tips are not necessary. . . . A waiter or waitress overhearing remarks of this nature may find these particularly annoying.

Although staff people often express boredom with dancers' performances, the frequent change of faces and interests adds an element of novelty. While the staff do not have the length of time available to become as acquainted with the dancers as they often do with the hookers, the degree of intimacy between strippers and staff may range from intense mutual dislike to "serious romances" with dancers moving into a waiter's or bouncer's home, for example:

Perry seems to fall in love with a lot of the strippers. It's not just a little thing, but each time it's rather a very serious kind of romance. One he is in love with now is Daisy. The last one he fell in love with, the butchy one, stole all his money and took off. Daisy is going out with another guy, but brings him to the bar, where they carry on in front of Perry. It seems to mess his head up quite a bit, because when I'm working with him at the bar, all he'd be doing is talking about her, and he makes a lot of errors on the cash. . . . Now, Daisy's been gone for about two weeks. It has pretty well taken that long for Perry to get over her. . . . Alvin was saying that his brother Perry is a fool for falling in love with every stripper he comes across. He also expressed disapproval at Perry spending so much money on strippers. He said that Perry becomes upset if a stripper that he is fond of even talks with a customer, adding that Perry should know better than to become jealous, since he has been working in bars for a number of years. (notes)

SIDELINE INVOLVEMENTS

While the hookers and the strippers may represent some staff contact points with "the life," other routes are noteworthy. In part reflecting the new staff member's acceptance, and in part reflecting "the action" of the staff and/or the patrons wherein one works, a newcomer may find himself drinking, using drugs, going to after-hours clubs, the race-track, and so on, more heavily than he had anticipated. If this happens, the staff member may not only experience a further differentiation of self from "straight society," but may also cultivate spending habits making him more dependent on financial aspects of bar work. Where participation in a "faster life" is more extensive, bar employees may develop spending habits which could not be supported by a majority of legitimate salaries:[6]

> A number of the employees at Main and Central are heavily into the track, booze, and drugs. Many times, Perry loses a few hundred dollars at the track as does Norton, the bartender, and Jack, a desk clerk. . . . Frank, the bouncer is quite the gambler too. He bets on everything, hockey games, races, boxing, everything. A lot of other people at the bar are heavily into gambling. . . . One of the waiters is in trouble with the loansharks. He was very nervous tonight, because some guy he owes money to is after him. He was running around, trying to find someone to spot him the money. (notes)

> As a waiter at Main, he was making a hell of a lot of money. But, his apartment is nothing. He's got a t.v., and a couch, a chair, and a coffee table, but he don't have nothing like what you would expect. Both of them are working. She is a hooker and he is a waiter. Now that's a lot of money. They could have had a lot of things. He's got a car, but that's about it. I don't know what he does with his money, because you can't see nothing. Who knows where his money goes, because I tell you, they're making easily over a $1000 a week. But this guy, and nearly all these waiters, they live in dives, a lot of them do, they live in shitty places. (bartender)

In addition to regular bar work and hustles, bar employees may find that contacts with hustlers provide opportunities to develop lucrative side-line hustles such as shylocking, bookmaking, drug dealing, fencing, and pimping. Although only some will become involved, bar people experiencing financial difficulties seem particularly susceptible to these side-line involvements and, on becoming involved, are advantaged in providing or distributing other services:

> Frank, the doorman, sold me a suit. We also made a deal that on any future sales I could steer to him, I would get ten bucks. He is always trying to unload something. He has a diamond ring, a watch. Different times he will also ask me if I want to make $150 bucks by going out of town, dropping off a package somewhere. He always has these kind of deals. . . . This merchandising in illegal goods is a pretty common occurrence. . . . Felix, the bartender, also runs a bookie service and does some loansharking. One of the waitresses has a booze can, an after-hours place. It is kind of a meeting place for people in the

---

[6] The parallels to involvements of persons involved in gambling (Lesieur, 1977) and card and dice hustlers in "action" (Prus and Sharper, 1977) are striking, suggesting that spending habits may represent an important continuance element in deviant careers.

fringes, in the underlife. Also, a number of the staff people have bootlegging enterprises or have had over the years. (notes)

Although these sideline involvements are apt to be more characteristic of staff at "action bars," they are far from limited to these. Not only do many hustlers frequent a plurality of bars, but the staff are also relatively mobile across bars in respect to both their work and patron roles.

CONTINUITY[7]

Representing demanding, confusing, disrespectable, and sometimes frightening work settings, the question of continuity in bar careers becomes a rather interesting one. For in spite of its disrespectability and demanding work conditions, bar work represents the major life career for many people. Proportionately few of the other staff people we have encountered have developed the extensive side-line involvements tending to characterize the staff at "action bars" but, with time, most bar staff come to define themselves increasingly as "bar people" and tend to find themselves less open (and less likely to be considered in reference) to other lines of work:

If they can get past the first 6 weeks, then they're going to stay, until either I get rid of them or they move on to other positions. But they aren't going to quit because they dislike the job. (manager)

It's a problem to get out. Once you're in this business, it gets under your skin. You start to develop the pattern of living at night and sleeping in the day, and you develop the rather carefree attitude towards life which working in a bar requires. You go to work and yet you enjoy it. It's not like going to an office job. It's hard to get away from that, very hard. The lady I was talking to last night, at the Top Spot, said that she'd never work any place other than a bar and she's almost 50 years old. She's worked in bars and restaurants for 30 years, been at the Top Spot for 20 years. She just loves it. She wouldn't do anything else. . . . Right now, I'm trying to find a different job. Taking a job as a manager of another bar is no problem, but my experience here, as a manager, does not weigh heavily with employers from other types of industries, even though I operate and control a staff of over 40 people, which is a large staff. They don't accept that readily. They figure it's a Mickey Mouse operation. It's not a business, the way they look at it. If they only knew that a room of this size could employ 40 people a week and can produce $700,000 a year. It just would boggle their minds. They can't realize that this industry is that lucrative and there is that much involved in it. A lot of people put you down for that. (manager)

Not only is there something of a negative sentiment towards "straight work" among bar workers, but few jobs offer the financial rewards or diversity one encounters in bar life:

Melissa mentioned that although she has worked in a office, she will probably not work there again. She said that she has received an offer to work for a local

---

[7] For another statement on continuity in bar work, see Hearn and Stoll (1975).

newspaper as a junior reporter or secretary, but they could not offer her the money that she could be making at Main. She said that she has gotten "spoiled" at Main by making so much money and that it would probably take her a while to get used to living on less. . . . Melissa said that Main was taking up a great deal of her time and that it was becoming the centre of her social life as well . . . that she was becoming concerned about what was happening to her at Main. She thought that she was becoming hardened and sleazy, because of the way people were treating her . . . customers often take liberties with her because they see her kidding around with the staff and think that they can do the same. She said that her reputation was also a problem, because she felt that people were losing respect for her . . . she also felt that she was losing her sense of identity at Main because of the "topless waitress image" being thrust upon her. She said, however, that she found the job more enjoyable than any straight job she had ever had, "Everyday's an adventure and you never know how it's going to turn out or all that will happen. Sometimes it's good and sometimes it's bad, but it's never a routine." (notes)

There's maybe other things I might be doing, but it's not so bad, and the money is a lot better than I could make, say in construction, or in a factory. And it's a lot easier, and a lot more interesting working here. (waiter)

Bar work may provide more diversity than some other jobs, but these diversions are not all positively experienced. Persons working in bars are likely to find themselves confronted with drunk and other troublesome patrons, on the one hand, and encounter indications of disrespectability from more conventional citizens on the other. Although some persons may continue to work in bars with attitudes of disgust or pity that many straights associate with drunks, toughs, and the like, long-term staff tend to become acclimatized to these concerns:

It's taught me not to empathize with everybody, to be more distant, more calloused too. When I see some guy get beaten up now, I just sort of turn around the other way. I don't like it, but at the same time, I'm willing to ignore it. Before, it used to leave me shaking for the rest of the night when I saw it. Now I just have a tendency to ignore it. . . . If you see someone getting drunk, the same thing. Like you used to say, "Oh Christ!" I still ask people if they're driving home. I don't like to see things happen to anybody and I always tell them at the end of the night to drive carefully when they leave, because a lot of stupid, foolish things have happened because people are drunk. I used to feel a little bit responsible, because you're the one that's doing the pushing and the hustling, but I don't feel anything about it now. Too bad if they don't have the brains to handle themselves. That's their problem. (waitress)

At first, like a lot of waitresses, I used to go around telling everybody, "This is only part time. I'm going through school and I'm going to be a teacher." Now I figure, being a waitress, there's an awful lot to being a waitress, I've found that out. You have to be a special kind of person. You have to have a smile on your face at all times, you have to learn to take complaints from customers. You can't get excited, you can't get hyper. I'm no longer justifying my reasons for being a waitress. (waitress)

As persons "fit in" to the hotel community, they typically find themselves more firmly embedded in bar life than they had anticipated, and much more of their social and personal identity becomes synonymous with bar life. Even on leaving one bar job, they are most likely, through kinship or friendship ties, as well as through "work experience," to find themselves in another hotel job. Regardless of their initial routings, on becoming more established in this "subculture," bar employees are apt to find that continued involvements are easier and more rewarding means of realizing personal interests than are attempts at disengagement:

> *The bartender, I told him that I had this brilliant idea, that I thought about going to school part time. He said I would never do it because the money was too good. At first I didn't think it would be hard, but I'm finding it hard because I'm getting wrapped into the life and I know it's going to be hard when I'm taking another course.* (waitress)

> *When I started seeing the money, and when my parents started seeing how much was coming in, their whole attitude was completely changed. I realized that I could never go back to that first job, it wasn't that good. Even though you do work really hard for say six, seven hours, it does pay off in the end.* (waitress)

> *Sometimes you like the job so much, and other times you just can't stand it at all, and you think, "Oh, I should quit. I should quit." But it's hard for anybody. If you've got a job, it's hard to go out and get another one, because you just don't have the initiative. If you don't have a job, it makes it easier because you have to, but if you don't have to, you just sort of end up staying where you are. And the money's good.* (waitress)

While we would not, as Lemert (1951, 1967) encourages, ignore preliminary deviance routings, it is clearly the case that the responses of "receiving audiences" (those whose "world" one enters) are much more critical in career deviance than is generally implied in sociological analysis. Fitting into the staff community has important implications for one's early involvements in bar work, but it is also exceedingly important vis-à-vis continuity. Not only does the bar become a less distant, less threatening, and more lucrative setting in which to work as persons become more integrated into the staff community, but as persons become more embedded in a series of activities and relationships within the staff community, the bar assumes much more meaning than it does to outsiders. Insofar as one develops bonds of friendship, love and sexuality, and as persons spend proportionately more of their off duty time at the bar, disinvolvement becomes increasingly difficult:

> *If you're working regular hours, 8 to 5 or 8 to 6 or whatever it is, you can say, "Well, I've got my evening free. I don't need to worry about this or that." In the hotel business, you might be there all fucking night and then you come in and work a double the next day. You're always in that hotel. If you're not at home, "Well, where is he?" "Well, he's right down there." It got so bad that even on my days off, I was there all the time. There's really nothing there, just sort of a lot of plastic people running around trying to impress everybody else. Now, all the time I was there, I was turning into one of these plastic people. Like I'd be standing at the bar, talking to people, buy this one a drink, buy that one a drink. I'd leave my wife at home, and go down to the hotel, every day.* (bartender)

> *The waitresses here, they're the centre of attention. They like the attention they get. They can come across any male they want, they can probably take home*

any male they want, even if they're dogs, really dogs, ugly looking girls. They'll still get approached because they're the easiest thing to approach in a bar. And a lot of girls take that as an ego building trip rather than what it should be taken as, a bunch of drunken bums coming on to you. But it is an ego trip, because no matter how ugly you are, you always get approached in the bar by some male. . . . So if a girl was to leave, she'd miss that, definitely. Myself included. (waitress)

I like it and I really don't know what else I could do, I only have an 11th grade education. Besides, I make good money. I have a late model car and good spending money. But with me, I like the competition, I like the hustle, and I really don't have any plans of quitting. . . . I like to be with people and mixing with them more. I'm always around, I'm circulating, talking to people. The thing is that you're always on, you're always with the people and if you're having problems at home or anything, well you just can't let that show. You always have to be on your best because if you want to make tips then you have to be more pleasant towards people. (waiter)

Although many people voluntarily leave bar work after a few days or a few weeks, and others are dismissed as unacceptable within a short period of time, those who "fit in" the hotel community and realize the lucrative potential bar work offers, seldom quit. Unless they find themselves in a series of heavy interpersonal conflicts, or have better opportunities in other bars, they are likely to leave only when discharged. However, given limited unionization in bars, and the opportunities employees have to steal, most dismissals are apt to be abrupt:

Doris, a new topless waitress, is fairly loud and haughty when she talks. A customer sitting beside me commented, "This girl won't last very long." He was right. The next day they told her they didn't need her as a waitress any longer. . . . (P.S.) Hadn't seen Doris for a few weeks but she's back again, this time working as a hooker. (notes)

The place was good for making money, but there wasn't any security there. They fired people all the time. Like if somebody finished work on a Saturday night, the management would say, "Well listen, don't bother coming in any more." The person might have been there a year, years, you know. Nobody gets any notice. There's a basic reason why they won't give you notice in the hotel, because you'd just rip them off, left and right. You'd say, "Fuck it, if I'm getting canned this week, I might as well make some money." You would have to do it, and then bang, you're into everything. You don't stop at nothing. If you're getting fired, you just take what you can get, and that's the way people do it. What the hell, if they're getting fired and they knew it, they'd bring their own bottles in. . . . I've got no education, and if I go somewhere and somebody says, "Were you in any kind of school or something?" I would have to say, "No, I was here and there," right? Now, if he wants to be a real prick and I've got to get references, and they phone in, he could say, "Well geez, you know, we had to fire him." (bartender)

Still, many of these dismissals are open to reconsideration or negotiation, as employers find that "good" new people are not so readily obtained in the short time span they often have in which to replace employees:

Edgar was fired Monday, but he's going to be rehired again. . . . Perry also was fired, but was rehired a couple days later. That seems to happen a lot around there. . . . The desk clerk, Simon, an old guy, was fired and hired two times. He gets drunk a lot and I guess that's part of his problem. One time, he drank two bottles of cough medicine and was wiped out. They had to call the ambulance for him. . . . A somewhat similar thing happened when the new management took over. They dismissed four of the old staff the next day, when they came into work. Two days later, they wanted to know where they could find these people so they could rehire them. (notes)

IN CONTEXT

Although our research originated in hooker bars, we endeavored to assess the representativeness of our material by examining staff routines in many other "types" of bars. The parallels were striking, suggesting an integrated discussion.[8] Thus, although some bars are "rougher" or more "action oriented" than others, concerns with service and "peacekeeping" are prominent across bars. Similarly, while "hustling" may assume a variety of forms, and is more common in some bars than others, very few bars seem void of this activity. Likewise, while one may find some romance involving staff in hooker and stripper bars, staff people in many other bars find themselves romantically involved with other staff or patrons. The notion of a "staff community" also seems in evidence across bars, and a newcomer's acceptance by that group can dramatically affect not only one's work routines, but one's social life more generally. In short, regardless of whether one is discussing a "cement floored, bootstomping beer joint," or a "posh, sophisticated night club," once one looks past the "packaging" and concentrates on activities, staff work is highly consistent across bars. A minority of staff people are extensively involved in "the life," but most staff people have some contact with "action" people, suggesting that bar staff, on the whole, are more "street-wise" than people in most occupational groupings. Staff people with more extensive contact with people in "the life" are apt to have greater opportunities to participate and may find their lives more complicated as a result. This does not, however, effectively replace other staff concerns. Further similarities among staff across bars will be evident in the following chapter on patrons.

---

[8] We had initially organized the bar material with respect to hooker and non-hooker bars, but found so much redundancy as to preclude this format. A qualified, but integrated statement seemed much more feasible.

Chapter 6

Being Patrons: Regulars, Rounders, and Heavies

In discussing the patrons and the ways in which they fit into the hotel community, we first provide an overview of generally operative bar norms, indicating how these coincide with patron identities. We then consider a number of "types of patrons" commonly encountered in bar settings. Other aspects of "being patrons" are examined in reference to "being somebody," "drinking," and "being entertained." The focus then shifts to "rounders," a category of patrons of critical significance for understanding the social life in "action bars." The chapter concludes with a discussion of "area restaurants" and "after-hours clubs." While this removes us somewhat from the bar itself, it is important to recognize the extent to which bar life spills over into the larger community. Much of "the action" takes place in bars, but a consideration of these other settings is essential for a fuller understanding of the "hotel community."

So far as possible, we will be discussing bar patrons in general. Patrons in some bars may be more interested in hookers and strippers than male patrons in some other bars, and proportionately more of the patrons in "action bars" are apt to be considered "rounders" than patrons at most other bars. However, while the particular mixes of patron interests are likely to vary between bars, the "social types" (Klapp, 1971) characterizing bar routines and their forms of association are sufficiently generic across bars to justify a de-emphasis of action bars in discussing patron roles.

BAR INVOLVEMENTS

In spite of all the research on alcoholism and drinking, we know surprisingly little about patron life in bars. For the most part, researchers have been content to survey individuals in other (sober) settings, endeavoring to find background correlates with liquor consumption. Given the number of bars in our society there has been surprisingly little recognition of drinking establishments as social settings. While Moore (1897) argued for the "social value of the saloon," sociologists have largely neglected this aspect of urban culture. Where sociologists have considered bars, it has been largely in terms of categorizing them (for example, skid row taverns, cocktail lounges) and describing the backgrounds of their clientele rather than indicating the ways in which persons in bars relate to one another. The commonly cited studies by Macrory (1952), Gottlieb (1957), and Clinard (1962) add little to our knowledge of social life in bars, however, the following are more useful in this sense: Paul Cressey's (1932) seldom cited work on the taxi-dance hall; Sheri Cavan's (1966) discussion of bar etiquette; Spradley and Mann's (1975) portrayal of the cocktail waitress; and Roebuck and Frese's (1976) analysis of an "after-hours club."[1]

Some earlier research (Macrory, 1952; Gottlieb, 1957; and Clinard, 1962) has emphasized differences among drinking establishments in reference to such things as geographical location, physical structures, and the like but, as Cavan (1966) notes, these distinctions tend to miss commonalities across bars. Cavan's suggestion that bars be examined more extensively in terms of function is well taken: for Cavan, "convenience bars" refer to accessible places in which to drink; "night spots" are bars highlighting stage entertainment; "marketplace bars" provide settings for a variety of sexual (and other) exchanges and hustles; and "home territory bars" represent a "home away from home" or in some cases, the "home." Cavan also takes issue with those who see function largely determined by the type of bar the place is alleged to be (skid row tavern, nightclub, neighborhood tavern). She correctly contends that many activities occur across bar types and may occur concurrently within the same bar.

While it is useful to recognize the variety of functions any bar may serve, our observations also suggest that it is important to recognize the variety of functions any bar may serve patrons each time they enter and over the course of their stay. For example, Henry may go to a bar with the intention of drinking, only to find himself absorbed in the entertainment or a newly formed friendship. Likewise, Tom, going to the same bar to "have a good time," may find the evening dull and disappointing, and may end up "getting drunk." Functions sensitize us to activities, but they do not inform us of the ways in which activities are worked out among the involved parties. Another step towards understanding bar life is to examine the normative frameworks generally operative in bar settings:

1.   Although "public drinking places" are seemingly open to all, "openness" varies not only from bar to bar, but also within the same bar over time and among the patrons in attendance. In part, initial receptiveness reflects the way in which each "stranger" is defined (for example, attractive female, dress style, time spent in the bar). The general patron norm is not to mix where you are not invited or have not received some initial indications of receptiveness to your company (such as a smile, a nod).

2.   The latitude of permitted behavior varies by bar and patron(s) involved. The management and staff are the main rule definers and enforcers, but both take cues from licencing and policing agencies and their anticipated/existing patrons. Strangers are especially likely to encounter stringent applications of bar rules. While more "boisterous behavior" is tolerated in bars than in many other settings, there is a concern that an individual's activities not disturb other patrons to the point of promoting extensive departures.

3.   There is a rather firm expectation that people in bars will drink and persons, especially newcomers, are expected to evidence drinking behavior.

---

[1] While it is not our intent, herein, to present an extensive analysis on the drinking activities of bar patrons, we suggest that only as researchers begin to study persons engaged in drinking (in their "natural" drinking settings) can they hope to achieve a more adequate understanding of drinking as a social activity. For indications of the sorts of literature on drinking presently available, see Whitehead et al. (1973) and Robinson (1976).

Some stigma is attached to the non-drinker, although this is generally diminished when the non-drinker is a female.

4.   While patrons often take turns paying for drinks in rounds, this practice is often encouraged by staff as a means of expediting (and occasionally hustling) orders. Persons of more or less equal status will tend to reciprocate drinks. Where one of the parties is financially more established, he may more frequently treat the others.

5.   Who may initiate conversation among strangers, and over what distance varies not only with the bar status of the initiator, but also the degree of crowding, and the loudness of the music. No matter who initiates the encounter, persons have different notions of appropriate terminations ("Hey, I'm talking to you. . . .") and may not appreciate subsequent inattention.

6.   Persons may initiate encounters with strangers on a variety of bases, but one common way of expressing interest is to offer to buy the other person a drink. Acceptance of a gift drink suggests a willingness to converse to some extent with the other. Refusing an offered drink is an effective means of promoting social distance. Once one has begun drinking with another person it may be easier to leave the bar than to disengage oneself from that other patron.

While this listing of bar norms is somewhat at variance with those suggested by Cavan (1966) in her discussion of "bar etiquette," we see the differences not as reflecting differences among bars sampled, but rather reflecting her limited contact with ongoing bar life. In what follows, we indicate the normative parameters in effect for each category of patron, keeping in mind the problems of fitting people neatly into categories.

THE PATRONS

The following "categories of patrons" are introduced with relatively little regard for the entertainment particular bars feature—country music, disco, strippers, and so on. These patron categories seem applicable across bars, although the "mixes" of patrons may vary considerably.

"NO ACCOUNTS"

Regardless of the bar, some persons are likely to be defined as either unsuitable for entry or inconsequential for business. In some cases, a bar's location or reputation will act as a preliminary screening device, keeping out "bums," "drunks," "trouble makers," and the like, so that "no accounts" are not often encountered. In other settings, however, they are much more obvious and one finds that staff and patrons may be highly intolerant of these persons. The "no account's" actual behavior is largely insignificant; he simply does not qualify for "general acknowledgement":

> An old man, wearing a skirt and rubber boots, whom I had earlier noticed on the street, tried to enter the bar at Central. He had just come in a few steps when one of the waiters turned him around and shoved him out the door. On returning, he commented, "We can't have weirdos like that coming around,

eh!''. . . . Generally speaking, although there are a lot of "winos" in the area, you see very few at either Main or Central. The drinks are more expensive there than at many other bars, and although this man in the skirt and rubbers was quite unusual, the staff at these places try to discourage the "rubbies" from entry even when they have the money. (notes)

TOURISTS

Generally speaking, persons identified as "tourists" attend bars in groups on special occasions. They tend to be of minimal concern to the staff, but larger, noisier groups are more readily noted. The general bar norms apply to the tourists more than to the "no accounts," but they are often exempted from the usual notions of propriety. For example, members of an out-of-town fraternal organization or a group of men holding a stag in the bar may be allowed liberties with the waitresses or noise levels that the same people would not achieve were they an unidentified collection of local residents. Tourists are seen as "one-time" business prospects and attempts are made to accommodate them:

There were about forty soldiers sitting in one section of the bar. The D.J. made something of a fuss over them, both while they were there and later as they were leaving. One of the soldiers had a birthday. The D.J. prompted the stripper working at the time to go over and give the lieutenant a kiss and then one to the guy who had a birthday that day. Apparently some of the boys enjoyed the show because six returned later on in the evening. (notes)

STRANGERS

When unknown persons go to bars individually or in small groups, they are more apt to be defined as "strangers" than tourists. It is interesting to note that although these people are much less familiar with the local rules, it is they to whom the "general normative framework" is likely to be most stringently applied. This is particularly the case for males entering alone. Single females tend to receive the largest range of tolerance, from rejection based entirely on her gender or the suspicion that she is hooking, to an acceptance of a variety of behaviors unlikely to be tolerated of any male patrons or staff. Solitary males, the most common strangers in most bars, are the patrons most likely to be defined as "outsiders," and are considered the most desirable targets for any hustles or animosities:

I dislike going to new bars. You never know what's going on and if anybody is going to come on to you. It's like you don't have anybody who's a friend there, and you have to watch yourself more, what you do or say. . . . If you get talking with a group of regulars there, then it's all different. You get treated better, more like one of them. Then you're not so much a stranger anymore. (patron)

OCCASIONALS

"Occasionals" are patrons whom staff persons recognize as people who frequent their bar on a now-and-then basis. When occasionals come in groups, they are not only more likely to be treated with more consideration, but are more likely to be remembered, especially if they return with the same people. Overall, however, occasionals are likely to be treated much like strangers, and be subjected to the "general normative framework." Like strangers, they are also seen as good prospects for any hustles the staff or other patrons are eager to promote:

> *You have a lot of people who come by now and then. You really don't get to know what they're all about. You maybe have a nodding acquaintance with some of them, but they're really not that important to you. A lot of them will remember you, but you can't really keep track of them.* (bartender)

REGULARS

Referring to persons fairly well-known by the staff, regulars are typically individuals who spend a few hours drinking at a particular bar two or three (or more) times a week. Regardless of whether bars are hooker bars, stripper bars, ones that feature comedians, jazz, bands, and so on, or whether they provide little more than "just a place to go and drink," few bars seem able to remain financially viable without a supporting cast of regulars. While some bars will, by virtue of their entertainment, attact more "tourists," and some will, by virtue of their location, represent convenient "watering holes" for those passing by, "regulars" represent an integral element in the social and financial life of most bars:

> *A regular is somebody who's always in here, that knows everybody around. . . . He's there every other day, or every three days, at least the weekends, Friday, Saturday. Sometimes, they're people that you've partied with, you've taken time off to party with. They're people who know you. Even though you don't know all of them, they're the regulars, they know me. . . . They look at the place as their own place, and they're free to do what they want, provided they keep it within limitations.* (waitress)

> *The regular customers coming in, they're the most important part of your business. Some of them will be big spenders when they come in. Some will be in like every day, and not spend that much, but yet they're there every day spending. And that's what I've found makes a difference in the business, if you have the regulars or if you don't.* (manager)

Although some regulars are largely "regular drinkers," many become more integral to the social life of the bar. In this respect, they contrast somewhat with the "occasional" who may come for one purpose only (for instance for a quick drink after work, or to find a hooker) and who is not so willing to take the time (or effort) required to "fit in" as a regular:

> *This place, I've known it under four different owners. I probably know it better than most of the staff working here.* (patron)

> *People will often hang out at a bar. They'll just hang out there. You know 20 or 25 people are going to be regulars. Like, I've been hanging out at the Jubilee, for two and a half years. . . . I'm a regular there. On my days off, I'm there all the time. During the days, if I've got time off, often by the time the bar opens, I'm there drinking with the boys. There's a few of us, we just hang out there. We all love the bar. And we're there whether the band's good or not. We like the*

place. We get treated well. If we want a special kind of beer, it's always on call, because they know that I'm going to want that if I'm around. And they stock that for me. . . . Like I walked in just before Christmas, and the first beer was on the house. Fuck, man! I spend two or three thousand dollars a year in that bar, yet they bought me one beer, and that made me feel so special. You wouldn't have believed how I felt! Man, have one beer bought for me at Christmas time. Now I just, "Hey, man, I'm going to come back here every time I can. The first chance I get, I'm going to come back here, because they made me feel like a million dollars!" The Jubilee's my bar. I live there. It's my hangout. And the regulars feel that way. The regulars are regulars, and nothing is going to stop them. Like, Wilson has been a regular there for 18 years. I've been a regular for two and a half years. No matter what happens, I'm going to be a regular there. I love the bar. (patron)

Generally speaking, the regulars do gain some familiarity with one another, but do not have the extensive knowledge of one another that is gained by members of the staff. Not only are the staff likely to have the advantage of sheer time spent in the bar setting, and opportunities to exchange patron information with other staff and patrons, but their work positions afford them levels of mobility and ease of contact patrons are generally not accorded. It should be noted that regulars, being viewed as "good for business," tend to be exempted from some generally applicable rules. These exemptions, however, tend to be very minor in nature. At the same time, while bar staff and patrons are apt to be more cautious in hustling "regulars," they are also likely to be more aware of their weaknesses. The extracts following provide more insight into the role of the regular:

Regulars have a somewhat inflated idea of their ability to get away with things. Many have a swollen head as to their importance in the business. They see how many dollars they're spending week after week and, the common joke around here was, "I paid for the washrooms," "I paid for the new bar stools." I had one girl that swore that she personally paid for the mirrors on that side, and I just said, "Well, what about the rest of us who work day after day after day after day. What do we do?" (manager)

Dale goes to Main three or four times a week. He said it was a "damned good place to drink" and that was mainly why he goes, that he "likes the atmosphere. . . ." He is a former teacher and now he has a small business. He is also an occasional client of the hookers. . . . Dale referred to himself as "an alcoholic at thirty" and there was support for that statement. He did get pretty well "sloshed" and when he was getting ready to leave, he sort of banged off the wall and back to the bar and fell over the cigarette machine, onto the floor. We helped him up and straightened him around. He sat down for a bit, complaining that his head hurt and then left. (notes)

Accompanying staff people to other bars was a worthwhile experience. Not only do they know staff people in other bars, and are quick to disclose their occupations to other newly encountered staff people, but they also seem to know a fair number of regulars at these other bars. . . . The patrons will sometimes mention that they have two or three preferred drinking places, but it was interesting to see the extent to which the same patrons were known in other bars. (notes)

To a large extent, we have directed this discussion of regulars towards solitary males. We should note that one may also speak of "regular females," and "regular groups." In general, these other regulars, while less frequent overall, are more apt to be readily defined as regulars given equal visits to the bar. Larger groups can more quickly and extensively "color" the atmosphere of the bar and are more likely to attract the attention of the management. Most female regulars with whom we are familiar attend bars in the same or mixed gender groups, but we have also encountered a number of solitary (non-hustler) female regulars. In most cases, they are persons who have known other people in the bar prior to their solitary entrances:

> Doreen was telling me that she first became involved with Central through Shannon, "We were taking some music lessons together. She invited me to come down and see what the place is like. I went down and began liking it." Doreen has now been a regular there for a number of years. She seems to know a lot of the people and indicated that she came down tonight because she owed one of the bartenders some money. She had brought her daughter to Central with her this time. (notes)

While the groups of individuals constituting the regulars at bars need not be "the crowd" the management desired to have as regulars, they can be exceedingly important in defining the "atmosphere of the bar" and the experiences of the management, staff, and entertainers, as well as any patrons. As a bar becomes known as a particular kind of bar, this reputation serves as a basis on which it may be assessed as a feasible "drinking" place by a variety of persons. The regular clientele may shift somewhat with time, but the significance of reputations in promoting/deterring other customers should not be neglected.

INSIDE REGULARS

As Spradley and Mann (1975: 76-79) note, patrons considered to be "friends of the management" (and in some cases, other staff) are likely to expect and receive deferential treatment. The "general normative framework" is considered largely inapplicable to them, and they may have greater licence in bar behavior than regular staff. Recognizing these insiders' abilities to communicate dissatisfaction to the management, staff persons generally endeavor to be overtly considerate of them. Although frequently resented by the staff, the "inside regulars" tend to view the bar as a home territory and recreational area:

> I also get some regulars, who are always trying to con you around, through the manager or the owner. They'll say, "Well, he said I'm good for it," or "I'll take mine on credit," or whatever it is. And you sort of wonder, "Do they have cent one?" Like you're worried about being stuck with the bill yourself. You hate having these people around because you don't make money off them and you never know where you stand with them. A guy will run up a 50 or 60 dollar tab and you figure, "Well, what am I going to do with it afterwards." And you're on the bar, you're busy working with people and they want their service right now, "Snap, snap!" You just get a little annoyed with them. But then, if you don't give them service before the other regulars, well, they run off to the boss, "Hey, what's the matter with this guy, he's not giving us good service."

I'm the only one on the bar and working my ass off as it is, and I'm not making any money off these guys and if I don't serve the other people, they're going to walk out too. These guys might run up a $50 tab and they'll say, "We'll straighten it up tomorrow," and they might go back and pay the boss. But what do you get out of it, just a headache, listening to these guys bullshit. (bartender)

Friends of the owners, they are the biggest pain in the rump that you'd ever want to find. You always have your free loaders, friends of the owners. My outlook on them was, "If the owner's here, he'll buy you a drink, if he's not here, you're just the same as everybody else to me. Here you get a lot of these old business men come in. They know they're safe from view of their wives and their wives'll never walk in here. They come in to hustle the young chicks and they can get pretty out of hand, but you've got to be careful with them. You can't go roughing up a lawyer or something like that the same way you can rough up a kid who's causing trouble. . . . They're always making plays for waitresses. The friends of the owner, they assume that they have little ins with waitresses. They always try and it's really funny because they're what you call the laughing stock of the place, because everybody knew what was going on. They were moochers and they were just in here for a free ride and everybody's laughing at them behind their backs. Since they were friends of the owners, you couldn't really say anything to them, but you had to deal with them. (manager)

HEAVIES

Another category of patrons meriting attention in the bar setting are the "heavies" or the "toughs." Although these people may represent all the earlier mentioned patron categories they tend to stand out from many other patrons as a consequence of their "disruptive potential":

We have had some heavies in here and you have to give them extra special attention. You have to be a little pleasant to them without asking for trouble, especially, like a waitress talking to some heavy duty. You don't want to lead them on to think that you're interested in them, but you just to have be a lot more friendly to avoid any trouble and sort of make a friend type image. Like I'm your friend, or maybe I'm your little sister sort of thing, and then they're less likely to cause any trouble. It's true. (waitress)

When I first started here, we had a lot of trouble with bikers. You don't want to get known as a bikers' spot. So you just kept kicking them out as soon as they walked in. You just called the police and out they went. They didn't get served. We didn't try to stop them, because if you did, you'd have a gang war on your hands. So you just let them walk in, you'd call the policemen and they'd walk back out again. You do that enough times and you don't have any more problems with them. They know that they aren't wanted, and most of them would be carrying dope on them and that and the least amount of contact with the police they had, the better they liked it. . . . So the police would come in and I'd have to ask them to leave in front of the police officer. Then, the police officer could say, "Come on, he's asked you to go. Get out of here." (manager)

Where toughs constitute a larger or more visible regular element in a particular bar, that bar is apt to acquire a reputation for roughness, finding that its subsequent clientele reflects its reputation:

> *I was working at this one hotel and what happened was that the heavies, the toughs, they just took over the place. The owner had his money tied up and that and he really didn't know what to do. He wanted the business, but everything was just getting so much out of hand, so I just quit there. And you get a hotel owner that's scared of the roughness, then those people will be running the hotel and the decent people are going to stay away. The hotel is going to lose in the end. I've seen it happen to hotels where the rough element sort of took over, and it wasn't bikers, it was just very tough people.* (waitress)

> *I've been to the Bluegrass a few times. The first time I went, I remember thinking that I'd never seen such a weird place. I never went down there with less than seven or eight of my friends, because some of the people there are really tough. . . . I thought I was raised in a pretty rough area, and hung around with some pretty tough characters, but this place was something else. Like when I went there with some guys from the club, we never wanted to fight down there. . . . There were always two or three cruisers floating around there, and when I was there somebody was usually fighting. It was a weird place, I couldn't handle it. . . . It wasn't a place where colors weren't effective. There were some guys down there five times as tough as guys in my gang. And a lot of them carried pieces or knives and wouldn't hesitate to use it on you without a moment's notice. . . . The Brass Bugle's different. There's often bikes outside, but I like going there. You figure something interesting might happen there. It has a reputation as a rough bar, but it's not like the Bluegrass.* (biker)

While roughness is to some extent associated with the presence of rounders, either or both elements may be affected by the hiring practices of the management. Where "rounders" or "heavies" are hired, they may not only attract former acquaintances, but they are likely to feel more comfortable in the presence of hustlers and toughs than are many other staff people.

> *The only time we actually have any heavies coming around is if they're knowing someone in the band. Or sometimes, if they know people who are working here, they'll come around. Those people sort of draw them in. . . . Sometimes if we have a group of heavies coming in, I'll actually ask the doorman to stay away from them. Then I'll just go and ask them to quiet down or whatever, and if there's any problem, I'll just call the police. But sometimes, they are looking for a fight and it's very easy for the bouncer to get drawn into that.* (manager)

In discussing "roughness" in bars, we should also distinguish between "rough looking bars" and bars in which violent physical exchanges are common. In general, fights are more common in rougher looking bars, but fights are not common in all rougher looking bars:

> *Spruce Springs is an older, run-down hotel with two large beverage rooms and a cocktail lounge. A few younger people drink there, but the hotel is patronized predominately by persons 45-50 years of age and up. About a third of the patrons are females. Nearly all drink beer. According to the waiter, they have problems with some of the patrons when they get drunk and a little obnoxious, but fights are not very common.* (notes)

BEING PATRONS

To this point, we have outlined the more general normative frameworks in bars, vis-à-vis patrons, and have indicated some variations of patron treatment by staff classification. These normative frameworks and the earlier mentioned "functions" of bars are certainly useful in helping us to understand bar life, but they neglect the dynamic aspects of "being patrons," they miss "the activity of bar life." Bars are social places, and only when one begins to take account of the shifting interests and ongoing exchanges of those involved, can one achieve a more adequate understanding of that social setting. Bars are not simply places in which to drink. Although patrons may go to bars with any number of things in mind, as they participate in an ongoing situation, as their own actions and those of others unfold, bar life may assume a meaningfulness not earlier anticipated. As a means of portraying this sense of ongoing group life, we would like to briefly discuss "being somebody," "drinking," and "being entertained." Although these represent areas in which individuals may influence ongoing group life, their experiences are also affected by those with whom they relate; the staff, the entertainers, and the other patrons.

BEING SOMEBODY

The earlier discussion of patron typings suggests one basis on which patrons may be more or less esteemed in a bar. It should be noted, however, that patron activities may be much more instrumental in determining recognition than are these categorizations. For example, if a patron is more generous in purchasing drinks, he becomes "somebody." Some may consider him "foolish," but this practice can also be a way of generating friendship and respect:

When I was working the bar, this guy came over and sat down and ordered a round. I noticed that he was alone and I asked, "A round for who?" He said "a round for the bar" indicating the dozen or so patrons seated at the stool bar. I thought that this was a little unusual and I was concerned whether the man could pay for it. However, he pulled out a roll of money to show he was good for it. The man wasn't drunk or anything, but just seemed to be "on the impress" with the people there. (notes)

Tipping practices are another means of establishing oneself in a bar. Certainly, persons flashing a roll of money around will be noticed, but a stranger may be able to acquire service superior to that of a "regular" or a "friend of the management" if he is a "good tipper":

What I do is I go in and she brings a round to the table, I give her $2.50 for maybe a $7.00 round. She figures, "Okay, the guy's a tipper!" That's not bad, it's a pretty good tip. The next time she comes, I give her $2.50 again. But if you keep doing that, she's going to slack off, because she figures she's going to get it every time. The next time, you don't give her a penny. She's back just like that. She's trying to figure out what she did wrong. And then you give her the $2.50 again. That will pretty well do it. You will get excellent service all night from then on. (patron)

If I'm a patron, when the waitress comes around I'm going to tip her real well, the first thing. That way I'm going to get good service. Then, regardless of how

I'm dressed and the other people there. She's going to know that I'm around.
(waitress)

Generous tippers are also likely to be granted more extensive behavioral licences:

Well, you wouldn't mind so much if they're tipping you good, but if they're not tipping, and they want service like "snap, snap," and then they're making a little play for you, well you just can't put up with that. (waitress)

One way of "being somebody" in a bar setting is to receive special or unique privileges. It should not be assumed, however, that "being somebody" necessarily hinges on "extreme privileges":

You never see anybody else sitting in this chair. They'll sit here, and here, and here, and there, but not in this chair. This chair is mine. Like, this chair that you're sitting in, that chair shouldn't be there. See the one over there, with the cracked arm. That's the one that should be here, right at this table. I was going to mention it to the waitress earlier, but I forgot. . . . This other place I used to drink, I had a stool that was mine. That was my stool whenever I went there. The other people sitting there, they would get up and say, "Sorry about that. Here's your stool." That was my stool. It's sort of like you belong in a place and they make room for you and that's your place. (patron)

The big thing is simply if the waitress notices somebody coming in and they're talking to them and they're very cheerful and if the person's going to the bar now and then, then they'll probably come back to this place, so that helps a lot. And then, if they bring their friends and you recognize them, well that's really great because then they're recognized and to their friends, they're somebody in that bar. (bartender)

Being somebody is not limited to recognition derived from generosity or regular patronage. While individual and group concerns with, and notions of, esteem can vary greatly, one can also "be somebody" by "being tough," "drinking," and "by being entertained." Bars are social settings, and each activity represents a basis on which persons may "be somebody" to themselves and/or others.

DRINKING

Although some people will occasionally (or even regularly) go to a bar "to get drunk," for most people, on most occasions, drinking places are more nebulous settings. Some customers will have a limited budget, and this may affect their drinking practices but, to a large extent, how much people drink in a particular evening is highly problematic. While customarily heavy drinkers are more apt to continue drinking heavily, the consumption of alcohol for many others depends on: those with whom they drink; their opportunities for side involvements; and the efforts of the staff and entertainment to promote drinking activities, either by their direct actions or by encouraging them to remain in that setting for longer periods of time. People may become caught up in drinking as a solitary activity, but the drinking practices of most patrons seem intelligible only within the contexts in which drinking occurs:

If a guy's out of town, where does he go to meet people, he's sitting there in a motel room. He's a trucker or something on the road, what's he going to do?

Watch TV? So he comes down to the tavern. Maybe score a broad, meet somebody. You never know. He's kind of open to the possibilities, drinking, women, whatever's there. (patron)

The staff can influence how much a person drinks, just by keeping him there. If you keep him there and you keep them happy, in good spirits, where they're having a good time, then they're more likely to drink more. (waitress)

We can suggest, which we do a lot, by singing a lot of drinking songs. If you mention to a person they should drink a lot of beer and get drunk, you mention it to them 25 times a night, he'll probably be more apt to do it than if you didn't mention it to him. And we mention it a lot in our show. So we will probably get a higher till than another band who doesn't mention drinking as much as we do, because it's in the back of their minds. Like whether they want to or not, we're pushing the alcohol down their throats. (musician)

For further indication of the problematic and negotiable aspects of drinking, readers may refer to earlier discussions of drinking among entertainers and staff, as well as the earlier material on "pushing drinks" as a means of the staff increasing tips.

BEING ENTERTAINED

People going to bars tend to be somewhat open to a variety of forms of entertainment. Some people will patronize a particular bar because it offers a particular form of entertainment, such as strippers, hookers, disco music, show bands, singles night, and the like, but the "what and how" of the evening's entertainment depends to a very large extent on the contributions of those present:

It depends on what you want to do, or who you're with, as to where you go. Like me, and lots of other people I've noticed, you don't drink real close to home when you want to unwind. When you want a little excitement, you don't want everybody to find out. (patron)

An analysis of "being entertained" becomes further complicated when one realizes that any audience may itself be quite diverse, even when a bar regularly features a particular kind of entertainment:

It is really frustrating playing music in bars. People in the bars, you don't know if they're here to hear the music, see their friends, or just to get drunk. You never quite know, or a combination. (musician)

A lot of bands make that mistake of believing they are all of the barroom scene rather than a part of the barroom scene, and we accept that fact, that we are a part of what's going on. We're part of the pinball machines, the pool table, the fucking tits in the house, the little games, we're all part of it. (musician)

In addition to structured entertainment of the sort provided by musical performances, pool tables, shuffleboards, jukeboxes, and pinball machines, bars also represent places in which sexual and romantic involvements may take place. Bars may, by featuring exotic dancers, topless waitresses, bar girls, hookers and the like, cater to those interests. And although some bars may promote themselves as "singles bars," which specifically purport to encourage romantic-sexual involvements, patrons in many other bars find this an entertaining aspect of bar life:

I have travelled all around the country, and one thing I have noticed is that bars are pretty much the same. It doesn't matter whether you're in the north, west or south, or around here in Eastville. The one big thing about bars is that guys follow pussy. Where the pussy hangs out, the guys will follow. Like certain places have ladies' night, at which they hand out roses or a free drink to the ladies every Wednesday. If the women are going down there to get free roses, the guys are going to follow. And the guys are going to go there and buy them drinks, trying to impress them, to get them to hop into the sack with them. And, if you want to impress a woman, you've got to spend. And you'll spend as much as you can to get her drunk so she doesn't know what she's doing. . . . We sing a lot of barroom songs, one of them is called, "The girls all get prettier at closing time." The guy goes to the bar looking, and he's got his taste up there. You see, if you rank a girl on a scale from one to ten, he's looking for a 9, even an 8 won't fit right in. A few more drinks and he'll walk up to a 5 or even a 4, but when tomorrow morning comes and he wakes up with a 1, he says he'll never do this anymore. . . . But he's basically a lonely person, so when it comes to the end of the night, he'll ask that one over there. She's maybe not the best looking dame in the world, but he figures, "Well, it's better than going home to a pillow." Or maybe at the last call, the one he was going for has gone. . . . There's another song, "She's looking better every beer." A guy goes in a bar, and the more he drinks, the more he notices how pretty she looks. . . . We can be realistic in a way, but we have to do it in a humorous way, or else people are going to go out and shoot themselves. Like you don't sing, "The girls all get prettier at closing time," right at closing time. If you do that, you're going to get shot! If some guy was moving in on a woman over there who was not that great a looker, he's going to come up. . . . I had that happen to me, five guys threw me up against the bar wall, "Don't you ever do that again, you son of a bitch!". . . . You don't sing songs like that right at closing time. (musician)

The "entertainment" the patrons experience is in many ways inseparable from that experienced by the staff and the "entertainers":

The regulars can get to be a lot like family and if you're away they're concerned, "Where were you? Were you sick? Why didn't you tell us you were going to be away." Also they might bring in their friends and sometimes relatives and make a big fuss over you. It's something like a family to a number of them. These are people sometimes who never tip, but you get to liking them because they're around and they're always nice to you, they seem to care for you, and so even if they're not tipping, you still get to feel very fond of them. I would never leave the bar job. It's something that I like very much and I'd miss the people. I seem to fit in there. I wouldn't like to quit. (waitress)

A lot of the waitresses, if they left, they would miss the popularity. A lot of girls who are married or have boyfriends, it's a perfect chance for them to talk to a bunch of different guys, meet a bunch of different people without having to worry about becoming involved with them. It's a way of socializing without having a chance of involvement. For the single girl, it's a perfect chance to socialize and be in total control because at any time, she can just walk away and end the conversation, where if she was here as a customer, she would be in a awkward situation, she would be moving to another table. Where the waitress, if she meets somebody who's interesting, she can spend as much or as little time as the job will allow. On a busy night she might not have time, but she can always say, "Hey, why don't you come back on a night when we're not so busy. I'll be able to sit down and talk to you." (manager)

Sometimes you get a regular customer and maybe he doesn't drink all that much, but maybe one night he'll get bombed and he'll be there kind of entertaining everybody. It's kind of a lark. Its so funny just to see them. It's entertaining. (bartender)

Finally, as the following extracts suggest, a lack of "entertainment" can also be a form of entertainment:

I'm not a country and western fan. I'm not a rock and roll fan either, or disco. I don't really care for any of those things, but I'll listen to it. The main thing to me is that the place be reasonably quiet, I can go and relax there while I'm drinking. (patron)

Different bars do different kinds of things for you. Some places you can't really go and have any peace of mind because somebody is going to be bugging you or hustling you. It depends on what kind of mood I'm in, if I want to mix with people then I'll go to a different bar than if I want to be alone. (patron)

As the preceding material suggests, bars have a plurality of meanings for those whose lives intersect in that setting. Typologies of bars (cocktail lounges, corner taverns, and the like) while tending to denote class backgrounds of the clientele neglect both the commonality of functions and the inner dynamics of bar life. While certain features of bars, such as decor, location, or entertainment, tend to attract persons with particular interests, bars are places in which persons, in addition to being entertained, live out aspects of their lives with others. Drinking is an important aspect of bar life, but there are more attractions to bars than the serving of liquor:

A lot of the people at bars are lonely and maybe come for a little companion-ship. You'll find people, they'll have televisions at home, yet they'll come down to the bar and watch the television, because there'll be somebody else there they can talk about the game with or whatever it is. . . . But a lot of the guys come down to meet girls. And it's not that they get lucky very often, because they don't. But what seems to be happening is that this way, they feel they've got a chance. Sitting at home, they don't have anything going for them. . . . Quite a few people are interested in coming out to listen to the music, but I don't think we can kid ourselves and say that the people come all that much to hear us, because we're the biggest thing that ever hit. . . . A bar is a melding of many different things, melding of staff who have to work there, entertainers who come in week by week and have to feel the place out, feel the clients out, and then there's the people, the regulars. The atmosphere is created by whatever they want, if they want a band, or they want strippers, or they have amateur contests, or any gimmick to draw people into consume alcohol. The manager is basically interested in getting people to consume alcohol because he's got an investment there. He's got a certain number of dollars invested in the hotel and he wants to make it pay off. . . . There are no scruples in this business.

Anything to make a buck in a bar. And, anything can make a buck, if it's "wet T-shirt contests," or "bikini contests," or if it's "gong shows," or like the Play Pen with its topless waitresses. . . . Bars are also social places. Peopl will go out for an evening and hang out there for a number of hours. And they'. get tired of watching TV and they go there because guys want to meet women and women want to meet guys. You get women going there so that guys can buy them drinks all night, where they take a liking to each other you might have a little romantic interlude. (musician)

ROUNDERS

While the roles and activities of "straight" patrons are important in understanding bar life in general, another noteworthy and often neglected group of patrons are "rounders." Referring to "streetwise people" generally having other than legitimate means of support, someone capable of survival in a downtown urban setting, "rounders" are particularly important in enabling us to understand not only the underlife of the hotel community, but also the "thief subculture:"[2,3]

The bars, that's where it all comes together. The straight world and the underworld, the straights and the hustlers. And there's so much the straight world don't know about the hustlers. Like in your study, you're only going to scratch the surface. (rounder)

To a very large extent, the terms "rounder," "hustler," "thief," and "grifte are interchangeable. Uses vary somewhat from area to area and, at any given ti~ one or other terms may be in vogue. Although rounders are not equally encoi tered across bars, it should perhaps be noted that people working and drinking in bars seem generally more informed about street life, commercial sexuality, gambling, and hustles, than those who do not frequent bars. The extent to which bar patrons and staff approximate "rounder knowledge" is, however, highly variable. As persons (1) spend more time in bars, (2) interact more extensively with a variety of patrons (rather than drinking in specific groups), and (3) spend time in a variety of bars, they are more likely to acquire higher levels of "street-wisdom."

One may find some rounder-like persons in most bars, but it is predominately in "action bars," that one finds a greater concentration of rounders. Not only are these the places to go to meet interested parties and make deals, but those involved in rounding more extensively seem most comfortable in settings in which they are likely to encounter fewer "straight" people among the patrons and the staff.

In discussing rounders, we will first endeavor to provide readers with an image of the sorts of persons to whom the term "rounder" might be applied. Then we will indicate the dimensions and activities a rounder life-style assumes. Follow. this, the role of the rounder in the hotel community will be discussed, indicating

---

[2] For other discussions of "rounder-like" persons and lifestyles, see Stebbins (1971), Sutter (1972) Letkemann (1973), West (1974), Binderman et al. (1975), English and Stephens (1975), S~ (1976:68-78), Klein and Montague (1977), Lesieur (1977) and Prus and Sharper (1977:21-30). W~ Sutherland (1937), Maurer (1941, 1955), and Prus and Sharper (1977) for more complete depictions of "professional" thieves and hustlers.

[3] In contrast to Irwin's (1970) distinction between thieves, hustlers, dope fiends, etc., we suggest that i is analytically productive to use the terms "thief" and "hustler" more generically.

how rounders negotiate aspects of their hustles and work out their personal lives with staff, strippers, hookers, and other rounders.

Many rounders are bar regulars, but persons need not frequent bars to be known as "rounders" by people within the bars. One will also encounter rounders in a variety of other places (pinball arcades, pool halls, restaurants, race tracks and so on):

> A rounder, that's a guy whose gone through a lot of things, done a lot of things, who can hustle around. It's a prestige term. . . . Sometimes people call me a rounder which is quite good, because I'm still young and I am getting this recognition. (rounder)

> Fawna's old man, he's a rounder. He more or less is into a lot of things. He does some bookmaking, a little pimping, that sort of thing and whatever else. I don't know all what he's into, he keeps it fairly quiet. He's a really nice guy. He's just a regular rounder, but he's one of the better ones. He's always high, but a nice guy. You can talk to the guy, he's reasonable. He's done a lot of things in his life. He's a pretty smart fellow, but he's in a little bit of shit. He got busted for doping. He'll get out of it, he always has been able to work things out like that. He's smart. (rounder)

> When you're a rounder, you see a lot of things that most people don't see. You also see things a little differently because you're on the other side of the fence most of the time. Take the coppers for instance, most squares think they're decent guys who play by the rules and protect the public. Now every rounder knows this is bullshit. Coppers fuck whores in their cars, blackmail people, receive payoffs, beat up on you for no reason, frame innocent people, etc., etc. Most squares don't know this because they never see this side of the police. The only thing they know about police is what they see on T.V. (rounder)

Although rounders may vary considerably in community prestige, a top ranking rounder would be: (1) knowledgeable about street life; (2) capable of hustling; (3) "well connected"; (4) "solid"; and (5) heavily into "the action." Rounders also tend to be free of formal organizational ties, but only some could be characterized as "drifters."

FRINGE ROUNDERS

Given the characteristics of the ideal rounder, most of the "rounders" are best seen as approximations, and persons are frequently referenced as "a bit of a rounder" or "a kind of a rounder."[4] Even these acknowledgments are important, however, for they help to distinguish these people from "squares" or "straights." They serve to denote others thought to possess some larceny sense, and who are likely to have had trouble with the law or minimally have unfavorable attitudes towards the police. Referring to people achieving limited recognition as rounders, concept "fringe rounder" encompasses a variety of persons, ranging from ice or prospective rounders looking for a break, to the "has beens," persons

---

etkemann (1973) does not acknowledge these "lesser rounders," but instead uses the term rounder to refer only to the "true criminal," someone deeply committed to an illegitimate life-style. His usage more closely corresponds with what we term "established rounders."

who might have been well established at one time but who, through drinking, drugs, or inactivity associated with age, have been relegated to a lower status. Some other "fringe rounders" are persons who have left hustling as a way of life in pursuit of other activities, but who still frequent some of the rounder places. There also exists a group of "perpetual" fringe rounders, persons who routinely venture into rounder settings, but who have other basic sources of income and commitment, people who show no evidence of desiring extensive thief involvements. All of these people, however, tend to be tolerant of those involved in theft and hustling and although not considered "solid," are open to some dealings with the more established rounders:

> James said that Nat was in the process of becoming a rounder. He said that it involved being around other thieves, strippers, and hookers all day and having these people become the central social element in one's life. . . . I also asked James if he would consider social workers in this neighborhood to be rounders. He replied, "No I wouldn't, because their life is not on the street and in bars. Sure, they may know something of what's going on, but they don't experience it the same way as rounders. When they finish work, they go back to a straight life at home. A rounder doesn't have many straight relationships." (notes)

> There's a lot of different levels of street people, all within a small area. There's guys with a lot of respect, real rounders and there's the guys who bum dimes, doing petty shit. . . . They run across each other, but I wouldn't call that getting close. The only time you really talk to the punks is to get them to run errands for you. (rounder)

ROUNDING AS A WAY OF LIFE

> There's two worlds. Yours and ours. It's different here. We don't make commitments to mortgages and things like that. We do what we feel like doing, we're not tied down. Like in our world, if a girl wants to become a hooker or a stripper, that's her choice. We don't ask, "Why?" or "What's wrong with you?" It's like her trip, her thing. She's not bothering you, so why interfere with her. (rounder)

> The rounder's life, that to me is normal. The average citizen's life is all fucked up. I don't want that routine for nothing. (rounder)

In contrast to the fringe rounders, "solid rounders" or "established rounders" are people extensively involved in the thief subculture. They are what Letkemann (1973:20) would term "the true criminal," persons whose life-styles have been extensively shaped by their illegitimate involvements, and whose financial success is dependent almost totally on their continued involvement in theft. Theft is both a business and a way of life:

> A rounder is someone who doesn't have to work to make money, he makes his money hustling. Rounders can have straight jobs, but they are also making money hustling even if they do have a straight job. . . . The main thing that differentiates a rounder from a heavy is that the rounder is able to get the money from people without having to get violent with them. He is able to steer people around and he is a good talker. He might hang around the hotel a lot, but he's

different from a regular. . . . A regular is someone who spends a fair bit of time in the hotel and who would maybe know a lot of people in the hotel, but who wouldn't be hustling. . . . The rounders usually stick together in the hotel, and if it happens that one of these people gets into a fight with people from the outside, well, then the other rounders would come in and help him out. (rounder)

A rounder, that's somebody who's done time, and he's been around. Like they've got all the answers. A rounder, there's just not much he hasn't done. Sometimes they're in the hotel, and they'll pretty well run that hotel. . . . I grew up among these people, the gamblers and the prostitutes, and the people at the race track. And these people, they're into that from the time they're five years old. It's hard for just anybody to become a rounder, but a kid growing up in that world, he's going to be a rounder, he's got to. . . . Hustler, that's another name for rounder. To me, a hustler's into everything, not just some guy who's hustling women. He would be at the track and bookmaking, or whatever, that would be a hustler. (rounder)

In discussing "rounding as a way of life," six aspects of rounding become prominent: street-wisdom; hustling skills; contacts; reputations; mobility; and action. While some overlap between these elements is inevitable, each points to features significant in delineating rounders from others. In the process of discussing these dimensions, we will provide indications of both "routes to rounder status" and "rounding as a way of life." Consequently, while our major focus is on rounders in the hotel, a broader conceptualization of rounding than that emerging within the hotel community per se is essential for understanding rounders within the hotel community more specifically.

STREET WISDOM

If one is to "play the streets," be it for survival, fun, or profit, some knowledge of "what's happening" seems essential. A first requisite to being a rounder is to have some knowledge of the "underlife." Street knowledge can vary considerably: for example, from knowing where or how to "score a free meal" or "finding a place to crash" to having a detailed knowledge of the underlife business operations in an area of the city or having an extensive set of working contacts among underworld persons:

Being streetwise means being hep to what's happening. It means having a certain kind of attitude, where you're not normally shocked or affronted by what's happening, like if somebody gets ripped off. . . . Knowing where the action is happening, knowing what's happening at different hotels, or where the card games are, knowing the after-hour places, who's just gotten out of prison or on parole, who's got a lot of heat on him, basically knowing the people on the street. What they're doing and what they're into, who's successful and who isn't. . . . It means not being easily duped, so if they approach you, you know the score. Or if you get busted, you know what to say to the cops, or what not to say to them. Like you know who the stool pidgeons are and what to keep to yourself. Knowing to keep your mouth shut about other people, that sort of thing. (rounder)

A further element of street wisdom involves knowing "who to tell what." Given the precarious position of rounders vis-à-vis the police, and the problematics of trust in the thief subculture, streetwise people tend to be discreet in discussing their activities (and those of others) with other parties. While they may like to tell others of their successes, or their close calls, concerns with personal safety deter many disclosures:

> *A rounder minds his own business. He doesn't start shit for no reason and he knows how to keep his mouth shut. Real rounders do. Some of them are publicity freaks though, they just love to tell everyone about how good they're doing. These guys go down mostly, unless they know how to handle their shit. James is an exception, he's flashy and loud, but he keeps his business to himself. He doesn't say anything that can be used against him. He's got angles, he knows what he's doing.* (rounder)

HUSTLING

Although any number of "straight" persons, such as car dealers, insurance salesmen, and politicians can be considered "hustlers" in that they attempt to realize their own interests at the expense of others, they can be distinguished somewhat from other hustlers in that their "edge-taking" activities are more apt to be regarded as "legitimate."[5] They also tend to be less explicit in defining targets as "suckers" or "marks" than are those involved in illegitimate or quasi-legitimate hustles and, as a rule, the "legitimates" tend to have little exposure to persons in other underlife activities:

> *A sucker, that's anyone who's not a thief. Sometimes you'll call another hustler a sucker, but usually you just use the word for straight people that you're getting money from.* (rounder)

When one focusses on persons involved in activities conventionally associated with the thief subculture (such as burglary, robbery, auto theft, pickpocketing, and drug dealing), it is important to further distinguish hustlers in the extent to which their hustling activities are specialized as opposed to being diversified. Although one has to take the level of dedication of the hustler into account, persons engaging in specialized hustles tend to be more successful overall in terms of both making money and avoiding incarceration. Insofar as competent specialization is contingent on tutelage by "professionals" (Sutherland, 1937; Maurer, 1955; Prus and Sharper, 1977), it tends to be a somewhat elite achievement. However, as West (1974) suggests, diversification should not be seen as necessarily dysfunctional. Many hustling attributes are generalizable across situations and diversity may promote longevity in one's career as a hustler, particularly among the less competent. Likewise when rounders are arrested, diversity may serve as a buffer against the longer sentences which tend to occur more frequently when the offender persists in a singular activity. Finally, in spite of the advantages of being able to work one hustle with considerable fluency, the financial opportunities it affords may simply be inadequate:

---

[5] The concept of "white collar crime" (see Sutherland, 1941; Geis and Meier, 1977) has narrowed the differences between "thieves" and "legitimate businessmen" somewhat, and an argument can be made for the operation of a "thief subculture" in the context of legitimate business enterprise.

I don't really care that much what type of hustle I'm doing. I'll do whatever it takes to get the money from them. . . . One of the things I'll do is go and approach one of the customers, maybe someone who's older or looks a little better off and I'll go and strike up a conversation with him and I'll let him know that I know a number of hookers and that I can set him up with this or that girl. And you try to make it seem like you are doing the guy a favor. You say, "Well, you know, if you want this girl, I'll be able to get her for you, but it'll cost like $50." So you get the guy to slip you the money and then you go over and you sit down and you talk to the girl for a little while and it might be anything, "Hello, how are you? What are you drinking?", just to give the impression that you're there and that you're making this business transaction for this guy. Then you might pass her something, "Would you like a joint?" or whatever. You reach into your pocket and you get one for her and you give it to her. The guy at the bar, he's probably watching and he thinks that you are giving her the money so he thinks everything is getting set up. Then you tell him, "Everything is set up. Go to room 314 or whatever, and she'll be there within twenty minutes or so. Everything is set up for you." Well, then you kind of finish your drink and then you say goodbye to the guy. You tell him that you have to leave, and away you go. The guy may go up to the room, but he won't get in, or he finds that there's somebody there, but they don't know what he's talking about and then he'll maybe get a little hot or whatever, and come back. Then if the girl's still there, like she hasn't gotten another date in the meantime, well he'll approach her and want to know where's his money, or what's going on and she'll say that she hasn't gotten the money from me, that she doesn't know what the guy is talking about. So then you can go to another bar and see what you can set up there. So in an evening you might go to 3 or 4 or 5 or 6 bars and maybe make two or three or four hundred dollars and each time setting people up. Now, if you make a big score, well then you stay away from that hotel for a couple days, because the guy might just be hanging around wanting to see you. But after a couple days he's likely to give up or he has to leave, he has business that he has to attend to and away he goes. You try and find out beforehand if the guy is passing through and if he's going to be staying longer and you sort of plan accordingly. . . . Another thing I'll do is, when the guy is drinking, I'll doctor his drink so that he figures that he's getting drunk or high or whatever, and I'll be trying to help him to his room, or to his cab, to get him out of the bar. So you might take the guy upstairs and get in the room, and take his wallet and away you go, or you might take him outside and you let the guy pass out and you get his wallet as he's going down. You might then wake him up and put him in a cab telling him that he should be going home. (rounder)

Certainly not all hustles require extensive social skills (for instance burglary, drug dealing), but persons in the thief subculture generally attribute prestige to those hustlers who rely more extensively on their "wits." The ability to "con" — promote definitions favorable to one's interests — regardless of whether one is dealing with targets, the police, or other rounders is considered both "smart" (resourceful) and "cool" (operating under pressure):[6]

---

[6] There is extensive agreement on the prestige attached to social skills in the thief subculture. See Sutherland (1937), Maurer (1955), Irwin (1970), Letkemann (1973), and Prus and Sharper (1977).

I'd say James is exceptionally good at conning people. I really mean exceptional. He's about the best I've seen, and I have seen many. I've seen him talk his way out of situations that I thought were totally hopeless. He can construct a complete, consistent alibi almost spontaneously and he won't slip up. Really fast thinker. . . . He can turn a situation around, so that he makes his accusers think they're in the wrong, meanwhile he's been caught redhanded. . . . He can talk people into anything, talk them right out of their money and get them to thank him besides. He can tell a lie as well as he tells the truth. There's no difference in his expression at all, its all the same. (rounder)

You have to be able to withstand pressure. When you've got a job to do, you have to do it, with no excuses. You don't need excuses. So you want a guy who will take that chance, because maybe everything else depends on him. You don't want some guy who says, "Well, it was a little tough, you know." It's always tough, you just have to get the job done. (rounder)

Generally speaking, persons seriously into hustling exhibit little concern for the targets. Their goal is to obtain possession of their valuables in the safest, surest way possible:

My attitude toward theft is that as long as it's not from a friend, it's okay. There's no real thrill in it anymore, it's just another way to make money, a way to make a lot of money fast. Never from a friend, though. All the other suckers on the street are fair game. Rounders don't have any real compassion for your average citizen. . . . That's my opinion though, I know other rounders who would steal from their own mothers, but to me, they are not real rounders, they're just two-bit hustlers. (rounder)

Not all hustling activity is directed towards "straights"; other hustlers also represent "fair game" both in "open" contests and as targets for hustles. There is normative support for the notion that "one does not hustle friends," but concerns with making money tend to weaken the "honor among thieves" principle:

There is honesty among thieves, but if they don't need you, you have to watch them because then they will rip you off whenever they can. It's good if you're honest with your partners because that reduces a lot of bickering, but otherwise you're in that environment where you're used to taking shots at other people, so you have to watch for that. (rounder)

A lot of times, rounders will hustle each other. They could be the best of friends and they would rip each other off. It's funny how someone will be real solid with you in some situations and fuck you in others. Like this one guy who owed me money and hunted me down to give it to me. Real solid, right? The cocksucker went and broke into my house the following day. (rounder)

It is not uncommon to hear persons expressing threats or intents to injure or kill others who have violated their notions of fair play, however, these threats are carried out relatively infrequently. A more likely response is that of "slandering" the offender and encouraging others to avoid any dealings with him. While some friendships reflect working partnerships among equals, other forms of respect and loyalty may also be sought. For example, a rounder may treat other persons very well with some anticipation of "being owed a favor." This is, perhaps, most evident in the development of a protégé, wherein a more established rounder develops a loyalty oriented relationship with a newcomer by showing this understudy considerate and helpful treatment. Hence, while intimidation remains one method of promoting respect, generosity and friendship are other, often more effective, ways of achieving these ends.

CONTACTS

Possibly the least dramatic element of becoming a rounder, but certainly a most important one, is that of "making contacts." Established rounders are on working terms with many rounders and/or can readily access other rounders through existing acquaintances. While one can achieve "nodding" acknowledgments with persons fairly easily, it generally takes a considerable amount of time to become "well connected."

Although bars, after-hours places, pool halls, race tracks, and "action-oriented" streets are some of the places habituated by rounders, this is not to suggest that all such places are heavily frequented by rounders or that rounders will constitute the majority of persons in any particular setting. These "hangouts" are important, however, for they represent places where one is more likely to find or learn of "a little action" and places where one might meet other rounders and "action people" (monied individuals looking for a little excitement):

Going to bars is not an essential part of being a rounder. There are some rounders who never go to bars and its the last place you would ever look for them. A lot of rounders go to bars to see what's happening, looking for some action. Now, some "big shot" rounders never go looking for action, the action comes to them. They pick and choose what they want to do. . . . They are very hard people to see, you hardly ever see them walking the streets. (rounder)

Rounders are likely to hang out almost anywhere. Sure, it could be places like booze cans and bars, but it could also be at other places like restaurants or certain apartments where everyone goes. As far as leisure time goes, rounders do the same things other people do, like going to the cottage, picnics, barbeques in the backyard. Rounders like to do things that everybody likes to do. It's just that rounders have these underworld hangouts as well. (rounder)

Involvement in delinquent groupings represents one possible way of making contacts with established rounders, but these links are much less effective than one might expect. One typically has to establish a personal relationship with someone who is into rounding more extensively. Thus, kinship ties (father, uncle, brother, brother-in-law) play a bigger role than does "being in a delinquent gang."[7] Similarly, by obtaining legitimate work in a "hangout," one is more apt to have an opportunity to become a rounder. "Joint" experience (prison or even reform school) may also qualify persons as rounder candidates[8] but, like the delinquents, these persons need someone to introduce them to rounders at the "work place":

---

[7] This is not to deny the value of delinquent experiences for developing thief orientations or composure. As Letkemann (1973:119) notes, delinquent involvements provide some rudimentary skills and an early testing of one's suitability as a criminal.

[8] While not "the best school of crime," prison does provide a setting in which some contacts may be made and some skills learned. Perhaps more significantly, however, prison experiences (and the inmate code) reinforce norms operative in both the street and thief subcultures, suggesting that persons stand up for themselves, grabbing what they can, however they can, settling any differences between themselves without recourse to outside authorities. For a fuller discussion of the dynamics of prison life, see Irwin (1970).

Rocky claimed that his father's record had a great effect on how he was and is treated. He found that some people opened up to him and treated him very well, while others were hostile because of who his father was. He also claimed that he has been unduly hassled by police because of his last name. (notes)

I've been in a lot of places where you come into contact with these people, like bootleggers' joints, where you have boosters, and B & E men, and stick-up men, bank robbers, where you don't know who you're talking to. You can't say to the guy, "Hey, what business are you in?" But you get talking to them and feel them out, or maybe somebody you know will fill you in on them. . . . And with Leo, the way he would get me in with them was that people recognized him as a loanshark from before and he was still respected for his muscle. And he'd say, "Well, I'll just drop a few hints to let them know that you're okay. Nobody will ask you right out, but they'll be wanting to know who you are." And it worked out okay, they relaxed after that with me. Thieves and B & E men, they're often into loansharks, and so he's accustomed to being around these people. Like they'll go to him and say, "I need a G note for this or that, to pull off this or that job." They never hold onto their money, they spend it on booze or gambling, or women, so they're always broke. They spend money like there's no end. It's not a fallacy. They spend big money, they really do. . . . Some of them, from what I could gather, were top people and still they couldn't hold on to their money. (rounder)

Although people may "hang out" at a particular spot for a variety of reasons (for example they work there, they meet friends there, they are looking for something exciting), once they become part of a setting in which rounders are present, their own chances of becoming known as "rounders" increase. This is particularly the case if existing rounders define the newcomer as reasonably congenial, trustworthy, and tolerant of underlife people and activities, but his opportunities largely depend on those taking an interest in him. If the newcomer orients himself towards younger rounders, or others primarily interested in having a "good time," he is more likely to find his opportunities limited to "rougher hustles." If, however, a more established rounder finds his company tolerable and begins to take an interest in him, a newcomer may find that, although he has to prove himself, he has opportunities to become involved in more systematic and profitable hustling in which the likelihood of using force and intimidation decreases:

Hustlers don't go out of their way to help other hustlers. It's not like a group of boy scouts. Now if you're partners, well you'll try to help him or warn him about this or that where it's your ass as well. But you don't go out of your way to help some other guy, it's not like that. (rounder)

If a more established rounder likes the newcomer's style he may involve the newcomer in his routines, but, by and large, his major influences are those of (1) alerting the newcomer to hustling more generally and (2) helping the newcomer become established by introducing him to other rounders. These other contacts in turn expand and define the nature of the newcomer's affiliational network:

Hank got me in with this group. He had to build me up like hell, just to get me in, and even then, they wanted to check me out little by little. They never came right out and opened it up to me, but with time I got to see a little more of how they worked. But they were very secretive, and that was part of the reason they didn't have me doing much at first, because the more you're doing, the more you are going to learn of what's going on. (rounder)

As many hustles require the co-operation of two or more persons (even those hustles which may be effectively worked on a solitary basis are often facilitated by the efforts of a partner), it is inaccurate to speak of hustling without reference to contacts. Likewise, as it is difficult to sustain involvements on a solitary basis, it is useful to have many contacts, and stronger contacts with established rounders are especially valued:[9]

Every rounder has to have good connections to some degree or other. A guy could be the best thief in the world, but it doesn't do him a bit of good if he can't process the goods. (rounder)

Connections are really important. If a guy is well connected, he could have a sweet life as a rounder. He could get in on the best scores, and be able to beat the rap if he was ever caught. . . . A rounder with top-notch connections can make a good buck just getting other rounders in touch with each other. Like a guy could set up a burglary crew, suggest a good place to hit, get a piece of the action for his efforts and never take part in the actual burglary. I've known a few guys that knew every score and every rounder, really solidly connected. But there's not very many like that, they're more or less an elite, older guys. (rounder)

REPUTATIONS

Becoming a rounder is not like joining a tightly-knit organization, but as a newcomer becomes acquainted with more established hustlers and as they define him as more "solid," he is "en route" to becoming an "established rounder" himself. It should be emphasized, however, that becoming "established" requires dedication on the part of the novice. Although he is unlikely to anticipate this at an early level of his involvement, it requires that he be prepared to organize his life around these people, their activities, and their settings.

Somewhat comparable to hustling skills and contacts, establishing a reputation as "solid" is one of the better labels one could achieve in the thief subculture. While it is assumed that rounders would possess "larceny sense," a "solid" person is someone who is thought not only capable of taking care of himself, but also someone upon whom others can place considerable confidence under pressure. Not only is reliability valued in terms of expediting ongoing hustles but, as many of their activities involve illegal pursuits, rounders place particular value on personal integrity. Some degree of trust is generated by the shared recognition that "we're all doing things we're not supposed to," but when trouble arises in dealing

---

[9] Contacts are also needed for the distribution of goods and services. For example, while a fence may represent a regular customer for a thief crew, he may be approached by safecrackers wishing to purchase "grease" (nitroglycerine) or wanting to find a third person to assist in "pulling off a job." As Letkemann (1973) contends, these sorts of interconnections are instrumental in building bonds among persons otherwise diversely involved in the thief community. For a recent discussion of the significance of networks in respect to "fencing," see Walsh (1977:116-146).

with targets or the police, concerns with one's associates being "solid" are maximized:[10]

> *The way I see it, if you're busted, you keep your mouth shut. You don't name names, you don't make deals, you just ask for your lawyer. Sure, the coppers will probably punch you out if you don't co-operate, but what the fuck, you don't send a guy to the joint over a lousy shot in the mouth. You would be surprised sometimes with some of the guys that turn stool pigeon. They act tough and they know a lot of gangsters, but as soon as the coppers threaten them, you have to put a zipper on their mouths to keep them quiet.* (rounder)

Another aspect of being solid, is that of "being able to deliver." While it is to a rounder's advantage vis-a-vis securing partners to have others believe in his abilities to hustle, keep their confidences, and the like, it is also incumbent on these persons to live up to their reputations in this sense as well:

> *A lot of partnerships are formed in jail. You have a lot of time on your hands when you're in the joint and you find out who's into what. Some guys you get along with and they seem solid so you make plans for when you get out. A lot of guys bullshit though. They say, "Oh, I can do this and I can do that," trying to be the big man in the pen. But when they hit the streets, the only thing they can do is bum nickels and dimes.* (rounder)

> *You look for somebody who's dependable and honest, like if the guy isn't there when you have something planned, or he has a drinking problem, you can have problems. Like I've worked with drunks, and they can get very reckless or careless, and you don't want that.* (rounder)

Concerns with the integrity of prospective partners are most accentuated among more established rounders. Relative newcomers are seldom aware of the reputations of those with whom they associate and, are apt to find that the more established rounders have no particular interest in opening any opportunities up to them. Once a person becomes known as "solid," however, he is likely to find that other rounders will both confide in him more extensively and that he has increased opportunities to become involved in other hustles. If a "solid" individual is also considered a capable hustler, then he will be extremely well received:

> *There's two basic things that you look for in a partner, ability and trust. Now if you're going to crack a safe, you want to work with a guy that's good at it. But you also have to be able to trust the guy, he's got to be solid. You have to trust him to split it evenly with you and if you get nabbed you have to rely on him to try to raise your bail or bond and get out of the joint fast. . . . If you're working with a guy like that, you've got a good partner.* (rounder)

Being "solid" also suggests that one is able to take care of oneself. For example, if a person is able to "give a good account of himself" in a fight, to where other persons would not want to "mess with him," this would also contribute to his

---

[10] While it would be erroneous to think of the thief subculture as a tightly-knit group, some parallels to Simmel's (1950) "secret society" may be noted. There is concern with secrecy of activities, and condemnation of betrayals. Newcomers may also be instructed in the value and practical necessity of exercising caution in any disclosures made to other persons (including other rounders.)

image as "solid." It should be noted, however, that persons need not be "toughs" or "heavies" to be solid, and persons thought too reliant on physical force as a means of doing business or resolving difficulties tend to be distrusted. They may be humored because of their force potential, but they are often avoided lest they disrupt routines and/or draw unwelcome "heat" (the police) to others. Additionally, to the extent one is considered "solid," he will tend to have other rounders supporting him. However, if he is seen capable of handling threatening situations independently with composure and tact, his overall prestige among his peers is likely to be enhanced:

> *The big thing about reputations is the other people you have behind you. Like you have to show yourself to be solid at first, right? But, if you have any trouble, well then the hotel people, the other rounders, they'll be behind you.* (rounder)

> *It's not so much that a rounder has to be physically tough, but he can't let somebody shit on him. If someone tries to walk all over him or insults him, he can't just let the guy do it. He's got to stand for his own or else he'll lose it. Even if he's five feet high and some huge guy is trying to intimidate him, he's got to stand up to him. Most often when the other guy sees this, he'll back off and respect him for it.* (rounder)

MOBILITY

Although rounders do "get around," this mobility is often not of a "cross-country" variety. While persons "drifting" or "bumming" around from city to city are apt to pick up some rounder qualities, much of a rounder's "mobility" involves either searching for action (excitement, hustling opportunities, and such like) or attempting to avoid trouble (for instance, police or debts). Rounders may be mobile, but this is typically within one section of the city:

> *Most of the rounders I know grew up in the same neighborhood they hustle in now. Some leave and return, but a lot of them are still in the same neighborhood, without ever really leaving.* (rounder)

> *I guess Todd's about the biggest gambler around. I don't know if he is now, but he used to be. He lost everything he ever owned. His wife, house, everything. He lost a lot of money gambling. He gets a lot of girls, no doubt about that, but he loses a lot of things through gambling. He owed everybody money, he was always ducking. You won't find him sometimes for months. For months, he's hiding and hiding till he gets some bread together to pay some people he owes. . . . The only thing that keeps him up now is the girls he has working for him. I guess he's doing all right now because he's around. If he was wanted by anybody he wouldn't be here, you wouldn't hear from him in six months.* (rounder)

While rounders value autonomy and freedom from obligations and may seek out more promising areas, they can more comfortably hustle in an area in which they are known and accepted by other rounders. Someone who ventures into other territories may make new contacts and may become more exposed to variations of the thief subculture, but he is likely to encounter loneliness and frustration in his attempts to do so. Additionally, mobility can be both time-consuming and fatiguing in itself and, although one may capitalize on existing concepts of street wisdom in new settings, a major problem for the mobile rounder is that of "fitting into a new setting." He has to identify the "local players" and learn the "local rules." And if he wishes to remain, he has to establish his own rights in a potentially hostile setting. Thus, while some hustlers (for instance professional thieves, cheque forgers, card and dice hustlers) are extremely mobile, most rounders seem reluctant to leave the advantages familiarity with the local places and people afford in their hustling endeavors.

In addition to geographical mobility, one may also consider the movement of persons in and out of "rounder activities." For example, although one finds considerable continuity in the more general underlife setting, it is not uncommon for persons to get married and to settle down for periods of time and/or to acquire jobs that take them away from hangouts or consume those hours (8 p.m. – 4 a.m.) most common for rounder encounters. Short-term disinvolvements are common for most rounders and, although many have periods during which they spend a great deal of time at "hangouts," for many, "rounding" is mixed with a variety of other pursuits.

Given the precarious life of the rounder and the relative looseness of the "organizational structure" of the rounder world, persons who leave are often readily (although not always satisfactorily) replaced and the returning rounder has to fit into the existing networks. As discussed before, rounders viewed as "solid," well connected, and capable, will be given preference over others. Somewhat like the newcomer, however, a long-term absentee rounder may find that he has to not only refamiliarize himself with the situation, but may also have to re-establish his contacts and his credibility.

ACTION INVOLVEMENTS

Another aspect of rounding involves "being where the action is." In contrast to daily routines, participation in "dramatic events" adds an element of excitement to life, and represents one of the attractions of persons to a "rounder life-style." Activities thought challenging, daring, or illegitimate are particularly likely to be seen as providing action.

To some extent, one's hustle(s) represents a source of action and although, with time, hustling tends to be viewed as mundane activity, even the "old pro" may find the occasional target so challenging (or lucrative) as to offer a sense of excitement. Likewise, while concerns with the police can be annoying, the sporadic "paranoia" rounding generates tends to make life more dramatic for street people than persons engaged in office work, for example. While "hustling" is most likely to appear exciting to the newcomer, "big scores" and the fear of detection can generate some drama for any rounder.

A second source of excitement for rounders comes from involvement in "action situations." It is important to recognize that excitement is very much a social phenomenon. Not only do rounders seek out (and cluster in) action spots, but "dramatic events" tend to shape the careers of individual rounders, as well as defining parameters of specific groups of rounders. While rounders may group somewhat by their definition of excitement (be it gambling, women, booze, or drugs), it should be noted that: (1) participants tend to be accorded more prestige than observers; (2) persons more intensively involved in action are deemed more noteworthy; (3) persons spending more time in action, both in long-term and full-time respects, are apt to receive more recognition; and (4) winners of contests are much more esteemed than losers:

> *A good action person is one who knows what's happening around town and in the streets. He knows the booze cans and he knows about the big scores that are going down. He's got to have good connections to know these things, he has to know how to relate to people in order to develop connections in the first place. . . . A good action person has to have something magnetic about him, something that draws people to him and makes them want to make him a part of what they are doing.* (rounder)

> *Part of it is that pool-room setting. Because you figure that pimps, runners, B & E men, where are they likely to go? Bars, bootleggers, and pool rooms. So they get together and they create action and then maybe it's off to the racetrack or find some women. In a pool room, these contacts start to snowball. . . . But like these pimps at the pool room, we rated them suckers and they were always good money in the pool hustle. Their old lady was out making them fifty or a hundred a day and they have five or six chicks working for them. So if they didn't blow all their money on dope, you'd get it in the pool room. They're suckers for it. Where else can they go and say, "Look at this diamond ring I've got. Look at all these nice clothes I've got," but the pool room. Like all the guys are there.* (rounder)

"Being somebody" is a third form of action. While none of the sources of action discussed herein are limited to "street people," amongst rounders there are certain ways of "being somebody" that do not correspond with the ideals of the "straight world." Whether one is discussing bikers customizing their bikes, persons carrying (and flashing) their paper money in rolls or leaving unusually big tips, hookers taking pride in turning the most tricks, or pimps trying to create their own distinctive style, "being somebody" ("Eat your heart out!") generates an element of excitement. Not only may being somebody frequently stretch to the limit one's ingenuity and resources, but it puts out an implicit challenge to one's companions. For example, while styles of "being somebody" can vary considerably among rounders, "blowing money" in ways in which others are reluctant to do so attracts attention and generates excitement. Although some prestige will be accorded "rounders" who have successfully accumulated possessions, the most immediate and intense acknowledgment is directed towards those who "are somebody" on a here and now basis, someone dramatically making the scene:

> *It's fantastic how these hustlers will gamble with each other, especially if they think the game is on the level, like barbut, the dice game. We were in this game, and this one guy, he flew home to get more money. The game lasted for over two days, and like my partner he lost over $12,000. . . . And here, these guys liked to go for broke, to get all the money. And they really liked to go after the elites. Everyone wanted to bet against them, like I can beat you heads up!* (rounder)

Although persons may engage in certain practices as a means of self-expression, "being somebody" can also have important consequences for one's life in the community. Attempting to be respected within their own circle of acquaintances, rounders seem particularly concerned about giving off the impression that they are solid, competent, and successful. Thus, while some rounders perceive clear advantages to remaining in the background, others envision their image and their hustles as contingent on the ways in which they present themselves to others:[11]

Lucky said that he needed to have diamonds, good clothes and big cars to keep up his image. He said that he could not continue his pimping activities if he let his appearance drop. He could not "let himself go" because the girls would lose respect for him. . . . Lucky is very particular about his appearance. One time he got busted and was upset that he was wearing jeans at the time. He wanted to look good when he got busted. (notes)

As a rounder, you have to create a total front and project an image that is not what you really are. I try to project the image that I'm a cold-blooded dude that you don't mess around with. If you notice that around here, no one gets on my case. I'm not really that bad, but if someone tests me, I've got to play the role right to the end, otherwise I'll blow my shit, right there and then. It's the same thing when me and my partners pull a job in a bank. When we get in that bank, we have to make those motherfuckers believe that we're for real. (rounder)

FITTING IN THE HOTEL COMMUNITY

For rounders, bars may represent both work places and social settings. Not only are they likely to make contacts with other rounders in this setting, and find opportunities conducive to hustling, but their non-work interests tend to be extensively interwoven with those of other bar people. This seems to be the case particularly in "action bars." Each action bar, however, tends to cater to a specific set of rounders and although some intermixing occurs, one may speak of sets of rounders constituting regulars in particular bars:

There are some rounders at Central and the Bluegrass that are there all the time. These guys don't really come here (Main) that much. They like to stay around the place they're best known. (rounder)

ROUNDER-STAFF RELATIONSHIPS

The relationship between staff persons and rounders is considerably more complicated than that of staff and the "straight" patrons in the bar. As the bar is both a work place and a source of community identity for rounders, it is important that they maintain good relations with the staff. Not only may staff persons tolerate and facilitate rounder hustles, but the recognition they accord a particular rounder in the bar has important implications for the rounder's overall reputation among his peers:

A rounder can walk in another bar outside his own circle and he's nobody in there. They don't know who he is or what he does and if he lets them know, they would probably look down on him. But if he goes in at Central, he's somebody special. The people look up to him there and treat him with respect. Take me,

---

[11] See Goffman (1959) and Prus and Sharper (1977) for further indications of the complexities of impression management.

for instance. Some straight people would think I was pretty low, but in my own circle I'm respected. (rounder)

As routine hustling activities taking place within bars partially depend on the staff's tolerance, it is in the rounder's best interest to consolidate himself with some staff members and to generally maintain a reasonably congenial relationship with the others:

> *It's important to be well-liked by the staff, the waiters and bartenders, because different times, somebody might have a roll of hundreds, a little bank roll, and they're drinking and these people will tip you off. Now, they'll want a little something for their help too, so you make sure that you don't forget them, but they can help you out a lot. If you know the guy has got money and you figure that you're able to get it, well you don't mind spending thirty or forty dollars getting the guy hammered, because you figure that you're going to be getting the money in the end. So after you'd probably give those people who helped you out some money and how much you give them might depend on how much you thought that they figured the guy had. Or the desk clerks, you might give them twenty or thirty dollars just to forget that you were there, like if you took the guy up to the room and rolled him there. And also, if you are in the bar or whatever, then you'll tip the waiters or the waitresses because when you are in the bar hustling, you want it to appear that people know you, that you are a well-liked guy and tipping is something that helps that way. When you are with the mark, then you want to show them that you are knowledgeable about what's going on there, and that you are trustworthy.* (rounder)

By generously tipping bar staff, buying them drinks, and helping out in troublesome situations, rounders become more preferred patrons, making the special concessions they demand (or assume) more tolerable overall:

> *Sure, there are some problems with rounders in the bar, but generally they provide a stable influence in the bar. If there is a major fight in the bar, and it looks like the waiters can't handle it, you can count on the rounders to help out. Also, when the other customers see rounders getting involved, they think twice about raising any shit themselves.* (waitress)

The relationship between rounders and staff assumes new dimensions, however, when one recognizes that many of the staff people at hookers' bars and rougher bars have themselves been (or still are) rounders, and may have been affiliated with many of the rounders before taking their present hotel jobs. Additionally, many of the rounders have worked in this or other bars at some point in their lives. In some cases, staff persons may effectively use bar work as a "front" and contact spot for carrying on a variety of hustles:

> *It's very easy for them to get involved with the hustlers, pushing dope, selling merchandise, something like that. If you're staff, and you're around for a while, you're going to get to know what everybody's doing. Who the hookers are, who the pushers are, who the hustlers are.* (waitress)

Rounders and bar staff also tend to socialize outside the bar setting. Working similar hours, and sharing similar definitions of desirable entertainment and acquaintances, they frequently attend the same after-hours clubs, private parties, and restaurants. Additionally, rounders not infrequently date waitresses and other women from the same pool of available females as the staff, thus promoting further alignments. Finally, as each is more apt to define the other as "hip insiders," this common perspective, along with some shared contempt for "squares," tends to promote more meaningful and satisfying exchanges for both parties:

> The real rounders spend most of their time with other rounders, hookers, strippers, and waiters. These are the people you have a good time with, because squares wouldn't have any idea of where I'm coming from. (doorman)

Although staff-rounder relations tend to be smoother than those characteristic of rounders one to another, one does find the occasional confrontation. Typically these incidents reflect differential notions of respect and service appropriate to particular rounders:

> Mark asked me to serve him a drink after closing time. I told him that all the liquor had been put away and that the cash was locked up. He became quite upset and threatened to "put my lights out" if I dared treat him like a "nobody." Then he called the owner over and got involved in a heated discussion with him. A number of staff then gathered around and were talking with him. The owner told me to leave, so I really don't know what happened after that. (bartender)

ROUNDERS AND STRIPPERS

Not only are strippers likely to develop some rounder-like qualities and identities as a consequence of bar work and the mobility their job entails but, representing elements of diversity, romance, and business in the bar setting, they are likely to have numerous encounters with rounders:

> When you are in that surrounding, automatically you meet those people. You don't have to go out and look for them, they are there. And even after work you end up going to the same places that they will be going to after work, so you will meet them there too. (dancer)

Not all rounders become involved with strippers, but most bar rounders will have some dealings with them. While some prestige is generally attributed to anyone in the bar able to "make it" with one of the entertainment features, rounders (like other patrons) may find themselves drawn towards the bar as a consequence of their attractions towards particular strippers or the prospects each new set of girls appears to offer.

Should a rounder find a particular dancer interesting in one or other ways, his chances of making a "successful" contact are much greater than those of straight patrons. Not only are rounders more apt to be noticed by the girls as "a some-body" in the bar, as a consequence of their attire, bar liberties, and friendly relations with staff and management but, by utilizing bar staff as agents for introductions, rounders can much more readily access the dancers than most other patrons:

> I was sitting with Lucky, Buddy, and Hans at Central when Lucky noticed Sapphire, a black stripper. She was drinking at the bar and Lucky commented on how beautiful she was and how he would like to meet her. When the waiter

came by, Lucky asked him to tell her to come to our table and "put a good word in for him." The waiter did this and Sapphire came over to our table. (notes)

Romantic Involvements

While rounders and strippers share a sense of empathy arising from the disrespectability associated with their activities and the bar setting more generally, the rounders' involvement in local action and the strippers' interest in "doing something" or "going someplace" tends to make romantic involvements more likely. Although not all strippers are so inclined, when the girls are interested in going to an after-hours club or a private party with "cool people," the contacts rounders have place them at a considerable advantage over straight patrons.

Stripper-rounder involvements tend to be of a short-term nature, given the mobility of the stripper and the precarious life-style of the rounder. Some encounters result in long-term relationships but both parties, through experience, are unlikely to anticipate this outcome:

You have to have an open mind when you're involved with strippers. A lot of straight guys get all fucked up over them. They fall in love and then get upset because she's fooling around with another guy. Rounders know better, at least most of them do. When a rounder is going out with a stripper, it's usually understood by both that it's going to be a short-term thing. A rounder has his old lady and the stripper usually has her old man in her home town, so when they become involved it's understood that it's only for a short time. . . . Strippers are hep to this, sometimes I think more so than rounders, that is, the more experienced strippers at least. (rounder)

This generally casual attitude of rounders towards strippers is fairly typical of rounder attitudes towards women more extensively. Thus, while most rounders attempt to remain emotionally aloof in their affairs with strippers, they tend to view women generally as less trustworthy than men:

Rounders will usually dump a broad once they get tired of her. Some broads can't take the action so they leave, but most of the time they get hooked up with another rounder and they're into the same old shit. Yeah, a lot of these broads get bounced around from rounder to rounder. (rounder)

There's no way that I'll ever respect women. You can't trust them, there's very few who you can call solid. They're very gullible. You can talk them into doing anything, even things that they don't want to do. The trouble is, so can any other rounder who's got some smarts. So he can turn your old lady against you. Also, if they find that they can have the upper hand in a relationship, they'll exploit the hell out of the guy and then dump him. If a broad feels that she can dump a guy, she'll dump him and hard too. No, I don't respect women. (rounder)

Hustling the Strippers

Recognizing that the dancers receive fairly lucrative weekly pay cheques the rounders also view them as targets for financial hustles. These hustles tend, however, to assume a somewhat haphazard form. They are not only very much dependent on the interests of the particular dancers, but they are also limited by the typical weekly mobility of the dancers:

> *I don't like to hang around the strippers very much because mostly they are just looking for some guy to buy them drinks all night. A lot of the girls have been around so much, the strippers, that they are not really very gullible and it's sort of a waste of time trying to put a move on them.* (rounder)

> *You don't find too many rounders being supported by strippers. You never know where they are half the time, so it would be stupid to have to rely on them to come through money-wise in a crucial situation. Basically, rounders just want to get a good fuck out of a stripper, that's all.* (rounder)

Representing customers for rounders' goods and services, strippers are perceived to be in the market for items such as jewellery, furs, drugs and the like:

> *Elmo often comes around Main trying to sell jewellery and drugs to the dancers. He seems to do all right for himself since he unloads a lot of merchandise at Main.* (notes)

> *Mahogany was showing me a ring that she bought from James. She seemed quite happy with the deal she got since she figured that the same ring would cost several hundred dollars more in a store. She assumed that the ring was hot, but did not show any apprehension about this.* (notes)

Further, in contrast to stable "insiders," the transient strippers are often seen as incapable of taking effective retributory action and are, thus, more susceptible to dealers who misrepresent the quality and/or quantity of their merchandise:

> *There used to be this rounder that made a lot of bread off the strippers at Bluegrass. He'd come in, get to know them and then offer them good deals on furs, dresses, coke, pot, almost anything. The only thing was that it was all fake. Fake furs, fake coke, and oregano for pot. The strippers were there for only a week and they had shows to do so what could they do? It's funny. A lot of them didn't know they were ripped off at all, they'd smoke the oregano and get off on it!* (rounder)

In addition to purchasing goods from rounders, strippers occasionally contact rounders involved in the money-lending business. As dancers are often unfamiliar with the city, the possibility of bank loans are diminished, and loansharks are often seen as the best option. Due to the strippers' high mobility, rounders are cautious about lending large amounts of money to the girls but, knowing when and how they are going to be paid, lenders can plan to be there at the right time, to help her collect. Finally, although the strippers are seen as poorer prospects than are hookers, when rounders find that dancers have become particularly fond of them, they may attempt to obtain some money from them:

> *Eric said that he gets money from Val and that she often buys him gifts. However, he said that she couldn't help him as much as a hooker. "These hookers make $200-300 a day if they are any good. You can't rely on a stripper to make that much. Besides, they travel so much, it's hard to keep track of them."* (notes)

ROUNDERS AND HOOKERS

Although the highly mobile strippers possess some rounder-like qualities, it is the hookers who are more likely to be considered "rounders" in the bar setting. This is in large part due to their hustling orientation and greater tendency to be both "well connected" and involved in other hustles.[12]

Romantic Involvements

Not only are the hookers (as hustlers) apt to be more orientationally compatible with the rounders than are the strippers but, being more geographically fixed, they are much more likely to encounter the same rounders (males) over a period of time, in a variety of contexts:

> *You meet hookers in a lot of different places. If you're a rounder, it's really difficult to avoid them. If you go to a party where there's a few rounders or a card game, you're bound to find a hooker or two there. Or if you're in the bar and you're sitting with a few rounders and then some women come over to join you, chances are that the broads are hookers. . . . Where there's hookers there's rounders and where there's rounders there's hookers.* (rounder)

While many of these relationships are highly transitory, these relationships tend to be some of the more stable ones in the lives of the involved persons:

> *I've noticed that some couples such as James and Betsy, Buddy and Carol, Gerald and Rosemary, Dave and Lisa appear to have fairly stable relationships. When visiting their homes I found their interaction to be very similar to that of most straight married couples I've observed.* (notes)

> *Sure, some rounders "settle down" with hookers if you want to call it that. They'll spend maybe 10 years with this one, 10 years with that one, they'll go on like that till they're ready to be put in an old folks home. In the meantime, however, they're fucking other whores as well, but they try to keep that away from their old ladies.* (rounder)

Rounder-Pimps

Intimate relations between rounders and hookers bring about the possibility of pimping—pimping being an accepted part of their shared subculture. In contrast to black pimps (Chapter 2), white rounder-pimps tend to be less reliant on hookers for the major source of their income. In most cases, however, rounders view pimping as a profitable sideline and tend to be receptive to these arrangements:

> *I don't see nothing wrong in taking money off these broads. Why not? They give up their money to somebody, so why not give it to me.* (rounder)

> *I don't really know if you can call rounders "pimps." I guess it depends on what you mean by pimps. A rounder won't get too heavy on a hooker if she*

---

[12] This is not to suggest that mobile strippers may not become street-wise, but rather to note that performers who remain in one setting for an extended period of time have greater opportunities to become involved with local rounders (and their action).

doesn't make a certain amount. Sure he might kick her ass if she doesn't pull her weight, but he doesn't kill her if she has an off day like some of these black pimps do. . . . A rounder, if he's any kind of rounder, will have another way of making money so he won't have to depend on broads. (rounder)

When I was talking with Lucky, a hooker from Central came up and said that this black girl, Joyce, was telling everyone that Lucky was her old man. She described the girl but Lucky didn't know her. Lucky then started to check up on this girl, trying to find out what she was like. She was around 19 or 20 and he found her very attractive. Later, she approached him, saying, "You're with me, right?" Lucky replied, "It's not quite that easy, you know. I'd like that, but you've got to help me out money-wise." She gave him about $200.00, to which he replied, "Well, you're going to need a little more than that." She said, "Okay," and went off down the street. She gets most of her tricks off the street. . . . Lucky said that he'd really like to take her to bed and then discuss money later, but he said he really couldn't do that. He seemed quite impressed, saying, "She really looks good. She talks sense too, and she dresses well, a classy broad.". . . . Later another girl, a friend of Joyce's, also approached Lucky, wanting to work for him too. But she was only 15 or 16 years old and Lucky didn't want to get involved with her because of that, "I really can't have anything to do with her. She'll draw too much heat if she's busted." (notes)

In discussing the prospects of having a hooker work for them, the rounders are somewhat at variance with one another in terms of pimping styles. Some prefer an experienced hooker with whom to establish a long-lasting relationship and a dependable income, while others want an inexperienced girl:

I like to find a girl that's totally naive to the scene, that she's never done it before and I like to introduce it to her myself, because if other people do it, well then you don't know what you're up against. If you can find a girl who's maybe just gotten thrown out of home, or she's lost her boyfriend or she's a little down in her luck to where she's sort of looking for someone that she can depend upon, well then that's the best situation. Then you start to take care of her and spend some money on her. What you want to do is give her the impression that you're really taking care of her and that you care about her. And someplace along the line, you try and introduce the idea that she could be making more money and doing a lot better if she was doing something else than say a straight job. . . . You try and work it so that you have some plans and that you're going to handle the money for her and take care of her and it's there if she needs it. Then you just try and give her enough money to just get around on. And the other thing you do, if you bring a girl in, is take her around and introduce her to your friends to where she starts feeling comfortable in that situation and that becomes part of her world. And you try to give her the impression that you don't really want her to go out and work there, but in terms of the situation, what else can she really do. You tell her you're going to be saving this money for her or investing it, or putting it in the bank or something. After a few months, she's going to start to catch on, so it's hard to know how long they'll last. It might just last three or four months. You give her the impression that you are caring for her, but yourself, you can't care whether she comes or goes. You just have to play it that way with her. If she wants her money, you just tell her to get lost. That's what you have to do if you're hustling like that. You really can't afford to have feelings for the girls. (rounder)

Any hooker I've been involved with was a hooker before I met her. These new broads are a pain in the ass. You always have to keep after them and they're always going through some change or other. They're good for a fuck, but they're homicide to live with. (rounder)

Although rounders will try to make the best deals for themselves, they will on occasion refer hookers to one another. Typically, these references follow lines of friendship, but "agent fees" are also expected:

James said that he has turned a few hookers over to Lucky. If he knows of a hooker who's looking for an old man, he will refer her to Lucky. This works on occasion and when it does, James receives a kickback. . . . James said that he referred one of the hookers to one of the black pimps whose girls work the hotel. James was talking to this girl and she indicated that she found this black guy attractive. He later went to the pimp and told him that he could introduce him to a hooker, but that the pimp had to pay him $500 if he "copped" her. The pimp agreed to this and as it turned out, he did get her. The pimp, however, did not pay James and James said that he would have Ray put some pressure on him. (notes)

Female Rounders

The interrelatedness of rounders and hookers is by no means limited to romantic and financial involvements. Whereas strippers are largely involved in hustles as "customers," the hookers are more likely to engage in sideline activities, such as picking pockets, boosting, and fencing. Just as one finds an overlapping of identities among "rounder" and "staff," the identities of (female) rounder and hooker also overlap. Most hookers have rounder-type sidelines and female rounders (women more extensively involved in theft, drug dealing, fencing, and so on) often have hooking sidelines. Like other rounders, female hustling involvements may vary over a period of time. For example, a girl may be more exclusively involved in boosting one season, and then drift more extensively into hooking the next, or she may be heavily engaged in both over a period of time. The following extracts illustrate these overlapping aspects of female rounder involvements:

Frieda's father was a big person in the hotel at one time. He was a very tough person and he had a lot of people backing him. But I haven't heard nothing from him lately. But she's been hanging around all these people, with the rounders since God knows how long. They're going to gladly accept her. Look at her, you can tell yourself. She'd fit in anywhere. She's a pretty classy chick, too, as a matter of fact, in her own way, but she's a rough person too. When she gets going, she don't care what. She'll smash a guy's face with a glass, and she's done it too. Don't underestimate this girl. She's a beautiful looking girl, nice and tight, but she's a fucking wild rat when she gets going. Her and another chick ripped up the Village Inn one time. It was a big fight. They were just throwing chairs through windows and whatnot. They were fighting together with some other people, but they tore the place up, literally. . . . She's also quite a little booster. All her clothes, she's dressed good all the time. She just walks in and walks out, her and a couple of other girls. They just clean the place out, whatever they want. . . . They used to come down and sell it around the hotels, or you could tell them what you want and they'd go get it for you, "What size? What color?" They'd let it go like a third of the price. I don't know if she's into it now. . . . Plus she hooks on the side. She's into a little bit of everything. (rounder)

Kim's a stripper, but she's a hooker, she's a booster, she's into dope, she's into everything. She's a stripper right now as a matter of fact. But once her gig is finished, she comes off the stage, goes and puts on something else. Then she comes and hustles at the bar downstairs, whatever she can. She's into that quite a bit, and boosting, stuff like that. (rounder)

One of the hookers, Betty from Central, is Sam's main contact for marijuana. Her old man is one of the dealers in the area and she supplies a number of the people in the area. She was discussing a recent bust, saying that her old man recently got picked up for possession of some chemicals. She figured that he should've just stuck to grass because the chemicals are likely to "draw the heat." (notes)

Greer's not really much of a hooker. She usually picks people off the street, or wherever she can. She's not too much to look at. She's gotten very skinny, but a few years ago she was quite good looking and I've gone to bed with her a few times myself. But she gets fucking smashed and hangs around with a lot of rough people. . . . She's a very sloppy girl. She doesn't care who she picks up. She's in the Parkside a lot and picks up whatever she can. She also rips a lot of people off. She'll do it right in front of them. Like if a guy pulls out a wad of money, she'll grab it and run. . . . She's into all kinds of drugs. Whatever she can get a hold of she'll probably use. I don't think she's into heroin, but speed, acid, whatever she can get. . . . If you're a friend though, she's a great person to know. She's always passing you dope, "Here, have a couple of joints," or whatever. She's not stingy. She treats her friends good, but if she doesn't know you and you happen to have a buck on you, she'll weasel it out of you. . . . She's a very poor hooker, but she does make money. She'll take people right into her house. She charges the guy $20 and takes him right into her house so that the guy doesn't have to blow an extra $15 or $20 on the hotel. But, she's been punched out a lot by tricks and she doesn't seem to be trying to use the safety the hotel provides. (rounder)

Rounders' women are usually into something themselves. A little hooking, a little boosting, hustling at the bar, stuff like that. A lot of strippers and waitresses get caught up with rounders too. You take Joyce. She started working at the Blue Moon and she started going out with Hector. Now he's a junkie and he's into grand theft. Pretty soon he's got her helping him and they both get pinched. Now she's got a record whereas before she was clean. (rounder)

Given the hookers' rounder status in the hotel, it should not be surprising to find them co-operating with the other rounders in their hustles, or turning to the other rounders for assistance:

Where you're kind of using the girls to steer somebody to you and getting his money, well the girls don't get too upset about that usually because they understand that you're there hustling too. And they also know that different times, if they're having trouble, I'll help them out, and so it's not like they're not getting anything out of it. So say she has some customer that is getting a little rough with her and threatening her, well I'll step in and she'll know that I will help her out different times, so they really don't mind that too much. (rounder)

Almost all of the girls are into the loansharks. Most of them that borrowed money, it wasn't because the guy needs some heavy money. Sure they borrow it. But in most cases, it's not their pimps who tell them to do it. They do not allow them to borrow money, "Don't you ever borrow money from the loansharks!" So when they do, it's for their stash, their money on the side that they're not telling their man about. Some of them are smart enough to put money away for themselves. If they make $150, they're only going to give them $100, if they make $300, they're only going to give them $200, or whatever. But if they need some extra money for their stash, say they're buying things for themselves and they're paying off bills that he doesn't know about, they can't ask him for the money. If they're saving for his birthday present or his Christmas present and they don't have enough. Or maybe he's been out of town for a month and she's supposed to have $2500 and she's only got $1800, and, "Why didn't you have the rest?" If he's that kind, that strict about it, she could be in trouble. Well, borrow it. Different things like that, I've known a few cases where the guy's just been heavy in his debt, he's a gambler or he's in trouble or he's got a case going and he needs to pay the lawyer off. If she can't make it, she'll borrow it. (hooker)

DISINVOLVEMENT

Insofar as rounders may (1) pursue similar activities in other settings, (2) become less obvious while continuing to hustle in the same setting, or (3) resume former hustles at a later point in time, it becomes difficult to achieve an adequate statement on disinvolvement. Generally speaking, total withdrawal from intensive rounding activities seems infrequent. Much like bar staff, rounders become reliant on the revenue illegitimate activities can generate. Additionally, they also become accustomed to "being their own boss." Further, to the extent individual rounders have become involved in the "action," more conventional work and life-styles appear rather shallow or unrealistic:

Rounders are not really interested in the home life. They stay away from it. It holds very little interest for them. Rounders who try to establish a home life usually fuck it up somewhere along the line, and the marriage ends in divorce or separation. It's tough on the kids too, it's no life for them, no security whatsoever. Their old man could take off at any time or he could be busted and put away for years. It's really bad on the kids. Usually they end up doing the same shit their old man is doing. (rounder)

Some rounders appear to go straight after a while. They make their money on the streets and then they go legit, buy a business. Some of them really make it legit, but they always will have larceny in their heart. None of them are honest in their business dealings, they're forever ripping people off, but doing it legit. You also find these guys still hanging around places, like Main, Central and Bluegrass, talking about old times with other rounders. Once you get the life in your blood, it's hard to stay away from the action. (rounder)

Rounders never really get out of the life. There's the friendships, the good times and the closeness you develop with your partners. Besides, there's always a phone call, you know, asking if you want in on a big score. It's hard to get away from it. (rounder)

Persons may also become disengaged from rounding activity by losing their ability to hustle effectively. This is usually facilitated by advanced age, an inability to "handle their booze," or a "loss of nerve." When this occurs, the rounder gradually loses his desirability as a "partner" and his hustling opportunities diminish. Some of these people move into minor straight roles, but others become drifters and "skid row bums":

This area used to be more of a rounders' area 20 years ago than it is now. I mean really tough rounders. Most of these guys now are either doing time or dead. Mostly dead though, a lot of them got bumped off, a lot died in the pen. Some of them are rubbies. They hang around bars all the time and then turn into alcoholics. Pretty soon they blow all their money and they can't hustle. They get old and they got no family, so they end up on the street as rubbies. (rounder)

IN SUM

Clearly not all hotel people are "rounders," but some appreciation of "rounding as a way of life" is necessary for an understanding of both the hotel community and the criminal subculture, and the ways in which they overlap. "Rounder" is a generic term, one which links together aspects of the lives of persons involved in a wide variety of activities. Not only are hustlers, thieves, and confidence men involved in rounding, but the concept also touches, in varying degrees, persons involved in biker clubs, cab driving, drug dealing, hotel patronage and work (staff and management), gambling, prostitution, bootlegging, fencing, street vending, and entertainment (strippers, musicians and so on). Insofar as these people are involved in a number of these activities, either on a concurrent or sequential basis, the term "rounder" serves to highlight both the commonalities across these activities and their interrelatedness. Although necessarily encompassing, a concept such as "rounder" is essential in linking together seemingly individualistic involvements in a variety of illegitimate pursuits. While, for example, one finds materials focussing on "occupational types," such as thieves and hookers, there has been very little written on how these people work out aspects of their lives in conjunction with one another. Hopefully, the preceding discussion makes evident the significance of contacts and affiliational networks for understanding "rounder" involvements. Career theft and the like cannot be adequately understood without examining the social settings in which these people are embedded. The following statement on "area restaurants" and "after-hours places" has relevance for the larger hotel community, but it also indicates another facet of "rounding as a way of life."

AREA RESTAURANTS AND AFTER-HOURS PLACES

Representing places in which a variety of hotel and street people may be found, area restaurants and after-hours places add to our overall understanding of "people in the life." While night people, action people, and the like, gravitate towards after-hours places, some restaurants have particular significance for the hotel (and street) communities. In addition to presenting some glimpses into after-hours places, we will provide some indications of the interrelatedness of area restaurants with "people in the life."

AREA RESTAURANTS

Restaurants frequented by hotel people range rather extensively in decor, hours open, and the extent to which they are dependent on hotel people and/or rounders as their major clientele. Although these places may be patronized during the day by the hotel people, many area restaurants assume the greatest significance after the bars close. Some staff people will "hang around" the bar setting, perhaps having a drink after cleaning up, and some will be leaving for home, but others will be going out for "breakfasts" and/or to after-hours clubs.

Some of these restaurants are also "action places" insofar as hustling activities, such as dope deals and hooking arrangements, are carried out on the premises. It might be noted, however, that bar staff and bar hookers tend to view restaurants more exclusively as places in which to relax than do street hookers and rounders, who are more apt to be seeking action:

A lot of the people from Main and Central meet at Biffy's for breakfast after work. For most, it seems a place to unwind. Not everyone goes, and it's not the same people every night, but usually one will find some of the hookers and some of the staff people there after work, and often when they take a break there during the day. The strippers sometimes go to Biffy's, but usually only if someone takes them there, because it's relatively inconspicuous. The hookers especially seem to like the place and although they sometimes get a little loud, they are usually tolerated. In general, everyone seems very relaxed when they're there, nobody's trying to hustle anyone. . . . The Purple Cow is another place the hotel people in the Main-Central-Flamingo area frequent. It does a fairly "straight" business during the day, but the hotel people more or less take over the place in the early morning hours. The staff is not keen on the hotel crowd, but the business and the tips makes them more tolerable. . . . Syd's Steakhouse serves much the same function as Biffy's, except that it caters to the Hillcrest crowd and a couple of other bars in that immediate area. It's a place where some of the staff and the "action people" meet during the day and particularly after the bars close. You also find some street people that you seldom see in bars there, mixing with the hookers or rounders and the staff. Some of these people, like Nancy and Nolan, are very well connected with a wide cross-section of people and services. (notes)

The Oasis is a 24-hour restaurant frequented by the street hookers as both a place to relax and to do business. A lot of young hookers stop at the Oasis for a coffee or a snack, or to sit down and talk after cruising Delta Drive. . . . The Teddy Bear, a relatively low-line restaurant, is another place habituated by some of the street hookers. Like the Oasis, the Teddy Bear is known as a place wherein hookers can be found, and it is not that uncommon to see dates being arranged on the premises. (notes)

Area restaurants also lend themselves to some very interesting exchanges, as bar staff, hookers and rounders intermingle much more freely than they do in the bar setting. "Within-bar" statuses are less significant in restaurant settings and one finds, for example, that staff, hookers and strippers are less constrained in maintaining role-related social distance. Further, freed of bar roles, persons tend to develop other ways of indicating that they are "somebody." As customers, they may, through their purchasing habits, tips, or special treatment received from the restaurant staff, establish identities somewhat distinct from their work roles:

The bar staff and the hookers will talk about everything at Biffy's. Not just their work problems, but their families, and holidays and just about everything. It's also a bit of a show place. It's much quieter there than in the bar, and if someone wants more people to know about something, like a new ring a girl received from her old man, that's a good place to mention it and show it around. You definitely see other sides of the people in this setting. A girl might seem really callous in the bar, but now you see the other side, where she might be very considerate and concerned for another hooker or staff person. (notes)

Offering a quieter and more relaxed setting than the bar, these restaurants also facilitate extended discussions of preceding hotel occurrences and anticipated events. Here, difficulties with work, fellow workers, management, patrons and outsiders can be discussed at length with staff members often exchanging advice as how to best deal with these aspects of bar work. These discussions not only define a group of insiders but, so far as they generate in-group support or solutions to ongoing problems, also facilitate continuity in their work.

While locational convenience promotes some regular attendance of staff people at area restaurants, the linkages are often more extensive than this. For example, even where interaction is minimal, restaurant people and hotel personnel may share similar concerns (trouble off the street, handling drunks and so on) and mutual acquaintances (hookers, hustlers, rubbies), promoting a sense of affinity. The restaurant people also recognize the dollar value of their associations with the hotel people; not only are they generally good tippers but may be some of the biggest spenders the restaurant possesses. While affinity and economics may promote a tolerance of the hotel crowd, as a place becomes more widely acknowledged by the hotel staff and rounders (becomes something of a "hangout"), one finds that the lives of the hotel and restaurant people are more likely to become intertwined. Not only may they cross-patronize one another's businesses, but they may also become involved in joint ventures of both a social (such as going to the track, romance), and business (lending money, hooking, and so on) nature:

Tony's Tacos is a small restaurant in the area. It's a little surprising to see the amount of business it receives from people in one way or another connected with the hotel community. Tony is fairly straight overall, but he is quite friendly with a lot of the rounders and spends some evenings drinking at Main and Central. In addition to the people you might meet there, you can also leave messages with the staff for other customers. Ralph, Tony's helper, spends very little time in bars, but he has been hustled by a few of the hookers who drop by for a coffee now and then. (notes)

Given these sorts of contacts, one finds the restaurant and hotel people further intertwined as a consequence of staff interchanges. Becoming familiar with the hotel staff and management, restaurant workers may be presented with employment opportunities in area bars and vice-versa:

> *Some of the hotel staff (Rocky, Nick, Jack, and Mike) at Main have worked at Tony's Tacos. A lot of the people working at Main and Central were cab drivers, or waiters or waitresses at other places in the area. . . . I have also noticed that a few bar staff people have taken jobs in restaurants when they've been dismissed or wanted a change of pace, but restaurant work seldom pays as well.* (notes)

Recognizing their business value, the restaurant staff generally try to accommodate the hotel and street people. Insofar as they have other patrons, however, they tend to be concerned about their more general business image. In attempting to minimize incidents between these patrons and other customers, some area restaurants "segregate" hotel and street people from others by seating them in different areas of the restaurants. While providing more privacy for the hotel and street people, this practice also means that the other patrons are less likely to become aware of the range of clientele to whom the restaurant caters. Should difficulties arise, the restaurant staff will usually attempt to manage the situation informally.

Should these difficulties become more pronounced, the restaurant staff may receive assistance from their regulars. They will occasionally call the police but generally, like the bars, they prefer to handle most difficulties informally.

AFTER-HOURS PLACES

After-hours places are settings in which persons may socialize after the regular bars close. Although we cannot provide the sort of information Roebuck and Frese (1976) present in their case study of the Rendezvous (an after-hours club), after-hours places are significant elements for people "in the life."

In respect to decor, atmosphere, and clientele, after-hours places are no less variable than the bars one finds open under "liquor licence" approval. While catering to "night people," be these people "in the life" or persons desiring to be "with it," after-hours places reflect both managerial interests and those of the patrons. For example, some places (usually those illegally distributing liquor) may put very stringent limitations on "membership criteria," while others are open to almost anyone. Entertainment can also vary considerably, from providing "only a place to gather" to musicians and floor shows. Although it seems useful to differentiate between legitimate and illegitimate after-hours places, it should be noted that there may be some spillover of activities, patrons, and staff between these two sets of after-hours places, making even these seemingly basic distinctions less significant than they may first appear.

Legitimate After-Hours Places

Legitimate after-hours clubs are more likely to be open to the public, collecting revenues through cover charges and/or the sales of coffee, soft drinks, and snacks. In some ways these places are more restaurant-like than bars, but they differ from most late-night restaurants by offering entertainment and in being known as "after-hours clubs." While the staff in some of these places will covertly sell liquor to known patrons, and/or patrons may bring liquor with them, with varying degrees of club tolerance, these places purport to be "legitimate." Initially, some of these clubs cater to a wide variety of patrons but, with time, they tend to become known for catering to particular types of clientele:

> *The Grass Hut is an after-hours club that some of the hotel people go to. It's official status is a "social club," wherein one can buy soft drinks and dance, but insiders can buy liquor from the doorman. It's a rougher type of after-hours club. It's located in a welfare neighborhood and a lot of the younger street people go there. The decor of the club is of rather poor quality. Everything looks well-used and patched-up. Some hotel people refuse to go there because of its "cheapness."* (notes)

While rounders and hotel people may represent significant clientele at some licensed after-hours clubs, it should be noted that many of these places cater to relatively "straight clientele." Providing entertainment of various sorts, these places resemble "straight" bars, discos, and the like, with the exception of a visible liquor trade.

Illegitimate After-Hours Places

In contrast to legitimate after-hours clubs "booze cans," "blind pigs," or "bootlegger joints," are more likely to be located in residential dwellings, sans advertising. As it is difficult to conceal the sale of liquor from those already on the premises, the screening of patrons is of considerable concern for the operators of "booze cans." One finds, consequently, that operators tend to "do business" with personal acquaintances or those vouched for by trusted others:

> *Pat's place, it's beautiful! It's a real nice quiet place, never no fights down there. A lot of musicians go there, musicians, waiters, bartenders. Like we opened the place up, we were the first ones there, when it first opened up. We sort of started the place off and we've been going there all the time. You've got to have a key to get in there. She doesn't answer the doorbell. She made a bunch of keys, and only certain people get the keys. So when we go down there, just open the door, go on upstairs. It's usually a good time. She's open about three days a week. That's all she has to be open, because she gets a packed house all the time. People are just standing all over, there's no room to sit. It's always packed. It's a beautiful place to go, and it's not expensive. Like I run a tab, and when I pay it, I pay it. I don't have to pay it that night. But when I pay it, it's never really that much, and you're, "Give him a drink, give him a drink." You're buying people drinks all the time. . . . A little bit of dope goes around, a little bit of coke might float by. It doesn't go through the whole house, but if you happen to be there when the guy's just sort of passing some out to some friends, "Like a snort?" But never anything heavy there. She's never been raided at all. Pat's a very smart woman. She takes precautions all the time. She'll be open for like three months and then she'll close for a month or two weeks, or whatever. She does this quite often. Every now and then she'll just say, "We're closing up for three weeks." Then she'll give you a call or something or you bump into her somewhere, and she'll say, "Well, I'm opening up again" and you just go down.* (rounder)

Cleon's booze can is located in a rougher, older neighborhood. From the outside it looks like an average working-class type of house. When I arrived, there were some people partying on the porch. What first struck me was the visibility of the activity. The neighbors, it seemed, would be aware of what was happening, because it wasn't a quiet party by any means and there were a few people pretty drunk, right out on the porch. . . . The kitchen was used more or less for the bar and the owner's wife was working as the bar maid. She had the liquor set up over a kitchen table, along with the coke, and plastic glasses. There were some people in the kitchen, singing and drinking, with the radio on. In the two other adjacent rooms, were more people sitting around, talking and singing, and even along in the hallway, there were people milling around with drinks. In the front room was another group of people, drinking and talking with each other. Most of the people were there in couples, but most of them were quite drunk, staggering, and slurring their words. (notes)

Ginger Bread, a dancer, runs a booze can in a residential neighborhood, located in the basement of a house. However, it's been extensively remodelled to look like a bar. There is a stool bar large enough to seat 12 customers, and she seems to have an ample supply and variety of liquors. There is even a pinball machine and jukebox. When I was there, the place seemed fairly full and there were a number of people from the Pink Panther (a hookers' bar) present. Ginger's hostess, Nola, is a hooker at the Pink Panther. She said that she generally spent a lot of time in after-hours bars and quite liked her arrangement with Ginger. (notes)

Booze cans, like area restaurants, represent places in which people "in the life" (hotel staff, hookers, entertainers, cab drivers, and so on) can relax and enjoy themselves in the company of "sympathetic others." As places less likely to be frequented or managed by "squares," after-hours places allow these persons to be themselves and yet avoid the sort of indignation they might encounter in more respectable society:

I go to Cleon's to relax, have a drink, maybe pick up a broad. I like it better than a bar because there I know I'm with my own kind. There ain't very many straight people at the booze can. (rounder)

At most of the after-hours places, you'll find a lot of wrongdoers, people who have been in the life. There's some straight people, but a lot of them would have been in trouble with the law or would be involved in some illegal activity. (rounder)

Apart from convenience and tolerance, after-hours places can also serve as "show places" for those in attendance. Insofar as persons frequent the same clubs as their friends and associates, these are places in which one can "be somebody," unencumbered by one's job or hustle. Although one may envision pimps and hookers trying to outdress one another, "show boating" is by no means limited to them. Persons may flash "success" signs by the jewellery they wear, their spending habits, the people accompanying them, and their "pull" with the staff and management:

The Triangle and the Lily Pad, that's where the cool people go. That's where the young pimps take their ladies and do a little dope, a little coke, a little grass, whatever they got. (hooker)

Not all hotel staff and rounders go to after-hours clubs, but "illegitimate" places in particular have important links to both the hotel community and the thief subculture. Not only are "booze can" staff often drawn from the hotel setting but the clientele is, to a large extent, likely to reflect hotel and rounder networks. Further, while after-hours clubs represent arenas in which the social lives of people "in the life" may be extended, they also facilitate contacts among rounders and hustling activities more generally:

> The Ebony, that's a real action bar. Like you have the pimps and the hookers, but it's a good place to unload things. Some of the pimps are into fencing and dealing drugs and whatnot, so it's good for them. But I can fit in there. You can't. It is not a place for white men to go. (hooker)

> Fritz had this booze can. Mostly for very rough people. . . . If somebody just happened to maybe crack accidentally, well, they were already up and, "Do you want to fight?" Right away! This booze can was a real dive, it was dirty and it kind of stunk, but you'd find all the heavies there. . . . This place has been just literally torn up many times and they'll still use the chairs where the backs are torn up, torn off or whatever. Usually they open it up right after work and you get all these heavies there, and they'd be talking about the joint all the time. A lot of them have been in prison or have just gotten out. . . . I was there one night and things were getting a little hot and then suddenly you hear some shots through the window. Everybody was down on the floor and I was sort of scared to make a move. All of a sudden, I saw all these guns coming out and a few people are firing back in some general direction. I didn't think they had guns. I just thought they were all here for a sociable drink, or whatever, but out comes the guns. A couple of hours passed by and everybody's just sort of hanging around, just sitting there, and finally one guy walked out and it was safe, so after a bit I left. I went back a couple of times after that, but I made sure I didn't stay for any length of time. (rounder)

> Willow's, that's a hustler's place. A lot of the hustlers come by and sell dope and things, or they might go there and watch for people leaving the club that they could roll. . . . Sometimes the hustlers will take a straight guy around to different places and let the straight guy pick up the tabs. If the guy wants to see some of the life, then they have to make it worth the hustler's time. . . . A lot of these people are into pimping, fencing, different cons, whatever they can do to make a buck. Mostly, it's a mental thing, where they'll be around somebody that they knew had money, and then try to figure some way of getting that money from him. It's sort of like the way the pimps approach the girls. They try to show how they're a big man about town, with their jewellery and cars, and how they know everybody. The same way they impress a chick. (rounder)

Getting Established

Although booze cans may seem relatively easy to establish, there are a number of concerns with which prospective operators must come to terms if they wish to be successful. In addition to finding a reasonably accessible but discreet location, they are also faced with the problems of finding the staff, establishing adequate safety measures to avoid legal entanglements and, most importantly, developing a viable clientele. Given these concerns, many plans to establish booze cans do not materialize:

Clint's booze can was a very posh place, but it just didn't work out financially. He didn't have the overhead to see it through a slow start. Also, it was located a fair distance from the clientele he hoped to attract. He had intended the place as a rather exclusive gathering spot for the hotel people, the staff, the hookers and some of the better action patrons. . . . Nancy, Luis, and several other people have all individually expressed plans to establish an after-hours club. Each has made some commitments in this direction, but none has materialized. In general, their plans for a "beautiful place" required more resources than they could accumulate. (notes)

Precluded from normal advertising and open-door admission practices, operators wishing to develop a more extensive clientele in illegitimate settings must tap into previously developed networks. They may also involve women in patron and staff roles, assuming that the presence of women in the club will attract more males as customers, but one needs a base from which to draw an audience. Thus, while strippers and hookers are welcomed in many after-hours clubs, established, well-connected rounders, representing a drawing card vis-à-vis their contacts, may be particularly valued as patrons.

One of the most significant sources of trouble for operators revolves around the illegality of their enterprise. For instance, while they may take a variety of precautions — such as requiring that guests park a block or more away, that they avoid disturbing neighbors, that they be very careful about those whom they bring to the party, and by using lookouts and heavily bolted doors to give themselves more time to make a business venture appear more like a friendly party — it seems only a matter of time until a place is raided. And, generally, the more popular the after-hours club, the greater the likelihood that it will come to the attention of the police. The vulnerability of after-hours places is not, however, limited to the illegal dispensing of liquor. Not only may some of the patrons be fugitives from the law, but others may be subject to arrest for illegal possession, distribution, and usage of drugs other than alcohol.

In addition to staying "a step ahead of the law," one of the major concerns of the operators of after-hours places is managing troublesome patrons. Since the possibility of calling in the police is virtually eliminated, almost all incidents must be handled informally. Aware of this precarious situation, both the staff and patrons often attempt to resolve difficulties with a minimum of outside interference:

At Cleon's, Glen's buddy, a man he met in jail, was talking about different things he'd done. The more he spoke, the more claims he made. . . . About half way through his story, a young woman walked in the room and listened to the man for a couple of minutes or so. When he finished, she said, "Well, all that's bullshit, you're really nothing." Glen's buddy got pretty upset at this. He had a drink in his hand and he threw it at her. He missed her face and the glass hit the wall behind her. She didn't react much to this, but just looked at him saying, "That's what I'd expect from you. You've got no class." He was then threatening to hit her, but the other people by this time were trying to get his attention away from her, trying to humor him. Glen was making a special effort, saying, "Don't do that. Not in here. We're here to have a good time, not to argue." The man said, "Yeah, that's right, we're not going to argue, we're here to have a good time, and to drink." He seemed to forget the matter until the girl brought it up again, and then he got angry again. At this point, other people in the room the other girls were starting to say things to this girl, telling her, "Come on, don't do that. Don't be so bitchy with the guy." Glen also pulled her aside and told her, "Listen, you don't start messing with people when they're drunk. You don't start calling them things like that. You don't upset them. There's no telling what he might do. Just play it cool. Don't bother this guy while he's drunk." Finally she quieted down and ended up leaving. Glen's buddy ended up falling asleep on the couch. (notes)

IN CONTEXT

Beginning with a discussion of patron roles generally in evidence across bars, and concluding with a statement on area restaurants and after-hours places, this chapter has examined the ways in which patrons (and rounders) fit into the hotel community. Although the patron-staff distinction is an important one in many respects, we also find that the roles are not as sharply defined or as mutually exclusive as they might first seem. Not only are staff people and entertainers likely to be some of the most dedicated patrons a bar may have, but patrons are also instrumental in defining an atmosphere, promoting social order in the bar, and providing some entertainment. Their drinking activities, their attempts to "be somebody," their concerns with entertainment, and their hustles, along with the activities of the "staff" and the "entertainment" define the bar as a social setting. The hotel community does not, however, cease activity with the closing of the bar. Patrons and staff vary greatly in the extent to which they are also involved in the "night life"; but for many, after-hours activities represent salient elements of their lives. Not only is the night life more likely to be void of "squares," but places catering to these people are more likely to represent "action spots," and as such cannot be neglected in discussions of the hotel community.

Chapter 7

In Perspective

At Greenview, we started talking with Doug, a used-car dealer. On learning that we were from the university, he asked what we were doing there. I didn't know where he fitted into things there, so I said, "We heard about this place at Spring Gardens and thought we should check it out. I thought maybe we could learn something about people." He replied, "Yeah, that's a good idea. All those things you learn in books, and I've read a lot of books myself, they don't do you any good when you're dealing with people. . . . A lot of people, writers and university people, they think that they are better than anybody else. Then, they just don't find out what's happening in those people's lives. If you want to find out about people, real people, you have to go to places like this. You have to go to the upper levels and the lower levels, places like this and Sunset, the hookers' bar, or maybe Spring Gardens, where you were, it's one of the roughest places in town." (notes)

Many people have asked us why we studied the hotel community. Some of them shudder at the thought of these places and some others assume that people studying "disreputable" persons in "disreputable" places must also be "disreputable" characters. Still others have chastized us for not studying "real problems" or for studying "exotic" subjects like hookers and strippers rather than "everyday people." Although all of these people are entitled to their views, the hotel community for us represented a setting of unusual richness. It was a setting about which many people are interested but, more than this, it provided invaluable contrasts with our more conventional routines and suggested considerable potential for showing how "categories of deviants" were intertwined. Like Doug, we share the impression that much of the material written about people bears little resemblance to their everyday lives. This seems particularly true in reference to "deviants," about whom a great deal is often written on the basis of very limited and superficial (if any) contact with the "subjects." The hotel setting is one in which a variety of people are coming together and working out their lives in the context of others and, so far as possible, we have attempted to depict this setting, with its animosities, uncertainties, hustles, and action.

DEVIANCE AS INTERACTION

As a means of qualifying the subsequent discussion, it seems advisable to stipulate a number of (interactionist) assumptions basic to the understanding of deviance as a process.[1] First among these is the assumption that humans operate in "symbolic

---

[1] For somewhat related statements on the problematic nature of reality, see Berger and Luckmann (1966), Blumer (1969), and Lyman and Scott (1970). See Charon (1979) for an excellent introductory statement on symbolic interactionism.

realities" rather than "objective" or "stimulus" realities. The meanings people attach to objects are derived through ongoing interaction with their associates (Blumer, 1969); perceptions and knowledge of phenomena are shaped by the social contexts in which people find themselves. While people tend to attribute "objective" or "immutable" qualities to those objects and events in which they perceive widespread consensus,[2] it is analytically useful to think in terms of "multiple realities" (Schutz, 1971). Rather than assume that our perspectives are shared by others, it is necessary to ascertain the perspectives from which those whom we wish to understand operate. Further, insofar as realities are ongoing products of association they are continually subject to negotiation on the part of involved persons. Thus, while each encounter need not result in any change in participants' perceptives, each encounter provides an occasion in which some conception of the "world-as-known" may undergo change for the involved parties.

A second assumption is that humans have the capacity for "self-reflectivity" (Mead, 1934: Blumer, 1969). Not only are humans seen to develop versions of the symbolic frameworks utilized by those with whom they have contact, but they have the ability to be "objects unto themselves." Hence they are both symbolically-minded, and self-aware. Not only do persons act towards others as they (symbolically) envision these others but they also act towards, and in terms of, a symbolically envisioned self. These "self-other identities" (and resulting concerns with labels and reputations)[3] thus have extensive significance for everyday life. Additionally, like other aspects of persons' (symbolic) realities, persons' images of self (and others) are subject to change and redefinition as a consequence of interaction. This capacity for self-reflectivity is significant in another sense as well. It means that persons are social beings, not only in their direct interaction with others, and in terms of their (symbolic) conceptualizations of the world, but also in terms of self-conversations, assessments, aspirations, plans, rehearsals, and daydreams.

The third assumption is that human association is problematic and negotiable. While reflecting previously developed meanings and structures, interaction has an emergent quality as participants endeavor to work out their interests in the context of unfolding exchanges. This is not to suggest that interaction cannot or does not have a systematic quality to it, only that the "normative parameters" operative are not as precise, consistent, relevant, or continually valued by the participants, as would be required to make ensuing lines of interaction highly predictable. The situation becomes further complicated when one recognizes that two or more interacting parties may not only have somewhat different world views, but also different self-attributed interests, introducing negotiation into already problematic encounters. Interactants may be interested in what others have to offer (resources, explanations, desired qualities, and so on), as well as desire to promote their own perspectives and interests; consequently, encounters lend themselves to negotiated outcomes. Further, insofar as persons may also stimulate or dissipate the interests

---

[2] Schutz (1971) uses the term "intersubjective consensus" to refer to a group sense of reality or objectivity.

[3] I attribute the term "self-other identities," referring to self and other definitions and the corresponding behavioral expectations, to Carl Couch. As he very succinctly puts it, "Self-other identities are the guts of social structure."

of others in various pursuits as the interaction sequence unfolds, each party may find his interests shifting as the exchanges take place. As a result of the problematic and negotiable nature of interaction, outcomes are seen as the result of ongoing activities rather than products of the forces defining the background characteristics of the persons involved. Activities are not predetermined products, they are the realization of social life. As Blumer (1969) suggests, social life is a continual process of working out and linking activities. Regardless of the time span (short run—long term), degree of structure (casual—formal), the number of individuals involved, or the cultural context, social life is contingent on activities and their interpretations.

A fourth premise, and one basic to this research, is that one does not need "one theory for the deviants" and "one theory for the normals." Thus an attempt is made to develop a theory "applicable to anyone." Investigations of "deviance phenomena" are examined in the more general context of human behavior.

To a large extent the present analysis fits into the "subcultural research" tradition. We are indebted to a wide variety of largely interactionist-oriented studies focussing on aspects of life (and deviance) within subcultural contexts. See, for example, Finestone's (1957) article on "cats, kicks, and color"; Goffman's (1961) Asylums; Reiss's (1961) analysis of "peers and queers"; Ray's (1961) discussion of heroin user relapses; Becker's (1963) statement on jazz musicians; Simmons' (1964) and Lofland's (1966) depictions of religious cults; Weinberg's (1965) treatment of nudists; Scott's (1968) monograph on "the racing game"; Rubington's (1968) portrayal of skid row drunks; and Irwin's (1970) description of prison experiences. While these and other ethnographic accounts are invaluable in sensitizing us to the highly variable social aspects of group life, it is important to more explicitly distinguish the following features of community life: (1) norms; (2) interrelatedness; and (3) activity. We begin with a statement on "deviance as normative," indicating the orientational frames most evident in hotel community. "Deviance as interrelatedness" portrays the significance of affiliational networks and the individual person's embeddedness therein, not only for reputations and career involvements, but for the overall life of the community as well. Following this, we consider "deviance as activity," endeavoring at this point to indicate the problematic, emergent, and negotiable aspects of activities frequently considered deviant.

DEVIANCE AS NORMATIVE

Although some sociologists would suggest that deviance is best defined as "norm violating behavior" (for example Cohen, 1957), we would suggest that much of what is labelled "deviance" is best understood as "normative behavior." That is, while behavior which violates the norms (expectancies) groups (and individuals) use as standards may be defined as "deviant" by these audiences, "norm violating behavior" is best understood within the context in which it occurs. In this respect, regardless of whether one is discussing hookers, strippers, staff, or hustlers, simply calling these people "deviants" or "norm violators" is to miss the entire effect of the subcultural framework in which they are operating. It is in this context that a notion of "multiple realities" (Schutz, 1971; Berger and Luckmann, 1966), suggesting that there are multiple frameworks in which to conceptualize activity, is so valuable. From this perspective, activity is neither good nor bad, right or wrong in itself; "deviance" is a quality conferred on an activity by some audience (Becker, 1963). Each group can be seen as having its own ethos, or style of life, making the activities of its members not only (seem) "natural," but "objectively correct," For example, while hookers are aware of conventional definitions of morality, when these females are at work the woman making the most money is apt to be the most esteemed. Likewise, rounders may have difficulty understanding another rounder who passes up a good opportunity to steal some merchandise or who refuses to accept money from a hooker or stripper. To illustrate the relevance of normative frames for the hotel community, three aspects of community life (hustling, drinking, and violence) have been selected. Presented in summary form, these discussions indicate some of the normative frames operative in "action" bars more specifically, but in most bars to some extent.

HUSTLING AS NORMATIVE

Hustling as a way of life can vary considerably across bars, but the normative parameters of hustling are applicable across a wide variety of people at action bars. Although neglecting some particularistic features of the normative frameworks employed by hookers, rounders, and staff people "taking an edge," the following points sensitize us to the more generic components of the hustling subculture:

1. Hustling (and theft) is a respectable and profitable way of making money. In general, persons making more money as hustlers are accorded more prestige, and persons utilizing non-violent hustles are deemed more respectable.

2. Hustlers, in principle, are "always on the hustle." Persons involved in hustling are expected to be knowledgeable, alert, and resourceful. Hustlers, thus, not only capitalize on existing opportunities, but are also expected to create or promote situations favorable to hustles they can manage.

3. Hustlers are expected to "know their way around," to know places and people conducive to "action" and to know how to minimize risks and avoid trouble.

4. Hustlers are expected to be self-oriented, "looking out for number one." They can, however, be expected to co-operate when it is perceived to their advantage to do so. While some partnerships reflect loyalty and friendship, many (particulary among those of limited acquaintance) are viewed with "natural" suspicion and distrust.

5. Ideally, a hustler has "no feelings" for the target. Everyone with money is a prospective target for a hustle. It is a matter of finding their weaknesses or developing an interest relevant to one's resources. The hustler's task is to relieve the target of his valuables; any sense of moral responsibility, ethics, or sympathy, thus represents an obstacle a hustler is expected to overcome en route to becoming a "bona fide" hustler.

6. Hustlers, themselves, should not be "suckers" for other hustlers. Although most hustlers end up being hustled by other hustlers, it is expected that any self-respecting hustler would not be extensively and consistently "duped" by others.

7. Hustlers are not expected to go out of their way to help other hustlers; however, it is expected that they not interfere with hustles that other hustlers are working.

8. Hustlers are expected to be "cool," not only in reference to maintaining composure in difficult situations, but also in remaining relatively disinterested in any activities or involvements on the part of others which do not affect them in any direct personal way.

DRINKING AS NORMATIVE

While drinking is one of the most common bar activities, this research was not undertaken with the intent of providing material on drinking. However, as we spent more time in bar research, it seemed that we might be able to suggest some aspects of bar life affecting drinking behavior. As such, the present focus is different from a somewhat related listing of bar norms developed in Chapter 6:

1. Drinking is an acceptable, enjoyable and expected behavior in the bar setting. Drinking is a means of establishing congeniality among persons in groups, and a means of "feeling good" on a personal level.[4]

2. Being able to manage oneself while under the influence of alcohol is an expected norm and, while persons defined incapable of doing so are viewed as less competent, some prestige will accrue to persons able to maintain their composure while consuming noticeably higher levels of alcohol than their peers ("Boy, he can really hold his booze!").

3. Although even the "solitary" bar drinker is sensitive to self-indications and cues proffered by bar staff, drinking behavior occurring within groups is especially vulnerable to normative parameters. While participation in joint drinking situations indicates self-other acceptance, part of "being someone" (a good sport, a big spender) in this situation is that of buying others drinks. Once the practice of "buying rounds" has been initiated, however, one finds that persons in the group tend to feel obligated not only to buy their fair share, but also to consume their fair share of alcohol. Likewise, once groups form, anyone wishing to cease drinking is likely to find that he is obligated to provide a "good account" for doing so. Anyone admitting that he is having problems holding his liquor is apt to lose some status in the group.

4. Given the group context, drinking may also be defined in competitive terms and it may, thus, be challenging for persons to try to top one another in either implicit and/or explicit liquor consumption contests.

5. There is no predetermined or fixed point at which to stop drinking. Persons are expected to stop "once they have had more than they can handle," but this is a rather ambiguous cut-off point.

6. From the management's perspective, the bar's major business is selling liquor. Therefore, one indicator of an effective staff is the volume of liquor

---

[4] Although we have not explicitly tested Becker's (1963) statement on "becoming a marijuana user" in respect to "becoming a drinker," the model he develops therein seems generally applicable.

sold. While some managers explicitly pressure staff people to "push drinks," staff members also tend to view a more extensive liquor trade as a means of promoting tips and/or hustles.

7. Although bars are not to sell liquor to "already intoxicated" persons, this simple mandate is complicated by bar staff interests in selling liquor and getting tips, and by the problematics of defining when someone is intoxicated.

VIOLENCE AS NORMATIVE

While fights are more common in some bars than others, it should be noted that compared to drinking and hustling, violent physical exchanges are relatively infrequent, even in the "rougher" bars:

1. Although violence can be expected to occur more frequently in bars than in many other settings, even in rough bars, expectations of violence have a sporadic rather than a continuous quality. It may happen that on some occasions an earlier event may lead to longer lasting expectations of trouble but, as persons become involved in other activities, anticipations of violent exchanges tend to dissipate. Fights represent some of the more dramatic events in bars and, to the extent they reflect upon the reputations and prestige of involved parties, they are more likely to be frequent topics of conversation than are many other events. Because fights represent exciting, entertaining events to many bar patrons (particularly in predominately male bars), unless observers deem their personal interests (or those of close friends) to be jeopardized, they are unlikely to discourage violent exchanges.

2. To the extent one honors the norm that "one has to stand up for his rights," any indication that one's rights have been unduly transgressed represents an occasion for becoming retributive in one's responses towards the offender. Insofar as persons view their identity as dependent on the opinions of any witnesses, any "transgression" becomes more serious when it is noticed by these others. While early and widely pronounced apologies offset the likelihood of violent reprisals, physically attacking an offender is considered an acceptable way of handling transgressions in many bars.

3. Persons in bars are deemed generally less deserving of civil respect than persons in many other settings. This freedom from moral restraints inhibiting violence,[5] is particularly evident in reference to "no accounts" ("drunks," "punks," "queers") who are considered liable targets for mistreatment. Others, however, such as "tough insiders" may be generally acknowledged as unfeasible targets. For example, while persons transgressed by inferiors or peers may lose some prestige by not responding assertively, a failure to confront a tough insider may be considered "wise."

4. Persons are more likely to initiate violent exchanges when they define themselves in bars in which they anticipate support. The expectation is that friends will help one another out. Persons anticipating support may more readily assume liberties with others with whom they find fault.

---

[5] Matza (1964) uses the term "drift" to refer to a situation in which persons feel freed from usual moral obligations. For a more extensive discussion of drift in reference to violence, see Prus (1978).

5. Once the fight has begun, it is considered desirable to "get in the first and last punch." Thus persons experience some latitude in using "whatever it takes to stop the other fellow," endeavoring not to let the other person retaliate. "Fair fight" rules are generally ineffective in bar encounters and, unless there is a somewhat balanced opposition, it may be considered "fair play" for a group of persons in a bar setting to gang up on a person (even though any one of his opponents might well be able to better him in a refereed event).

6. In general, participants in bar fights exhibit little concern for the long-term suffering any fight may have for their opponents. Participants expect to be held less accountable for damages to other persons in bar settings than in many other contexts. Injuries sustained by others are seen to reflect their "just rewards."[6]

7. Staff perspectives on fights tend towards a "peacekeeping" model. In general, they try to avoid violent exchanges and the ensuing damages to property or to patron attendance. They are particularly concerned with maintaining the goodwill of their "regulars" and when incidents do occur, the staff, unless personally involved, are apt to assume positions they feel represent the best long-term interests of the bar. In general, while the police may be called in more extreme cases, attempts are made to handle trouble in the bar on an informal basis.

While subcultural norms may be used to depict a "way of life" characterizing a group of people, these summary statements represent but a starting point in the analysis of "deviant behavior." Depicting the norms of those we study establishes a context and indicates that "deviance" is a relative phenomenon, reflecting prevailing social definitions; it does not, however, indicate how the referenced behavior unfolds, or how the people fit their activities and lives together.

DEVIANCE AS INTERRELATEDNESS

As we spent more time within the hotel setting, it became increasingly apparent that persons involved therein could not be simply understood as categories of actors enacting norms. Not only did we find people occupying a plurality of roles in the hotel community concurrently or over time, but we also found that persons were often closely affiliated through friendship, marriage, or family ties, with others involved in a variety of pursuits. In the first instance, a girl might be a waitress, a hooker, and a stripper on either a sequential or overlapping basis; the same girl might be dating the manager, and her brother may be a rounder best known for his involvements in boosting and drug dealing. While it makes sense to discuss involvements in particular roles, as persons become more extensively involved in the hotel setting the notion of "interrelatedness' is essential for understanding the "career contingencies" of those persons. Further, although one might attempt to develop hierarchical power charts by activity these tend to be rather misleading. Much of the power and prestige accruing to persons in specific positions is extensively qualified by their affiliations with others in the community and by their own multiple involvements. A waiter may be a loanshark, a janitor may be a top-ranking rounder's son. One's overall reputation within the commun-

---

[6] See Athens (1974) and Dietz (1978) for other statements on (street) violence norms.

ity thus tends to depend more on the individual's contacts and his recognition as "solid," than upon any particular role involvements.

The concept of interrelatedness also has basic implications for the understanding of activity as a process. Although it is commonly assumed that persons engage in activities as a consequence of attitudes favorable to that activity ("seekership") or a lack of options ("closure"), our research suggests that involvements to a very large extent reflect fortuitous contacts, selective recruitment, and the negotiations of all involved. Not only are the "recruitment tactics" of others relevant, but also significant are the ways in which persons, on an ongoing basis, define their interests and the situations in which they find themselves. While persons lacking specific contacts may have little opportunity to engage in certain activities, where this exposure does take place participation in these activities depends considerably on the role of these contact persons. For example, one may speak of a person's interests in drinking as being at a particular level on entering a bar on a specific occasion; once therein, however, that person's "decisions" to order a drink, continue drinking, and to stop drinking, may depend much more on the ways in which the other people in the bar act towards him than his earlier interest (or his more general attitudes towards drinking).

CAREER CONTINGENCIES

One of the reasons it is difficult to come to terms with the concept of "career contingencies" (Becker, 1963; Prus and Sharper, 1977) is that not one, but four sets of "careers" are intertwined. One may speak of "careers of role participation" (bartender, hooker, drinker). This is the most common usage of "career." If one envisions "identity careers" as one's image of self over time,[7] a second set of contingencies, those affecting one's self-identity over time becomes prominent. Identity careers would link the various role careers in which individuals become involved simultaneously, and over time.

A third usage of the career concept refers to the "career of an activity" or event (for example, fight, game, hustle, party), wherein one looks at the contributions of the people involved as the event begins, develops, and concludes. The participants, individually, may be at any stage in their role and identity careers, but insofar as each activity has a career of its own, they collectively participate in its unfolding. This notion, while highly consistent with interactionist theory, has received surprisingly little attention. Just as persons may become more or less intensively involved in forms of activity over varying lengths of time, so can activities escalate or dissipate in intensity and persist for varying lengths of time. For example, one may speak of the career contingencies of confrontations (Prus, 1978), of performances, and of negotiations (such as hooker-client exchanges).

A fourth usage focusses on "careers of relationships": how relationships between persons emerge and when they are likely to intensify or dissipate. For instance, while one may speak of the career of a thief, one can also speak of the relationships of that thief with particular others, each relationship having a career of its own. Likewise, while one can speak of the careers of specific hooker-trick exchanges, one can also delineate the contingencies affecting the careers of hooker-trick relationships.

---

[7] Goffman (1961) uses the term "moral career" to convey a related notion of self-image over time.

Career as applied to ''role participation'' provides substantive continuity for the individuals on whom one focusses; career as applied to ''self-identity'' provides individual continuity across role careers; career as applied to ''activities'' provides continuity within a setting, as all involved parties are considered; career as applied to a ''relationship'' provides continuity betwixt two or more persons, but only where their activities overlap. Each of these notions of career deserves attention. The four sets of careers, while requiring analytical attention individually, cannot be understood without reference to one another. ''Role'' careers cut across self-identities, activities, and relationships; ''self-identities'' span and are shaped by role participation, activities, and relationships; ''activities'' intersect with role careers, self-identities, and relationships; and ''relationships'' transverse roles, identities, and activities. Unfortunately, we have only relatively recently been explicitly sorting out these components of ''career contingencies.'' Nevertheless, by focussing explicitly on the ''interrelatedness'' of the people constituting the hotel community we have, in addition to examining the career contingencies affecting role involvements, also introduced material dealing with the career contingencies of self identities, activities, and relationships.

In what immediately follows, the significance of ''interrelatedness'' is discussed with particular emphasis on persons' role careers in deviance. Focussing on initial involvements, continuities, and disinvolvements from deviance, we are particularly concerned with the ways in which persons ''fit into'' ongoing sets of relationships. This is something largely neglected in sociology and may reflect a tendency on the part of both the proponents and the critics of labelling theory to focus on the role of control agencies (as opposed to the ''receiving audiences'') in the making of deviants.[8] Certainly this is an important issue but the ''receiving audience,'' the ''deviant group'' to which the actor is exposed, also seems critical in affecting subsequent involvements in deviance.

INITIAL INVOLVEMENTS

If one considers initial involvements in deviance then, in addition to accidental or unwitting participation, three major routings are in evidence: closure, seekership, and recruitment.

Closure

When persons become involved in deviance as a means of obtaining goals thought unattainable by conventional routes, we may speak of ''closure.'' Lemert (1953) introduced the term ''closure'' to describe a situation in which some people, finding themselves pressured to resolve financially uncomfortable situations in the most immediately expedient way, wrote cheques on accounts unlikely to be adequate to cover the amount. If one envisions closure with respect to ''felt obligations'' or responsibilities more generally, then as a concept it assumes considerable relevance for the explanation of deviance. When one's sense of obligation is very strong, and other options are closed, deviance options may be seriously entertained ''out of necessity.'' Closure may assume financial dimen-

---

[8] Although aspects of labelling theory can be traced back to Tannenbaum (1937), ''labelling theory'' is most commonly associated with the works of Lemert (1951, 1967) and Becker (1963). For more detailed statements on the complexities and issues of labelling theory, see Prus (1975a,b).

sions, but other loyalties (such as friendship, family) are also relevant in defining the viability of options.

Insofar as "financial necessity" is one of the more common reasons outsiders have proffered as to why people go into prostitution, hustling, and theft, some caution seems advisable. Our observations suggest that this is one of the least likely and least effective (continuity-wise) routes of involvement in the hotel community. Not only do many persons "in need of work" dismiss hotel jobs (and career theft) as unacceptable for them, but many of those who do inquire into, or begin, these jobs find themselves very uncomfortable in this setting. For example, many persons who assume positions as barboys or waitresses envision these as short-term work situations and often continue to seek out other work and may change jobs at their earliest convenience. Of the people beginning bar work "out of necessity," only those fitting into the hotel life and/or finding the job unusually lucrative are apt to remain. The bar can be an unfriendly and intimidating setting, even for staff people, and anyone not reasonably well accepted by the other participants is unlikely to stay. While certain deviant activities may represent ways of making or saving money, we should note that the type of activities in which persons participate, and the regularity with which they do so, depends to a large extent on their contacts and their ability to overcome any reservations (moral, health, and so on) they associate with the activity.

Although closure is situational and time-situated, any lines of action in which persons embark as means of solving their problems may be extremely consequential for their subsequent involvements in deviance. In this regard, people experiencing a sense of desperation seem particularly likely to react in ways which tend to further disadvantage them over the long run.

While persons may, through their own actions, find themselves in pressing situations, the role of other persons should not be neglected. For not only may others pressure a person to make good any claims or promises he has made but they may also (inadvertently or otherwise) place him in a situation wherein, as a matter of principle or responsibility, he finds himself obligated to act in a certain fashion. Persons may experience closure as a consequence of principles or beliefs they hold dear or concern with certain self-images; but a great deal of the closure people experience reflects their entanglements with others.

Closure frequently prompts more desperate action, but it should be recognized as a negotiable phenomenon in its diffusion as well as in its development. Particularly significant in this respect is the proffering and acknowledgment of "accounts" (see Lyman and Scott, 1970; Prus, 1975b). Explanations, justifications, apologies, and the like, may jeopardize some images persons might like to sustain, but these accounts may enable users to extricate themselves from otherwise demanding situations.[9]

Seekership

In contrast to closure, wherein one feels little choice but to engage in an activity, seekership assumes a "self-defined attraction towards, or fascination with, an activity."[10] Perceiving oneself as having certain kinds of interests, the task then

---

[9] For a more extensive discussion of closure, entanglements, and techniques of disentanglement as these pertain to violence, see Prus (1978).

[10] Somewhat similar notions of seekership are expressed by Lofland and Stark (1965) and Klapp (1969).

becomes one of seeking out settings in which these interests seem most likely to be realized. While one's interests may be seen to reflect one's general orientation towards the world, interests have a situational and negotiable quality. Not only may one's interests shift over time, and vary by context, but other people may significantly promote or discourage interests. As an involvement route, however, the immediate concern is not with the basis of one's interests but rather with their direction and intensity, as these latter aspects prompt involvements. It may happen that persons experience (external) closure and fascination in reference to the same activity, but the two can operate quite independently.

The significance of "seekership," like that of "closure," is moderated by one's contacts. While there are people who very much want to become involved in particular activities characterizing the hotel community, unless these people have or are able to make contacts with the "right people," their chances of realizing their ambitions are diminished considerably. A number of the fringe rounders, for example, are people who want to make "the big time" through criminal activities. They do not, however, have access to persons involved in crime on a more sustained basis and unless they are content to "kick around" for an undefined period of time their chances of making it are greatly reduced. A more common pattern is that of persons seeking a life-style and then settling for what seems the best available approximation. Some dancers, for example, hold aspirations of celebrity fame. Although a few of these have sought jobs as strippers as a consequence, this is seldom their first priority. It does, however, move them closer to the "stardust" they seek. Seekership as a means of involvement has some impact but is to a large extent dependent on existing contacts.

Recruitment

Recruitment is used herein to refer to the attempts of others to involve (or facilitate involvement of) the target in a particular activity and/or life-style.[11] As such, recruitment ranges from explicit, "high pressure" attempts to involve persons in an activity, to a "grudging consent" to give the individual a chance to become involved; from a very structured, formalized approach, subsuming a highly elaborated ideology, to a very casual kind of joint agreement to do something together. Regardless of how "hard" or "soft" the attempt to involve someone, few activities can be explained by reference to the individual alone.

To illustrate the range of recruitment, three levels of explicitness are examined: inadvertent involvements, sponsored involvements, and solicited involvements. "Inadvertent involvements" reflect situations in which persons find themselves experiencing unanticipated options (typically where one activity intersects with another). For example, a regular patron may be offered an opportunity "to make a few bucks" on a particular evening when a waiter suddenly quits. The patron may have been laid off from work or may simply find bar work preferable to his regular job and may ask, or be asked, to continue this job on a regular basis. Persons becoming involved in this way are unlikely to feel offended by bar life and they are more likely to be accepted by both staff and patrons than are outside applicants. Similarly, a thief may meet a hooker at an after-hours club, find her company pleasurable, and subsequently become her "old man."

"Sponsored involvements" are somewhat akin to inadvertent involvements but

---

[11] For discussions of other aspects of recruitment, see Prus (1976) and Prus and Sharper (1977).

denote insiders who, in effect, "set the person up." The insiders (typically friends or family) may be in a position not only to arrange initial involvements but, more importantly, to facilitate the newcomer's adjustment therein. One finds instances of facilitated involvements not only in reference to bar work, but also in stripping, hooking, rounding, and drinking. Sponsored involvements, building on pre-existing bonds, tend to be more stable than those arising from necessity and, overall, represent one of the most common forms of involvement.

"Solicited involvements" refer to situations in which persons more explicitly endeavor to involve others in particular activities. For instance, agents may advertise in newspapers for exotic dancers, hotel owners may seek out a particular person in another bar to manage their places, pimps may endeavor to obtain additional "hos," and hustlers may attempt to locate "marks." Sometimes the targets are aware that they are being solicited and may use this to their advantage in bargaining. At other times, however, the targets may be relatively naive about the plans the other persons have for them. In any event, the target is apt to find that the situation is being defined as one befitting a person of his (her) particular interests, as the agent tries to make the prospects more enticing. Although not always effective, the definitions proffered by the agent are likely to increase the possibility of the target's involvement. While solicited involvements are sometimes based on a confidence game model (Prus and Sharper, 1977), they seem most effective when combined with sponsored involvements. For example, a pimp may use a variation of "the con" in attempting to involve a girl in prostitution, but if he can introduce the prospect to a hooker with whom she becomes good friends (a "sponsor" who will facilitate the prospect's entry into the work role), he is more apt to be successful in "turning her out."

Drift

Regardless of whether one is discussing "closure," "seekership," or "recruitment," prospective actors have to overcome any reservations they associate with the activities under consideration. As a result, concerns with "drift" are relevant in each case. Matza (1964) uses the term "drift" to refer to circumstances in which persons feel less constrained than usual to act in conventional ways. Although he uses the term primarily to refer to "freedom from moral restraints," our research suggests that a similar notion is also viable in denoting situations in which persons feel released from other normally operative constraints, such as concerns with physical injury or financial loss. Therefore a more generic conceptualization of drift, referring to situations in which persons feel freedom from "normal concerns" or limitations, seems desirable.

Drift is best conceptualized, as Matza suggests, as "situational and transient," such that persons over time and across situations may experience varying levels of drift. It is also important to recognize, as Matza notes, that under conditions of release from restraints, persons may engage in activities which they might generally condemn as in one or other ways undesirable, immoral, foolish, and the like. To illustrate, persons may define places (bars) or persons (drunks) as contextual elements making "normally deviant activities" (such as being rude to, or hitting, persons) seem more reasonable, particularly if one is operating as a community control agent (a bouncer) or has been "personally violated" (insulted).

While drift may be experienced cognitively on an individual level, it can also be affected by situational definitions one receives verbally from others (such as, "It's okay, everybody has to unwind sometimes"), as well as by their behavioral examples. It would also seem that once one has engaged in a particular activity without any significant loss of respect, finances, or other injury, the degree of drift necessary for persons to repeat that activity is likely to be less.

Like "closure," drift entails a situational quality. It is different, however, in that while closure results from obligations to realize (or avoid) certain outcomes, drift represents freedom from obligations.

Multiple Routings

Although three forms of involvement (closure, seekership, and recruitment) have been delineated, there is no reason to assume that only one route is operative for any given person. For instance, while a girl may seek to become an exotic dancer, she may find that agents are out to recruit new talent, and that a high school friend offers to introduce her around, help her with her costumes, and otherwise facilitate her career as a dancer. Overall, each additional base of involvement operative in a given case appears to enhance the likelihood of a stabilized involvement. Thus, while we will be discussing continuity contingencies next, the basis of initial involvement can have considerable impact on one's subsequent involvement in that activity. Closure, seekership, and recruitment are experienced by individuals, but these experiences are very much a product of the interactional context in which the persons find themselves.

CONTINUITY

In discussing aspects of career contingencies conducive to continued involvements in deviance, five themes are prominent: conversion; continuance commitments; activity entanglements; embeddedness in the social life of the (deviant) community; and self-other identities.

Conversion

In contrast to the accepting orientation of those involved in activities they view as natural, "conversion" suggests that some redefinition of an activity is necessary before one becomes a regular practitioner. It further suggests that a person more generally foregoes one life-style (and its accompanying world view) for another.[12] While the notion of conversion is useful in sensitizing us to the dynamics of activity stabilization, some qualification is necessary. First, the two life-styles may not be as sharply differentiated as is typically inferred in a conversion model. Conversion in fact seems to occur most readily and most commonly among persons whose present life-style is more compatible with the prospective one. For example, women working in bars as waitresses, or strippers, on becoming more familiar with "underlife" people, would tend to fit into the hooker community more readily than women in many other occupations.

---

[12] For other discussions of recruitment and conversion, see Karsh et al. (1953); Becker (1963); Festinger et al. (1956); Lofland and Stark (1965); Matza (1969); Gerlach and Hine (1971); Della Cava (1975), Prus (1976), and Prus and Sharper (1977). It seems instructive to view recruitment as an ongoing concern throughout the career of the follower.

Secondly, "prospective recruits" may vary greatly in their explicit recognition of the life-style in which they are supposedly being involved. While some may seek out (or resist) recognized life-styles, others may find themselves extensively involved in an activity before they acknowledge the more general subculture in which "persons like them" are involved. Thus, conversion need not be dramatic, nor need it require extensive changes in one's former life-style. It may reflect one's present activities albeit with the now explicit recognition that one is, for example, a "hooker" and that once one accepts that, one can hustle more effectively.

Thirdly, the degree of "formal organization" encountered, and "lines of recruitment" may vary considerably for converts to different activities. Not only may there not be a clearly defined hierarchy among some groups, but any recruitment (such as it is) may be extremely haphazard and may depend much more on the acceptance of newcomers than any outreaching activities on the part of the insiders. While the conditions of entry for some life-styles (for example, formal religions, secret societies) are clearly prescribed, there may be no well-defined routes for involvement in other life-styles such as rounding, hooking, or stripping. Likewise, although the "ideology" may be highly developed in some cases, in other instances "members" may have difficulty articulating "central group beliefs."

Conversion to a "deviant perspective" typically entails not only tolerance of the practitioners of activities conventionally defined as deviant, but also living with the knowledge that more conventional citizens would consider oneself disrespectable (or at least suspect) as a consequence of one's "deviant affiliations." While this sense of rejection may be effective in promoting internal solidarity among a group of deviants (Simmel, 1955), it may become an obstacle to conversion; persons more sensitive to concerns with respectability may find themselves endeavoring to disengage themselves from deviant involvements at a relatively early stage. As most persons experience these sorts of reservations on an occasional basis, some desensitization to respectability concerns seems fundamental to continuity. For instance, a novice rounder who is very selective in those from whom he steals and tries to educate other rounders to his way of thinking is likely to find that not only is he unable to support himself as a rounder, but also that the other rounders do not want him around. Similarly, a hooker unable to adopt a hustling orientation to sex is apt to find that she is undergoing a series of internal crises as she goes from trick to trick, and that she is likely to have more trouble handling her dates in the room; both of which make hooking a more precarious activity.

While conversion (or some variation thereof) is often viewed as an individual experience, it is best seen as a "group phenomenon." Not only are there explicit instances of recruitment (such as a pimp trying to "turn out a ho"), but even when persons are trying to establish a place among a group (for example a new hooker in a bar), the receiving audience (insiders) can play a major part in determining whether or not they remain. Further, although newly developing affiliational networks are of considerable significance vis-à-vis conversion of the newcomer, pre-existing networks may be instrumental in determining the extent to which conversion takes place. For instance, while the career of a stripper may depend very much on how she is received at the first few places she works (by patrons, staff, and the other dancers), the likelihood of her being absorbed in a stripper life-style may reflect her previous affiliations (parents, boyfriend, former employer). Strong opposition may deter some prospects (and minimally dramatize decisions) but, where previous associates remain more accepting of the individual and attempt to involve the person more extensively in their activities, conversion is less likely to be either extensive or lasting.

Although conversion suggests a lasting quality, it is best viewed as problematic. Persons may be attracted to certain aspects of a new life-style, and yet find other components disenchanting, or find that they miss former activities. Likewise, where conversion has hinged largely on particular affiliational networks, a dramatic change in these may result in "seeming converts" leaving the newly chosen life-style. However, insofar as particular conversion experiences involve irretrievable investments, disrupted life-styles, ongoing intensive relationships, and altered identities, presently disenchanted converts may find it extremely difficult to become disinvolved even when they desire to do so.

Finally, while systematic involvements frequently entail conversion, the essential routineness of the "focal activity" should not be overlooked. Over time, the activity becomes very much "a matter of fact," and little thought may be given to any morals involved. On becoming regularized practitioners, persons may find not only that the activity loses some of the mystique they had earlier associated with it, but that the contingencies affecting continuity may be quite different from those affecting initial involvements or those promoting more intensive participation in the activity. Insofar as it provides a rationale for an activity, conversion promotes continuity, but it is not necessary for continued involvements.

Continuance Commitments

Continuance commitments (Stebbins, 1970; Hearn and Stoll, 1975) refer to aspects of an activity that make alternatives seem unfeasible, thus "forcing" persons to continue these activities. Exotic dancers may, for example, find that they are unable to make as much money in a legitimate job, or that few other jobs available to them offer the "limelight' stripping does. Similarly, persons involved in rounding or bar work may find that few other jobs pay as well.

Further, it should be noted that one's sense of financial dependency on a job is very much dependent on one's spending habits. The hotel community, for instance, tends to be an expensive environment in which to live. Not only may one develop a habit of paying for a wide variety of services, but as one becomes more heavily involved in "action" one is likely to find that few "straight" jobs are adequate to cover the expenses.

Finally, even where people are willing to forego hotel life, they may find it difficult to convince prospective employers that they have not become irrevocably "tainted" by their previous work. Thus, regardless of the initial route of involvement, persons may experience "closure" in contemplating withdrawal.

Activity Entanglements

While overcoming the deviant mystique allows persons to be more comfortable in the presence of others in the hotel community, and while continuance commitments represent deterrents to disaffiliation, continuity in individual careers is very much influenced by the relative acceptance of the newcomer by the insiders. For instance, not only may an accepting audience make the bar seem a more pleasant place to work but accepting audiences are also more likely to "convert" newcomers to their way of life. This is particularly significant in terms of developing hustling interdependencies and in embedding the newcomers in the social life of the group.

Although hustling skills sharpen the degree of continuance commitments persons are likely to associate with bar work or hustling more generally, it is critical to recognize that the initial development of these skills is largely contingent on the extent to which other staff/hustlers are willing to share their knowledge. An observant individual may pick up some techniques for "taking an edge" merely by hanging around in that setting, but generally it is only when someone explains things to the newcomer that the significance of a series of activities or routines begins to crystallize in his mind. Insiders may also be instrumental in providing direct or implicit social support for the idea that the newcomer, too, should be "on the hustle."

Other hustling interdependencies reflect the value of partnerships (and/or assumed support) for expediting both long-term (bookmaking, boosting, shylocking) and short-run (shortchanging customers, rolling drunks) hustles. As persons establish a series of working relationships with others, not only are they likely to find hustling more lucrative (continuance commitment) but they are likely to find that these associations further promote this way of life. They become more knowledgeable about whom to approach regarding certain hustles and they are more likely to find that others are approaching them, in this way more fully absorbing them into the thief subculture. While expenditures promote commitment, working contacts tend to consolidate persons in the community. Where these contacts are more extensive and more productive they create the sort of "closure in options" one finds characterizing high levels of continuance commitments.

Finally, as persons become involved in a greater assortment of hustles they are likely to find that not only "is there always something going on," but that any thoughts of leaving are more complicated. One does not have the clearer starts and endings a single activity entails, rather one is more continuously faced with the problem of completing activities and "tying up loose ends."

The tendency towards continuity in a rounder life-style is also promoted by the awareness that problems or bad experiences in one hustle do not preclude other hustles. For example, while a person may find himself somewhat disenchanted working as a waiter or a booster, any contacts he has established during his exposure to the hotel setting may provide him with alternatives which might seem more appealing. He may find that he has opportunities to become involved in bootlegging, drug dealing, pimping, or loansharking. The very flexibility afforded persons in a hustling subculture promotes continuity.

Embeddedness in the Social Life

Continuity is also critically affected by one's social-life affiliations. While this tends to be most powerful when other insiders (family, friends) sponsor the individual's induction into the hotel community, as newcomers become more extensively involved with others in the context of recreation, friendship or romance, they are likely to find their careers extended. Thus, although friendships promote continuity in most settings, many of the friendships developing in the hotel community affect hustling contacts and opportunities, frequently creating multiple bonds among the involved parties. A waiter dating a hooker, for example, may not only have an opportunity to become involved in pimping but through this girl (or her good friend or relative) may also have opportunities to become involved in drug-dealing and fencing. These friendship and family ties are particularly significant in structuring one's hustling opportunities. They suggest specific individuals whom persons involved in some aspect of hustling may trust, and to whom they may disclose their plans and operations.

Involvement in the social lives and activities of other hotel people is also conducive to "climatizing" and "converting" newcomers to a rounder life-style. As the insiders are more accepting and invite newcomers to their gatherings and to participate in any ongoing "action," they are not only likely to demystify themselves in his eyes, but are also more likely to become significant reference points in shaping the newcomers' definitions of "the good life." Regardless of whether individuals are recruited very deliberately or quite inadvertently, as they more extensively participate in the activities of the receiving audience they are more likely to find themselves orientationally committed to this new way of life.

Reputations and Identities

Apart from conversion and recruitment, the significance of acknowledging an identity as a thief, hustler, or hooker, for example, should not be overlooked vis-à-vis continuity. Generally speaking, the sooner and more totally persons accept identities of this nature, the more likely they are to continue these pursuits. Not only are they now apt to feel more confident in dealing with any rebuffs they may encounter but once these identities have crystallized, participants are more likely to intensively involve themselves in these activities and the life-styles they associate with these activities.

A sense of personal identity seems a generally much more effective source of continuity among hustlers than what might be termed "loyalty to the community." Although we have occasional references to this latter bond, it is one of the least powerful sources of individual continuity in the hotel community. Persons may experience a sense of loyalty to their partners, and individuals leaving the hotel scene may be occasionally chastised for "going straight" but, lacking clear structural referents, the idea of a general loyalty to other hotel people or hustlers seems generally ineffective as an element promoting continuance.

In contrast to community loyalties, reputations within the hotel community play a significant role in affecting people's continuity therein.[13] Reputations are dependent not only on what persons do (or do not do) but also upon those with whom they are most closely affiliated. As suggested in chapter 6, for instance, one of the best overall labels a rounder could achieve is that of "being solid." However, persons are much more likely to be characterized as such when they are sponsored or otherwise associated with other "solid" people in the community. Likewise, while a newcomer may have a much better opportunity to become a "sharp operator" when accepted by an established rounder, the knowledge that he is affiliated with a solid rounder is likely to protect him from being hustled, as well as open up other avenues of knowledge, thus giving him the appearance of being

---

[13] The notion of a singular reputation is rather misleading. While one finds more consensus in reference to the reputations of certain persons, or in reference to one or other qualities attributed to persons, it is more accurate to think in terms of persons having multiple reputations, reflecting the values and interests of the various audiences and experiences they have had with those persons.

"hip" before he has matured in this respect. Contacts are "not everything," but "being tight with the right people" can be a very powerful mechanism in establishing a newcomer's identity in the community.

As persons spend more time in a setting they are also likely to develop reputations apart from those reflecting their hustles and affiliations. While many qualities attributed to these people reflect their "dispositions" ("great sense of humor," "gets angry too easily," "a real scatterbrain," and such like), another set of identities refers to their encounters with trouble. Images pertaining to pleasant dispositions and the like are significant in the development of friendships, but trouble tends to introduce a more dramatic (and often threatening) element in the situation. People's reputations for starting trouble ("shit disturber," "loud-mouth," "drunk") and/or the ways in which they handle trouble ("tough," "fink," "cool"), can consequently have major consequences for their acceptance in the hotel community.

Another aspect of social identity involves "being somebody," with participants endeavoring to convey a distinctiveness making them noteworthy among others. For instance, being the "best ho," the "sharpest operator," or the "biggest dealer," ensures one of community recognition, but it also reflects on one's image of self (respectability). Not only may persons believe in the parts they are playing but they may also find themselves cultivating these roles more extensively than they had anticipated.

Operating in a setting considered disrespectable by conventional standards, even the most "dedicated" may experience some difficulty coming to terms with self-respectability. This is not to suggest that hustlers and the like are bothered by each "misdeed" but, on occasion, they may find themselves doubting their own moral worth.[14] It should be noted that while crisis events prompt self-reflections, concerns with self-worth are apt to be most acutely experienced by newcomers, particularly those lacking successful models (success, it seems, tends to render moral concerns less effective). Other self-doubts may be dispelled as newcomers demystify activities and practioners. One finds persons reconciling concerns with respectability on "being converted,"[15] but perhaps more important than this is the rather arduous, uncertain, and frequently tempestuous life-circumstances many hotel people experience. Concerns with "getting by" (working out hustles, handling pressing problems) in a relatively ambiguous setting, and involvements in action and trouble, combined with "highs" and "hangovers," leave relatively little time for extensive self-reflection. Thus persons come to accept the idea that they are thieves, hustlers, hookers and the like, because those are the activities in which they are engaged. And, while they may think they should or could do better, their involvements in "the life" generally leave little time or energy for consider-

---

[14] See Ball (1970) and Douglas (1970) for two insightful discussions on the problematics of respectability. For another statement on the reconciliation of doubt, see Prus (1976).

[15] One may distinguish ideologies conducive to specific hustles, from "hustling as a way of life." One will encounter the occasional individual who "proselytizes" on this basis but, in general, commitment to ideologies of these sorts seem limited. While there is a strong tendency to distinguish "straights" from "people like us," and while one may elicit rationales for activities from these people, we have found [as did Bryan (1966) in his study of call girls] that such ideological concerns are rarely expressed in day-to-day work situation. Among hustlers, one does not need to justify hustling. . . it is "taken for granted."

ing or pursuing alternatives. Hence there is a certain resignation to disrespectability, "Well, what can you do?" By defining their activities (partially at least) as beyond their control, persons reduce the extent to which they consider themselves accountable for their activities. This is not to suggest that these persons enjoy being thought of as disrespectable. However, more thought and effort may be directed towards "being respectable" than towards handling concerns with disrespectability.[16]

Overall, while there are many people whose self-images preclude any thoughts of involvement in the hotel setting, for those finding themselves in that setting, the relationships they develop with the "receiving audiences" seem much more instrumental than their self-images in affecting their involvements. Not only are self-images open to some change over time, and are persons able to reconcile themselves to less than desirable circumstances, but a wide variety of relatively common interests (friendship, loyalty, romance, excitement, and recognition) are attainable in the hotel setting. In spite of concerns with respectability the participants may still have an opportunity to approximate "the kinds of persons they want to be."

DISINVOLVEMENT

Once persons have come to terms with the initial rebuffs (drinking, disrespectability and so on) associated with bar life they are apt to remain in that setting indefinitely. Although participants frequently express disenchantment over their work situations (such as the dishonesty, roughness, and unreliability of hotel people; the unpredictable incomes derived from hustling; and legal "hassles"), and frequently mention "leaving this scene," departures do not as readily materialize.

Part of the difficulty persons desiring to leave bar life encounter reflects their very success in "making it" in hotel life. The same patterns facilitating adjustment, once established, deter disinvolvement. The investments persons make to ensure success, and the affiliational networks they develop in order to promote business and/or good times tend to "lock" participants in the community. As persons become more embedded in the hotel setting, more effort and planning may be required for successful disengagement. There is extensive support for Lemert's (1967) claim that a major element affecting continuity in "secondary deviance" is the costs involved in the transition to a more conventional life-style. The "costs" are, however, not limited to the relative payoffs of the alternative lines of action but also reflect "the problematics of disentanglement."

If the prospect also plans to change the life-style of another person(s), the matter becomes further complicated. A waiter may, for example, fall in love with a hooker and wish for the two of them to leave together. However, even if she is willing to do so, they may find that the times conducive to her disengagement may not coincide with his, and vice versa. Each person becomes involved in a web of affiliations and it is often not possible to sever all the ties at one point in time. If, the departure is delayed, however, then any subsequent developments (for

---

[16] Respectability and disrespectability seem best conceptualized as two dimensions rather than opposite ends of the same dimension. Thus persons can be resigned to disrespectability and yet strive for respectability.

example, new contacts, acquiring debts) can make the prospects of disinvolvement less imminent.

While disenchantment with bar life prompts interest in "straight" work—most hustlers, for instance, have looked for legitimate work at some point in their careers — such things as an unsteady work record, a lack of references, limited education, and a prison record, disadvantage persons for many jobs. And, at the same time, their own disinclinations to do "routine, square" work mitigates against obtaining employment. So long as persons envision hustling as a viable comparison point, the prospects of finding acceptable, conventional work are limited. Legitimate work may be obtained, but typically this is only after the occurrence of an event or circumstance generating an extensive questioning of one's activity as viable.

On occasion, "getting married" may be the event promoting disinvolvement from bar life or hustling. In general, however, this event tends to be more effective in disinvolving females, and is contingent on "her old man" being willing and able to support her. Should she later find the marriage disagreeable, she may return to the bar setting. Overall, the event has less effect on the male. While a "straight wife" may pressure her spouse to leave the bar, it is somewhat unlikely that he will do so. Not only may he have difficulty obtaining a satisfactory straight job, but he may have some difficulty disentangling himself from his former associates. When males "settle down" with females from that setting, as is often the case, little change on the part of either may be expected. The woman is likely to assume a more domestic role but she may still remain very much a part of "the life."

Another event leading to disinvolvement from bar life, albeit relatively infrequent, is the accumulation of sufficient funds to establish one's own business. Even here, however, the businesses are likely to reflect the proprietors' interests, knowledge, and contacts and are, thus, often related to hotel life. Not only may they locate in the same areas, and find that some of their customers are hotel people, but they may also employ other (trusted) hotel people in their operations. While many bar people express hopes of realizing a venture of this sort, few have been successful in saving the money required.

One also finds some disinvolvement from active hustling arising from "disqualification" or "rejection" of individuals as acceptable associates. For instance, rounders being defined as "too old," "drinking too much," and the like, may find themselves unwanted and excluded from dealings with others. Finding their alternatives extensively limited, these "rejects" may seek out other more tolerant bar settings, or may resign themselves to the streets becoming "rubbies," or "winos," remaining rounders of sorts, but now being more frequently characterized as "no accounts." Similarly, although dancers and hookers may find themselves being less selective in the bars they work, or their clientele, they too may encounter "rejection from the bar before they reject bar life."

Of the more sustained disinvolvements from hotel life, the more dramatic and more common of these derive from internal conflicts, job dismissals, and arrests. Most of the internal conflicts and dismissals are "patched up" by the involved parties, but they occasionally entail serious concerns with personal safety and reputations. In these instances, at least temporarily, persons may define a particular bar or area as an unfeasible setting in which to operate. While this may present no great problem to persons who are geographically mobile (strippers for example) or who have more extensive outside contacts (such as some boosters, thieves), many hotel people have very few or only weak contacts beyond the "locals." For this latter set of persons, this immediate lack of external alternatives is likely to result in some (typically) frustrating "kicking around" the streets and other bars and/or a more concerted effort to find legitimate employment. This "crisis" event is often instrumental in persons rethinking their situation and, in the process, viewing the hotel scene from a new perspective. Further, provided that the individuals are not pressured by people to whom they owe money, these crisis events may also promote breaks with their spending habits, making legitimate salaries more acceptable than was previously the case.

Being arrested can also promote disinvolvement but its impact tends to be greatest among the novices, and particularly among those who find themselves with little community involvement or support. In addition to the fearful prospects of doing time, acquiring a record, and/or disrupting other aspects of one's life (job, marriage), being arrested also promotes a reassessment of one's situation. It makes very real another element of hustling, and, as such, tends to promote disinvolvement. Like other events suggesting disinvolvement, this would be more effective when persons consider themselves to have reasonably viable legitimate alternatives to "the life." Otherwise, "getting busted" and/or "doing time" may not only result in the target feeling a greater affinity with other hustlers, but may also result in these others defining the target as more worthy ("solid") of their association.

DEVIANCE AS ACTIVITY

Activity, as used herein, refers to a sequence of behavior organized around a theme or focal point. Activities may be conducted on a solitary basis (such as decision-making, daydreaming, or planning) or in the context of exchanges involving two or more actors (partying, fighting, or entertaining, for instance). Further, although both the ways in which activities develop and their outcomes are problematic, they represent occasions of meaningful ("minded") behavior for the participants.

The concept of "activity," like "interrelatedness" is basic to the present study. Not only were the chapters organized around activities (hooking, working the bar, being patrons, and so on), but activities (like hustling, keeping order, drinking, providing service, putting on a show) constitute the essence of bar life. So powerful are these "forms" (Simmel, 1950) that they provide considerable continuity across bars varying greatly in decor, setting, clientele, and entertainment.

Activities consist of people working out interests (preceding and emerging) in a (social) setting. Some of these activities have a solitary quality, such as a bartender mixing drinks, a hooker at a table waiting for customers, or a stripper readying herself for her next performance, but even these activities are only intelligible within the settings in which they take place. Much solitary activity either reflects anticipated encounters or comes about as a result of earlier exchanges. And, just as newcomers face the problematics of fitting into bar settings, so do performers face the task of integrating solitary activities (or their products) with the activities (and products) of others. The bartender is expected to mix "the right drinks," a hooker is expected to be somewhat receptive to customers, and a stripper is expected to provide a certain type of performance. It is at this point that Blumer's (1969) concept of "joint activity," referring to the fitting together of activities of two or more people becomes so central in the study of social life. It is apparent, however, as Goffman (1959) suggests, that a great deal of "front region" activity reflects "back region" preparations as well as ongoing supportive behavior on the part of others. Further, while persons may, as a result of disenchantment, insight, or curiosity, alter solitary activities and "routines," activities involving others are even more susceptible to situational contingencies. The bartender may mix the right drinks, only to find that the patrons have changed their minds or have left; the hooker may be accessible, but may find that the customers would rather watch a football game; and the stripper may find that her act is "not strong enough" by local standards. Only when one begins to recognize that joint action consists of an ongoing series of alignments and realignments, does its emergent and negotiable features become prominent.

The analysis of activities becomes further noteworthy in the sense that any "joint activity" may have somewhat different implications for all involved. Not only may persons note discrepancies between their own activities and their present (or earlier) interests, but each of the participants may view each of the components constituting an event differently (and all may view the event differently from the "objective observer"). An earlier analysis of "violent encounters" (Prus, 1978) suggests, for instance, that two confrontations actually took place when two persons became involved in a confrontation (the confrontation A was having with B, and the confrontation B was having with A). An observer (C), witnessing the exchanges, could describe a third confrontation (the one he saw take place between A and B). If this is the case, then the study of joint activity becomes exceedingly demanding of the researcher. However, as joint activities are emerging, negotiable phenomena, and may involve persons in ways quite different than they had earlier anticipated (or would have predicted as plausible), it seems that an explanation of deviance which does not consider the role of joint activity would be unduly limited.

Involving persons with differential interests, levels of preparation, and interactional styles, activities constitute basic features of human life. Thus, regardless of whether one focusses on (1) the definitions of reality on a broader community level (developing explanations or moral and legal positions), (2) the problematics of keeping order (enforcing rules and regulations, implementing policies, or peace keeping), or (3) the problematics of managing interpersonal relations (labelling and reputations, intimacy and distancing, hustling, recruitment, confrontations), a consideration of activities seems critical.[17]

In discussing career contingencies, some elements critical to understanding activities were earlier introduced. Notions of "closure," "seekership," and "recruitment" affecting initial involvements, along with conditions promoting continuity, represent themes permeating our understanding of activities. At the same time, however, each focal activity (for instance, drinking, keeping order) deserves consideration on its own. Therefore, we would argue for a sociology more sensitive to "activities as social processes."

---

[17] For negotiations vis-à-vis reality definitions on a broader community level, see for example, Garfinkel (1956), Bergerand Luckmann (1966), and Shibutani (1966), Goffman (1961), Skolnick (1966) and Martin (1975) provide indications of the extent to which "keeping order" is negotiable. For material focussing on interpersonal relations, see Goffman (1959), Davis (1961), Daniels (1970) and Emerson (1970).

DEVIANCE AS COMMUNITY

Reviewing the community literature, Hillary (1955) suggests that a community consists most basically of a group of people interacting with one another in a geographical setting. Sinclair and Westhues (1974) note that geographical settings do not define communities, arguing instead that communities are better demarcated by orientations, activity, and a sense of belongingness. Our notions of community correspond closely with those of Sinclair and Westhues. Interaction is necessary for community, and so is continuity, but a sense of "group distinctiveness" seems much more instrumental in defining communities than is geographical location per se. While physical settings may generate notions of distinctiveness, more important in defining a community are outsider and insider identifications and practices. In this sense, one may speak not only of a general hotel community bounded by interactions within and across hotels in North America (facilitated, for example, by chain hotels, mobile entertainers and staff, patrons and hustlers), but also of each hotel or bar as constituting a geographical setting in which a particular "hotel community" is housed. Similarly, one may speak of "hooker communities," "staff communities," and the like.[18]

Our research suggests that "deviance is a community phenomenon par excellence." It is social, not only in definition (and in the emergence of those definitions) but also in terms of group activities and sentiments, and individual involvements and the working out of interests in ongoing group life. As Simmel (1955) argues, one cannot separate the individual from the group. Only in studying the group does one learn about "the deviants."

In developing this project, we sought to examine the relatedness of persons coming together in an environment characterized by a number of deviant pursuits. Although we have also provided some insight into the "career contingencies" of, and "activities" in which, persons in the hotel community find themselves, some emphasis on concepts such as "interrelatedness" and "embeddedness" is essential if we are to understand deviance involvements. Unfortunately, in attempting to account for particular forms of deviant involvements, researchers have seldom been concerned with articulating the ways in which persons work out their lives in conjunction with others. However, regardless of whether one is discussing initial involvements, continuities, or disinvolvements, some consideration of interrelatedness seems critical to understanding deviant involvements in both the short-run (such as ongoing hustles, handling disruptions) and long-term (career contingencies, maintenance of the community) instances. Orientations and techniques are learned through association with others (as Sutherland, 1947, suggests), but the extent to which persons become involved in particular activities is to a very large extent dependent upon others who variously encourage, support, and facilitate these involvements in both short- and long-run terms. Orientations towards, and involvements in, activities are best seen in process terms, as persons negotiate lines of action with others. Accordingly, any research (such as surveys, census data) which decontextualizes outcomes from the settings in which they arise is apt to miss integral components of group life. Likewise, while we can learn

---

[18] Although the term "subculture" is largely synonymous with the present usage of community, we prefer the term "community." Not only does this usage overcome some of the "deviance mystique" often associated with the term "subculture," but it more explicitly suggests notions of interaction and affiliation.

a great deal about people by studying fleeting encounters between strangers (see Davis, 1959; Goffman, 1959), it is exceedingly important to examine the ways in which relationships develop, persist, and dissipate over time within the context of ongoing group life.

RESEARCH PROBLEMATICS AND PROCESSES

To further put the present material in perspective, we would like to indicate how the project developed and how the data was obtained, noting some of the difficulties involved in the process.

GETTING STARTED

This project originated through a chance meeting of the authors. At this time, mutual interests in the study of deviance and communities were discussed and we made some tentative plans to keep in touch:

> I first met Stylios when he dropped around to inquire about deviance courses at Waterloo. I was just finishing a book dealing with card and dice hustlers, and on learning that he was working at a hotel as a desk clerk, my interest level was greater than otherwise might have been the case. As Stylios described the hotel at which he worked, the setting seemed very promising. I asked him to keep notes on the everyday happenings at Main and, although I didn't know if he would do so, he returned about a month later with a couple of tapes of observations he had made.

The idea of doing an ethnographic account of the hotel community seemed worthwhile since we found existing literature on bars, hotels, and the like, to be very limited, offering little that we could use as a prototype.[19] Assuming an interactionist perspective, we were interested in such things as career contingencies, joint action, impression management, negotiation of identities, and interpersonal manoeuvering, but lacked a model emphasizing "the interrelatedness of a group of persons." This is, of course, a basic theme in symbolic interactionism, but most research focusses on the careers of individual involvements over time or the situated negotiation of activities and identities. Both of these elements were present in our situation, but we were also dealing with a plurality of interlocking careers and relationships, as well as negotiations of activity and identity over time.

As we became more familiar with the hotel setting and the people whose lives intermeshed therein, we became increasingly aware, not only of our own lack of knowledge in respect to this life-style, but also of the comparatively shallow accounts of hotel life and bars existing in the literature. Given the plurality of involved actors in the hotel setting, we often felt overwhelmed during the project. While finding that we were continually learning about hotels and people in general, our experience throughout was somewhat akin to putting together a jigsaw puzzle, not knowing how many pieces there were or what the final picture would look like. As a result, we attempted to keep ourselves open to new sources of information, issues, and organizational strategies. Orienting ourselves to the

---

[19] Other than Goffman's *Asylums*, we found Cressey's (1932) discussion of Taxi-Dance Halls to be the study closest to our own.

ways in which activities were worked out by the parties involved, and the ways in which persons were interrelated, it was not until after six months in the field that we developed from our field observations and interviews a working outline of our major research interests. In general, however, our procedure was to gather as much material as possible about as many things as possible, with a particular emphasis on obtaining detailed information on the everyday experiences of the participants.

While our most intensive research was done from August '76 to January '79, our field work activities did not cease when we began writing this book. We continued to collect material into the later stages of writing. This seemed a very productive strategy in two senses. First, in attempting to come to terms with material we had already collected, we sometimes found that other information was required to more accurately or completely discuss hotel life. Second, we found it very useful in trying to analyse the material to return to the field and discuss various ideas we had with former and recent contacts, attempting to obtain their assessments of the material as it developed.

MAKING CONTACTS

One of the most crucial aspects of ethnographic research is establishing working contacts with those whose life-style one wishes to study. Given the variety of interests, activities, and actors cross-cutting the hotel community, we found that "making contacts" was an ongoing concern throughout the project. Although Stylios' job-related contacts were vital in initially accessing the hotel community, and in establishing us within this setting, a large number of the contacts we eventually made involved persons whom we subsequently met in a variety of ways: through "friends in the field" introducing us to other acquaintances, through fortuitous contacts, and through persons whom we simply approached (lacking an "in"), hoping for the best.

Generally speaking, it appears that our task would have been greatly simplified if we had limited ourselves to one category of persons (hookers, dancers, or waitresses), but all our observations, preliminary and subsequent, suggested that we attempt to tap as many different sources in the community as possible. Consequently, while the people we talked to were not uniformly helpful, we made a number of key contacts in most of the categories of persons who together compromise the hotel community. We found that one could obtain some useful information from most people, but clearly some people were much more articulate and attuned to ongoing group life than others. We might add that there did not seem to be much correlation between an educated person and an informative one. Some grade school dropouts were much more observant than many university educated people. It did appear, however, that persons who became easily morally indignant about hotel life tended to be of the least assistance in providing careful, detailed statements about hotel life.

"FITTING IN"

As might be expected from the preceding chapters on the hotel community, "fitting in" is as much a two-way phenomenon for a researcher as for any other person in the hotel community. Not only does the researcher have to overcome any awkwardness or reservations he faces in dealing with a group of people, but if he wishes to gain an intimate understanding of their life, he is obligated to help them become accepting of his presence. Our experiences suggest that persons do not want you to be just like them, but they don't want any differences to threaten them. Everyone, it seems, has some "quirks" and the hotel people are no exception. Not only would it be impossible for any researcher to be "just like" a variety of people but it does not seem necessary, provided he gives the other people the opportunity to feel familiar with his style. While acceptance of a researcher is apt to be very limited when he is perceived intolerant of the way of life of the group he is studying, other idiosyncrasies may be overcome.

Our personal quirks were most readily accepted with time and humor, but we also found a team approach useful in obtaining information, as individually we have had differential success approaching particular people in the hotel community. In a similar vein, we also found it helpful to be accompanied by a female research assistant. Not only did this tend to relax any females we encountered, but we found that the males tended to be more interested in talking to us.

It seems that almost anyone will fit into a setting, in some capacity, if allowed to remain in the presence of a group of others over a period of time. Our concern was, however, not this limited. Not only did we wish to be tolerated by the people we were studying, but we also wanted to obtain an intimate understanding of their lives in a reasonably short period of time. For while our earlier observations suggested that we would be dependent on others for "the inside story," our subsequent experience confirmed this. A careful observer can learn some things about the life-style of a group but, unless he delves into the experiences and definitions of the persons living that life he is likely to miss a great deal of group life. Good observation can sensitize researchers to social phenomena, and it can be invaluable in detecting both consistencies and inconsistencies. Observation, however, regardless of its quality, cannot replace firsthand accounts of life-experiences.

PLAYING THE FIELD

Different times, when discussing this project with other people, we have encountered comments to the effect, "That must be fun!", "Wish I could do some research in bars! Ho, ho, ho!" and the like. It's true that bar research can be interesting and even exciting at times but it can also be time consuming, costly, boring and frustrating. Like the professional ball player, the serious researcher realizes that "playing the field" entails a lot of hard work.

Although we did not have what we would call "typical days," so far as we did, a "typical day" in the field might go something like this. Unless we had an earlier appointment with someone, we started out in the field around noon. From this point we moved around, depending on where we thought we might encounter any of the cast of persons constituting the hotel community. Individually or together (usually in groups no larger than two), we would visit any number of bars, hotels, street corners, restaurants, strip joints, and the like, endeavoring to contact people "in the life" and/or any action events.[20]

---

[20] As a caveat, we might note that although action events were often good places to make contacts, they tended to be poor places for inquiring into aspects of hotel life with particular persons. Not only might the central event distract persons, but they might not be willing or able to discuss aspects of their lives while in the "mood of the event" or in the presence of other people. In this sense, for

In general, we tried to arrange meeting times and places, but found that the somewhat haphazard life-styles of many of the hotel people made regular planning precarious. Not only did we encounter a sizeable proportion of people who tried to avoid scheduling their lives, but also found that many did not keep their appointments very faithfully. Initially, we were inclined to view these "evasions" as particular to us but with time found these not atypical of people in the life more generally. Best friends might not keep previously made appointments, and some of the people who seemed to be avoiding us turned out to be extremely helpful when we eventually found them in. We do not suggest that people in the hotel community are unreliable, but found that we could not structure appointments in the way one might in the business world or with a group of clergymen. The hotel people were more likely to: encounter problems with the police, find themselves suddenly involved in hustles, become intoxicated or high, and find themselves caught up in upsetting interpersonal conflicts. Consequently, although we made a concerted effort to keep all our appointments, we began to find ourselves regarding these as "tentative" and trying to be as flexible as possible with time, places, and contacts.

Given the multiplicity of people and activities with which we were concerned, we found it much more useful to focus on topics than to employ formal interview schedules. In general, we asked questions in line with our working outlines, but endeavored to keep these as open as possible. "What can you tell me about. . .," "Can you tell me how. . .," "I was wondering about. . . ." We tried to avoid "yes" and "no" questions and answers, allowing our respondents to speak as long as they were willing on any aspect of life pertaining in one or other ways to the hotel community, prompting them wherever it seemed feasible, "Hmmm," "Interesting," "Then what?" "How's that?" If the respondents were willing and the situation favorable, we taped our interviews. Otherwise, we made notes at the earliest convenience. These "interviews" took place in bars, restaurants, homes, cars, parks, offices, and on the street. Sometimes we anticipated having a few hours to talk with the person, other times we expected the person to leave in a few minutes. Actual interview time, however, not unlike our appointments, tended to be problematic.

So far as possible we endeavored to maintain a conversational flow in the interviews, trying to work our topics into the conversation as it developed. In general, our stance was that of being open-minded and curious. We saw our task as one of obtaining a careful, detailed description of hotel life. We were not there to educate or to reform our respondents, or to change their lives in any way. As we told them, "We are not interested in whether something's good or bad, right or wrong. We just want to know what happens, and how it takes place. We don't need names, dates, or places, just what happened and how things worked out." We were also concerned that we not appear too knowledgeable, lest respondents assume that we already knew whatever they might have to say; and yet, at the same time, we didn't want to appear too naive, lest persons try to conceal something from us. While trying to be open "to an education," we also tried to follow-up on points the respondents for one reason or another neglected, "Hmmm, you were saying such and such. I was just wondering. . . . The other day, I noticed that you

---

example, while Thursday, Friday and Saturday might be better action nights, Mondays and Tuesdays might be better nights in which to talk to people. Similarly, persons may be more open to encounters before and after work or other events.

did it a little differently. I was wondering if you could explain that to me.'' We wanted to gain a thorough understanding of hotel life, but we also wanted to verify previous information and to sort out any inconsistencies we encountered.

Another feature of the project making one's daily routine more difficult was that we didn't know where we would be going from one point in time to the next, nor did we know with whom we would be talking. For instance, while we might decide to ''check out'' a particular setting, someone we met there or on the way might want to go to another location and, depending on what was happening in the first place, or whether we had made any arrangements to meet someone else, we might go along to the second place, and from there. . . . We found that if one wishes to learn about groups of people, one has to go to their places and adjust inquiries to their life-styles.

We also found it highly productive to observe people across situations and over time. Not only was this useful in showing us other sides of the same people, but it also helped us to understand the interrelatedness of people in the hotel community. Each time we met a new person, we had the task of trying to figure out where he/she fitted into the total context. While persons might establish new friendships and partnerships, on a day-to-day basis, we found that people were often not as ''role-bound'' as they might appear. A ''patron'' might be a dealer or a pimp; a ''stripper'' might be a hooker, a thief, and a rounder's ''old lady.'' Thus, part of our daily routine involved the continual sorting out of people, as well as endeavoring to obtain information on their activities.

In addition to the more routine research-oriented aspects of our daily rounds, we also found that we had opportunities to ''go native,'' to assume one or other roles operative in the hotel community. These opportunities varied considerably from time to time, but amongst other things included getting involved in hooking as a client and pimp, getting involved in drug use and sales, becoming a boy-friend/travelling companion to an exotic dancer, working other bars and partici-pating in bar hustles, chauffeuring for an escort service, and working in an after-hours place. Probably the easiest role for a researcher doing research on bars to slip into, is that of ''becoming a drunk.'' In general, we managed to stay disinvolved from these activities, but note that it would be considerably easier for persons lacking a strong research commitment to find themselves participating much more fully ''in the life,'' particularly if they were working alone.

As the reader might also infer from the first six chapters, another daily concern we had was that of doing research in a potentially volatile setting. While, in general, we found the hotel community relatively non-threatening, we found ourselves feeling somewhat uneasy at times. First, although we found that even intoxicated persons can generally be reasoned with to the point of avoiding aggression, bar-room fights often occur so quickly that one may not have the opportunity to adequately remove oneself from the central combatants. While we were not injured as a consequence of any bar fracas, any time an incident erupted it introduced that possibility. We also noted, however, that the people we were with occasionally put us in awkward situations as a consequence of their behavior. For example, on a couple of different occasions, some dancers we were with had gotten into verbal confrontations with other people, who then began wanting to settle the matter with us.

While making initial contacts with people was always problematic, as was hanging around individuals long enough to get to know them, for the most part we found hotel people rather congenial. We did encounter a few people who did not believe that we were actually doing a study of the hotel community, and some who were reluctant to talk to us, as well as a few who seemed especially concerned that we might be undercover agents.[21]

Although we tried to avoid making conclusions on a day-to-day basis, we were concerned with establishing verifications of any material collected earlier on a day-to-day basis. Thus, in addition to continually seeking new information and new contacts, we also sought to establish the validity of previously collected information and to situate it in a larger context. Placing significance on this concern, we not only endeavored to check seemingly mundane information with persons involved in the same activities, but also expanded our research field to include a great many more people and places than we had originally anticipated. As the field expanded, our daily routine while sometimes more readily structured, tended to become more diverse. Our research often resulted in late hours wherein, around four or five in the morning, we would find a quiet place to have some coffee or a meal, and sort out the day's events, writing whatever further notes we could recall. On rising, we would review the last day's events and attempt to develop some plans for "the next typical day."

PUTTING IT TOGETHER

In producing a jointly authored book we found that the project was one in which our relative contributions varied. Stylios assumed a larger role in the early stages of the research, with his observations and contacts representing the resource core for the project. The theoretical orientation and the organizational features of the project are largely Bob's designs. We both spent time observing and interviewing people for each chapter, although Stylios directed his attention more towards the desk personnel and other staff at Main, the rounders, and the after-hours places, while Bob focussed on the hookers, the entertainers, the staff in other bars, and the patrons. We hadn't planned to divide the roles up in this fashion, but this was how they took shape. Stylios's work roles advantaged us in certain respects, but were limiting in other ways. Further, his subsequent involvements in graduate school ended up being more time-consuming than we had anticipated, so that most of the writing was done by Bob. We conducted some of the research together in settings, but also gathered data individually, thus giving us access to more people, settings, and activities. To a large extent, the theoretical material developed in *Road Hustler* (Prus and Sharper, 1977) served as the frame of reference in organizing the incoming data, but we more explicitly incorporated notions of "interrelatedness" and "activity" into our working outlines.

In addition to expanding our theoretical base in this fashion we also found that as

---

[21] These responses in many ways did not surprise us much as some of the reactions we received from some members of the academic community. Some of these people did not see any value in studying the hotel community, and some did not see how we could spend our time hanging around such "seedy" people and places, suggesting that we also might become corrupted, had this not already happened! We found the hotel people to be "regular people" working in a socially disrespected setting. We also found that although they also engaged in some "fronting," the hotel people were in many ways more open about their activities than many "respectables."

the research was developing our notions of the hotel community were broadening. Focussing on careers, interrelationships, and activities, we not only found ourselves conducting research in many bars other than Main and Central, but also found that attempts to understand hookers, rounders, entertainers, et al took us to burlesque theatres, after-hours places, area restaurants, and the streets. Each of these settings added valuable comparative data but in the process made it increasingly difficult to handle the material we gathered within the printing limitations of this book.

In closing, many potential bar and street-life related topics come to mind but we would like to emphasize "interrelatedness" "fitting in," "reputations," "conversion and recruitment," and "career contingencies," as concerns of significance not only in the hotel community and the street scene, but that also permeate our social lives in areas quite removed from the bar scene. While we would like to see researchers investigating other aspects of bar and street life and are, through our existing contacts, likely to continue to do so ourselves, we see these settings as being of most significance when we can generate from them insights applicable to other areas of life. Research on bars can be useful in rounding out our overall knowledge of society, but it is most valuable when we can in the process of studying bar life learn about life in hospitals, prisons, office buildings, factories, and any other settings in which persons find themselves:

Bars, they're a mixture of sex, alcohol, cigarettes, pinball machines, pool tables, and shuffleboard. And music, that's just another part of it. . . . Bars are places where you can get away from it all. We've got a lot of money invested in the bars in this country and we organize a lot of our social lives around bars and drinking. . . . Some people are into religion and some are into politics, but a lot of them are into bars. (musician)

APPENDIX A

THE SAMPLE

Attempts to neatly define the sample on which this book is based seem rather elusive. For example, we started our research in one bar, and over the three years we were involved in the project we gathered information on life in well over fifty bars—not to mention the "outside-the-bar" life of many participants. In no way, however, should the material on all these bars be seen as equally relevant to the study at hand. First, not only did we not spend equal time in each bar but we did not have equal access to "insider" information in all these settings. Further, through contact with staff and patrons, we found that we learned a considerable amount about some bars in which we ourselves spent very little time. Somewhat surprising in this sense is the extent to which we encountered staff and patron interchange across seemingly unconnected Eastville bars. Additionally, in contrast to some bars we initially attended as "strangers," on many occasions we were taken to particular bars by people whom the bar staff defined as "insiders." Thus, even an initial visit under these circumstances provided opportunities to gather information which was in many ways superior to that which a careful observer spending a great deal more time in the same setting might be able to gather.

Interviews and observations of individuals are no more easily tallied. Not only were many people able to provide some information on two or more activities (for instance, hooking, stripping, waitressing) as a consequence of their role shifts, but many "observations" were necessarily limited as we tried to gather material around existing routines. Additionally, we often found that there was not enough time in which to obtain "full" interviews with a mobile, action-oriented collection of people. While we gathered some information from a seemingly unlimited number of people, most of which bears direct relevance for the activities discussed herein, we found that some people were much more informative than others. Not only did we find participants differentially accessible but, clearly, "one interview" does not equal "one interview" as one goes from one person to the next.

Another aspect of the study obscuring "counting routines" is that many activities and conversations took place in settings involving a number of people who may have been "contributing" to the situation in markedly different ways and with vastly different levels of impact on the ongoing activities.

Had we remained in one bar for the duration of the study, we could have more easily (but not easily) defined the parameters of the "sample." But, as one moves further from a "captive" or a "quota" sample, and considers people involved in a variety of activities over time, it becomes increasingly difficult to describe with exactness the nature of the sample. Accordingly, although the following estimates are somewhat "problematic," given (1) the difficulties of counting discrete individuals and activities within the context of shifting social settings, (2) the tendencies of people to have multiple involvements, (3) the problematics of "non-uniform completeness" of the data, and (4) *the power of contact with the people/activities being studied in a variety of contexts and over time,"* they are provided to satisfy somewhat those wanting to know "sample sizes."

In arriving at the following tallies, each person was counted only once (this represents a somewhat conservative indication of the sample as persons are "forced into a central activity," regardless of the multiplicity of their involvements). We also made distinctions between (1) those with whom we had "extensive" contact; (2) those with whom we had explicit contact which resulted in "significant" information on some aspect of their involvements being obtained; and (3) those whom we recognized as participants in particular activities or settings but with whom we had little or only fleeting contact. While even this latter category of data has some value in suggesting the general representativeness of particular activities, we provide estimates only for the two more easily tabulated former categories:

Chapter 2	Extensive Contacts	Significant Contacts[1]
bar hookers[2]	37	110
street hookers[2]	8	35
massage parlor girls[2]	2	23
call girls[2]	5	7

Chapter 3	Extensive Contacts	Significant Contacts
clerks (hooker hotels)	14	6
clerks (other hotels)	10	8
bellhops	4	5
security people	5	9

Chapter 4	Extensive Contacts	Significant Contacts
exotic dancers	48	150
agents	3	4
musicians[3]	9	30
d.j.'s	3	6
comedians	2	3

Chapter 5	Extensive Contacts	Significant Contacts
bar staff (action bars)	27	80
bar staff (other bars)	55	120

Chapter 6	Extensive Contacts	Significant Contacts
patrons	40	300
rounders (male)	34	60
rounders (female)	4	7
area restaurants	8	9
after-hours places	4	11

---

[1] "Significant contacts" do not include "extensive contacts."

[2] These categories at best represent "central operating" styles at the time of the study. They are subject to considerable overlap and thus tend to underestimate significantly persons who have had experience in any particular hooking routine. Likewise, the numbers fail to indicate the degree of category overlap among strippers, hookers, waitresses, and female rounders, as each person is counted only once in their "designated central category."

[3] Even the counting of something as seemingly distinct as "musicians" or "disc jockeys" is misleading when one realizes that these people may not only be involved in other aspects of the life, such as drug dealing, pimping, or being a stripper's "old man" on a concurrent basis, but may also intermittently or subsequently become involved in staff routines, or rounding, or may also be bar and/or hooker patrons.

In concluding this discussion of the "the sample," we caution readers against attaching strong significances to particular subsamples. There is much more to a community than the numbers of participants considered, and it is strikingly the case that time spent associating with these people across settings and over time cannot be replaced by samples of any size. For example, observing (and interacting with) hookers in bars, lobbies, area restaurants, after-hours places, and associating with their friends (hookers, boyfriends, staff, and so on) and families (children, parents, "old man") introduce data one may be otherwise unable to attain.

APPENDIX B

MAIN

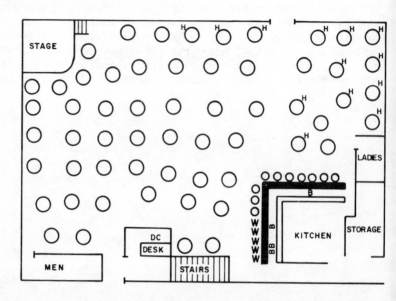

CENTRAL

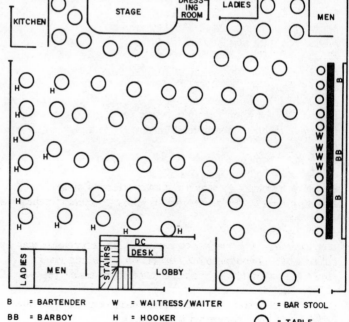

B = BARTENDER	W = WAITRESS/WAITER	○ = BAR STOOL
BB = BARBOY	H = HOOKER	◯ = TABLE
	DC = DESK CLERK	

Glossary of Terms

action   activity of a more venturesome nature; hustling

action bars   bars habituated by hustlers and/or offering "illicit" (especially hookers) entertainment

after-hours places   places open after regular bar hours. May be legitimate or illegitimate

B&E men   burglars who "break and enter" a building

bar   (1) drinking place; (2) prohibit entry

beaver   female pubic hair/vagina, used in reference to a stripper

bennies   amphetamines; stimulants

bi   bisexual

biker broad   female extensively involved with bikers (motorcycle club)

black culture   Black American styles, entertainers, etc.

blow job   fellatio; oral sex

blind pig   illegitimate drinking house

body rub   massage parlor

book (the)   hooker's list of clients

bookmaker   illegal odds-making entrepreneur

booster   a thief involved in shoplifting

bootlegger   someone illegitimately selling liquor

bootlegger's joint   illegitimate drinking house

booze   liquor

booze can   illegitimate drinking house

bottom lady   a pimp's main hooker

burlesque theatre   a strip-tease theatre

bust   arrest

candy ass   someone unable to stand up to others

chippy score   cheap, easily attainable

choosing   process by which a hooker selects a pimp

choosing money   the money paid by hooker to a pimp for the privilege of working for him

coke   cocaine

con, conning   (1) confidence gaming; (2) interpersonal manoeuvering

connections   knowing other hustlers on a working level

cool   (1) tolerant; (2) maintain composure under pressure; (3) someone in "the life"

cop   (1) policeman; (2) obtain possession (e.g., copped some drugs)

crack   jest, joke somewhat sarcastically

cruising   looking for action, business

dancer   exotic dancer, stripper

date   hooker's client; also "John," "trick"

dildo   instrument used to simulate a penis

dope   drugs; marijuana (pot, grass) is the most common overall, but almost anything might be tried by some

doper   (1) a regular user of drugs; (2) a heavy user of drugs

doubles   (1) a hooker doing two tricks in succession; (2) a stripper working two bars/theatres in the same day; (3) a bar drink containing twice the amount of alcohol

downers   sedatives; barbiturates

drunk   (1) intoxicated; (2) a skid row person, wino, rubbie. A word much preferred to "alcoholic" by street people

escort services   agencies arranging commercial dates

ethnography   study of the way of life of a group of people

fencing   selling stolen merchandise

fink   someone who sells, exchanges, or gives information to the police

flash   (1) someone making the scene (presenting himself) in a flamboyant fashion; (2) a stripper lowering her G string

front   an activity or setting concealing back region and/or illegitimate activities

frenched (getting)   fellatio; oral sex

G string   narrow loincloth held up by a cord

gaff   a hustle

gay   homosexual

grass   marijuana

greek   homosexual interests/activities

grifter   a hustler, thief, rounder

heat   police; also "narc," "the man," "morality"

heavy   (1) a "tough"; (2) a well-connected individual

hip (hep)   someone attuned to "the life"

ho   whore (southern pronunciation); a prostitute

hooker   prostitute

house   (1) bar; (2) house of prostitution

house girl   (1) stripper with an indefinite stay at one club; (2) hookers in houses of prostitution

hustler   someone with other than legitimate means of income; grifter, rounder

inside regulars   privileged bar patrons

jacking off   masturbating

john   a hooker's client; trick

joint   (1) marijuana cigarette; (2) prison; (3) a place such as a house, apartment, bar

jug   (1) a bottle or pitcher; (2) jail

learning the ropes   becoming familiar with an activity, role, or life-style

life, the   the world of hustlers, thieves and hookers; their orientations, places, and activities

loanshark   someone who lends money at greater than the legal prevailing rates of interest

lush   a drunk

main lady   a pimp's "number one" hooker; bottom lady

mark   target for a hustle; sucker

narc   (1) undercover police officer; (2) narcotics agent

old lady   (1) a pimp's hooker; (2) a man's female companion
old man   (1) a hooker's boyfriend/pimp; (2) a woman's male companion
pasties   devices designed to cover the nipples of an exotic dancer
pimp   (1) a man who receives money from a hooker on a somewhat regular basis;
   (2) someone into the game of "hustling ho's."
player   (1) black pimp, someone in the game of "hustling ho's;" (2) slick hustler
pushing drinks   encouraging patrons to purchase more liquor than they would
   otherwise buy
pussy   vagina
queer   male homosexual
rap   (1) talk, discussion; (2) criminal charge
regulars   patrons who frequent the same bar over a period of time
rehash   resell the same items (e.g. rooms, drinks)
round (buy)   simultaneously purchasing drinks for all those at one's table
rounders   hustlers, grifters, streetwise persons with other than legitimate
   means of support
rounds (making the)   frequenting a number of bars, action spots
rubber   prophylactic; condom
rubbies   skid row people, winos; drunks
S & M   sadism/masochism
safe   prophylactic, condom
score   (1) attain one's goal; (2) a good deal
shit   (1) drugs; (2) activities; (3) put-on, fabricate; (4) lowly
shooting gallery   place where drugs are frequently used (and obtained)
shortchange   intentionally giving patrons insufficient change
short shot   putting less than the legal amount of liquor in a drink
shylocking   loansharking
smoke   (1) cigarettes; (2) other drugs, especially marijuana
snitch   inform on others
solid   someone trustworthy, dependable, reliable
speed   stimulants; amphetamines; also "whiz"
square   conventional; "straight"
stable   a pimp's hookers
stag   an all-male party
stash   (1) hiding place for drugs; (2) money set aside for safe-keeping
stool pidgeon (stoolie)   police informant
straight   (1) conventional; (2) not part of the bar scene; (3) not part of "the life"
strip joint   burlesque theatre; bar featuring strippers
strippers   exotic dancers
the life   the world of the hustlers, thieves and hookers; their places and activities
thief   someone who steals for a living; a hustler, rounder, grifter
trick   a hooker's client
trick pad   an apartment rented for the purpose of "entertaining tricks"
underlife (underworld)   the thief subculture; their contacts, places, and activities
uppers   stimulants; amphetamines
valium   a barbituate; sedative
wives-in-law   two or more hookers sharing the same pimp
wino   skid row person; drunk
working girl   (1) hooker; (2) career woman

References

Athens, Lonnie. "The Self and the Violent Criminal Act," *Urban Life*, 1974, 3:98-112.

Ball, Donald W. "The Problematics of Respectability," in J. D. Douglas (ed.), *Deviance and Respectability*. New York: Basic Books, Inc., 1970, pp. 326-372.

Becker, Howard S. *Outsiders: Studies in The Sociology of Deviance*. New York: The Free Press, 1963.

Berger, Peter and Thomas Luckmann. *The Social Construction of Reality*. New York: Anchor Books, 1966.

Binderman, Murray, Dennis Wepman, and Ronald Newman. "A Portrait of 'The Life'," *Urban Life*, 1975, 4:213-225.

Bittner, Egan. "The Police on Skid Row: A Study of Peace-Keeping," *American Sociological Review*, 1967, 32:699-715.

Black, Donald J. "Production of Crime Rates," *American Sociological Review*, 1970, 35:733-747.

Black, Donald J. and Albert J. Reiss, Jr. "Police Control of Juveniles," *American Sociological Review*, 1970, 35:63-77.

Blumer, Herbert. *Symbolic Interaction*. Englewood Cliffs, N.J.: Prentice-Hall, Inc., 1969.

———. "Social Problems as Collective Behavior," *Social Problems*, 1971, 18:298-306.

Boles, Jacqueline and Albino Garbin. "The Strip Club and Stripper-Customer Patterns of Interaction," *Sociology and Social Research*, 1974, 58:136-144.

Bryan, James H. "Apprenticeships in Prostitution." *Social Problems*, 1965, 12:286-297.

Bryan, James H. "Occupational Ideologies and Individual Attitudes of Call Girls," *Social Problems*, 1966, 13:441-450.

Bryant, Clifton D. and Eddie Palmer. "Massage Parlors and 'Hand Whores': Some Sociological Observations," *The Journal of Sex Research*, 1975, 11:227-241.

Carter, Barbara. "Race, Sex and Gangs," *Society*, 1973, 11:36-43.

Cavan, Sheri. *Liquor Licence*. Chicago: Aldine Publishing Co., 1966.

Charon, Joel. *Symbolic Interactionism*. Englewood Cliffs, N.J.: Prentice-Hall, Inc., 1979.

Clinard, Marshall. "The Public Drinking House and Society," in D. J. Pittman and C. R. Snyder (eds.), *Alcohol, Culture and Drinking Patterns*. New York: John Wiley & Sons, Inc., 1962, pp. 270-292.

Cohen, Albert. *Deviance and Control*. Englewood Cliffs, N.J.: Prentice-Hall, Inc., 1957.

Cressey, Donald. *Other Peoples' Money*. New York: The Free Press, 1953.

Cressey, Paul. *The Taxi-Dance Hall*. Chicago: University of Chicago Press, 1932.

Daniels, Arlene Kaplan. "The Social Construction of Military Diagnoses," in H. P. Drietzel (ed.), *Recent Sociology No. 2*, 1970, New York: Macmillan, Inc., pp. 181-208.

Davis, Fred. "The Cab Driver and His Fare: Facets of a Fleeting Relationship," *American Journal of Sociology*, 1959, 65:158-165.

_____. "Deviance Disavowal: The Management of Strained Interaction Among the Visibly Handicapped," *Social Problems*, 1961, 9:120-132.

Davis, Nannette J. "The Prostitute: Developing a Deviant Identity," in James Henslin (ed.), *Studies in the Sociology of Sex*, New York: Appleton-Century-Crofts, 1971.

Della Cava, Frances A. "Becoming an Ex-Priest: The Process of Leaving a High Commitment Status," *Sociological Inquiry*, 1975, 45:41-50.

Dietz, Mary Lou. "The Violent Subculture: The Genesis of Violence," in M. A. B. Gammon (ed.), *Violence in Canada*. Toronto: Methuen Publications, 1978, pp. 13-39.

Douglas, Jack D. *Deviance and Respectability*. New York: Basic Books, Inc., 1970.

Driscoll, James P. "Transsexuals." *Transaction*, 1971, 8:28-37, 66.

Emerson, Joan. "Behavior in Private Places: Sustaining Definitions of Reality in Gynecological Examinations," in H. P. Drietzel (ed.), *Recent Sociology No. 2*, 1970, pp. 73-100. New York: Macmillan, Inc.

English, Clifford and Joyce Stephens. "On Being Excluded: An Analysis of Elderly and Adolescent Street Hustlers," *Urban Life*, 1975, 4:201-212.

Ermann, M. D. and R. J. Lundman. *Corporate and Governmental Deviance*. New York: Oxford University Press, Inc., 1978.

Festinger, Leon, Henry W. Riecken and Stanley Schachter. *When Prophecy Fails*. New York: Harper and Row Publishers, Inc., 1956.

Finestone, Harold. "Cats, Kicks and Color," *Social Problems*, 1957, 5:3-13.

Garfinkel, Harold. "Conditions of Successful Degradation Ceremonies," *American Journal of Sociology*, 1956, 66:420-424.

_____. *Studies in Ethnomethodology*. Englewood Cliffs, N.J.: Prentice-Hall, Inc., 1967.

Geis, Gilbert and Robert Meier. *White Collar Crime*. New York: The Free Press, 1977.

Gerlach, Luther P. and Virginia H. Hine. *People, Power and Change: Movements of Social Transformation*. Indianapolis: Bobbs-Merrill Co. Inc., 1970.

Giallombardo, Rose. *Society of Women: A Study of a Women's Prison*. New York: John Wiley & Sons, Inc., 1966.

Goffman, Erving. *Presentation of Self in Everyday Life*. New York: Anchor Books, 1959.

_____. *Asylums*. New York: Anchor Books, 1961.

_____. *Stigma: Notes on the Management of Spoiled Identity*. Englewood Cliffs, N.J.: Prentice-Hall, Inc., 1963.

Gottlieb, David. "The Neighborhood Tavern and the Cocktail Lounge, A Study of Class Differences," *American Journal of Sociology*, 1957, 62:559-562.

Gray, Diana. "Turning-Out: A Study of Teenage Prostitution," *Urban Life and Culture*, 1973, 1:401-425.

Greenwald, Harold. *The Call Girl*. New York: Ballantine Books, Inc., 1958.

Hall, Susan. *Ladies of the Night*. New York: Trident Press, 1973.

Hall, Susan and Bob Adelman. *Gentleman of Leisure*. New York: Prairie House, New American Library, 1972.

Hayner, Norman S. *Hotel Life*. College Park, Maryland: McGrath Publishing Co., 1969 [1936].

Hearn, H. L. and Patricia Stoll. "Continuance Commitments in Low-Status Occupations: The Cocktail Waitress." *The Sociological Quarterly*, 1975, 16:105-114.

Henslin, James. "Craps and Magic," *American Journal of Sociology*, 1967, 73:316-330.

Hillary, George. "Definitions of Community: Areas of Agreement," *Rural Sociology*, 1955, 20:111-123.

Hollingshead, August B. *Elmtown's Youth*. New York: John Wiley & Sons, Inc., 1949.

Hong, Lawrence, William Darrough, and Robert Duff. "The Sensuous Rip-Off: Consumer Fraud Turns Blue," *Urban Life and Culture*, 1975, 3:464-470.

Horning, Donald. "Blue Collar Theft: Conceptions of Property, Attitudes Towards Pilfering, and Work Group Norms in a Modern Industrial Plant," in G. D. Smigel and R. L. Ross (eds.) *Crimes Against Bureaucracy*. New York: Van Nostrand Reinhold Company, 1970.

Irwin, John. *The Felon*. Englewood Cliffs, N.J.: Prentice-Hall, Inc. 1970.

Karp, David A. "Hiding in Pornographic Bookstores," *Urban Life and Culture*, 1973, 1:427-451.

Karsh, Bernard, Joel Seidman and D. M. Lilienthal. "The Union Organizer and His Tactics: A Case Study," *American Journal of Sociology* 1953, 59:113-122.

Klapp, Orrin. *Collective Search for Identity*. New York: Holt, Rinehart & Winston, 1969.

———. *Social Types: Process, Structure and Ethos*. San Diego: Aegis, 1971.

Klein, John and Arthur Montague. *Check Forgers*. Lexington, Mass.: Lexington Books, 1977.

LeMasters, E. E. "Social Life in a Working Class Tavern," *Urban Life and Culture*, 1973, 2:27-52.

Lemert, Edwin. *Social Pathology*. New York: McGraw-Hill, Inc., 1951.

———. *Human Deviance, Social Problems, and Social Control*. Englewood Cliffs, N.J.: Prentice-Hall, Inc., 1967.

Lesieur, Henry. *The Chase*. New York: Anchor Books, 1977.

Letkemann, Peter. *Crime as Work*. Englewood Cliffs, N.J.: Prentice-Hall, Inc., 1973.

Liebow, Elliot. *Tally's Corner*. New York: Little, Brown & Company, 1967.

Lilly, Robert J. and Richard Ball. "No-Tell Motel: The Social Organization of a Low-Rent Rendezvous." Paper presented at American Sociological Association meetings in San Francisco, 1978.

Lofland, John. *Deviance and Identity*. Englewood Cliffs, N.J.: Prentice-Hall, Inc., 1967.

Lofland, John and Rodney Stark. "Becoming A World Saver: A Theory of Conversion to a Deviant Perspective," *American Sociological Review*, 1965, 30:862-875.

Lyman, Sanford and Marvin Scott. *Sociology of the Absurd*. New York: Appleton-Century-Crofts, 1970.

Macrory, Boyd. "The Tavern and the Community," *Quarterly Journal of Studies on Alcohol*, 1952, 13:609-637.

Martin, Wilfred. "Teacher-Pupil Interactions," *Canadian Review of Sociology and Anthropology*, 1975, 12:529-540.

Matza, David. *Delinquency and Drift*. New York: John Wiley & Sons, Inc., 1964.

———. *Becoming Deviant*. Englewood Cliffs, N.J.: Prentice-Hall, Inc., 1969.

Maurer, David W. *The Big Con*. Indianapolis: Bobbs-Merrill Co. Inc., 1940.

———. *Whiz Mob*. New Haven, Conn.: College and University Press, 1955.

McCaghy, Charles H., and James K. Skipper, Jr. "Lesbian Behavior as an Adaptation to the Occupation of Stripping," *Social Problems*, 1969, 17:262-271.

McManus, Virginia. *Not for Love*. New York: G. P. Putnam's Sons, 1960.

Mead, George H. *Mind, Self and Society*. Chicago: University of Chicago Press, 1934.

Milner, Christina and Richard Milner. *Black Players*. Boston: Little, Brown & Company, 1972.

"Misty". *Strip!* Toronto: New Press, 1973.

Moore, E. C. "The Social Value of the Saloon," *American Journal of Sociology*, 1897, 3:1-12.

Orwell, George. *Down and Out in Paris and London*. New York: Penguin Books, 1940.

Parnas, Raymond. "The Police Response to Domestic Disturbances," *Wisconsin Law Review*, 1967, 914-960.

Platt, Anthony. *The Child Savers*. Chicago: University of Chicago Press, 1969.

Polsky, Ned. *Hustlers, Beats and Others*. Chicago: Aldine Publishing Company, 1967.

Prus, Robert. "Labeling Theory: A Reconceptualization and a Propositional Statement on Typing," *Sociological Focus*, 1975, 8:79-96.

———. "Resisting Designations: An Extension of Attribution Theory into a Negotiated Context," *Sociological Inquiry*, 1975, 45:3-14.

———. "Religious Recruitment and the Management of Dissonance: A Sociological Perspective," *Sociological Inquiry*, 1976, 46:127-134.

———. "From Barrooms to Bedrooms: Towards a Theory of Interpersonal Violence" in M.A.B. Gammon (ed.), *Violence in Canada*, Toronto: Methuen Publications, 1978, pp. 51-73.

Prus, Robert and C. R. D. Sharper. *Road Hustler*. Lexington, Mass.: Lexington Books, 1977 (Gage paperback, 1979).

Rasmussen, Paul and Lauren Kuhn. "The New Masseuse: Play For Pay," *Urban Life*, 1976, 5:271-292.

Ray, Marsh. "Abstinence Cycles and Heroin Addicts," *Social Problems*, 1961, 9:132-140.

Reiss, Albert J. "The Social Integration of Queers and Peers," *Social Problems*, 1961, 9:102-120.

Rettig, R. P., M. J. Torres, and G. R. Garret. *Manny: a Criminal Addict's Story*. Boston: Houghton Mifflin Company, 1977.

Richards, Cara E. "City Taverns," *Human Organization*, 1964, 22:260-268.

Robinson, David. *From Drinking to Alcoholism: A Sociological Commentary*.

New York: John Wiley & Sons, Inc., 1976.

Roebuck, Julian and Wolfgang Frese. *The Rendezvous: A Case Study of an After-Hours Club*. New York: The Free Press, 1976.

Roebuck, Julian and Patrick McNamara. "Ficheras and Free-lancers: Prostitution in a Mexican Border City," *Archives of Sexual Behavior*, 1973, 2:231-244.

Roebuck, Julian and S. Lee Sprey. "The Cocktail Lounge: A Study of Heterosexual Relations in a Public Organization," *American Journal of Sociology*, 1967, 72:388-395.

Roy, Donald. "Sex in the Factory: Informal Heterosexual Relations Between Supervisors and Work Groups," in C. D. Bryant (ed.), *Deviant Behavior*. Chicago: Rand McNally & Company, 1974, pp. 44-66.

Rubington, Earl. "Variations in Bottle-Gang Controls," in E. Rubington and M. Weinberg (eds.), *Deviance: The Interactionist Perspective*. New York: Macmillan, Inc., 1968, pp. 308-316.

Salutin, Marilyn. "Stripper Morality," in C. Boydell, C. Grindstaff, and P. Whitehead (eds.), *Deviant Behaviour*. Toronto: Holt, Rinehart & Winston of Canada Limited, 1971, pp. 532-545.

Schutz, Alfred. *Collected Papers I: The Problem of Social Reality* (Maurice Natanson, ed.). The Hague: Martinus Nijhoff, 1971.

Scott, Marvin. *The Racing Game*. Chicago: Aldine Publishing Company, 1968.

Shover, Neal. "Structures and Careers in Burglary." *Journal of Criminal Law, Criminology, and Police Sciences*, 1972, 63:540-549.

Shibutani, Tamotsu. *Improvised News: A Sociological Study of Rumor*. Indianapolis: The Bobbs-Merrill Co., Inc., 1966.

Simmel, Georg. *The Sociology of George Simmel* (Kurt Wolff, editor). New York: The Free Press, 1950.

———. *Conflict and the Web of Group-Affiliations*. New York: The Free Press, 1955.

Simmons, J. L. "On Maintaining Deviant Belief Systems: A Case Study," *Social Problems*, 1964, 11:250-256.

Sinclair, Peter and Kenneth Westhues. *Village in Crisis*. Toronto: Holt, Rinehart & Winston of Canada Limited, 1974.

Skipper, James K. and Charles H. McCaghy. "Stripteasing: A Sex-Oriented Occupation," in J. Henslin (ed.), *Studies in the Sociology of Sex*. New York: Appelton-Century-Crofts, 1971, pp. 275-296.

Skolnick, Jerome. *Justice Without Trial*. New York: John Wiley & Sons, Inc., 1966.

Slade, Joseph. "Pornographic Theatres off Times Square," *Transaction*, 1971, 9:35-43.

Spradley, James and Brenda Mann. *The Cocktail Waitress*. New York: John Wiley & Sons, Inc., 1975.

Stebbins, Robert. "On Misunderstanding the Concept of Commitment," *Social Forces*, 1970, 48:526-529.

———. *Commitment to Deviance: The Nonprofessional Criminal in the Community*. Westport, Conn.: Greenwood Press, Inc., 1971.

Stein, Martha L. *Lovers, Friends, Slaves: The Nine Male Sexual Types*. Berkeley: G. P. Putnam's Sons, 1974.

Stephens, Joyce. *Loners, Losers and Lovers: Elderly Tenants in a Slum Hotel*. Seattle: University of Washington Press, 1976.

Sundholm, Charles A. "The Pornographic Arcade," *Urban Life and Culture*, 1973, 2:85-104.

Sutherland, Edwin H. *The Professional Thief*. Chicago: University of Chicago Press, 1937.

———. *Principles of Criminology*, 4th ed., Philadelphia: J. B. Lippincott Company, 1947.

———. "The Diffusion of Sexual Psychopath Laws," *American Journal of Sociology*, 1950, 56:142-148.

———. *White Collar Crime*. New York: Dryden Press, 1959.

Sutter, Alan. "Playing A Cold Game: Phases of a Ghetto Career," *Urban Life*, 1972, 1:77-91.

Tannenbaum, Frank. *Crime and Community*. New York: Columbia University Press, 1938.

Vaz, Edmund. "The Metropolitan Taxi Driver: His Work and Self Conception." M.A. Thesis. McGill University, 1955.

Velarde, Albert J. "Becoming Prostituted," *British Journal of Criminology*, 1975, 15:251-263.

Velarde, Albert J. and Mark Warlick. "Massage Parlors: The Sensuality Business," *Society*, 1973, 11:63-74.

Walsh, Marilyn E. *The Fence*. Westport, Conn.: Greenwood Press, Inc., 1977.

Weinberg, Martin. "Sexual Modesty and the Nudist Camp," *Social Problems*, 1965, 12:311-318.

Werthman, Carl and Irving Piliavin. "Gang Members and the Police," in D. J. Bordua (ed.), *The Police*. New York: John Wiley & Sons, Inc., 1967, pp. 50-98.

West, W. G. "Serious Thieves: Lower Class Adolescent Males in a Short-Term Deviant Occupation," University of Chicago: doctoral dissertation, 1974.

Whitehead, P. C., C. F. Grindstaff, and C. L. Boydell. *Alcohol and Other Drugs*. Toronto: Holt, Rinehart & Winston of Canada, Limited, 1973.

Whyte, William F. *Street Corner Society*. Chicago: University of Chicago Press, 1943.

———. *Action Research for Management*. Homewood, Ill.: Irwin-Dorsey Limited, 1964.